ATMAN

A RECONSTRUCTION OF THE SOLAR
COSMOLOGY OF THE INDO-EUROPEANS

ALEXANDER JACOB

Atman: A Reconstruction of the Solar Cosmology of the Indo-Europeans
Alexander Jacob

978–1–7638613–2–9

Second Edition: Manticore Press, Melbourne, 2025

First edition: Georg Olms Verlag, Hildesheim, 2012.
This edition published by kind permission of Georg Olms Verlag, Baden–Baden.

Thema Classification: QRD (Hinduism), QRDF1 (Hindu Texts), 1QBA (Ancient History) QRS (Ancient Religions).

MANTICORE PRESS
WWW.MANTICORE.PRESS

yatparam brahma sarvatma vishvasyāyatanam mahat
sukshmat sukshmataram nityam tat tvam eva tvam eva tat

(That, the supreme Brahman, the Soul of the universe,
the principal Foundation of the world,
Subtler than the subtle, eternal, that is indeed thy self,
that even art thou.)

Kaivalya Upanishad, 16

CONTENTS

ACKNOWLEDGEMENTS

This attempt to fathom the ultimate cosmological source of the religions of the ancient world is a result of the profound impression made upon me in my youth by the Brāhmanical rituals of India, which seem to me to retain, more fully than any other, the form as well as the significance of the religious worship of the ancients.

Because of the fragmentary nature of much of the documentary evidence from the ancient Near East, my study necessarily exhibits a mosaic quality and – this being a pioneering work – I hope that I have fitted the myriad pieces of literary and archaeological evidence in their right positions in my reconstruction. While it is impossible to be absolutely certain of the original form of a religion that is at least eight thousand years old, I shall consider my work not to have been in vain if it succeeds in evoking with sufficient verisimilitude the extraordinary depth of vision and spiritual power of the prisca theologia.

I should like to thank here Prof. Ronald Sweet, Prof. Emeritus of the Department of Near Eastern Studies, University of Toronto, and Prof. Ronald Leprohon, of the same department, for their constant, and unstinting, help in checking and correcting translations from the Sumero-Akkadian and Egyptian, respectively.

I should also thank Miss Lari Langford of the Robarts Library, University of Toronto, for her gracious help over the years with the collections in her care. Finally, I must thank Dr. Dmitri Filimonov of the Department of Chemistry, The Lomonosov Moscow State University, for his generous assistance in preparing my manuscript for publication.

Moscow, 2004
Alexander Jacob

ABBREVIATIONS

AW	*Akkadisches Wörterbuch*
DED	*Dravidian Etymological Dictionary*
HW	*The Hindu World: An Encylopedic Survey of Hinduism*
DNM	*Dictionary of Nordic Mythology*
MW	*Moslem World*
EB	*Encyclopedia Britannica*
ER	*Encyclopedia of Religion*

INDIC

BP	*Bhāgavata Purāna*
BrP	*Brahma Purāna*
BrvP	*Brahmavaivarta Purāna*
BrdP	*Brahmānda Purāna*
LP	*Linga Purāna*
MP	*Matsya Purāna*
SP	*Skanda Purāna*
ShP	*Shiva Purāna*
PP	*Padma Purāna*
MBh	*Mahābhārata*
AV	*Atharva Veda*
RV	*Rg Veda*
KYV	*Krishna [= Taittirīya] Yajur Veda*
SYV	*Shukla [=Vājasaneyi] Yajur Veda*
TS	*Taittirīya Samhita*
VS	*Vājasaneyi Samhita*
AB	*Aitareya Brāhmana*
GB	*Gopatha Brāhmana*
KB	*Kaushītiki Brāhmana*
SB	*Shatapatha Brāhmana*
TB	*Taittirīya Brāhmana*
BAU	*Brhadāranyaka Upanishad*

MESOPOTAMIAN

AGH   *Die akkadische Gebetsserie "Handerhebung", I*, ed. E. Ebeling.
AKF   *Archiv für Keilschriftforschung*
AO   *Archiv Orientalia*
A.O.   *Antiquités Orientales du Louvre*
AfO   *Archiv für Orientforschung*
ANET   *Ancient Near Eastern Texts relating to the Old Testament*, ed. J.B.
        Pritchard.
ARM   *Archives royales de Mari*
ATAT   *Altorientalische Texte und Bilder zum Alten Testamente*, ed. H.
        Gressmann, Vol.I.
BA   *Beiträge zur Assyriologie*
BE   *Babylonian Expedition of the University of Pennsylvania, Series A:
        Cuneiform Texts*
BIFAO   *Bulletin de l'institut français d'archaeologie orientale*
BSOAS   *Bulletin of the School of Oriental and African Studies*
CAD   *Chicago Assyrian Dictionary*
CAH   *Cambridge Ancient History*
CSMS   *The Canadian Society for Mesopotamian Studies*
CT   *Cuneiform Texts from Babylonian Tablets in the British Museum,
        London*
EE   *Enuma Elish*
FAOS   *Freiburger Altorientalische Studien*
JCS   *Journal of Cuneiform Studies*
JAOS   *Journal of the American Oriental Society*
JEOL   *Jaarbericht van het vooraziatisch–egyptisch Genootschap 'Ex
        Oriente Lux'*
K   *Kuyunjik Collection, British Museum.*
KAR   *Keilschrifttexte aus Assyrien religiösen Inhalts*
MVAG   *Mitteilungen der vorderasiatischen Gesellschaft*
R   *The Cuneiform Inscriptions of Western Asia*, ed. H. Rawlinson.
RLA   *Reallexikon der Assyriologie.*
SAK   *Die sumerischen und akkadischen Königsinschriften*, ed. F.
        Thureau–Dangin.
SEL   *Studi Epigraphici e Linguistici*
Sp.   *Spartoli Collection, British Museum.*
STT   *The Sultantepe Tablets*, ed. O.R. Gurney, J.J. Falkenstein, P. Hulin.
TCL   *Textes Cuneiformes du Louvre.*
VAT   *Vorderasiatisches Museum, Berlin.*
W   *Warka*
W.B.   Weld–Blundell Collection, Ashmolean Museum, Oxford.

HITTITE

CTH   *Catalogue des textes hittites*, Paris, 1971, by E. Laroche.
KUB   *Keilschrifturkunden aus Boghazköi*
Kbo   *Keilschrifttexte aus Boghazköi*
RHA   *Revue hittite et asianique*

EGYPTIAN

BD   *The Book of the Dead*, tr. E.A.W. Budge.
CT   *The Ancient Egyptian Coffin Texts*, tr. R.O. Faulkner.
DAWW *Denkschriften der (kaiserlichen) Akademie der Wissenschaften in Wien*
JEOL   *Jaarbericht van het vooraziatisch–egyptisch gezelschap Ex Oriente Lux*
LÄ   *Lexicon der Ägyptologie*
OEAG   *The Oxford Encylopedia of Ancient Egypt*
PT   *The Ancient Egyptian Pyramid Texts*, tr. R.O. Faulkner.
UC   *Petrie Museum of Egyptian Archaeology, University College, London.*
W   *Wörterbuch der aegyptischen Sprache*, ed. A .Erman and H. Grapow, 1926– 31.
ZÄS   *Zeitschrift für ägyptische Sprache und Altertumkunde*

PURĀNA

INTRODUCTION – HISTORICAL

The comprehension of the full significance of the ancient cosmological religions of the Near East has hitherto been hampered by the isolation in which the documents of Egypt, Mesopotamia, and their Āryan neighbours have most often been studied. Examining the documents of these apparently distinct regions of the ancient Near East together presents a much more coherent and comprehensive picture of the cosmological scheme which underlies the religions of the area. Apart from the very fragmentary state in which most of the religious documents are preserved, another major obstacle to a sympathetic understanding of these religions has been the modern, empirical sensibility which many scholars in the field have unfortunately brought to bear in their examination of sacred materials from the distant past. As N. Wyatt rightly pointed out recently, referring to the so-called "seasonal" interpretation of Near Eastern mythology,

> It is full of inner contradictions, in that no overall coherent or consistent system can be derived from the various approaches: no two expositions are consistent with one another. Nor does it reduce the whole body of material to an allegory … but reduces entire panthea into nothing more than ciphers for the weather, rather like the clouds and raindrops on a television forecast. This is the ultimate trivialization of myth.[1]

---

[1] N. Wyatt, "Arms and the King. The earliest allusions to the Chaoskampf motif and their implications for the interpretation of the Ugaritic and biblical traditions", *Und Mose schrieb dieses Lied auf: Studien zum alten Testament und zum alten Orient, Festschrift für Oswald Loretz*, ed. M. Dietrich and I. Kottsieper, Münster: Ugarit Verlag, 1998, p.854. For examples of the unfortunate persistence of the seasonal approach to mythology, see T. Jacobsen's exposition of the Ninurta mythology in terms of the "hydraulic cyle and the

The simplistic classification of the ancient religions as polytheistic, in contrast to Hebrew monotheism, has contributed further to the confusion of the former with animism and pantheism. In 1860, however, Max Mueller had recourse to a neologism in describing Āryan religion as 'henotheism', or a religion which maintains that god is one but not that he is the only one – as is strenuously held by the monotheistic Semitic cults following Judaism.[2] The radical difference between Hebraic monotheism, which began and continues today not so much as a worship of any universal spiritual forces but, rather, as a political doctrine of mono-nationalism (that is, the unique concentration on the history of the Israelites as the destiny of mankind) and ancient henotheism is that the latter is a genuinely universal religion based on the scientific and philosophical understanding of the cosmos, whereas the Abrahamic revolution represents a repudiation of this religiosity for an obscurantist anthropocentric – and Judeocentric – ethics. The Abrahamic aversion to cosmological religion is evident from the references in Josephus' *Jewish Antiquities*, I,157 and Philo the Jew's *De mutatione nominum*, 72-6.[3] As Renan pointed out in his *Histoire Générale et Système Comparé des Langues Sémitiques* (1863), monotheism, far from representing a higher stage of religious consciousness, is "en realité, le fruit d'une race qui a peu de besoins religieux. C'est comme minimum de religion, en fait de dogmes et en fait de pratiques extérieures, que le monothéisme est surtout accommodé aux besoins des populations nomades".[4] While Renan considered this phenomenon to be a result of the "religious instinct" of the Semitic peoples, Max Mueller more accurately considered it to be due to "their belief in a national god – a god chosen by his people as his people had been chosen by him".[5]

---

spring thunderstorm in the mountains" (T. Jacobsen, *Treasures of Darkness: A History of Mesopotamian Religion*, New Haven: Yale University Press, 1976, p.133); cf. also Kinnier–Wilson's study of cosmic events as geological ones in *The Rebel Lands: An Investigation into the Origins of early Mesopotamian Mythology*, Cambridge: Cambridge University Press, 1979.

[2] 'Semitic Monotheism' in *Selected Essays* (1881), II:415.

[3] For a discussion of the nomadic "habiru" (Hebrews) as dangerous brigands and mercenaries of the ancient Near East, see J. Bottero, *Le problème des habiru*, Paris, 1954; cf. S. Smith, *Early History of Assyria*, London: Chatto and Windus, 1928, p.192. The equation of "habiru" with "Hebrew" is confirmed by Philo the Jew's explanation of the latter term as "migrant" (*De Migratione Abrahami*, 20).

[4] E. Renan, *Histoire Générale et Système Comparé des Langues Sémitiques*, Paris: Levy, 1863, p.432.

[5] As G. Garbini remarked, "the whole of the Old Testament is a testimony to the work of demythologization carried out by some Hebrew religious circles who have transferred the work of the deity from nature to history" (*History and Ideology in Ancient Israel*, tr. J. Bowden, London: SCM Press, 1988, p.xi), a tendency which is repeated in the New

My reconstruction of the pristine cosmology of the Āryan as well as the Mesopotamian and Egyptian religions will confirm the accuracy of Max Mueller's description of these religions as henotheistic by demonstrating how the various principal deities of all these related religions of the ancient Near East express different manifest forms of one principal and ineffable cosmic reality, the One.[6] The fiery desire, Agni, of this primal and universal Soul (Ātman)[7] is the source of the various divine transformations which constitute the subject of religious adoration among the various ethnic groups considered in this study. As it is chanted in *RV* II,2,29, Agni is not only the first of the gods but indeed also all of them. Indeed, since all these gods represent the primal forces which engendered the cosmos, these ancient religions may equally be called a 'cosmotheism', for the cosmos is not only worshipped therein as the regulator of the course of the microcosmos, man, but is itself also continually sustained in its original moral order through the several sacred rituals which constitute the core of these religions.[8]

~

In reconstructing the supreme cosmic forces which are worshipped by the Āryans and their Mesopotamian and Egyptian neighbours, I shall rely principally on the literary evidence of the Purānas, the Vedas, the Brāhmanas, the Avesta, the records of the religions of Egypt, Sumer, Akkad, Assyria and the Hurrians, as well as the earliest western Āryan theogonies

---

Testament in the transformation of the originally Babylonian story of Marduk's ordeal into the sufferings and resurrection of a historical Jesus, a transformation which appropriated the Babylonian cosmological myth for Jewish Messianic purposes. That Christianity in its original form contained a Babylonian cosmological element, however, gives it a peculiar "solar" quality which elevates it above the two other Semitic religions.

[6]   Cf. the understanding of polytheism as "pluriform monotheism" in T.P. van Baaren, "Pluriform Monotheism", *Ned. Theol. Tijdschr.* 20 (1965-66), pp.321-8.

[7]   I have throughout this study used simplified transcriptional symbols to render the sounds of the various ancient languages cited in it.

[8]   The significance of the Vedic ritual for the sustenance of the cosmic order is already present in the Hurrian sacrificial rites, as, for instance, in the address to Telipinu in the following verse: "Behold, O Telipinu, I have sprinkled thy path with fine oil,/ Go now, Telipinu, on the path sprinkled with fine oil". (V. Haas and G. Wilhelm, *Hurritische und luwische Riten aus Kizzuwattna*, Kevelaer: Butzon und Bercker, 1974, p.9), where the sacrificer actually initiates the divine activity. While in India the Brāhman priests are the sole initiates into the divine system of the cosmos, in Egypt the pharaoh, as the representative or son of the sun (that is, as Horus the Younger), was equally invested with this divine knowledge, as well as with the concomitant responsibility of establishing divine justice on earth (see S. Quirke, *The Cult of Ra: Sun-Worship in Ancient Egypt*, London: Thames and Hudson, 2001, pp.17ff.).

of the Hittites, the proto-Stoic and Orphic Greeks, and the ancient Germans. Of the ancient religions, the Indic and the Zoroastrian reform of the ancient Iranian alone have survived as living religions. Since the Indic tradition, in particular, is preoccupied with the deepest spiritual aspects of the ancient religion from which it is derived, we may use its spiritual foci as an intellectual guide through the documents of the related religions as well. The esoteric, spiritual understanding of cosmology that is found, for instance, in the Upanishads is not a later development of religious culture but simultaneous with the first inspired insights into this cosmology. It is clear also that the deep penetration of the cosmos which informs the religions of all these cultures must have been obtained through a spiritual discipline such as that which yoga provides.[9]

On the other hand, the greater elaboration of the concepts of the cosmic egg and of the solar course in ancient Egypt happily gives us a more focussed view of the solar theology which served as the basis of the philosophical insights found in the Upanishads. It must be noted that the Mesopotamian and Āryan religions too were probably originally solar-centric, for the name of Babylon is itself derived from the name of the sun-god,[10] and the primal deities in the pantheon of the Hittites too are "sun-gods". However, the concentration on the solar aspect of the cosmology is most acute in Egypt and in Iranian Mithraism. The later Mithraic religion which arose from Persia and spread throughout the Roman Empire indeed attests to the persistence of the solar significance of the ancient Iranian religion.

The similarities between the cosmological religions of these different civilisations may be explained either by a mere transmission of religious ideas from one racial group to the other through incidental trade contacts, or else by the attribution of the creation and development of this cosmological world-view to priestly classes which were closely related to an original hieratic group. The fact that priests in the ancient cultures were extremely conservative and not likely to spread their essentially esoteric religions through commercial intermediaries suggests that the latter alternative is indeed the more probable one. And since priests are not likely to have migrated alone from one region to the other, it may be assumed that large sections of the original populations of these geographically

---

[9] See below p.50. We may refer also to the yogic pose in which a principal deity of the Indus peoples [perhaps Shiva] is represented on some of the Indus seals (see, for instance, M. Jansen, *Die Indus-Zivilisation: Wiederentdeckung einer frühen Hochkultur*, Köln: DuMont, 1986, pp.233f).

[10] See W. Lambert, "Studies in Marduk", *BSOAS* 47(1984), pp.8f. The original name was Bar.ki.bar (where "ki" denotes town).

distant lands were constituted of branches of one original ethnic group. The conservatism of the ancient religions itself is evidenced in the faithful preservation of the earliest cosmological insights through several generations by the priestly classes. Thus we find that the Assyrian priests writing at a much later stage in the history of Mesopotamian religion still possess the original understanding of the secret significance of the various deities of the Sumerian pantheon that their own religion was based upon.[11]

Of course, it must be noted that there are manifest differences too in the religious customs of the peoples considered in this study, such as, for instance, the preoccupation with the afterlife in Osirian Egypt which gave rise to the elaborate mummification and burial rites in that land[12] in contrast to the more exclusive focus on fire-rituals in India, where cremation became the prevalent funereal mode. However, the philosophical focus on the soul and its ultimate identity underlies both these apparently divergent customs. For, as the Egyptian books of the underworld reveal, the journey of the sun is not merely that of the cosmic light but of the individual soul itself. As Hornung pointed out,

> This nocturnal regeneration of the sun demonstrates, by way of example, what powers of renewal are at work on the far side of death. At the same time, the journey occurs in the spaces of the human soul, in which a renewal from the depths becomes possible.[13]

The tendency to distinguish, largely on the linguistic difference between agglutinative and inflected languages, the Egyptian civilisation from the Sumerian and both from the so-called 'Indo-European'[14] cultures of the Āryans and the Hittites and Greeks ignores the possibility that they may have all been derived from a common racial and linguistic source. The similarities between the cosmological religions of the three most ancient civilisations certainly give credence to this possibility. And the references in the Sumerian epic of *Enmerkar and the Lord of Aratta*, 141-6, to a time when all the peoples of the region "in unison/ To Enlil in one tongue [gave

---

[11] See, in this context, the excellent study by A. Livingstone, *Mystical and Mythological Explanatory Texts of Assyrian and Babylonian Scholars*, Oxford: Clarendon, 1986.

[12] cf., *inter alia*, *The Book of the Dead*, spells 42ff.

[13] See E. Hornung, *The Ancient Egyptian Books of the Afterlife*, tr. D. Lorton, Ithaca: Cornell University Press, 1999, p.27.

[14] For a clarification of the significance of the terms "Indo-European" and "Āryan", see below p.32n.

praise],"[15] as well as in *Genesis* 11:1 to the sons of Noah speaking the same tongue originally reinforce such a hypothesis. Charvat has also recently noted the emergence of the first "universal religion of Mesopotamia" already in the Chalcolithic cultures of Tel el Halaf and Ubaid.[16]

Of the several similarities of religious terminology between these three civilisations, we may mention just a few. In Egyptian cosmology, the description of Horus as the one who takes "wide strides" through the several regions of the universe is an exact equivalent of the Indic description of Vishnu's cosmic prowess.[17] Both in Sumer and Egypt the lunar god is called "the great light" in order to indicate its priority to the sun in the order of creation.[18] The name of the second pair of the Theban Ogdoad "Kuk" representing Darkness has the same significance as the Sumerian "$ku_{10}.ku_{10}$" meaning darkness.[19] Also, the characteristic opposition that is to be found in the Zoroastrian religion between the asuric representatives of the Truth and the demonic forces of the Lie is evident already in the mythology of Horus and of Thoth, who in a funerary text declares that he is "the writer of the truth, whose horror is the lie".[20] The designation of the fire-god as "child of the waters" is common to both Sumerian and Vedic literature.[21] The fire-god is said to have three births in the Vedas (*KYV* I,3,14) from Heaven, Earth and the Waters. Similarly, in the Egyptian *Book of the Night* the course of the sun is said to extend through the underworld [Earth], the Waters of

---

[15]   See S. N. Kramer, *Enmerkar and the Lord of Aratta*, Philadelphia: University Museum, 1952, p.15. The later divisions of this region include the mountain land of "Shubur" [the Hurrian homeland], the land of "Hamazi", the land of "Sumer", the land of "Uri", and the mountain land of "Martu" [the "westerners", the Amorites].

[16]   See P. Charvat, *Mesopotamia Before History*, London: Routledge, 2002, p.236. The fact that Halafian culture coincides mostly with the Subarian culture (see D. Frayne, *op.cit.*, p.23) makes it reasonable to assume that the proto-Hurrians were perhaps the most ancient practitioners of this ancient religion.

[17]   See below p.265.

[18]   ᵈGisnugal (the great light) is a name of the moon-god Sin in TCL 15,10,151, since the birth of the moon is, in Sumerian cosmology, prior to that of the sun (see below p.245).

[19]   See J. Bottero, *Mesopotamia*, tr. Z. Bahrani and M. Van de Mieroop, Chicago: University of Chicago Press, 1992, p.274. The vocalisation of this word, as of most Egyptian words, is uncertain and Budge reads the hieroglyphic k-k-y-w as Kekui (*The Gods of the Egyptians*, I:283). However, it may be noted that the Sumerian KI.KI for the underworld is also pronounced "kuku" (see *CAD*).

[20]   See C.J. Bleeker, *Hathor and Thoth: Two Key Figures of the Ancient Egyptian Religion*, Leiden: E.J. Brill, 1973, p.136. Horus is also sometimes represented as a two-headed god, "the one bearing the truth, the other the lie" (*BD* Spell 17, 64).

[21]   See M.J. Seux, *Hymnes et Prières aux Dieux de Babylonie et d'Assyrie*, Paris : Editions du Cerf, 1976, p.251.

Nun, and the Heavens, Nut.[22] The three forms of the supreme Soul, Vishnu, Brahman, Shiva form an indissoluble trinity[23] that appears in Mesopotamia too, as is evident from the frequent invocation of the triad An-Enlil-Ea in the earliest Sumerian cosmological fragments,[24] as well as in oaths and prayers from the time of the Larsa dynasty onwards.[25] The Akkadian term "apsu", the Sumerian "abzu", and the Egyptian "abtu" for the primeval Abyss which is at the base of the cosmologies of all the religions of the area are clearly related to the Indic word "ap" for water.[26]

The imperfect state of archaeological researches in the regions under investigation prohibits any definite identification of the "master-race" which created the spiritual culture of these earliest civilisations of mankind. Yet, the profundity of the cosmological insights which inform their religions leaves us in no doubt of the incomparable spiritual development of these ancient peoples. Since all these civilisations are situated in the south and, according to Gordon Childe, the predominant racial element in the earliest graves in the region from Elam to the Danube[27] is the 'Mediterranean', we may presume that these early cultures were founded by the genius of that broad racial group. The dolichocephalic Mediterranean, or "brown",[28] race[29] may thus have constituted the earliest strata of the populations of

---

[22] See E. Hornung, op.cit., p.125; cf. p.66 for similar evidence from The Book of Gates.

[23] See BrdP I,I,4,17ff.

[24] For instance, Nipp.10673,10652 and Ebeling, TAT, p.136 (see H. Wohlstein, op.cit., pp.4ff.).

[25] See H. Wohlstein, op.cit., pp.66ff; cf. H.D. Galter, op.cit., p.144.

[26] The fact that Akkadian preserves the original "p" phoneme whereas Sumerian substitutes "b" for it suggests that Akkadian is indeed closer to the Hurrian and Āryan languages and argues for the existence of a proto-Akkadian element in Elam/Ubaid along with the Hurrian (see below p.39). It is interesting, in this context, to note that G. Rubio has pointed out that many of the proto-Euphratean words detected in the earliest Sumerian texts from Uruk seem to have been Akkadian and Hurrian "loan-words" (see G. Rubio, "On the alleged 'Pre–Sumerian Substratum'", JCS, 51(1999), p.5).

[27] See G. Childe, The Dawn of European Civilization, London: K. Paul, Trench, Trubner and Co., 1961, p.109. The German evidence for this type dates from the late chalcolithic period (early 4th millennium B.C.) called Danube III.

[28] This is the term used by G.E. Smith, The Ancient Egyptians and the Origin of Civilization, London: Harper, 1923, p.69ff. to describe a race that includes the Semites as well as Hamites, Mediterraneans as well as extra-Mediterraneans.

[29] cf. H. Heras, Studies in Proto-Indo-Mediterranean Culture, Bombay: Indian Historical Research Institute, 1953, p.465: "The Mediterranean race, ethnologically considered, forms the brown sub-group within the white race, which is said to be found in Europe in the Iberian Peninsula, South France, South Italy, Islands of the Mediterranean and in continental Greece." By "brown" we are to understand "brunet" as well, since the proto-Dravidians are closely associated with the Hurrians (see below p.23). The Dravidian Brahui speakers of

Asia, Egypt and Europe. As we shall see below, this race may be called the "proto-Dravidian" or "proto-Hurrian". The Semitic, Hamitic and Japhetic peoples mentioned in the Bible are all closely related to this race. According to the 'Table of Nations' in *Genesis* 10:22, the Semites were situated first in Elam and contributed to the neighbouring Assyrian state as well as to the formation of the Aramean and Hebrew races. That the Japhetic branch too was early related to the same group is evidenced by the fact that the graves of the Āryan culture of Bishkent (1700-1500 B.C.) related to the northern BMAC have yielded mostly Mediterranean skeletons.[30]

In the Indian *BP* VIII,24, the survivor of the "flood", Manu (the counterpart of Noah) is himself called Satyavrata, King of Dravida. In the *MP* too, Manu is described as practising austerities (tapas) on Mt. Malaya, which is identified with a mountain in South India,[31] though it may have originally been the name of a mountain outside India associated with the proto-Dravidians. Some scholars have attempted to identify the Dravidians with the Sumerians.[32] The presence of Dravidian linguistic features in Sumerian, such as "gal" for great and "uru" for town, as well as the syntactical peculiarity whereby the verbal inflection varies according to whether the subject is a person or an object,[33] suggests the possibility that Sumerian is indeed related to Dravidian. It is not accidental also that the Dravidians of South India have best preserved the temple traditions of ancient Hinduism in a form resembling most closely the religious customs of ancient Mesopotamia and Egypt.[34] However, the evidence of the *BP*

Pakistan are racially akin to the Afghani Pashtuns and the Baluchis. cf. This group is well known through the deep green colour of the eyes, through the black colour of the hair and even through the colourless complexion and sometimes its tanned shade. All these typical features of the Hamites seem to be the inheritance of their father and founder, 'Ham' himself, whose name in Hebrew, from the root 'hatnam', "hot", means "the brown one", but on no occasion "black", which would be 'Hum'. This name was most likely given him, as was customary in those early days, after having seen his olive complexion. We may here refer to some ancient documents that mentioned this dark head, i.e. hair and complexion, of some ancient nations which are classified as Mediterranean.

[30] See A. Parpola, *op.cit.*, p.366.

[31] See D. Shulman, "The Tamil Flood Myths and the Cankam Legend", in *The Flood Myth*, ed. A. Dundes, Berkeley: University of California Press, 1988, p.296.

[32] See, for instance, H. Heras, *op.cit.*; cf. K.L. Muttarayan, "Sumer: Tamil of the First Cankam", *Journal of Tamil Studies*, 8 (1975), 40-61.

[33] See B. Landsberger, "The Sumerians" (1943), in *Three Essays on the Sumerians*, tr. M. DeJ. Ellis, Los Angeles: Undena Publications, n.d., p.6.

[34] See, in this context, R.F.G. Sweet, "A New Look at the 'Sacred Marriage' in Ancient Mesopotamia" in E. Robbins and S. Sandahl (ed.), *Corolla Torontonensis: Studies in Honour of Ronald Morton Smith*, Toronto: Tsar, 1994, 85-104; cf. K-H. Golzio, *Der Tempel im alten*

passage quoted suggests rather that the proto-Dravidians preceded the Sumerians, as well as the Semites and the Āryans, so that the Dravidian elements in the Sumerian language may only be vestiges from a proto-Dravidian, Noachidian language shared by all the three groups.

The proto-Dravidians are most probably identifiable with the proto-Hurrians. The geographical region in which the earliest Hurrians are found corresponds to the earliest Anatolian-Halafian settlements associated with the Subarians/Suwarians/Hurrians from the seventh millennium B.C.[35] These earliest Hurrians spoke a language that possessed Dravidian characteristics and F. Bork[36] and G.W. Brown[37] have revealed the intimate linguistic relationship between Hurrian (along with its Mitanni dialect),[38] Elamite, and Dravidian. Thus Elamite, which is today generally considered a Dravidian language,[39] is also related to the Hurrian. However, Elamite and Dravidian are possibly later dialects than the northern Hurrian, since they lack the initial 's' of Hurrian personal pronominal forms.[40] The Dravidian of the Brahui-speakers in northwestern India itself retains archaic elements resembling Hurrian which are lost in the southern Dravidian languages.[41] This confirms the route taken by the Dravidians from northern Syria and Elam to South India.

Although the Hurrians are attested in historical records only from the Old Akkadian period and more particularly in the following Ur III period,[42]

Mesopotamien und seine Parallelen in Indien: eine religionshistorische Studie, Leiden: E.J. Brill, 1983.

[35] See above p.20.

[36] See F. Bork, "Die Mitanni Sprache", *MVAG*, I and II, 1909.

[37] See G.W. Brown, "The Possibility of a Connection between Mitanni and the Dravidian languages", *JAOS*, 50 (1930), 273-305.

[38] For the dialectal relationship between the language of Tushratta's letter to Amenophis III and Hurrian, see Knudtzon, *Die el-Amarna Tafeln*, no.24; cf. S. Smith, *op.cit.*, p.71.

[39] See D. McAlpin, "Linguistic Prehistory: The Dravidian Situation", in M.M. Deshpande and P.E. Hook (ed.) *Aryan and Non-Aryan in India*, Ann Arbor, MI: Center for South and Souteast Asian Studies, The University of Michigan, 1979, 175-190.

[40] See G.W. Brown, *op.cit.*, p.290f. For further discussions of the connection between Dravidian and Āryan, see F.C. Southworth, in *Aryan and Non-Aryan in India*, 191-234; cf. also J. Harmatta, "Proto-Iranians and Proto-Indians in Cental Asia in the 2ⁿᵈ Millennium B.C. (Linguistic Evidence)", F.R. Allchin, "Archaeological and Language – Historical Evidence for the Movement of Indo-Aryan speaking Peoples into South Asia", in *Ethnic Problems of the History of Central Asia in the Early Period (second millennium B.C.)*, Moscow, 1981, and A. Parpola, "On the Protohistory of the Indian Languages in the Light of Archaeological Evidence: An Attempt at Integration", in *South Asian Archaeology*, Leiden, 1974, 90–100.

[41] See G.W. Brown, *op.cit.*, p.297.

[42] The calcite tablet of Tisadal, king of Urkis, composed entirely in Hurrian dates from this

the fact that the Hurrians, as Wilhelm has shown,[43] are in all probability identical to the Subarians may advance their presence in Mesopotamia to a much earlier date.[44] G. Wilhelm has suggested that even proto-Urartian may have been spoken around 2000 B.C. in the Transcaucasus.[45] Subartu itself may have referred later to the north-eastern lands bordering on the Tigris, and particularly Assyria,[46] but it is likely that the Elamites too formed a southern branch of the same people.[47] The gentilic "subari" is, according to Speiser, in its original form, "suwari", which suggests that it is indeed derived from the name of the sun-god "suvalliyat/suvariya" (Skt. sūrya/Av. hvare) which is also related to the later ethnic term "hurri".

The Hurrians, who are found widespread throughout the ancient Near East, are closely associated with the Indo-Āryans as well as with the Hittites in the seventeenth century B.C. So we may assume that the Hurrians formed an integral part of the original Āryans – Indians, Iranians and also Hittites. One of the earliest attested cultures of the Armenian region is indeed the Urartu, dating from the 9th-6th c. B.C., the language of which is related to the non-Āryan Hurrian,[48] though the culture in general is strongly influenced by the Assyrian.[49]

Of the three linguistic branches associated with the sons of Noah, the earliest literary evidence is indeed mostly of the Semitic proto-Akkadian. Many of the words of the earliest Uruk tablets that were designated as "proto-Euphratean" by B. Landsberger are most probably of proto-Akkadian origin, as G. Rubio has recently pointed out.[50] It is interesting to note, also, that, of twenty-two monarchs constituting the first dynasty of Kish (in the

---

period (see E.A. Speiser, "The Hurrian participation in the civilizations of Mesopotamia, Syria and Palestine", *Cahiers d'Histoire Mondiale*, I,2 (1953), p.313). Wilhelm points out that the Hurrians are first noticed in southern Mesopotamia mostly as slaves brought there after the northern wars of Sulgi (see G. Wilhelm, *The Hurrians*, tr. J. Barnes, Warminster: Aris and Phillips Ltd., 1989, p.14).

[43]   See G. Wilhelm, *op.cit.*, p.1.

[44]   In the Hebrew Bible, the Hurrians are referred to variously as Horites, Hivites or Jebusites (see *Interpreter's Bible*, p.665) and are not listed separately in the 'Table of Nations'.

[45]   See fn46 and 47 below; cf. G. Wilhelm, *op.cit.*, p.17.

[46]   See S. Smith, *Early History of Assyria*, p.70.

[47]   See G.Wilhelm, *ibid.*; cf. A. Ungnad, *Subartu*, pp.113f.

[48]   See E.A. Speiser, *Introduction to Hurrian*, p.10. In this context, it may be recalled that the Armenian epic of *Hayk and Bel* declares that Hor and Aramaneak were the sons (the latter being the elder) of the legendary hero Hayk (son of Tᶜorgom), for it is possible that Hor is a personification of the Hurrians.

[49]   See G. Wilhelm, *op.cit.*, p.58.

[50]   See G. Rubio, *op.cit.*, p.5.

north), the names of twelve are Semitic, while six are Sumerian and four are of uncertain provenance.[51] This suggests that the proto-Akkadian Semites were widespread throughout the region,[52] even though the first two kings of Kish (as also the last two) bear clearly Sumerian names.[53] Some scholars have even gone so far as to note that there are "few indications of the Sumerian language in the archaic tablets from Uruk and Jemdet Nasr; especially distressing is the dearth of recognizable Sumerian personal names".[54] Indeed, none of the oldest city names such as Urim, Uruk, Larsa, Adab, Lagas, and Zimbir is Sumerian but belong to what Landsberger called a "Proto-Euphratian" substrate,[55] which may be related to the proto-Akkadians. Langdon, however, noted that most of the Semitic names were concentrated in the north, "none of the southern pre-Sargonic dynasties, Erech, Ur and Adab, show Semitic names, whereas the northern dynasties Kish, Maer and Akshak have a mixed nomenclature", and this suggests the "entrance of the Semites into the northern area at Kish and Maer at a very early period".[56] The Semitic Akkadian culture of northern Mesopotamia must have been related also to that of Elam, which is described in *Genesis* 10:20 as a "son" of Shem.

The "proto-Euphratean" relics from the Ubaid culture have, interestingly, been described by Landsberger as indicative of a predominantly agricultural society, which mingled with a more 'professional' Sumerian stratum that included scribes, physicians, and judges.[57] Thus the indigenous Mesopotamians, proto-Dravidian and proto-Akkadian (G.E. Smith's "brown race") may have been less gifted in the direction of urban culture, which was due more to the dynastic Sumerians.

That Akkadian is an older language than Sumerian is suggested by the fact that the Akkadian vocabulary is closer to that of modern Dravidian than Sumerian itself, as the lexical lists presented recently by Muttarayan suggest.[58] This is in consonance with the traditional reverence for the sage

[51] See G. Roux, *Ancient Iraq*, London: George Allen and Unwin, 1964, p.102.

[52] See Poebel, *ZA* 39, p.149,n.2.

[53] See S. Langdon, *Excavations at Kish*, I, Paris: Librairie Orientaliste Paul Geuthner, 1924, p.57.

[54] J.S. Cooper, "Sumerian and Semitic Writing in most ancient Mesopotamia", in *Language and Cultures in Contact: At the Crossroads of Civilizations in the Syro-Mesopotamian Realm*, ed. K. van Lerberghe and G. Voet, Leuven: Uitgeverij Peeters, n.d., p.61.

[55] See B. Landsberger, *op.cit.*, p.9.

[56] See S. Langdon, *op.cit.*, p.58.

[57] See B. Landsberger, *op.cit.*, p.11f.

[58] See K.L. Muttarayan, *op.cit.*, p.42.

Akkathiya (Skt. Agastya) among the Tamils, who consider the latter to be the one who imparted Vedic learning to them.[59] The fact that the Tamils consider Akkathiya as their tutor suggests also that the Tamils (and the Sumerians) are not identical to the original proto-Dravidians/Hurrians of Elam/Akkad. However, Tamil curiously retains some archaic forms of the proto-Dravidic language compared to Akkadian, for the Tamil word "vitu", for house, is clearly more original than Akkadian "bitu", Tamil "panu" than Akkadian "ban", and Tamil "ālu" than the Akkadian umlaut variant "awilu". The greater general deviation of Sumerian from modern Dravidian than that of Akkadian indicates also the relative lateness of Sumerian compared to Akkadian. The Sumerian voiced transformation of the voiceless sibilant in the Akkadian "apsu" as "abzu" confirms the greater antiquity of Akkadian. Again, the fact that the Sumerian word for water itself, "a", drops the final consonant of the Sanskritic (or proto-Dravidian) "ap", even though this final consonant reappears euphonically in the term "abzu", shows that the Sumerian of the Uruk period is a late variant of the original proto-Dravidian language of the Elamites and the Ubaid folk. It seems clear also that Akkadian, on the other hand, is a very senior branch of proto-Dravidian.

It is not surprising that the earliest Akkadians were closely associated with Hurrian tribes as well, with whom they seem to have shared a common historical tradition. A Hurrian magical ritual text mentions historical figures of the northern kingdom of Akkad such as Sargon and Naram-Suen along with a certain "Autalumna of Elam", showing that both Akkad and Elam were considered as parts of an integral Hurrian-Akkadian domain.[60] We have here another indication of the great antiquity of the Semitic Akkadian family. The apparently Sanskritic words that Akkadian contains are no doubt derived from Hurrian/proto-Dravidian originals.[61] The Akkadian word for the Abyss, "apsu", is related to the "Sanskritic" word for water, "ap". The Akkadian term "sibittu" for seven is also remarkably similar

---

[59] See below p.53.

[60] *Ibid.*, p.101.

[61] D. Frayne ("Indo-Europeans and Sumerians: Evidence for their linguistic Contact", *CSMS Bulletin* 25 (1993), 19-42) has suggested that many words in the earliest Mesopotamian texts may have been loans from "Proto-Indo-European". But, apart from the fact that PIE itself is only a hypothetical reconstruction, Frayne seems to think that the Hurrian culture of Halafian Subartu – which he posits as the source of this language – itself may have been a "proto-Indo-European" one. However, we must bear in mind that proto-Indo-European is not the same as "Āryan", as most scholars who use the term PIE seem to think (see below p.32n).

to the Hurrian "šitta" and the Indo-Āryan "sapta".[62] Similarly, the Sanskrit term "hiranya" for "gold" is clearly related to the Akkadian "hurasu", though the source of them both may have been the Hurrian "hiyarruhe". The Akkadian word "atmanu" for "sanctum" (*Gilgamesh* V,249, *Anzu* I,56) is also clearly cognate with the Sanskritic "ātman", meaning soul, and is related as well to the Egyptian Amun (imin), who is called the "inner support" of the entire universe.[63] The Akkadian "atmanu" is the source also of the Sumero-Akkadian term "temmenu"/"temen" for a foundation-stone, particularly that of a temple.[64] The fact that the word "ātman" is no longer generally used for the sanctum or its deity in India itself suggests also that the Indic peoples were in Elam and Mesopotamia long before they migrated to India.

Following the biblical description of the sons of Noah – the Semites, the Hamites and the Japethites – we find that the original founders of both Sumer and Egypt are said to be the *Hamites*. Kush and Mestraim, the founders of Sumer and Egypt respectively, are said to be sons of Ham. In the Priestly version of *Genesis* 9:18, Ham is mentioned as the second son, after Shem,[65] so Japheth may be considered as the youngest. In *Genesis* 11:1, it is stated that the three sons of Noah found the plain in the land of Shinar (Sumer, from [Emesal] Shengir=[Sum.] Kengir) "as they journeyed from the east". The founding of the earliest towns of Sumer, especially Eridu, was thus probably due to immigrants from Elam or farther east. The attribution of the foundation of Eridu to the Subarians/Hurrians[66] suggests that the Hamites of the Bible may also be identified as a branch of Hurrians.

It may be noted that the most ancient bull cult in Anatolia dating from at least the seventh millennium B.C. is dedicated to a Hattic deity called Taru,[67] who was transformed into the Hurrian-Hittite weather-god Teshup. Heth is said to be a son of the Hamitic Canaan in *Genesis* 10:15. It is not surprising that the same bovine deity is found also among the Canaanites as Baal.[68] Speiser suggested that "Kina-hhi", the term for

[62] See E.A. Speiser, *Introduction to Hurrian*, AASOR XX (1941), p.82. The close relationship between the Hurrians and Indo-Āryans is discussed below p.34.

[63] See A. Annus, *The Standard Babylonian Epic of Anzu*, Helsinki: The Neo-Assyrian Text Corpus Project, 2001, p.xi.

[64] See W. von Soden, *Akkadisches Wörterbuch*, III:1346. This term is carried over into Greek as "τέμενος".

[65] Ham is, in the early Jahvist version of *Genesis*, considered to be the "youngest son of Noah" (see *The Interpreter's Bible*, N.Y.: Abingdon Press, 1952, I:560).

[66] See below p.39.

[67] See V. Haas, *Geschichte der hethitischen Religion*, Leiden: E.J. Brill, 1994, p.322.

[68] See V. Haas, *op.cit.*, p.320; cf. C.H. Gordon, "Canaanite Mythology", in S. Kramer (ed.),

Canaan, is itself of Hurrian provenance.[69] It is also attested in the Akkadian Amarna texts as "Kinahni". If the most ancient cultures of Anatolia and the Palestine, as well as of Sumer and Egypt, are to be attributed to Ham, it would seem that the Hamites, though described in the Bible as the "second" son of Noah, indeed played a particularly important role in the diffusion of the most ancient proto-Hurrian/Dravidian tradition, which they seem to have preserved very carefully.[70]

According to Sankuniathon of Beirut, Kronos (Kāla/Shiva) granted Attica to Athena (Anat, consort of Baal), Egypt to Taautos (Thoth),[71] Byblos to the goddess Baaltis or Dione (who may be a consort of El/Kronos himself), and Beirut to Poseidon and the Kabeiri, or Dioscuri.[72] Of the descendants of the Kabeiri, it was Chna (Canaan) who changed his name to Phoenix (Phoenicia).[73] It is clear therefore that the Hamitic Canaanite culture was a widespread one.

Indeed, the Zeus mythology of the Greeks derives in most part from Crete,[74] which in its Neolithic period seemed to Evans to be "an insular offshoot of an extensive Anatolian province".[75] The name of the legendary king Minos of Crete is cognate with Manu/Menes and this may be due to the arrival of Egyptians from the Delta in the period immediately following the Neolithic.[76] It is to be noted, at the same time, that the Cretan Zeus, who is the son of Chronos, is called Zagreus, which suggests an origin of the deity in the Zagros mountains.[77] This indicates that the Zeus cult is derived from the Enki/Varuna and Marduk/Ninurta cults first developed

---

Mythologies of the Ancient World, Garden City, NY: Doubleday, 1961, pp.181-215. In the Bible (*Genesis* X:15), Canaan also engenders the Amorite.

[69] See E. Speiser, *Mesopotamian Origins*, p.141.

[70] See G. Sergi, *The Mediterranean Race: A Study of the Origin of European Peoples*, London: W. Scott, 1909, p.150, where the author maintains that the indigenous peoples of Asia Minor as well as Syria are of the same type as the Egyptians and "derived from the same centre of diffusion". These Hamitic folk form part of the Mediterranean Race (*ibid.*, p.41).

[71] According to Malalas, Thoth came from "Italy" (see below p.49).

[72] The Kabeiri are also identified with the Korybantes and the Samothracians (see Philo of Byblos, *op.cit.*, p.47).

[73] *Ibid.*

[74] See A.B. Cook, *Zeus*, I:644ff.; cf. M.L. West, *The Orphic Poems*, Oxford: Clarendon Press, 1983, p.50.

[75] Quoted in G. Childe, *The Dawn of European Civilization*, p.17.

[76] See G. Childe, *op.cit.*, p.19; cf. Hesiod, *Catalogues of Women and Eoiae*, 74: "(Minos) who was most kingly of mortal kings and reigned over very many people dwelling round about, holding the sceptre of Zeus wherewith he ruled many."

[77] See below p.202.

in the Elamite region.[78] The Sumerian appearance of some of the statues in Crete,[79] however, suggests that it was the brachycephalic Sumerian race which spurred the Uruk development that may have crystallised the Cretan culture as well. The Sumerians may be a branch of the proto-Dravidians mixed with brachycephalic, perhaps Alpine, or even Uralic, elements.[80]

The Semites, Hamites and Japhetites may have all been early settled in Elam as proto-Hurrians/Dravidians. According to *Genesis* 11, the division of languages first occurred in Babel, in the north, after the settlement of Eridu/Ubaid by the three sons of Noah. So it is likely that the language of Elam/Eridu as well as of proto-Akkadian Kish was indeed a form of proto-Dravidian/Hurrian,[81] whereas the languages of the Uruk period were split into Sumerian, Akkadian and Elamite. The king associated with Babel is the Hamitic king, Nimrod.[82] As Nimrod is also called son of Kush in *Genesis* 10:8, it is difficult to discern the influx of a new racial element into the Hamitic in this biblical statement. Yet, as we shall see, there is a noticeable difference between an early stratum of Mediterranean folk and a later brachycephalic, or "Armenoid", one in the Uruk culture of Sumer as well as in early Egypt.

G.E. Smith, in the case of pre-dynastic Egyptians of Naga-ed-der and Giza, and W.M.F. Petrie, in the case of the Naqada "New Race" graves, have shown that the original founders of Egyptian civilization are to be distinguished from an incoming "*Armenoid*" race. Smith noticed the difference between the indigenous dolichocephalic variety and the alien brachycephalic type both at Naga-ed-der near Abydos and Giza in the Delta, that is, both in Upper and Lower Egypt.[83] This New Race was probably an Armenoid branch of the Indo-Europeans.[84] They may have

---

[78]   *Ibid.*

[79]   See, for instance, G. Childe, *op. cit.*

[80]   For the relation between Dravidian and Uralic, see S. Tyler, "Dravidian and Uralian: the lexical Evidence", *Language*, 44, pp.198-212.

[81]   See E. Speiser (*Mesopotamian Origins*, p.54n) suggests that the very name Agade has the same ending as Hurrian place-names such as Lub-di, Tai-di, Irri-di, so that it is very likely that "the available philological evidence confirms the theory that the oldest population of Akkad had much in common with the Elamitic group".

[82]   According to the Sumerian king-list, it was Enmerkar who was first established at Uruk (see T. Jacobsen, *The Sumerian King-list*, Chicago: University of Chicago Press, 1939, p.87).

[83]   See G.E. Smith, *op.cit.*

[84]   The Indo-Europeans are traditionally divided into three branches, the Mediterranean, the Alpine and the Nordic. Of these, the Nordic, or Āryan, is represented by Japheth in the biblical Table of Nations. We see that the Indo-Europeans are not identical to the Āryans since they include the Alpine "Armenoid" type identifiable with the Uruk Sumerians as well as the earliest proto-Dravidian/Hurrian Mediterranean type (see p.32n).

been characteristically brachycephalic, big boned and fair-skinned, whereas the Mediterraneans are dolichocephalic, small boned and brown-skinned. The "Hamitic" founders of Egyptian as well as of Ubaid Sumer belonged to the earlier Mediterranean type.

The newcomers may possibly be related to the "Beaker" folk, who were widely dispersed in Europe as well as in North Africa in the late chalcolithic era (corresponding to Danube III, ca.2500 B.C.).[85] The "Beaker" folk are brachycephalic[86] and interred in a contracted position in graves aligned in a north-south axis rather than the east-west axis followed by the preceding Corded Ware folk.[87] The beaker folk seem to have been effective traders as well as warriors, the graves of the latter being especially richly supplied with funerary goods.[88] Cremations too were performed by this community and may have been reserved for the upper classes or castes, since cremations in Moravia are seen to be especially furnished with beakers.[89] Though it is uncertain where this type originated, some claiming Andalusia as the original habitat and others Germany, Childe believes that they too were of "East Mediterranean stock."[90] The Beaker folk may perhaps be more accurately identified with the Alpine or Armenoid branch of the Indo-Europeans.[91]

This Armenoid type seems to have, already in the fourth millennium B.C., entered the Nile Delta from Palestine and Syria, but, as Petrie points out, the type is equally present in Libya and could have entered Egypt from the west as well. In fact, Petrie notices family resemblances between the "new race", as he calls them, and the Libyans, Palestinians, Amorites, as well as the earliest inhabitants of Mycenae, Cyprus and even central Italy.[92] The arrival of the new race is dated by Petrie to around 3200 B.C., that is, the time of the Uruk culture, the rise of which is also, as we shall

---

[85] See G. Childe, *op.cit.*, (1961 ed.),pp. 222-8; cf. R.J. Harrison, *The Beaker Folk*, London: Thames and Hudson, 1980.

[86] See K. Gerhardt, *Die Glockenbecherleute in Mittel- und Westdeutschland*, Stuttgart: Schweizerbart'sche Verlag, 1953; cf. R.J. Harrison, *op.cit.*, pp.160f.

[87] See G. Childe, *op.cit*, p.226; cf. R.J. Harrison, *op.cit.*, p.51.

[88] The Beaker folk seem also to have been associated with the ritual monuments of Britain including those at Stonehenge and Avebury (see Harrison, *op.cit.*, pp.94ff.).

[89] *Ibid.*, p.55.

[90] *Ibid.*, p.227.

[91] The Alpine type is said to have the same round skull as the Beaker folk except that it has a rounded occipital bone whereas the Beaker type has a flattened occipital bone (see R.J. Harrison, *op.cit.*, p.160).

[92] This may be the reason why Malalas mentions that Thoth arrived from Italy to rule Egypt after Mestraim (see below p.80).

see, dependent on the infusion of newcomers into a more indigenous Mesopotamian society. As in Mesopotamia, the arrival of the "New Race" in Naqada coincides with the emergence of a greater complexity of social organisation.[93]

The pottery of the area around Badari and Wadi Hammamat, on the other hand, is possibly indicative of the oldest Egyptian civilization, which we may characterise as Hamitic, following the Bible and Malalas.[94] This pottery bears decorations that are different in material, colour and subjects from that of the New Race. Petrie identified the group around Wadi Hammamat as "Punites", or the people who came from Punt and worshipped Min of Coptos.[95] Wilkinson however has recently claimed that the petroglyphs from the Badarian period (5000-4000 B.C.) indeed suggest that the origin of Egyptian civilization is to be found in the Eastern Desert itself.[96] Wilkinson maintains that the people who made the petroglyphs were indigenous Badarians since their boat drawings are earlier[97] than those of the Mesopotamians, whom Winkler had considered as the source of his hypothetical group of "Eastern Invaders".[98] However, even though the Badarians may have been long settled in Egypt, it is possible that the Badarians were not originally native to Egypt since the "rippling" evidenced in their ceramic decorations bears a resemblance to that of the Palestianians.[99] This Badarian or "Punite" race may have been the Hamitic branch of the proto-Dravidian/Hurrian race which first settled Elam as well as Anatolia and Palestine.[100]

The fact that the Badarians were followers of the most ancient religion is clear from the importance given to depictions of the boat as a funerary vehicle, for the motif of the solar barque persists in Egypt throughout its recorded history and points to the solar cosmology that informs all the most ancient cultures that we are studying. The bovine imagery found in

---

[93] See T. Wilkinson, *Genesis of the Pharoahs*, London: Thames and Hudson, 2003, p.185.

[94] See below p.80.

[95] See W.M.F. Petrie and J.E. Quibell, *Naqada and Ballas*, London: Bernard Quaritch, 1896, pp.59ff.

[96] See T. Wilkinson, *op.cit.*

[97] The pottery of Naqada I (4000-3600 B.C.) too reveals the same boat drawings that are found in the Eastern desert (see T. Wilkinson, *op.cit.*, p.69f.)

[98] See S. Mercer, *op.cit.*, pp.5ff.

[99] See *OEAG* III:63.

[100] See above p.11. G. Steindorf suggested that the Badarians were Hamites (see G. Steindorf, *Aniba*, Serv. des Antiquités del'Egypte, Glückstadt, 1935, p.2).

Anatolia is also noticed in the Eastern Desert petroglyphs.[101] Further, the red crown typical of Lower Egypt is already evident in the petroglyphs[102] and a depiction of the ithyphallic Min points to the earliest worship of Amun.[103] The culture of the later dynastic Egyptians probably involved a fusion of the original Badarian with the "New Race".

In the absence of any ancient early documentary evidence of a Sanskritic language in the region before the Mitanni of the second millennium B.C., it is difficult to determine what the linguistic peculiarities of proto-Āryan (eastern Japhetic)[104] may have been, and whether this language resembled the artificially reconstructed PIE at all.[105] The Indo-Āryans however emerge as a recognizable ethnos in the middle of the 16th c. B.C. as the Mitanni.[106] According to Herodotus (*Histories* VII,69), the Medes were originally called "Arians" and it is possible that the Mitanni were the same as the Medes. That Sanskrit, as we have seen, shares several words with Akkadian, is no doubt due to the close relationship between the Mitanni and the Hurrians and Akkadians of the region.[107] Also, the persistence of the proto-Dravidian/Hurrian language in the Āryan languages is attested by

---

[101]   See T. Wilkinson, *op.cit.*, pp.99f.

[102]   *Ibid.*, pp.80f.

[103]   *Ibid.*, p.191.

[104]   The eastern Āryan tribes are distinguished from the western Āryan ones by their 'shatem', as opposed to 'centum', linguistic peculiarities.

[105]   It will be necessary henceforth to rename the current linguistic term "Proto-Indo-European" as "Proto-Āryan", since "Proto-Indo-European" better denotes the proto-Dravidian/Hurrian language than the earliest form of the Japhetic/Āryan branch of it. Aurobindo Ghose pointed out that some of the obsolete or "high" Sanskrit words were indeed common Dravidian ones such as "sodara" for brother (instead of the typical Sanskritic "bratha") and "akka" for sister (see A. Ghose, "The Origins of Aryan Speech", Sri Aurobindo Birth Centenary Library, vol.10, p.560). Interestingly, the common Germanic word for son, "sohn", is similarly cognate with a high Sanskrit word, "sūnuh", rather than with the typical Sanskritic "putra" (*ibid.*). This confirms the relative lateness of the formation of Sanskrit. Proto-Indo-European must include Semitic elements as well since Semitic is one of the oldest branches of it. The modern opposition between "Indo-European" and "Semitic" is therefore to be reconstrued as a religious rather than a linguistic or racial one, based essentially on the radical opposition of one branch of Semites, the Hebrews, to the cosmological religion of the other branches of the Indo-European family (see above p.16).

[106]   See J. Klinger, "Überlegungen zu den Anfang des Mitanni-Staates", in V. Haas (ed.) *Hurriter und Hurritisch*, Konstanz: Universitätsverlag Konstanz, 1988,27-42.

[107]   See above p.26.

the numerous Dravidic words in Āryan, especially Indo-Iranian,[108] Hittite[109] and Greek.[110]

The Indo-Āryans as well as the Iranians are closely related to the northern Scythian branches of their Japhetic race.[111] The Sanskritic names of the Mitanni kings are distinguished by their charioteering affiliation, and this expertise is reflected also in the names (Keres-aspa, Pourus-aspa) of the Iranian branch of the Āryan family,[112] as well as in the extraordinary prestige ascribed to the horse by the Indo-Āryans in their sacred rituals.[113] The close relation between the Indo-Āryans and Iranians and the Scythians is confirmed by the veneration of the horse among the Scythians reported by Herodotus (IV,61).

G. Wilhelm conjectured that the equestrian expertise of the Mitanni may be evidence of an elite warrior caste (Marianni) among them, since the upkeep of horses and chariots was an expensive undertaking.[114] However, even the well-known Hittite treatise on horse-training was written by a Hurrian called Kikkuli.[115] Also, the first four-wheeled wagons were not imported by the Indo-Āryans but are found in Mesopotamia already in the fourth millennium B.C., whence they were transmitted northwards, and

---

[108] One of the most remarkable evidences of the persistence of Dravidian among the Āryans is the use of the Dravidian word 'kutirai' for horse – an animal typically associated with the Āryans – as 'kuzra' in one of the Dardic languages, Tirahi (see J. Harmatta, " Proto-Iranians and Proto-Indians in Central Asia in the 2nd Millennium B.C. (Linguistic Evidence)" in *Ethnic Problems of the History of Central Asia in the Early Period (second millennium B.C.)*, Moscow, 1981, p.81; cf. also F.C. Southworth, "Reconstructing social context from language: Indo-Aryan and Dravidian prehistory" in G. Erdosy (ed.), *The Indo-Aryans of South Asia*, pp.264ff).

[109] The Hittite word for father, "attas", is related to the Dravidian "attai" (see P. Kretschmer, "Indra und der hethitische Gott Indra", p.305).

[110] The Dravidian elements in Greek are obvious in such words as 'παῖς' (Tamil 'paian') for 'boy', and 'παλαιός' (Tamil 'palaia') for 'old'.

[111] See below below pp.63ff. The intimate relation between the ancient Indo-Āryans and the Scythians is attested also by the close similarity between Sanskrit and Russian (even modern Russian).

[112] For the characteristic association of charioteering with the Āryans see A. Parpola, "Aryan Languages, Archaeological Cultures and Sinkiang: Where did Proto-Iranian come into being and how did it spread?", in V.H. Mair (ed.) *The Bronze Age and Early Iron Age Peoples of Eastern Central Asia*, Washington, D.C.: Institute for the Study of Man, I:129.

[113] The horse sacrifice is attested also among the shamanistic Altaics, who no doubt derived the custom from the Scythians (see M. Eliade, *Shamanism: Archaic Techniques of Ecstasy*, N.Y.: Pantheon Books, 1964, pp.190ff.).

[114] See G. Wilhelm, *op.cit.*, p.27.

[115] See A. Kammenhuber, *Hippologia hethitica, Wiesbaden*: O. Harrassowitz, 1961,

even westwards to eastern Europe.[116] W.F. Albright and P.E. Dumont have also pointed out[117] that, though the horse-sacrifice seems to be typically "Indo-European" and attested among the Iranians, Greeks and Romans,[118] there are significant similarities in the processes of the royal horse-sacrifice described in *SB* XIII and those of two texts from Mesopotamia describing an ass – and a bull – sacrifice respectively. The first is an Assyrian text from around the second half of the second millennium B.C. and the second a Babylonian one from perhaps the third millennium B.C. It is likely therefore that the horse-sacrifice of the Āryans was modelled on the bull-sacrifices of Sumer and Akkad.

It is interesting to note that the Mitanni kings also often called themselves "kings of the Hurrians",[119] showing that the Āryans were closely associated with the Hurrian populations, though it is not certain if they were an exclusively ruling class or not, since, even though the Mitanni kings bear Sanskritic names, their consorts have Hurrian ones, and sometimes the kings too, as in the case of Kurtiwaza, who was called Kili-teshup.[120] The considerable number of Hurrian names among the warrior class called "Marianni" reveals that the aristocracy was not exclusively constituted of an invading Āryan elite among Hurrian plebeians.

The language used by the Mitanni too was the apparently Caucasian, and agglutinated, language, Hurrian – along with the official Akkadian. The fact that Sanskrit is not attested in their written records in a single complete sentence may be explained by the possibility that Sanskrit may have been reserved for the priestly caste (and the royalty) among the Mitanni and, as a sacred language ('daiva vāk'), could not be committed to writing.[121] The fact that Sanskritic names seem to have been reserved for the male members of the Mitanni royalty seems to be related to the fact that, in India too, Sanskrit was spoken only by the two upper castes and not by women or the lower castes, who only spoke Prākrit.

---

[116] See J.P. Mallory and V.H. Mair, *op.cit.*, pp.324ff.

[117] cf. W.F. Albright and P.E. Dumont, "A Parallel between Indic and Babylonian Sacrificial Ritual", *JAOS* 54 (1934), 107–28.

[118] See Herodotus, VII,113, Pausanias III,20,4.

[119] So in the case of Artadama I, Sudarna III, and Tuishratta.

[120] See A. Kammenhuber, *Die Indo-Arier im Vorderen Orient*, Heidelberg: C. Winter Verlag, 1968, p.71.

[121] G. Wilhelm (*op.cit.*, p.18) suggests that the absence of complete Sanskrit texts in the records of the period may be due to scribal incompetence in transcribing a foreign tongue. But this is unlikely, since, even in India, Sanskrit was not committed to writing until relatively recently.

If Sanskrit was indeed the oral language of the higher castes of the Mitanni, the inflection evident in its structure is nevertheless shared with Akkadian, which is a Semitic language. We have already noted the close unity between Hurrians and Akkadians,[122] and the fact that the Akkadians also have an inflected language suggests that inflection must have arisen among the peoples of northern Mesopotamia, where the Akkadians as well the Mitanni and their Hurrians were principally located. However, the greater phonetic, morphological and syntactical complexity of Sanskrit compared to Hamitic, Hurrian, or even Akkadian may have been due to the linguistic peculiarities of the Japhetic Āryans themselves.

~

As regards the original home of the people who developed the cosmological insights shared by the most ancient religions of the region, the only evidence we have is that of the so-called "Flood" story. The Flood story is clearly a cosmological account of the birth of the universe and its light after the destruction of the cosmos at the end of a cosmic age.[123] The "boat" which survives the flood bears the seeds of universal life and comes to rest atop a mountain, which is indeed the location in which the light of the universe arises – as the Egyptian evidence makes clear.[124] The story of the deluge however is transferred to a terrestrial setting in the popular flood stories of Sumer, India, and Israel. The "ark", or boat, which sails over the flood, lands on a terrestrial mountain and this mountain is considered to be the originating point of the race itself, since the survivor is described as a primeval king or sage.[125]

In the Indian account of the Flood in the BP, the boat of Manu comes to rest upon an unnamed "northern" mountain (VIII, 24). In the MP we have seen the same Manu practising penance on Mt. Malaya, a name still used for mountains in South India. In the Babylonian history of Berossos,

---

[122] See above p.26f.

[123] See P. Jensen ("Assyrio-Hebraïca", ZA IV (1889), p.272f) was one of the first scholars to point out the similarity of the term "tebitu" in the cosmological verse "sihhirutusu ina elippi tebitim sallum" (Hymn IV to Tammuz, R 30, no.2) to the ship of the deluge.

[124] See below p.166; cf. p.255 below, where the Sumerian "magur" boat which bears the sun is identified with the moon, the moon being the bearer of the seeds of universal life (see below p.258).

[125] In a Hurrian fragment of the flood story, Atrahasis, the survivor, is mentioned as being the son of Hamsa. (see H.G. Güterbock, Kumarbi, Istanbuler Schriften 16, 1946, p.30f.). In India, the sun is called the "swan (hamsa) in the sky" (see, for instance, Katha Upanishad, II,2). So it is possible that Atrahasis, like Manu (Vaivasvata), is the son of the sun (Vivasvant).

the boat of Xisouthros (corresponding to the Sumerian Ziusudra, the Babylonian Atrahasis[126] and Utnapishtim of the Gilgamesh epic[127]) lands in Armenia. According to Nikolaos of Damascus, a contemporary of Augustus,[128] the Armenian mountain on which the boat landed is the Baris mountain, which may be the same as Mt. Ararat (north of Lake Van) mentioned in the biblical Flood story of *Genesis* 8:3. According to Berossus, the Babylonians moved to different parts of Babylonia from Armenia.[129] In the Ethiopian 'Romance of Alexander', the Brāhmans are called the sons of Adam's son, Seth,[130] and Noah was considered a transmitter of the wisdom of Seth.[131] Since Adam is indeed the Cosmic Man and not a human, we may assume that the brāhmans referred to here are associated with the preservation of the Divine Consciousness of Brahman which arises from the Cosmic Egg and is later conveyed to humanity by the seventh Manu/ Noah.[132] Josephus declares that Seth

> strove after virtue and, being himself excellent, left descendants who imitated the same virtues. All of these, being virtuous, lived

---

[126] Usener suggested that the right form of this name may have been Hasis–Atra, which seems likely as the Babylonian version of the Sumerian Ziusudra (see H. Usener, *Die Sintflutsagen*, Bonn: Friedrich Cohen, 1899.

[127] In the Gilgamesh epic (XI,204), Utnapishtim is said to be beyond the Ocean in the region whence "the rivers flow forth". We may surmise that Utnapishtim, like Manu, must be resident in the region of the Moon, the lower heavens.

[128] Nikolaos is reported in Josephus' *Jewish Antiquities*, I,93.

[129] See Berossus in W. Lambert, *op.cit.*, p.136. Berossus, like all authors of terrestrial Flood stories, believes that the antediluvian history is also set on earth, in his case, in Babylonia.

[130] See E.A.W. Budge, *The Alexander Book in Ethiopia*, London: Oxford University Press, 1933, p.75. The identification of the Brāhmans with Seth may be glossed with the reference in the *BrdP* I,i,1,8ff. to the fact that the Purānas (or the original Purāna which was later divided into the several extant Purānas) were transmitted by the sage Vasishta (one of the seven sages) to other divine sages Parāsara, Jātukarnya, and Vyāsa (also called Dvaipāyana) and the last then transmitted this divine learning to the mortals Jaimini, Sumantu, Vaisampāyana, Pailava, and, finally, Lomaharshana *the Sūta*. A Sūta is not a Brāhman but the son of a kshatriya father and a brāhman mother (see, for instance, *Gautama Dharmasūtra*, 4,15), but the fact that it is a Suta who relates the contents of the *BrdP* – which may indeed reflect most closely those of the original Purāna – is significant. Annus identifies the Sutians with the Sethians since the name Suti'u seems related to the Amorite Šᵉti'u meaning "descendants of Šutu/Šitu" (*ibid.*, p.xxvi). But it is not likely that the Sutians, of whom little is known before the first half of the second millennium B.C. and first appear in the region of Mari as raiders, can be identified with the original sons of Seth who are associated with the Brāhmans in the *Ethiopian Romance of Alexander*.

[131] See A. Annus, *op.cit.*, p.xxix.

[132] See below p.74.

in happiness in the same land without civil strife, with nothing unpleasant coming upon them until after their death. And they discovered the science with regard to the heavenly bodies and their orderly arrangement.[133]

Josephus identifies the land of Seth as located around "Seiris", which is also the land of Noah, who is said to have preserved the wisdom of Seth. In the Christian *Opus Imperfectum in Matthaeum of Pseudo-Chrysostom*, the books of Seth were supposed to have been hidden by Noah in the land of Šir, and the so-called "cave of treasures" in which they were hidden is identifiable with Mt. Ararat.[134] In *Genesis* 14:6, the Horites, or Hurrians, are particularly identified with Mt. Seir, and we see again a close identification of the proto-Hurrians with the proto-Dravidians of BP, where Manu is King of Dravida. The Brahmans who are considered to be the "sons of Seth" must have originally constituted the priesthood of the proto-Hurrian/proto-Dravidian population.[135]

Since the earliest centres of high culture are those of the Canaanites, Hatti, Elamites, Sumerians, and Egyptians, it is possible that Mt. Ararat was the central region from whence the proto-Dravidians travelled to Palestine, Anatolia, Mesopotamia and Egypt. In one version of the Sumerian king-list, Ziusudra, the survivor of the Deluge, is also said to have lived in Shuruppak,[136] the last of the antediluvian cities, situated north of Uruk. In the Sumerian Gilgamesh epic, the mountain atop which the boat comes to rest is called Mt. Nimush (or Nisir), which may be in the Zagros.[137] If so, the region around this particular mountain may have been the home of

---

[133]   See Josephus, *Jewish Antiquities*, I:70-1. Mount Seiris may be a corruption of the name of Anzu's mountain Sarsar in the *Epic of Anzu* where Ninurta regains the tablet of destinies after battling Anzu (see A. Annus, *op.cit.*, p.xxviiiff.).

[134]   See G.G. Stroumsa, *Another Seed*, p.117.

[135]   The term Hurrian (derived from Suwariyat/Sūrya; see above p.51) however may not be equated with Āryan since both Iranian and Indian have distinct terms for the sun (sūrya, hvare) and for the community of Āryans (ārya, eira), respectively. Hurrian certainly includes a strong Dravidic element in it (see above p.23).

[136]   W–B 62, where Ubar-Tutu(k) the king of Shuruppak is mentioned as the father of SU-KUR-LAM (representing Shuruppak itself), whose son is said to be Zi–u–sud–ra (see T. Jacobsen, *Sumerian King-List*, pp.75f.).

[137]   The name of the mountain is sometimes read as Nisir. It is probable that Nimush is the original version of the name in the face of the evidence of the *BP* (cf. M.L. West, *East Face of Helicon*, Oxford: Clarendon Press, 1997, p.492); cf. Ashurnasirpal, *Annals* II:34 (see Streck, *ZA*, XV, 272-5). M.G. Kovacs has suggested that it might be the same as Pir Omar Gudrun in southern Kurdistan (see *The Epic of Gilgamesh*, tr. M.G. Kovacs, Stanford: Stanford University Press, 1985, p.113).

the originators of the Gilgamesh story. It is noteworthy that the *BP* begins
its long narratives at the hermitage of Suta in the forest of Naimish (*BP*
I,1,4), which may indeed be the same as the mountain mentioned in the
Gilgamesh epic.

It is possible that one of the earliest regions to be settled by the
Noachidian peoples from neighbouring Armenia was Anatolia.[138] This is
suggested by the great antiquity of the Neolithic archaeological finds at Çatal
Hüyük in (ca. 7th millennium B.C.). The civilisation of Syro-Palestine may
be even as old as that of Anatolia since settlements in Jordan are traceable
from the late 7th millennium B.C. and in Byblos from the 6th.[139] Following
the archaeological finds from Anatolia and Syro-Palestine are those from
Susa. Susa I dates from the sixth to the fifth millennium B.C. [Berossus'
history mentions as the first king after the flood Euekhoios,[140] whose name
may be a veiled Greek reference to Susa or a man (=king) of Susa (Greek
"eu" corresponding to Sanskrit "su"), since it does not seem to correspond
to the fragmentary name of the first king of Kish in the Sumerian king-
list (Ga...ur)]. The earlier settlements in the Elamite highlands than in the
neighbouring river-valleys may be due to the fact that it was not originally
possible to cultivate land in the swampy plains of Mesopotamia.[141] Speiser
considered Susa I to be related to similar cultures scattered across the
whole of Mesopotamia and Persia, as well as in Armenia, Baluchistan,
and a little later in Eridu.[142] He, along with Frankfort, conjectured that the
source of this culture may have been in Armenia itself, especially since the
farthest northern site to yield pottery of the Susa I type is Mt. Ararat.[143] So
it is possible that we have in Elam, as in earliest Anatolia and Palestine,
the same Noachidian proto-Dravidian people. As for the biblical account
of the earliest Elamites, we have noted that it considers Elam as a son of

---

[138] Though the urban Neolithic achievements at Çatal Hüyük seem to be older than those
in Armenia, there is evidence of similar development at the border of ancient Armenia in
Jarmo (see D. Lang, *Armenia: Cradle of Civilization*, London: George Allen and Unwin, 1980,
p.61).

[139] See G.W. Ahlstrom, *Ancient Palestine: A Historical Introduction*, Minneapolis: Fortress
Press, 2002; J. Cauvin, *Religions néolithiques de Syro-Palestine*, Paris: J. Maisonneuve,1972;
S.A. Cook, *op.cit* ; for Jericho, see K.M. Kenyon, *Digging up Jericho*, London: E. Benn, 1957.

[140] Reported by Alexander Polyhistor (see G. P.Verbrugghe and J.M. Wickersham, *Berossus
and Manetho, Introduced and Translated: Native Traditions in Ancient Mesopotamia and
Egypt,* Ann Arbor, MI: University of Michigan Press, 1996, p.51).

[141] See H. Nissen, *The Early History of the Ancient Near East 9000-2000 B.C.*, tr. E. Lutzeier
and K.J. Northcott, Chicago: University of Chicago Press, 1988, pp.55ff.

[142] See E. Speiser, *Mesopotamian Origins*, pp.63f.

[143] *Ibid.,* pp.65ff. Speiser placed the "original center" of the First Aenolithic culture
"somewhere between Anatolia and the Caspian" (p.66).

Shem. This suggests that the proto-Akkadian Semites formed a major constituent of the proto-Dravidian/Hurrian population in Elam. Though, these proto-Akkadians may well have been just proto-Dravidians speaking the Akkadian dialect of the "eldest son" of Noah, Shem. The resemblances to Sanskritic vocabulary in Akkadian must derive from the common proto-Dravidian source which produced both Akkadian and, later, Sanskrit.

Of the early Ubaid culture of southern Mesopotamia, Eridu, which dates from the sixth millennium B.C., shows marked Elamite affinities. In fact, as Frankfort pointed out, in Elam "the stage corresponding with al-Ubaid" was found "overlying that called 'Susa I'".[144] According to Speiser, the original name of Ku'ara (near Eridu) in the first dynasty of Uruk[145] – HA.Aki – may be of Subarian, or proto-Hurrian origin.[146] The very term "subari" or, more precisely, "suwari",[147] is clearly related to Suvalliyat (Suvariya)/Sūrya, which is also the Hititte/Indic name of the sun-god. Hurri then would be the Iranian pronunciation of the same name, as the Iranian name of the sun-god, "Hvare", suggests. The Subarians were traditionally identified as a northern highland people, though they may have moved south to Elam as well.[148] The presence of the Hurrians in southern Mesopotamia is attested from the Old Babylonian period since magical ritual tablets of this epoch contain Hurrian language texts.[149] The wide-ranging extent of the Ubaid culture is evident from the fact that even the most northern city of Nineveh was continuously occupied from the fifth millennium.[150]

The earliest sites of northern Mesopotamian culture are indeed to be found in Tel el Halaf, dating back to around 5000 B.C.[151] The powerful

---

[144]   H. Frankfort, *Archeology and the Sumerian Problem*, Chicago: Chicago University Press, 1932, p.19.

[145]   See T. Jacobsen, *The Sumerian King-List*, p.89. It may also be related to the original Akkadian A.a for Ea.

[146]   See E. Speiser, *Mesopotamian Origins*, p.38f.

[147]   *Ibid.*, p.39n; cf. the letter of Rîb-Aeldi, Prince of Byblos which refers to the land of Suru, which may be synonymous with Subartu (see A. Ungnad, *op.cit.*, p.50).

[148]   According to Landsberger, the pre-Sumerian "Proto-Euphratians" of the south are to be distinguished from the pre-Semitic "Proto-Tigridians" of the north (see B. Landsberger, "The Beginnings of Civilization in Mesopotamia" [1944], in *Three Essays*).

[149]   See G. Wilhelm, *Grundzüge der Geschichte und Kultur der Hurriter*, Darmstadt: Wissenschaftliche Buchgesellschaft, 1982, p.97.

[150]   See G. Leick, *Mesopotamia: The Invention of the City*, London: Penguin Books, 2000, p.222. Similarly Nippur, south of Babylon, was inhabited from the fifth millennium (*ibid.*, p.143) and Sippar, farther north, is mentioned in early cosmogonical texts, as one of the oldest cities in the land, much like Eridu (*ibid.*, p.172).

[151]   See J. Finegan, *Archaeological History of the Ancient Middle East*, Boulder, CO: Westview Press, 1979, p.7.

influence of the Halafian culture is attested in the imitations of its pottery in southern Armenia[152] as well as in northeastern Syria.[153] One major distinction of the northern culture is the aesthetically more advanced state of the pottery of the Tel al Halaf region in the north, which is contemporaneous with Ubaid I. The Ubaid I pottery of the delta, dating from even before 5000 B.C., on the other hand, is characterised by a much lower level of craftsmanship and artistry.[154] The Tel el Halaf pottery is marked by bucranium designs[155] which associate it with the seventh millennium shrines of Çatal Hüyük in eastern Anatolia,[156] which may have been established by the earliest proto-Dravidians or Hurrians.

Recently, Oates has shown that, in spite of their qualitative differences, there are generic similarities also between the Samarra and the Ubaid pottery.[157] And Charvat has revealed that the fundamental social and religious forms of later Mesopotamian culture, including that of Uruk, are evident already in embryonic form in the early chalcolithic sites of northern Mesopotamia.[158] Crematory practices associated with fire-rituals are noticed here[159] and Tell Arpachiyah (TT6) also gives the first evidence of the use of the white-red-black colour triad which persists from chalcolithic times to Uruk[160] and is representative of three of the four castes – the brāhman, kshatriya, and shudra – amongst the Āryans.[161] So we may assume that the proto-Dravidians including proto-Akkadians were present in the

---

[152] See D. Lang, *Armenia*, p.63.

[153] See G.W. Ahlström, *The History of Ancient Palestine*, p.107.

[154] *Ibid.*, p.9.

[155] *Ibid.*, p.7.

[156] For Çatal Hüyük, see J. Mellaart, *Çatal Hüyük: A Neolithic Town in Anatolia*, London: Thames and Hudson, 1967; also H. Nissen, *op.cit.*, p.35f.

[157] See J. Oates, "Ur and Eridu: the Prehistory", *Iraq* 22 (1960), p.42, where she suggests a common ancestry for both Samarra and early Eridu.

[158] See P. Charvat, *op.cit.*, pp.92,96.

[159] *Ibid.*, pp.45,90.

[160] *Ibid.*, p.92. In Greek antiquity, black may have denoted prime matter, red matter and white spirit (*ibid.*, p.93). This corresponds to the three basic energies in Indian philosophy, Tamas, Rajas, Sattva (see below p.74). In Egypt, Osiris is frequently represented with black skin, indicating perhaps his lordship of Earth and of the dead (see R.H. Wilkinson, *Symbol and Magic in Egyptian Art*, London: Thames and Hudson, 1994, p.109).The association of the three Indian castes with these colours is clearly due to the predominance of the sattvic, rajasic, and tāmasic elements, respectively, in them.

[161] See, for instance, *BrdP* I,ii,15,18ff. The vaishya caste is normally represented by the colour yellow. The absence of yellow in the pottery of this period suggests that the original caste-system of the Hurrians was a tripartite one comprised of priests, warriors and agriculturists (cf. the Iranian castes mentioned below p.157).

north as well as in Elam and Eridu. Since Armenia is the most likely place from which the cultures of both Çatal Hüyük and Tel el Halaf may have originated, it is probable that we are dealing, in the case of the sixth- and fifth millennium pottery of the north as well as the south, with the proto-Dravidian or Noachidian race.

The Uruk culture (from ca. 3500 B.C.), however, is significantly different from the earlier Susaite culture of the Ubaid period, and we may detect the arrival of the Armenoid, proto-Alpine founders of Sumerian culture in this period. It must be noted also that the earliest Uruk tablets are from both Kish and Uruk proper,[162] which suggests an extensive north-south migration of the new Sumerians. But the fact that the Sumerian king-list begins its postdiluvian section with the establishment of a kingdom at Kish in the north, which is more likely proto-Dravidian and proto-Akkadian, suggests that the political ascendancy of the Sumerians in Uruk was a gradual one, beginning with political accomodation with the original inhabitants of the north and ending with a final establishment of independence at Uruk.

The cuneiform system of writing emerges in the Uruk period and is transmitted in a simplified form to Elam. That the Sumerians were clearly the founders of the system of notation and writing which developed in the south is made clear by the fact that only Sumerian has the phoneme-values required to make the word for Enlil intelligible.[163] The first numerical tablets found at Uruk are from the Uruk IV period, whereas those in Elam date from the following Uruk III period,[164] showing that the transmission of writing to Elam was relatively late. The earliest tablets also give evidence of a sexagesimal system of measurement along with four other systems varied according to the objects being measured,[165] whereas the Elamites used mostly just the decimal system.[166] The Sumerians seem to have been responsible for both the administrative excellence attested by their invention of writing and the urban civilisation that the Uruk culture, which begins Sumerian civilisation proper, represents.[167]

---

[162] See J. Bottero, *op.cit.*, p.70.

[163] *Ibid.*, p.80.

[164] See H. Nissen, P. Damerow, R.K. Englund, *Archaic Bookkeeping*, Chicago: University of Chicago Press, 1993, p.5

[165] Thus discrete objects were measured mostly in the sexagesimal system whereas land measures were recorded through the Gan2 system (*ibid.*, pp.27,43,138,131).

[166] *Ibid.*, pp.93-5, pp.75-7.

[167] See G. Algaze, *The Uruk World-System: The Dynamics of Expansion of early Mesopotamian Civilization*, Chicago: Chicago University Press, 1993.

A noteworthy difference that is evident between the Ubaid and Uruk cultures is their respective customs of interment, with the former favoring an extended posture of the corpse and the latter a flexed.[168] We have noted that the Beaker folk of Europe also favoured this form of burial. It is to be noted that, while the skulls found in the graves of the Ubaid period are all dolichocephalic and "Mediterranean", those of the subsequent Uruk culture are mixed, showing at first a "predominance of brachycephali" which is gradually replaced by dolichocephali.[169] The brachycephalic skulls of Ubaid signal an Armenoid race, belonging either to the Alpine physical type or to the Uralic,[170] but the new race must have been assimilated into the older population. The language of the Sumerians may be a form of the original proto-Dravidian/Hurrian language modified by that of the new stock, either Alpine Indo-European or Uralic. The pictorial representations of the early Sumerians reveal markedly Anatolian, "Hittite" noses, and the Sumerian language, both the Main Dialect and Emesal, may have contributed to proto-Hittite itself.[171] We have seen also that the Cretan peoples may have been related to the Anatolian and the Uruk Sumerians.[172]

In the Susa II period (latter part of the fourth millennium B.C.), Elam too was "colonised" by the Sumerians, since the pottery of this period is remarkably different from that of the earlier Susa I period and bears a close similarity to that of Sumer.[173] Also, the use of a Sumerian name for the chief deity of Susa, Nin-shushinak, seems to confirm the predominance of Sumerian influence in Elam in the post-Susa I period.[174]

---

[168]   See J. Oates, "Ur and Eridu", p. 42; cf. the same flexed position in the Naqada graves studied by De Morgan (see G.E. Smith, *op.cit.*, p.89)

[169]   See H. Frankfort, *op.cit.*, p.9. The recurrence of dolichocephalic types suggests a successful absorption of the new brachycephalic type by the indigenous population.

[170]   It is possible to detect a mingling of proto-Āryan peoples with Ural-Altaic elements in a slightly later period, i.e., in the late Yamnaya culture (ca.2000 B.C.), which reveals a practice of skull deformation in infancy that was indulged in later, in the Iron Age, by the Mongoloid Huns (see J.P. Mallory and V.H. Mair, *The Tarim Mummies*, London: Thames and Hudson, 2000, p.239).

[171]   Cf., in this context, C. Autran, *Sumérien et Indo-Européen*, Paris: Librairie Orientaliste Paul Geuthner, 1925, p.169: "sous le rapport langue,Sumer représente, en tout cas, l'un des eléments qui, en des temps fort anciens, ont concwereouru à la formation de l'indo-européen, qu'il est, par suite, un témoin archaïque de l'un des dialects pré-indo-européens essentiels".

[172]   See above p.28.

[173]   See D.T. Potts, *The Archaeology of Elam*, Cambridge: Cambridge University Press, 1999, p.52.

[174]   See P. Steinkeller, "Early Political Development in Mesopotamia and the Origins of the

Farther east, we know that the ancient civilisation of the Indus Valley is also an extension of the Elamite culture. The first proto-Indus settlements are observed in Mundigak, Afghanistan, neighbouring on Elam, around 3000 B.C. (corresponding to the Jemdet Nasr culture of Mesopotamia)[175] The Kulli culture of southern Baluchistan also resembles Early Dynastic Mesopotamian (ca.2800 B.C.) in its pottery.[176] The presence of fish-offerings to the deity (most probably Enki) in the ruins of the shrines of the most ancient temples of Eridu (which are of pre-Uruk date) is matched by the ubiquitous presence of fish symbols on the seals of the Indus Valley civilisation. This suggests that the Indus culture is as indebted to the earliest, proto-Dravidian/Hurrian religion of Elam and Ubaid as the Sumerian is. Just as the principal Indic god Varuna is described in the *RV* V,48,6 as "four-faced and nobly clad, urging on the pious to his task", so too one of the seals of the Indus Valley civilisation reveals a four-faced deity.[177] The Indus Valley, which derives from Elam at a time of Sumerian domination (Jemdet Nasr being posterior to the Uruk period to which Sumerian ascendancy over Elam may be dated) was probably originally inhabited by peoples representing all the earliest sections of Elamite civilisation, proto-Dravidians/Hurrians, Semitic Akkadians and Uruk Sumerians.[178] The figurines of the Indus Valley reveal the physiognomy of the early Dravidian/Hurrian population with remarkable clarity and the resemblance of this type to that of the Old Kingdom in Egypt is worth noticing.[179]

As for the later, dynastic Akkadians, we find that, according to *Genesis* 10:10, Akkad is said to have emerged during the reign of the great Hamitic king, Nimrod, along with "Babel and Erech [Uruk] and ... Calneh, in the land of Shinar [Sumer]". The concentration of Akkadian power around Kish is made clear from the fact that Sargon, in the Sumerian king-

---

Sargonic Empire", in *Akkad, the First World Empire*, ed. M. Leverani, Padua: Sargon srl, 1993, p.111.

[175] See B. and R. Allchin, *The Birth of Indian Civilization*, Harmondsworth: Penguin Books, 1968, p.105.

[176] See S. Piggott, *Prehistoric India*, p.115.

[177] *Ibid.*, pp.233f.

[178] That the language of the Indus Valley peoples was Dravidian is the common consensus of most scholars today (see A. Parpola, "On the Proto-history of the Indian Languages in the Light of Archaeological, Linguistic and Religious Evidence: An Attempt at Integration", *South Asian Archaeology 1973*, Leiden: E.J. Brill,1974, 90-100; cf. D. McAlpin, *op.cit.*).

[179] See, for instance, M. Jansen, *Die Indus-Zivilisation*, p.226; cf. D. Arnold, *When the Pyramids were Built: Egyptian Art of the Old Kingdom*, N.Y.: Metropolitan Museum of Art, 1999, *passim*.

list, is described as having been a "cup-bearer" of Ur-Zababa(k) of the (18ᵗʰ) Sumerian dynasty, at Kish.[180] The Akkadians seem to have strengthened their political position in the north in the Jemdet Nasr (3000 B.C.) and Early Dynastic I (2800 B.C.) periods,[181] and finally established their rule over Mesopotamia in the Early Dynastic II period.[182]

Turning to the Assyrians, we find that *Genesis* X:11 refers to Assur too as going out of Shinar to build Nineveh, Rehoboth and Clah and Resen. The earliest archaeological evidence from Nineveh suggests the presence of a culture resembling Susa II[183] and undergoing the influence of the Late Uruk,[184] just as Kalah (modern Nimrud) also was occupied from around 3000 B.C.[185] So it is possible that the expansion of Uruk culture was partly due to the Assyrians. Asshur himself is classified as a son of Shem (22), and so the Assyrians may have been related to the earliest Akkadians who first established a powerful kingdom in the region. Indeed, the Assyrian language itself may be considered, if not a dialect of Akkadian,[186] certainly closely related to the latter so that both may have been derived from a common original.[187]

The *prisca theologia* first noticed in Susa and Eridu may have been the source of the Osiris-Horus-Seth cult of Upper Egypt[188] as well as of the Varuna-Mitra/Indra cult in the Elamite Indus Valley. The relatively dark

---

[180]   This is the fourth dynasty lodged at Kish (see T. Jacobsen, *op.cit.*, pp.107,111).

[181]   See B. Landsberger's classification of the earliest peoples in the north as Semitic "proto-Tigridians" above p.39n.

[182]   See P. Steinkeller, *op.cit.*, pp.115,128. The fall of the Akkadian empire was due to the invasion of Gutians, who were neighbours of the Subarians/Hurrians (see H. Weiss and M.-A. Courty, "The Genesis and Collapse of the Akkadian Empire: the Accidental Refraction of Historical Law", in *Akkad, the First World Empire*, p.142: "The localization of Gutium adjacent to Subir/Subartu/ the Habur Plains resolves perhaps the long-standing historical geographical cruxes of the equation of Gutium with Subartu and ARM VI, 27, 'the queen of Nawar' (Tell Brak) and her '10,000 Gutian troops' in the 'land of Subartu'"). The identity of the Gutians is uncertain, but they are quite possibly related to the Hurrians (see E. Speiser, *op.cit.*, p.100ff.). Both Gutian and Hurrian slaves are characterised in a cuneiform text by the same term "namrutim" (see Meissner, *Beiträge zum altbabylonischen Privatrecht*, no.4).

[183]   See R.C. Thompson, *A Century of Exploration at Nineveh*, London: Luzac, 1929, p.108.

[184]   See H. Nissen, *op.cit.*, p.119; cf. G. Leick, *Mesopotamia*, Ch.9.

[185]   See J. Finegan, *op.cit.*, p.105.

[186]   So F. Cornelius, *Geistesgeschichte der Frühzeit*, II, i, Leiden: E.J. Brill, 1962, p.7.

[187]   So S. Smith, *op.cit.*, p.105f.

[188]   See S. Mark, *From Egypt to Mesopotamia: A Study of Predynastic Trade Routes*, College Station, TX: Texas A & M University Press, 1997, p. 115. Osiris is originally the god of Abydos in Upper Egypt (see J.G.Griffiths, *The Origins of Osiris and his Cult*, Leiden: E.J. Brill, 1980, p.60).

complexion and facial features of the early Egyptians as revealed in scenes portraying Egyptians along with Semites may indeed be an indication of the most ancient protoDravidian/Hurrian racial element in their population.[189] The "New", Armenoid, race in Egypt is, as we have noted, considerably distinct from this type in physical stature as well as in physiognomy.[190] However, as the portraiture of the Old Kingdom reveals, the original type persists even after the arrival of the new race. This type is noticeable also in the relatively late culture of the Indus Valley.[191]

The Amun cult of Thebes (in Upper Egypt) seems to have derived its initial impulse from the south, since the divine figure of Amun is based on the earlier god Min (or Amin) of Coptos (at the mouth of Wadi Hammamat).[192] Min was identified with Horus the Elder as well.[193] We will note later in our study of the cosmological bases of the ancient religions that the identification of Min/Amun with Horus the Elder is possible only through the Upanishadic understanding of the equivalence of Ātman and Brahman (Horus the Elder/Mitra/the light of the Mind as well as of the Cosmos).[194] This is why Amun and Atum/Re are also frequently identified in Egypt. Min is traditionally remembered as having come from the land of "Punt" and the "eastern mountain".[195] Hornell suggested that Punt was the early Egyptian form of Pandu, the Dravidian dynasty.[196] However, it is

---

[189]   See, for instance, A.G. Shedid, *Die Felsgräber von Beni Hassan in Mittelägypten*, Mainz am Rhein: Verlag Philipp van Zabern, 1994, pp.60-1; cf. H. Heras, *op.cit.*, p.465.

[190]   See above p.42.

[191]   See above p.43.

[192]   The early Naqada culture of the south reveals, at El Amra, hieroglyphics possibly related to Min, with whom Horus the Elder was identified. These, like the comb with an animal resembling the Seth animal, may be indicative of the religion of the New Race or of the Badarians, who are found not far from them (see S. Mercer, *Horus Royal God of Egypt*, Grafton, MA: Society of Oriental Research, 1942, pp.7-8).

[193]   See the hymns to Min in A. Barucq and F. Daumas, *Hymnes et Prières de l'Egypte ancienne,* Paris: Cerf, 1980, p.367ff. Horus, Amun and Min equally bore the title "Bull of his Mother", Kamephis (cf. H. Grapow, *Die bildlichen Ausdrücke des Ägyptischen*, Leipzig, 1924, p.78). The mother of Horus the Elder is Hathor as Nut (Heaven). The Horus of the south is thus Horus the Elder (An), rather than Horus the Younger, who became Lord of Lower Egypt.

[194]   See the Upanishadic epigraph to this study, p.3 above.

[195]   See C.J. Bleeker, *Die Geburt eines Gottes: eine Studie über den ägyptischen Gott Min und sein Fest*, tr. M.J. Freie, Leiden: E.J. Brill, 1956, p.34ff. Horus too is said to have come from the divine land of Punt (cf. S. Mercer, *op.cit*, p.89).

[196]   See J. Hornell, "The Origins and Ethnological Significance of Indian Boat Designs", *Memoirs of the Asiatic Society of Bengal*, VII,3,139-256.

possible that Punt, like the Sumerian Dilmun,[197] represents a cosmological concept – that of the primordial hill form in which the material universe first emerges from the Abyss – rather than a geographical location, as the following verse from a Gebelein creation myth suggests:

> I [Ihy, son of Hathor, Horus] am the babe in the Primeval Waters
> ...
> I sought an abiding place in this my name of Hahu[198]
> And I found it in Punt. I built a house there on the hillside where my mother resides beneath the sycamores.[199]

We have noted however that Petrie pointed to a certain type of "Punite" pottery at Naqada which is different from that of the "New Race".[200] This probably belonged to a sea-faring group, and the designs on the pottery include a Min symbol, which is related to the sign with which prehistoric ships are.[201] It is not certain if the people who fashioned this pottery were indigenous, or originally entered Egypt through Wadi Hammamat after a maritime immigration from the Red Sea. However, this group already possesses the religion of Ātman/Amun-Brahman/Horus the Elder that informed the later Egyptians. The similarity of the Egyptian name Amun to the Sanskritic 'ātman' for the god representing the soul, life-breath, and wind may indeed not be an accident, especially since, as Manetho maintained, Amun represented both "that which has been concealed" and that which is "identical with the All", which is exactly what the Upanishads also maintain of the soul.[202] It is possible that the earliest Min-worshippers were proto-Dravidians/Hurrians who came by sea from western Asia.

As *Genesis* ascribes the foundation of Egypt as well as Sumer to the sons of Ham, we should not be surprised to find common elements in Egyptian and Sumerian religion. The resemblance of An to Atum, the divine light, is evident from the fact that both are born of primeval "fathers and mothers" such as the "21 fathers and mothers of An" of the An=Anum god-list and the Ogdoad of Thebes. The early Naqada graves of Upper

[197] See below p.53.

[198] Hahu is a form of Shu (see below p.99).

[199] See R.T. Rundle Clark, *Myth and Symbol in Ancient Egypt*, p.88.

[200] See above p.31.

[201] See C.J. Bleeker, *Geburt*, p.41.

[202] See Plutarch, *De Iside et Osiride*, 9 (cf. G. Verbrugghe and J. Wickersham, *op.cit*, p.168); see also the Upanishadic epigraph to this study.

Egypt however reveal the intrusion of an alien Armenoid element.[203] The Armenoid element which established the Uruk dynasties may have entered Egypt from the Levant, and perhaps equally from earlier settlements in western Africa, chiefly Libya. The Naqada graves also have connections to the most ancient Anatolian Çatal Hüyük culture, since offerings of bull's heads and haunches were found in them.[204] This suggests, significantly, that the religion of the "newcomers" was not different from that of the earliest proto-Dravidians/Hurrians, whose worship of their chief deity in the form of a bull is attested also in the Elamite temples adorned with bulls' horns exactly as the Dravidian temples of South India still are.[205]

The clay cones in the architecture of the Delta resembling the cones found at Susa and Mesopotamia during the Uruk period reveal the influence of the later Sumerian culture in Egypt.[206] The formation of dynastic rule in Egypt may indeed have been due to the political organisation of the Armenoid immigrants. The earliest recorded dynasties of Egypt (beginning with the traditional legendary king Menes/Manu)[207] were in all probability influenced by the Uruk Sumerian culture, which is, as we have seen, a largely Armenoid one, though spiritually influenced by the Ubaid/Elamite culture which preceded it. The white crown of Osiris associated with UpperEgypt[208] is, interestingly, also to be found in an early representation of it from the Later Uruk (Sumerian) period in Susa.[209]

The course of dynastic Egypt seems to have followed a south-north direction. The first dynasty in the king-list of Manetho[210] is said to be that of Menes of Thinis, a southern town that has been associated with Abydos.[211] According to Herodotus, Menes is supposed to have founded Memphis in Lower Egypt. This seems to be confirmed by the king-list of Manetho since the second dynasty, also from Thinis, is followed by a third and fourth from Memphis. Memphis, however, seems to have been a major religious centre

---

[203] See above p.29.

[204] See W.M. Flinders Petrie, op.cit, p.61.

[205] See W.M. Flinders Petrie, op.cit., p.63; cf. G.Sergi, op.cit., Ch.IV. See W. Hinz, *The Lost World of Elam*, tr. J. Barnes, London: Sidgwick and Jackson, 1972, p.56.

[206] See S. Mark, op.cit., pp. 66,106.

[207] Petrie dated the arrival of the "new race" rightly to "between 3300 and 3000 B.C.", but he identified this time period with the sixth dynasty rather than with the first, as is done nowadays (see, for instance, the chronology in J. Finnegan, op.cit., Ch.11).

[208] See J.G. Griffiths, op.cit., p.130.

[209] See S. Mark, *ibid*.

[210] See G.P. Verbrugghe and J.M. Wickersham, *Berossos and Manetho*, pp.95ff.

[211] See J. Finnegan, op.cit., p.187.

already in predynastic Egypt since the inscriptions at the temple of Horus at Edfu reveal that the temple was built according to a sacred tradition originating in a region "north of Memphis".[212]

It is difficult to determine whether the Horus-Osiris cult began in the north or in the south. Busiris in the Delta is the most ancient site of Osirian rituals,[213] though Abydos in Upper Egypt is also a major cult centre.[214] Herodotus identifies Khemmis, where Isis is said to have given birth to Horus, as an island in Buto.[215] Very ancient evidence of the cult of Osiris is present in the early Gerzean culture in the eastern Delta.[216] According to Plutarch, the Osiris cult was derived from Syria, since Osiris' burial place was at Byblos in Syria. The association of sun-worship with Syria is strengthened by the reference to Syria as the origin of such worship among the Egyptian pharaohs in the letter of Akizzi, governor of Katna, to Amenhetep III.[217] We have noted that Canaan too is said in the Bible to have been Hamitic, the name of the land itself being probably proto-Dravidian/Hurrian.[218] Syria, we have seen, was originally inhabited by Hamitic Canaanites. It is also not impossible that the Osiris cult was originally located in the south as well as in the north,[219] since Abydos (Abtu) in Upper Egypt seems to have been the Egyptian counterpart of Enki's most sacred seat at Eridu, which, as we have seen, was most probably founded by proto-Hurrians.

The heliocentric religion of Egypt also bears a strong resemblance to that of the Mithraism of the Iranian branch of the later Āryans. The Iranians' preference for Mithra over Indra, who is indeed considered a demon by them, is also reflected in the later denigration of Seth among the Egyptians.[220] The name "Horus" is, as we have noted, probably related to the Iranian word for the sun, Hvare.

---

[212] See E.A.E. Reymond, *The Mythical Origin of the Egyptian Temple*, Manchester: University of Manchester Press, 1969, pp.262f. Ptah is also considered the founder of temples in Egypt (see M. Sandman-Holmberg, *op.cit.*, pp.32ff.).

[213] Cf. PT 182a, b14, where Osiris is called the "dweller in Andjet", a district in the Eastern Delta of which the chief town is Busiris (J. Finegan, *op.cit.*, p.198).

[214] See R.T. Rundle Clark, *op.cit.*, pp.108, 124,131

[215] See J.G.Griffiths, *op.cit.*, p.129f.

[216] See S. Mercer, *op.cit.*, p.98; cf. Z. Saad, *Royal Excavations at Helwan*, Cairo, 1952, pl.xivb, for evidence of a symbol of Osiris at Helwan dating from around 3000 B.C.

[217] See E.A.W. Budge, *The Gods of the Egyptians, or Studies in Egyptian Mythology*, 2 vols., London: Methuen and Co., 1904, II, 23.

[218] See above p.28.

[219] See J.G. Griffiths, *op.cit.*, p.60.

[220] See H. Te Velde, *Seth God of Confusion*, pp.140ff.

The first representation of a Horus falcon is from El-Amra, near Abydos.[221] There is also evidence of the cults of both Horus and Seth in predynastic Naqada I and II.[222] The cult of Horus may thus have been instituted in Upper Egypt by the Badarians, who may have been sea-faring invaders who entered Egypt via the Wadi Hammamat.[223] Horus the Elder was indeed called "Lord of Upper Egypt".[224]

The religious records of the south however suggest an early focus on the *alter ego* of Horus the Elder-Osiris, Seth,[225] the ruler of Heaven (and, in political terms, Upper Egypt), in contradistinction to the ruler of Earth, Horus the Younger (who, in political terms, rules Lower Egypt).[226] POT 204a, 370b call Seth "lord of the land of the south" and "he of Ombos" (see Urk. IV, 1437,8 in J.G. Griffiths, *op.cit.*, pp.21, 99). Ombos is located near Coptos and is a site of the Naqada culture where the "New Race" settled. One of the finds at Naqada was a comb with a carved animal resembling the Seth animal.[227] Seth is, as we shall see, a close counterpart of Teshup among the Hurrians and Hittites, and Zeus among the Greeks, as well as, of Ganesha amongst the Indians.

The reference in Malalas' king-list to the arrival of Thoth from "Italy"[228] to succeed Mestraim, the original founder of Egypt,[229] suggests that the first institution of Heliopolitan theology by the Hamites was consolidated by "Armenoid" immigrants from the early cultures of Palestine and Greece that Sankuniathon refers to in his history.[230] A branch of the Armenoid type may have entered from Syria into the Delta and founded the Gerzean civilisation of Lower Egypt. Also the fact that Armenoid traits emerge in Lower Egypt even earlier than in the south, from Predynastic

---

[221]   See S. Mercer, *op.cit.*, p.88. The early El Amra culture of the south has yielded hieroglyphics possibly related to Min, with whom Horus the Elder was identified (*ibid.*).

[222]   *Ibid.*, p.122.

[223]   See S. Mercer, *op.cit.*, p.88.

[224]   See J. de Morgan, *Kom Ombos*, Vienna, 1895-1909, I, 300, 406 l.5 (cf. S. Mercer, *ibid.*, p.119).

[225]   See J. Finnegan, *op.cit.*, p.171.

[226]   In the Memphite Theology (see A. Erman, *Ein Denkmal memphitischer Theologie*, Sitzungsbericht Berliner Akademie, 1911, pp.916ff), which is older than the Pyramid Texts, Geb gives Upper Egypt to Seth and Lower Egypt to Horus (see S. Mercer, *op.cit.*, p.64); cf. below p.260.

[227]   See S. Mercer, *op.cit.*, p.8.

[228]   The reference to Thoth as "Italic" suggests that the Elamite race was early established in Italy too. Thoth is succeeded in the king-list of Malalas by Ptah and Helios.

[229]   See below p.80.

[230]   See above p.28.

times,[231] suggests that the "New Race" too entered from the north. Further, the Gerzean pottery exhibits influences related to the late Uruk, Jemdet Nasr, ED periods of Mesopotamia as well as to Palestine.[232] That the Armenoid newcomers shared the same religion generally as the Āryans/ Akkadians has been already noted. The epic of Enmerkar too reveals that the Sumerians were worshippers of Inanna, the consort of the solar deity An, as well as of Enlil (Shiva-Indra).[233]

The Amun cult – a more recognizably southern one – is clearly related to the earliest philosophical religion of the Soul, Ātman developed by the proto-Dravidians/Hurrians. The solar aspect of the Osiris-Horus cult of Egypt is well preserved in the cultures of both the earliest Egyptian and the Mesopotamian Hamites. It is also characteristic of the later Iranian Āryans. The Seth cult, on the other hand, may have been due to a segment of the population that was related to Hurrians of Western Asia who later developed the Indra/Teshup/Zeus cults among the Indic/Hittite/Greek Āryans. This segment, however, may have been introduced into Egypt along with the Armenoid "New Race".

~

As regards the cosmological and philosophical insights that inform the ancient religions of ancient Elam and Sumer, it is certain that they were developed first through yogic meditation, as the *BrdP* I,i,3,8, for instance, indicates. Besides, as we shall see, the real significance of the universal tree of life which features in the cosmologies of all these cultures is indeed a yogic one.[234] Since it is most likely that the Noachidian race was indeed a proto-Dravidian one, it is probable that this yogic knowledge is derived from it. *BP* VIII,14,3 informs us that the role of a "Manu", who in BP VIII,24,13 is, as we have seen, called King of Dravida, is to maintain the cosmic order at the time of the creation of the universe. So we may assume that Dravida and its king Satyavrata represent the first fully enlightened mankind. We have seen also that the brāhmans were considered the "sons of Seth", the son of Adam. Since Noah is a descendant of Seth and Noah is the same as Manu, who is a Dravidian "king" in *BP*, we have here a

---

[231] See G.E. Smith, *op.cit.*, p.143.

[232] See J. Finnegan, *op.cit.*, p.168; cf. T. Wilkinson, *op.cit.*, p.127. S. Smith (*op.cit.*, p.44) suggested that the common source of the cosmology of Osiris, Marduk, and Assur may have been Syria.

[233] Cf. the reference to the universal worship of Enlil in "Enmerkar and the Lord of Aratta" above p.19.

[234] See below p.302.

confirmation of the proto-Dravidian origin of the Brāhmanical religion.[235] F.E. Pargiter too maintained that Brāhmanism itself was not originally Āryan but adopted into Indo-Āryan religion from Dravidian.[236] However, Pargiter did not consider the possibility that both Āryan and later Dravidian may have been derived from a proto-Dravidian/Hurrian spiritual culture.

The proto-Hurrians are, as we have seen, most closely related to the earliest Noachidians or proto-Dravidians. The religion of the historical Hurrians based on the Enki cult is most probably derived from the original Dravidian religion. One evidence of the identity of the religion of the Hurrians with that of the proto-Dravidians/Indics is the use of their names Nara and Nārāyana for the primal form of the Lord of the Abyss, Vishnu/Varuna.[237] At the same time, some of their religious terminology reveals early cultural contacts with the Uruk Sumerians, since their pantheon includes Sumerian deities along with Hurrian. The Hurrians bear a highly simplified and popular, but nevertheless comprehensive, record of cosmogonical processes in their epic of "The Kingship in Heaven".[238] This record includes deities that have Sumerian names such as Alalu and Anu and may indicate an early contact between Hurrians and Sumero-Akkadians, perhaps in northern Mesopotamia itself.[239] In the Akkadian period, the cult of Nergal emerges as a particularly strong religious force among the Hurrians.[240]

We have noted the fact that the details of the solar aspect of the cosmology are most similar in the Hurrian and the Egyptian religions. The Egyptian name "Horus" itself may be related to the Iranian Hvare/ Hittite Suwalliyat/Skt. Sūrya, since only Iranian has the "centum" form of the name of the sun-god.[241] Similarly, the term "ka" for the essence of a

[235] See above p.37.

[236] See F.E. Pargiter, *Ancient Indian Historical Tradition,* London: Milford, 1922, Ch.26.

[237] See the list of Hurrian gods of the Hittite treaties discussed below p.62. J.P. Brereton has suggested that even the name "Varuna" may not be of Indo-European origin (see J.P. Brereton, *The Rgvedic Adityas,* New Haven, CT: American Oriental Society, 1981, p.64n).

[238] See H.G. Güterbock, "Hittite Mythology" in S. Kramer, *Mythologies of the Ancient World,* pp.155-161.

[239] For the relations between the Hurrians and the Akkadians in the first Akkadian period (ca.2230 B.C. - 2090 B.C.) see G. Wilhelm, *op.cit.,* p.7.

[240] See G. Wilhelm, *op.cit.,* p.12.

[241] S. Mercer (*op.cit.,* p.91) considered it possible that the name "Horus" may related to the term Hurrian. He is indeed right insofar as both Hurri and Horus are related to the Iranian name Hvare for the sun-god (see above p. 39). Mercer also points to the fact that Horus is derived from a root "hr"which also gives the word for heaven "hr.t" (see S. Mercer, *op.cit.,* p.97). However, it must be noted that the Hurrians themselves called their sun-god Tashmishu in the Akkadian manner (see above p.39, see below p.191).

person is no doubt related to the Iranian "khvarr" meaning the same.[242] In the Tir Yasht devoted to the god Tisthrya, the release of the waters is due to the destruction of Apaosa (Yasht VIII,29), a name which may be related to the Egyptian Apop. It is possible thus that the Egyptian-Hurrians were particularly closely related to the Iranian branch of the Āryans.[243]

For the identity of the founders of the Elam/Eridu culture we may turn to a set of liturgical texts relating to Nabu (texts 66,67)[244] – the divine force representing the moon, and counterpart of the Egyptian Thoth[245] – where Nabu is characterised as the one who founded Eridu. Nabu is one of the seven forms of Ninurta, and the counterpart of Soma, who is the moon-god of the Vedic Indians. Nabu's cosmological priority as the force within the moon – compared to Marduk, who is the force within the sun (which is formed later than the moon) – associates him with Ea and Eridu rather than with the three cities in the antediluvian section of the Sumerian king-list following it that are ruled by the solar divinities, An and Utu.[246] In the temple hymn W.B., 161, Enki himself is described as building the temple of Eridu with the blessings of An and Enlil of Nippur.[247] The close identification of Enki with his son Ninurta and the latter's two forms Nabu and Marduk is one we shall encounter again in other contexts.[248]

---

[242]   See *Greater Bundahishn*, Ch.XIV,2, in Zaehner, *The Teachings of the Magi*, London: George Allen and Unwin Ltd., 1956, p.75.

[243]   If the Elamite Aila dynasty was indeed a "lunar" dynasty, then the fact that the Egyptian religion imported from Mesopotamia is a predominantly solar one suggests that the immigration to Egypt took place after the rise of the solar Ikshvāku dynasty which we may tentatively identify with that of Kish (see below p.55).

[244]   See K. Al Nashef, "The Deities of Dilmun", in *Bahrain through the Ages: the Archaeology*, ed. S.H.A. Al Khalifa and M. Rice, London: KPI, 1986, p.347.

[245]   See below p.254.

[246]   See T. Jacobsen, *The Sumerian King-List*, pp.71-5.Though Nabu is also equated directly with Marduk in an Ersemma text (69,70), it is likely that he was originally distinct from Marduk/Nergal (Al Nashef, *ibid.*). However, the moon and the sun (Nabu and Marduk) are both, indeed, forms of Ninurta. In Susa, Inzak (Nabu) is mentioned *along with* Ea and Insusinak (*ibid.*, p.348). Interestingly, in the myth of "Enki and Ninhursag", Ensag of Dilmun (Nabu) is the child of Enki and Ninhursag. This points to the possibility that Ninsusinak is perhaps identical with or related to Ninhursag (thus a female, or androgynous, deity). If this were so, the name 'Susa' itself may be related to the Sumerian word for 'hills', the Sanskritic "s" being subject to transformation into "h" among most Iranian peoples.

[247]   See H. Wohlstein, *op.cit.*, p.55. In the building record for the Enki temple at Uruk too, Enki is called the first-born of An (*ibid.*, p.73). This Enki is clearly the Lord of Earth and not the primal Lord of the Abyss.

[248]   See, for instance, below p.248.

The Nabu associated with the founding of Eridu in the Nabu texts may then have been a proto-Hurrian god of Elam.[249] This possibility is reinforced by the fact that the Aila dynasty is considered to be a "lunar" one, derived from a daughter of Manu, rather than from a son, as the "solar" Ikshvāku dynasty was.

Nabu's original Elamite name is Enzak/Inzak, who is called the god of Dilmun, the 'pure land', in more than one god-list.[250] In the story of the Flood in the Babylonian *Atrahasis*, we will note that the first man of the present age, Atrahasis, is also blessed with the realm of Dilmun after the deluge. It is possible that Atrahasis' association with Dilmun is the same as that of Enzak, since the moon, in the Avestan accounts, bears the seed of the slaughtered Bull of Heaven (just as the ark of the flood-survivor bears the seeds of universal life). Dilmun is indeed not a geographical location but a cosmological one, signifying perhaps the same state of beatitude as the possibly cognate Sanskritic term 'Dharman'. The Assyrian reference to Dilmun as being "in the midst of the sea of the rising sun"[251] also refers to the "shrine" or mountain atop which the ship of life comes to rest during the flood. Dilmun may thus refer originally to the mountain from which the heavenly light emerges.

The literary references to the sage Agastya and his spiritual instruction of the Tamils seem to suggest that the proto-Tamils are related to the Sumerians of Uruk. In the Tamil Kallatam (10th c. A.D.), Skanda/ Muruga, or Subrahmanya ('perfect brāhmanhood'), is said to have bestowed the Vedic knowledge on Agastya – who may himself represent the Akkadians –,[252] who then transmitted this wisdom to "South India" having crossed the "Vindhya" mountain range.[253] It is possible that the sage Agastya (also called Maitravaruni since he was born of the Vedic gods Mitra-Varuna), is actually a reference to Akkad,[254] and the transmission of Vedic wisdom to "South India" a modern rendering of the traditional memory of a migration of proto-Akkadians from northern Mesopotamia to the Uruk

---

[249]   Nabu is racially not to be equated with his Egyptian counterpart, Hermes (Thoth), who is, in the king-list of Malalas, described as the "Italic" ruler of Egypt after its first foundation by the Hamitic Mestraim (see *Berosus and Manetho*, p.153. As we have seen, the proto-dynastic skeletons at Naqada, of a dolichocephalic Mediterranean type, may belong to the old Hurrian/Akkadian family.

[250]   See K. Al Nashef, *op.cit.*; cf. "Enki and Ninhursag", 45, 3-4.

[251]   See J. Finegan, *op.cit.*, p.17.

[252]   See below p.26.

[253]   See below p.54.

[254]   According to the Sumerian King-List, Akkad is said to have been founded by Ur-Zababa (see T. Jacobsen, *The Sumerian King-List*, p.111).

region of southern Mesopotamia. The reference to the "Vindhya" mountain range suggests that this immigration proceeded from a region north-east of Kish, since there are no high mountains south of Kish.

The Dravidians of the "South India" of the *Kallatam* may be proto-Tamils as distinguished from the proto-Dravidians. They seem curiously contemporaneous with the Armenoid rulers of Uruk. An interesting episode in the Sanskrit poem of Kalidāsa (5th c. A.D.), *Raghuvamsha* (VI,59ff.) refers to Agastya's being the officiating priest of a Pāndya (Tamil) king who is the contemporary of Aja (the grandfather of the Ikshvāku king Rama), and the capital of the Pāndya king here is called not Madurai, as one would have expected if the scene were set in South India, but rather "Uraga",[255] which might indeed refer to the Sumerian Uruk itself. Aja may be represented in the Sumerian king-list as Aka,[256] of the first dynasty of Kish, which preceded the foundation of Uruk. The first rulers of Kish were thus proto-Akkadians from whom the Ikshvākus were derived. Ikshvāku itself seems to be identical to Akshak[257] in the Sumerian King-List.[258] One of the extant Sumerian histories related to "Gilgamesh and Agga" too refers to the initial supremacy of Kish and the north under the king Agga, son of Enmebaraggesi, who demands the submission of Gilgamesh in Uruk.[259]

Agastya is said to have learned the "difficult language" of the Tamils from either Muruga or directly, from Muruga's father Shiva.[260] The reference in Kālidasa must be to a time when the Uruk Sumerians were still somewhat alien to the Akkadians. However, the fact that Agastya is said to have crossed the "Vindhya" mountains in order to reach Uraga suggests that the Kish dynastes included the earliest peoples who arrived from farther north and these we have suggested may have been proto-Dravidian or Hurrian. The presence of a king with the Sanskrit-like name Ūsîwatar (possibly from

---

[255]   See G.S. Ghurye, *Indian Acculturation: Agasthya and Skandha*, Bombay: Popular Prakashan, 1977, p.31.

[256]   The "centum" quality of Sumerian is also evident in the Sumerian word for "eye", "igi", which is closer to the Germanic "Auge" than to the Sanskritic "akshi".

[257]   Akshak was later called Upi (Gk. Opis) and may, like Kish, have been situated in the southern vicinity of modern Baghdad.

[258]   See T. Jacobsen, *op.cit.*, p.107. The first king of Akshak is recorded in the King-List as Unzi, though there was perhaps an earlier ruler called Zuzu (*ibid.*, p.181), who is the only historically verifiable king of Akshak. The first Akshak dynasty may have ended by 3400 B.C. (see *RLA* I:64).

[259]   See J.B. Pritchard, *ANET*, pp.44-7. In the Sumerian King-List, Aka is a king of the first dynasty (at Kish), though Gilgamesh follows apparently later in the second dynasty (at Uruk) after the fall of Kish (see T. Jacobsen, *op.cit.*, pp.85, 89–91).

[260]   See K. Zvelebil, *Tamil Traditions on Subrahmanya-Murugan*, Madras: Institute of Asian Studies, 1991, p.24.

(Skt.) vishva=universal) in the 13th dynasty (established at Kish) of the Sumerian king-list[261] also points to a continuing proto-Indic element in the earliest royal lineage of Mesopotamia.

If the "solar" Ikshvāku dynasty of the Indian king-lists be representative of the Kish/Akshak civilisation, the other "lunar" dynasty derived from Manu's daughter Ilā, the Aila, may well denote Elam.[262] These northern Mesopotamians and Elamites may have imparted their spiritual wisdom to the Sumerians of Uruk, whose political ascendancy seems to have been established first in the south. Both the Aila [Elamite] and the Ikshvāku [Kish] dynasties are derived from Manu, a Dravidian king (BP, VIII,24). If we were to draw up a tentative scheme of first beginnings, we may imagine Noah/Manu as representing an enlightened proto-Dravidian/Hurrian group which branched off into Semitic groups which flourished first in the northern and Elamite mountainous regions and later in northern Mesopotamia, while an Armenoid Indo-European group (perhaps related to proto-Tamil) spread first through north-westerly areas of the Near East and then entered Mesopotamia from the north to finally establish their political supremacy in Uruk.

The original Vedic system of esoteric wisdom elaborated by the proto-Hurrians/Dravidians was conveyed, through the mediation of Akkadians, to the Armenoid-proto-Tamil group which had consolidated their power in Uruk. It may be significant that, in the MBh, Aranyakaparva (IX,45, 87ff.), the title "Yogeshvara" (Lord of Yoga) is applied particularly to the chief god of the Dravidians, Muruga/Skanda.[263] The fact that the historic evidence of the entrance of the modern Dravidians (whom we may call Tamils, to distinguish them from the proto-Dravidians) into South India is of relatively recent date, perhaps around the thirteenth century B.C., means that there are only a few dim hints of the Near Eastern origins of the Dravidian peoples in the earliest archaeology and literature of South India. The earliest archaeological evidence (ca. 1200-80 B.C.) of the entrance of the Tamils into South India is from dolmen burial sites in Adichanallur (similar to those in Palestine and Cyprus), where some of the finds such as golden "mouth-pieces", bronze representations of cocks and spear-heads may be related to the worship of Muruga/Marduk/Ninurta.[264] The megalithic graves of the Madurai district dating from around 1000 B.C. also

---

[261] See T. Jacobsen, Ibid., p.109.

[262] It may be noted, in passing, that the Edda ('The Deluding of Gylfi') too records the first human beings as a girl called Embla and a boy called Ask.

[263] Cf. below p.239.

[264] See K. Zvelebil, op.cit., p.75f.

reveal resemblances to the early Iron Age graves of the Caucasus and Sialk Necropolis B.[265]

The earliest textual references to Muruga from the Dravidian literature of the first three or four centuries A.D. bear witness to a Dionysiac god who is capable of infusing women with love-sickness and possessing his devotees in a frenzy.[266] In this context, we may also note that Muruga's mother is Shiva's consort Parvathi in her form as "Korravai". The adjective 'kuravanji' (nowadays translated as "gypsy") is cognate with the Greek 'korybantes' (associated with the birth of Zeus/Dionysus) and refers originally to the deities of the mountain (which in Sumerian is called "kur"). In the Tamil lexicon, *Tivakaram*, dating from the 8th century A.D., we find a full-fledged religion of Muruga/Marduk among the Tamils since it lists all the titles of the god.[267]

In Mesopotamia itself, the incoming Uruk Sumerians clearly possessed a greater aptitude for urban culture and writing/computing than the proto-Dravidians/Hurrians or Akkadians. The Sumerian political domination of the latter caused their language to be adopted as the sacred language of the entire region and their religio-political system served as the model for all the later states, Elamite or Semitic, in the region. The fact that the later Akkadian religious culture is largely based on a Sumerian pantheon and even the extant Hurrian mythological literature includes references to Sumerian deities such as Alalu and An, indeed suggests, if not the originality of the latter, at least its political and religious predominance over the Akkadians.

When we consider the religion of the specifically Sumerian Uruk culture, however, we should not be surprised to find that there is a clear continuity between the temple forms of the earlier Eridu and the classical Uruk types. We have already seen that the founding of Eridu may have been due to the Elamite proto-Hurrians (who are probably the same as the eldest branch of the proto-Dravidians), since it precedes the immigration of the "Armenoid" type to Uruk. The fact that there are no written records earlier than the numerical tablets of Uruk IV thus does not mean that the most ancient societies of Susa and Eridu were not highly cultured, since the system of writing itself developed mainly for the purposes of computation and not for the preservation of sacred knowledge which, being esoteric, could not be committed to writing but was passed on from generation

---

[265] See B. and R. Allchin, *op.cit.*, p.230.

[266] See K. Zvelebil, *op.cit.*, p.78.

[267] *Ibid.*, p.73.

to generation in an oral tradition.[268] This suggests that the ancient proto-Dravidian religion may have been preserved in Elam and Ubaid in an oral Hurrian/Akkadian form before it was codified by the Sumerian intellectuals of Kish-Uruk.[269]

In passing, we may consider the fragmentary quasi-historical epic of "Enmerkar and the Lord of Aratta", which is set at the time of the founding of Uruk by Enmerkar.[270] In this poem, the latter king seeks to obtain the submission of the Lord of Aratta (probably called Ensukushsiranna). This may refer to the Sumerian subjugation of an older city-state situated east of Elam and Anshan [perhaps in Afghanistan], since it is said to be separated from Sumer by seven mountain ranges (l.171).[271] Aratta is also, interestingly, mentioned in the Indian epic *Mahābhārata* VIII, 30.35 (cf. 43,47) as a hostile mountainous land whence flow five rivers including the Sindhu, and which is peopled by the Balhikas, also called Vasatis, Sindhus, and Sauviras. It is a land that is to be avoided by the Āryas.[272] The Sumerian poem also refers to Aratta as the land cursed by Enki (l.119). It further states that, although Inanna was the goddess of Aratta, "she did not favor him like [she favored] the lord of Kullab [Enmerkar]".[273] The poem recounts Enmerkar's efforts to obtain Aratta's submission to him so that he may establish his kingdom at Uruk with the blessings of Enki of Eridu. It is interesting to note that the religion of Aratta, however, is the same as that of the Sumerians, since both Aratta and Uruk are mentioned in the poem as being devoted to Utu, the sun-god,[274] and his sister Inanna.

---

[268] See H. Nissen, *Archaic Bookkeeping*, p.21, where Nissen points out that, of the 5000 or so written documents retrieved from Uruk IV and Uruk III, "not one of them is clearly related to religious, narrative, or historical topics ... This fact strongly implies that such text genres were simply not written down".

[269] In this context, we may consider the curious passage in *Genesis* 9:22, which states that Ham "saw the nakedness" of his father Noah and told his brothers of it. This may refer to the public dissemination of the ancestral wisdom among the highly literate Hamitic civilisations of Sumer and Egypt, whereas the Āryans preserved it in purely oral form. For the tradition that Noah symbolises the wisdom of "Seth" see p.37 above.

[270] Enmerkar is credited in the epic (ll.504ff.) with the invention of cuneiform writing.

[271] See S.N. Kramer, *Enmerkar*, p.17. In l.177 of the epic, we note a possible indication of the seniority of Enmerkar vis-à-vis the Lord of Aratta, since the latter is called the "son" of the former, though this may just be a manner of political parlance.

[272] See M. Shendge, *The Aryas: Facts without Fancy and Fiction*, N. Delhi: Abhinav Publications, 1996, pp.98f.

[273] See S. Kramer, *op.cit.*, p.9.

[274] In fact, Enmerkar himself may probably have been deified in the Egyptian manner, since he is referred to as the "son of Utu" and as being born, exactly like Atum, "of the faithful Cow [Mehet Ouret] (see below p.150) in the heart of the highland" (l.185).

We have seen that the first settlements in Afghanistan resembling those of Elam and the Indus Valley are from ca.3000 B.C. in Mundigak. As the date of the occupation of Mundigak is somewhat later than that of Uruk, it is not certain if the Mundigak settlement represents Aratta, and whether the hostility represented in the poem of 'Enmerkar and the Lord of Aratta' as well as in the *MBh* is historical at all. For, indeed, like Dilmun, Aratta may have been a symbolic land expressing the opposite of Dharman/ Dilmun, since Dilmun and Aratta are represented together in an early Mesopotamian text as if they were the two poles of the universe.[275]

From 2200-1700 B.C., however, there is clear evidence of typical Indo-Āryan settlement in the BMAC complex, which is not far north of Mundigak.[276] It is difficult to determine whether these Āryans represent a continuation of the early Elamite Hurrians of Mundigak or are new immigrants from the Andronovo culture associated with the Indo-Āryans (1800-900 B.C.).[277] The latter is indeed the more probable. The Andronovo culture is itself derived from the Hut Grave and Catacomb Grave culture of 2800-2000 B.C.[278] and the Sintashta culture of the southeast Urals (2300-1900 B.C.),[279] which may have been proto-Āryan rather than proto-Indo-Āryan. The fact that there is clear evidence of fire-worship in the BMAC and little evidence of it in Mundigak suggests that the former is derived from the Andronovo rather than from the Elamite colonies. Elaborate fire altars are evident in the ruins of the BMAC complex which correspond to the Āryan fire-sacrifices. The temples also contain rooms with "all the necessary apparatus for the preparation of drinks extracted from poppy, hemp and ephedra" that may have been used for the soma-rituals.[280] The BMAC may have thus been the centre of cultural contact between the proto-Dravidian/ Hurrian peoples of Mundigak and the later Indo-Āryans.

---

[275] See H. Nissen, "Ortsnamen in den archaischen Texten aus Uruk", *Orientalia*, NS, 54, pp.228-30; cf. P. Charvat, *op.cit.*, p.156.

[276] Herodotus' description of the inhabitants of the various satrapies of Darius suggests that this region in Afghanistan may have been settled by Bactrians (Darius' 12th province) or Sattagydae, Gandaridae, Dadicae and Aparytae (7th province) (cf. J.P. Mallory and V. H. Mair, *op.cit.*, p.45f.; p.262).

[277] Andronovo type pottery has been found in the early layers of Margiana (see A. Parpola, "The problem of the Aryans", p.363).

[278] The Hut Grave culture apparently separated into the Timber Grave (proto-Iranian) and Andronovo (proto-Āryan) cultures. The fourth millennium predecessor of the Hut Grave and Catacomb Grave cultures may have been the Yamnaya dating from 3500-2800 B.C. (*ibid.*, p.356).

[279] See J.P. Mallory and V.H. Mair, *The Tarim Mummies*, pp.260f.

[280] *Ibid.*, p.262.

However, we must remember at the same time Herodotus' statement that the Iranians did not worship fire originally.[281] In the Purānas, too, Pururavas, the early Aila [=Elamite?] king, is said to have obtained sacrificial fire from the "Gandharvas", who also taught him the constitution of the three sacred fires of the Āryans.[282]This suggests that the early Hurrians of Elam and the earliest Iranians did not worship fire and learnt it from a later, more northerly wave of Āryans. However, even the Gandharas are included among the Aila [=Elamite?] dynasties in the Puranas, which suggests that they too were a northern and eastern branch of proto-Hurrians identifiable with the Japhetic.[283] The Japhetic tribes that moved northwards to the Pontic-Caspian steppes created the Yamnaya culture there, which is considered the major source of the Āryan tribes.[284]

The Gandaridae are also mentioned by Herodotus (III,91) as one of the Indian tribes of the seventh satrapy of Darius I (550-486 B.C.) and can be located near the Bactrians of the 12th satrapy. The archaeological evidence of the early Gandharvas may be that found in the Gandhara Grave culture of the Swat settled from 1700-1400 B.C., which followed the BMAC. The occupants of the BMAC may have been related to the same family as the later Gandhara. Since the Gandhara culture also bears the first evidence of cremation rituals in South Asia, we may consider them to have indeed consolidated the Vedic customs of the Indo-Āryans. Cremation is evidenced also in the Andronovo culture.[285] At the same time, the neighbouring Bishkent culture, which is contemporaneous with the Gandhara and is related to the northern BMAC type, exhibits also a curious

---

[281]   See Herodotus, *Histories*, I,132.

[282]   See F.E. Pargiter, *op.cit.*, p.309.

[283]   W. Bernard suggested that the human remains from Period I of Gandhara bore resemblances to those of Bronze Age and early Iron Age crania of 2500 B.C.-A.D. 500 from the Caucasus and Volga region as well as from Tepe Hissar in Iran (see K.A.R. Kennedy, "Have Aryans been identified in the prehistoric skeletal record from South Asia?" in G. Erdosy (ed.) *The Indo-Aryans of Ancient South Asia*, Berlin: Walter de Gruyter, 1995, p.49).

[284]   See A. Parpola, "The Problem of the Aryans and the Soma", in G. Erdosy (ed.), *op.cit*, p.356.

[285]   *Ibid.*, p.366. It is interesting to note, however, that the earliest Neolithic caves of Palestine in Gezer (7th millennium B.C.) already give evidence of a culture that practised cremation. Inhumation appears in these sites only much later in the fourth millennium B.C. (see S.A. Cook, *The Religion of ancient Palestine in the Light of Archaeology*, p.74). This confirms the possibility that Palestine and Anatolia were first inhabited by proto-Dravidians/Hurrians before they were settled by the Armenoid peoples who practised inhumation. The early neolithic/chalcolithic levels of Yarim Tepe II (7th millennium B.C.), near Assyrian Nineveh, also reveal crematory practices (see P. Charvat, *op.cit.*, p.45). So we may assume that cremation was the earliest funereal mode of the entire Noachidian race.

quasi–Scythian custom of inhumation involving the removal of the entrails and their replacement with clarified butter which may have persisted among the Vedic Indians, as is suggested by *SB* XII,5,2,5.[286]

The Pururuvas who adopted fire-worship from the Gandharas may thus represent an Elamite branch of the proto-Āryan family, while the Gandaridae, who may have arrived from the south-east Caspian region (since the BMAC culture is apparently derived from the latter)[287] may be a later, typically Indo-Āryan, north-eastern branch of the same family. That the Indic Vedic culture itself was developed after ist original formulation in the ancient Near East is suggested by the greater elaboration of the name of the god Tvorestar amongst the Iranians – representing the older religion of the proto-Āryans – compared to the Vedic Tvastr.[288] This eastward movement of proto-Dravidians-Hurrians (Ailas as well as Ikshvākus) with Elamite forms of religion (Brahmanism) may have encountered the more northerly fire-worshipping Gandaridae tribes to form the typically Indian branch of the Āryan family.

The importance of fire-worship is indeed most evident among the Vedic Indo-Āryans and the Avestan Iranians. However, it should be remembered that this fire-worship is employed in a religion which is little different from the solar religions of the Sumerians or Egyptians. In the Sumerian religion too, the chief sky-god An is equated to Girra, the fire-god (in an Assyrian exegetical text)[289] and Re in Egypt is the same as the solar force, Agni. So that it is possible that the adoration of the solar force as divine fire may have been recognized as an integral part of the original proto-Dravidian religion that was shared by Semites, Hamites, and Japhetites. But the actual fire-rituals may have been preserved more carefully by the Japhetic Indo-Āryan stock that had migrated at a very early date northwards to the Yamnaya and Andronovo cultures whence they moved southwards again later, in the second millennium B.C., towards northern Mesopotamia, Iran and India. In this context, it may be noted that the early neolithic/chalcolithic sites of Yarim Tepe II (7th millennium B.C.) also give some evidence of fire rituals in connection with funerary practices.[290]

---

[286] See A. Parpola, *op.cit.*, p.365.

[287] See J.P. Mallory and V.H. Mair, *op.cit.*, p.262.

[288] Cf. A. Jacob, "Cosmology and Ethics in the Religions of the Peoples of the Ancient Near East", *Mankind Quarterly* 140, no.1 (Fall 1999), p.96.

[289] RA 62–52,17-8 (see A. Livingstone, *op.cit.*, p.74); cf. K170+Rm520rev. (*ibid.*, pp.30ff.).

[290] See P. Charvat, *op.cit.*, p.90.

Pargiter has suggested that the Dravidian Brahmanical institution was also considerably transformed by the Āryans. While the original [proto-] Dravidian priesthood was characterised by the practice of yogic austerities (tapas) which gave them magical powers, the Āryan was preoccupied with the performance of sacrifices, especially revolving around the worship of fire.[291] The Indo-Āryan religion thus seems to have combined the ancient proto-Dravidian wisdom of the Elamite/Mesopotamian Hurrians with more northerly fire- and soma-rituals and horse-sacrifices. Also, the original proto-Dravidian or Noachidian wisdom[292] is best preserved in the cultivated [sanskrit=refined] and inflected language of the upper castes of the Indo-Āryans.

~

Of the three sons of Noah, the eastern Japhetic group of Āryans, that is, the Iranians and Indians,[293] seem to have preserved best, in their oral hieratic linguistic tradition, the philosophical import of the ancient cosmology of the proto-Dravidians/Hurrians. This spiritual focus is evident in all of the Indic Vedic and Sanskritic literature, which was originally oral and not committed to writing until relatively recently.[294] The Indo-Āryans are manifest first in the 16th century B.C. in northern Mesopotamia, in the kingdom of the Mitanni.[295] The original home of the Mitanni remains uncertain. It is possible that they may have arrived from the BMAC in Afghanistan (settled from 2200-1700 B.C.), where the evidence of fire-altars confirms the presence of Vedic Āryans.[296] That there was trade between Bactria and North Syria is also proved by the fact that from the 18th c. B.C. north Syrian seals show a typically Central Asian Bactrian camel such as is

---

[291] See F.E. Pargiter, op.cit., pp.308f.

[292] That the biblical Noah, a descendant of Adam's son, Seth, represents the wisdom of Seth is evident from the Gnostic tradition (see G.G. Stroumsa, *Another Seed: Studies in Gnostic Mythology,* Leiden:E.J. Brill, 1984, p.107). Josephus' *Jewish Antiquities,* I, 70-71 also makes clear the association of the line of Seth with cosmological learning (see A. Annus, *op.cit.,* p.xxvii).

[293] The Scythians form an integral part of the Indo-Iranian group, but their spiritual tradition seems less developed (see below pp.41f).

[294] For the early oral history of Sanskrit, see A.A. Macdonell, *A History of Sanskrit Literature,* Delhi: Munshiram Manoharlal, 1961, pp.20f. and C.K. Raja, *Survey of Sanskrit Literature,* Bombay: Bharatiya Vidya Bhavan, 1962, pp.11, 168.

[295] The original cuneiform spelling of the kingdom used by Suttarna I (early 16th c. B.C.) was apparently "Ma-i-ta-ni" (see I. Gelb, *Hurrians and Subarians,* p.70).

[296] This is the view of A. Parpola, *op.cit.,* p.369.

depicted in the BMAC seals.[297] However, there seems to be little evidence
of fire-altars in the Mitanni region itself and it is equally possible that the
Mitanni descended directly into Mesopotamia from the Caspian region
rather than moving westwards from Afghanistan. The Mitanni themselves
may be identifiable with the Medes, and, as Herodotus (VII,69) reveals, the
Medes were once universally called Arians,[298] as well as perhaps with the
proto-Iranians, since several Median words are traceable in Old Persian.[299]
It is clear that the Mitanni culture informs both the Indo-Āryan and the
Iranian.

The Mitanni exhibit an adherence to an Indo-Āryan, Vedic form
of religion along with the Hurrian. The Indo-Āryan culture, as we have
seen, may have been a combination of that of the earliest Elamite and
Mesopotamian Hurrians who adopted fire-rituals from the northern
"Gandaridae" of the BMAC no earlier than the 23rd c. B.C. The first
coherent list of Indic gods in the treaty of the Mitanni-Hurrian king
Šattiwaza and the Hittite king Šuppililiumas I dating from the sixteenth
century B.C. includes the names Mitra-Varuna, Indra, and Nāsatyas.[300] It
is important to note that the Hurro-Akkadian version of the Lord of the
Waters among the Mitanni is 'Uruwana' or 'Aruna'. In the Vedic GB, I,1,7,
Varana[301] is indeed the secret form of the name Varuna,[302] and this repeats
the penultimate vowel of both (Mitanni) "Uruwana" and (Gk.) "Ouranos".
The form "Aruna" is perhaps related to the Hittite term for "ocean"
"arunas".[303] Further, the Sumerian name of the sun-god Utu may have been

---

[297] *Ibid.*, p.362.

[298] That the name "Mede" may be related to the term Mitanni has been suggested by
J. Charpentier, "The Date of Zoroaster", *BSOS* 3 (1923-25), 747-55; B. Landsberger and
T. Bauer, "Zu neueröeffentlichen Geschichtsquellen", *ZA* 37 (1927), 61-98; E. Forrer,
"Stratification des langues et des peuples dans le Proche-Orient préhistorique", *JA* 217 (1930),
pp.227-52; and F. Cornelius, "Erin-Manda", *Iraq* 25 (1963), pp.167-70.

[299] See P.O. Skjaervo, in G.Erdosy, *op.cit.*, p.159.

[300] The text (CTH 51 and 52 (see D. Yoshida, *op.cit.*, p.12; cf. V. Haas, *Geschichte*, p.543)
reads "Dingir MešMitraššiel, Dingir MešUruwanaššiel, DIndar, Dingir MešNašattiyana", where the
uncertain suffix "šiel" may be a dual indicator.

[301] Following the example of the Latin pronunciation, we may assume that the original
Sanskrit of this region also favoured the "u" sound for the phoneme later transcribed with
a "v".

[302] "Being Varana, he is mystically called Varuna, because the gods love mysticism" (see U.
Chouduri, *op.cit.*, p.95).

[303] See G. Wilhelm, "Meer" in *RLA* VIII:3. Wilhelm suggests that this term is not of Indo-
European origin [by which he no doubt means that which is properly called Āryan; see p.
above], but, rather, Hattic.

conserved in the Vedic Brāhmanas as the secret name of Sūrya, Ud.[304]
The fact that some of the esoteric names of the Indo-Āryan deities, Agni
(as Agri) and Sūrya (as Ud), are possibly of Sumerian origin suggests that
Sanskrit itself must have been developed only after the establishment of the
Sumerian Uruk culture.[305] The priesthood at Uruk too must have included
a Brāhmanical element that persisted from Ubaid times. It is possible also
that the Brāhmanical language behind Akkadian "apsu" and Sumerian
"abzu" was ultimately proto-Dravidian, which was loaned into Akkadian,
Sumerian and Āryan equally.[306]

The presence of Indo-Āryan cultural elements in later Mesopotamia
is attested by the occurrence of the divine names Mitra, Gishnu [Vishnu][307]
and Surya [as 'Suliaat', from Hittite-Hurrian 'Suwaliyatta'][308] in the
Sumerian god-list contained in CT 25, which, though dating from Assyrian
times, around the seventh century B.C., must reflect a more ancient list of
Sumerian deities translated into Akkadian. The description of the fire-god
Girra as the "child of the Apsu" in an Akkadian hymn to the fire-god[309] also
corresponds exactly to Agni's typical appellation "apam napat", child of the
waters.

It may be noted that, in *Genesis* 9:2, the eldest son of Japheth
[the Āryan] is called Gamer, representing the Nordic Cimmerians, and
he is followed by the Magog[310] (Magi) and the Madai (Medes), Javan (the
Greeks), Tubal (uncertain), Meschech (uncertain) and Tiras (uncertain).
The Cimmerians themselves are described by Herodotus (IV, 14) as having
had their initial home "on the shores of the Black Sea". The sons of the
eldest son, Gamer, include Ashkenaz (the Scythians), Riphath (uncertain)
and Thokarmah (possibly the Tokharians, or else, the Armenians, whose
ancestor is called Tᵒorghom).[311] We see that the Nordic Cimmerians,
Iranians, Indians and Greeks are roughly contemporaneous while the
Scythians are a somewhat later branch of the Nordic. According to
Herodotus, the Scythians were located, in Darius' time, just north of

---

[304] See *Taittriyopanishad Brāhmana*, I, 45,4: "Yonder sun, that same is *ud*, fire is *gi* [cf. the Sumerian fire-god, Girra], the moon is *tham*".

[305] See above p.41.

[306] See p.26 above.

[307] The lack of the "w" phoneme accounts for the translation of Vishnu into Gishnu in the Sumerian, "g" regularly substituting "w" in that language.

[308] See H.G. Güterbock, "The god Suwalliyat reconsidered", *RHA* 19 (1961), 1–18.

[309] See M.-J. Seux, *op.cit.*, p.251.

[310] Gog and Magog are, in Ezekiel 39:2 and elsewhere, representatives of the utmost North.

[311] See A.E. Redgate, *The Armenians*, Oxford: Blackwell Publishers, 1998, p.14.

the Gandaridae (in the 15th satrapy), and considered themselves as the "youngest of all nations" (Herodotus IV,3).

However, the fact that neither the Cimmerians nor their "sons" the Scythians exhibit much sophistication in their religious rituals (Herodotus, IV,59) suggests that the Mitanni were not likely to have derived their cosmological insights from their northern kinsmen in Central Asia but from their earliest habitation amongst the Hurrians and Akkadians of northern Mesopotamia, whence they conveyed their wisdom to their Scythian neighbours.

The Elamites and Mesopotamians, of the first proto-Dravidian/ Hurrian stock, seem to have provided the basic religious culture for the later fire-worshipping Āryans of the BMAC and India deriving from the Hut Grave, Sintashta and Andronovo proto-Āryan cultures that migrated southwards at a later date. Indeed, both the Indians and the Avestan Iranians seem originally to have been nomadic peoples, as is attested by the language of the Old Avesta, wherein the cosmos is viewed as an enormous tent.[312] We may remember also Megasthenes' report that

> The Indians were in old times nomadic, like those Scythians who did not till the soil, but roamed about in their wagons, as the seasons varied, from one part of Scythia to another, neither dwelling in towns nor worshipping in temples;[313] and that the Indians likewise had neither towns nor temples of the gods, but were so barbarous that they wore the skins of such wild animals as they could kill ... they subsisted also on such wild animals as they could catch, eating the flesh raw, before, at least, the coming of Dionysus into India. Dionysus, however, when he came and had conquered the people, founded cities and gave laws to these cities, and introduced the use of wine among the Indians, as he had done among the Greeks, and taught them to sow the land, himself supplying seeds for the purpose ... It is also said that Dionysus first yoked oxen to the plough, and made many of the Indians husbandmen instead of nomads, and furnished them with the implements of agriculture; and that the Iindians worship the other gods, and Dionysus himself in particular, with cymbals and drums, because he so taught them ... and that he instructed the

---

[312]   See P.O. Skjaervo, "The Avesta as source for the early history of the Iranians", in G. Erdosy (ed.), op.cit., p.168.

[313]   The fact that the Scythians did not build temples or worship divine images is mentioned also by Herodotus, Histories, I,131.

Indians to let their hair grow long in honour of the god ....[314]

Since Dionysus is the same as An/Horus the Elder-Osiris,[315] we may assume that the cultural contact being referred to by Megasthenes is that between the early Scythian settlers of India and Elamite Dravidians/Hurrians from the Zagros region.

That the Scythians depended for their limited cosmological understanding and religious practices primarily on their Iranian kinsmen is clear from the fact that the word for hemp in most Central Asian cultures is derived from the Iranian "bhangha".[316] The predominance of the Iranian language in the regions inhabited by Cimmerians and Scythians, that is, from the Danube to the Dnieper, is evidenced also by the names of the Danube, Dnieper and Dniester, which employ the Avestan term "danu" for river.[317] Further, Darius I (522-486 B.C.) himself refers to the Sakas as "unruly" and not devoted to Ahura Mazda.[318] Herodotus' account of the religious customs of the Scythians (IV,59) indeed reveals their sharp focus on martial life, since they apparently did not set up altars or statues to any god except Ares, god of war. Eliade's researches also point to a very rudimentary practical application of the spiritual bases of the cosmological religion of the ancient Near East to quasi-shamanistic rituals.[319] This also explains their ancient designation as "hoamavarga", or "soma-drinking", Scythians.[320] The use of intoxicants for the acquisition of transcendental states is an inferior path in comparison to the inner spiritual discipline advocated by yoga,[321] and the reduction of yogic knowledge to ecstatic flights among the shamans[322] is an indication of a certain degeneration of the wisdom of the ancient Near East in its transmission to the north. As Eliade pointed out,

---

[314]   See Arrian, *Indica*, VII (in R.C. Majumdar, *The Classical Accounts of India*, Calcutta: Firma K.L. Mukhopadhyay, p.220f.).

[315]   See below p.180.

[316]   See M. Eliade, *op.cit.*, p.400f.

[317]   The Russian Slavic word for god "bog" is also derived from Iranian "bhaga".

[318]   See W.W. Malandra, *An Introduction to Ancient Iranian Religion: Readings from the Avesta and Achaemenid Inscriptions*, Minneapolis, MN: University of Minnesota Press, 1983, p.24.

[319]   cf. M. Eliade's discussion of shamanism among the Scythians, *op.cit.*, pp.394ff.

[320]   So in the inscriptions of Darius I (see P.O. Skjaervo, in G. Erdosy, *op.cit*, p.157).

[321]   See M. Eliade, *op.cit.*, p.401.

[322]   The term "shaman" may be related to the typical Indian brāhmanical patronymic "Sharman", the corresponding patronymics for the kshatriyas, vaishyas and shudras being "Varman", "Gupta" and "Dāsa" (see *VP* III,10,9).

> let us emphasize once again the structural difference that
> distinguishes classic Yoga from shamanism. Although the latter is
> not without certain techniques of concentration, ... its final goal is
> always ecstasy and the soul's ecstatic journey through the various
> cosmic regions, whereas Yoga pursues entasis, final concentration
> on the spirit and "escape" from the cosmos.[323]

The Iranians themselves may be recognized by their later hieratic name,
Magi, in the "Magog" of the biblical record. The Iranians are represented
in Herodotus as worshipping the "circle of heaven" (Ahura, from Ashur/
Anshar=circle of heaven) as well as the heavenly bodies. The incantation
that the priest utters during the animal sacrifice is supposed to evoke
the creation of the heavenly bodies. This is in accord with the Vedic
sacrifices, which mimic the creation of the universe. The Iranians
discussed by Herodotus however did not build temples or worship statuary
representations of their deities (I,131), and this emphasises their ancient
affiliation with the Scythians, while the Mitanni- and the Hittite-Hurrians,
however, were certainly not averse to such representations. Besides, the
Iranian rituals are described by Herodotus as not involving fire, even
though the later Zoroastrian religion – like the Indic – is indeed typified
by its worship of fire, Atar. This suggests once again that the Iranians, like
their Mitanni kinsmen, must have come into contact in the south with the
Pururuva Ailas [Elamites/Hurrians], who derived their worship of fire from
the Gandharvas who followed the settlers of the BMAC complex.

The first attestation of a western, 'centum' Āryan language is
among the Hittites, whose modern name is derived from the early settlers
of Anatolia called Hatti. The Hatti were most probably proto-Dravidians/
Hurrians since Heth is considered a son of Canaan, one of the sons of Ham,
in Gen. 10:15. The so-called Hittites were Āryans. The Hittite kingdom also
gives evidence of a strong neo-Hurrian cultural influence from the fifteenth
century B.C. and many of the Hittite queens bear Hurrian names, just as
in the case of the Mitanni. Thus the wives of Tudhaliya I (15th c. B.C.) and
Suppililuliumas (14th c. B.C.) are Nikalmati and Dadu-Khepu, respectively.
The Āryan language of the Hittites and Mitannis may have been limited
to the male members of an Āryan aristocracy.[324] The Hittite religion is
fully Sumero-Hurrian but has, as we shall see, particular affinities with
the Mitanni and Indo-Āryan as well.[325] The Hittite Āryans may indeed

---

[323] *Ibid.*, p.417.

[324] See above p.34.

[325] Cf., in this context, E. Laroche's comment that the dearth of exact Akkadian equivalents

have been related to the Uruk Sumerian "Armenoid" peoples, since this Armenoid Sumerian physical type is evident not only in Anatolia but also in the Aegean and in Italy.[326] In passing, it may also be noted that, in the *Prose Edda* ('Prologue'), the first humans, Ask and Embla, are said to have settled in Asgard, which is situated "in the middle of the world" and is identified with Anatolian Troy. The Anatolian location may be due to the fact that German culture is, according to Snorri Sturlusson, derived from that of the Anatolians. As for the convention of calling a homeland the "centre of the world", this is obviously a custom among all the ancient Āryan peoples since we find that the Iranians called the centre of the Earth Airyanem Vaego and the Indians Āryāvarta.[327]

The Greeks most probably arrived in the Helladic region around 2200 B.C. from Anatolia.[328] The pre-Āryan culture of Crete however was instrumental in developing the Linear A script (before 1700 B.C.) which preceded the Mycenean Linear B (1300 B.C.). Just as the Cretan script is at the base of the Āryan Mycenean, so too their religion is continued unchanged by the later immigrants. This religion is possibly the same as that of the proto-Dravidian/Hurrians. We note particularly a predominance of the Cretan Zeus (Zagreus/Dionysus) in Greek mythology, while the presence of Tvoreshtar/Tvashtr as Tartarus in the Hesiodic cosmogony shows the close relation of the Greeks to the Indic and Iranian Āryans. The deeper incursion of the Hittite Āryans into Europe is also evidenced in the fact that the Roman civilisation too traces its origins from Troy (Aeneas) and Hittite Anatolia.

---

to express the attributes of the primeval gods of Sumer in the Hittite treaties written in Akkadian "s'explique seulement, à notre sens, par l'hypothèse d'une transmission directe du sumérien au hourrite, sans intermédiare babylonien. La documentation anatolienne entraine cette conséquence paradoxale qu'elle oblige à poser le problème d'origine hors d'Asie Mineure, à plaçer l'élaboration des 'dieux antiques' hourro-hittites dans un milieu éthnique en contact immediat ave les spéculations mythologiques de Sumer, c'est-à-dire en Syrie ou en Mésopotamie septentrionale" (E. Laroche, "Les dénominations des dieux 'antiques' dans les texts hittites", in *Anatolian Studies Presented to Hans Gustav Güterbock*, ed. K. Bittel, P. H. H. Houwink Ten Cate, E. Reiner, Istanbul: Nederlands Historisch-Archaeologisch Institut, 1974, p.185.

[326] See above p.30.

[327] See below p.183. In fact, As-gard may be related even etymologically to the Indo-Iranian names. The substitution of 'g' for 'v' is evidenced also in the Sum. Gishnu/Ind. Vishnu (see p.40n above). If this be right, 'As' and the related 'Aesir' must be related to the term, "Āryans". The Aesir are gods, just as the original twin inhabitants of Asgard, Ask and Embla, are semi-divine beings (see "Gylfaginning" in *The Prose Edda*, tr. J.I. Young, Cambridge: Bowes and Bowes, 1954, pp.37,43). Human beings, on the other hand, live in Midgard.

[328] See J.P. Mallory, *In Search of the Indo-Europeans: Language, Archaeology and Myth*, London: Thames and Hudson, 1989, p.69.

Farther west, one of the oldest branches of the Germanic peoples is called the Alemanni, a name that is certainly related to Aryamanni, which may equally be the original of the term "Armenian". According to Snorri Sturlusson,[329] the author of the *Prose Edda*, the Germans first derived their religion from Anatolians who moved into Europe.[330] The first Anatolian (the "Aesir") who migrated into Germany is said to be "Voden" or "Odin", the god of Wind [the original Germanic form, Wotan, is clearly related to the Āryan Wata, god of Wind].[331] Odin, however, is said to be a distant descendant of "Tror" or "Thor",[332] the son of a Trojan king called Mennon or Munon who had married a daughter of King Priam. Thor himself first wandered to Thrace and then to other parts of the world. We will note that Thrace is also the source of the Dionysiac cult.[333] The date of the migration may have been around that of the Trojan War. Odin's three sons, Vegdeg, Beldeg (Baldur) and Sigi ruled over East Germany, Westphalia, and France, respectively. Further expeditions took Odin to Denmark, Sweden and Norway, whereby he succeeded in spreading the "language of Asia" all over Europe. Thus we see that, although the Nordic Cimmerians are, according to the biblical Table of Nations, the elder brothers of the Magi and the Medes, the Āryan languages of Europe are later derivatives of the Anatolian ones.

According to Tacitus, Mannus was the ancestor of the Germanic race, and he had three sons represented by the Ingaevones, Herminones, and Istaevones.[334] The first Germanic tribe to have crossed the Rhine and

---

[329] See *The Prose Edda*, p.25ff.

[330] This is confirmed by the earliest archaeology of Europe, where the first formation of the earliest Germanic cultures is to be located in the south, in modern day Czechoslovakia, which it may have reached from "the Mediterranean or Anatolia" (G. Childe, *op.cit.,* p.101). Geoffrey of Monmouth (*History of the Kings of Britain*, Chs.3-16) points to the Trojan origin of even the earliest Britons, since Britain was, according to him, first settled by a great grandson of Aeneas called Brute.

[331] See below p.201n.

[332] The name Thor seems to be derived from Taurit, the Anatolian bull-god who is later identified with Teshup, the son of Kumarbi/Chronos (see below p.197). Teshup is the counterpart of the younger Thor who battles the serpent (see below p.203). If this etymology be right, it would confirm Sturlusson's claims regarding the Anatolian origins of the Eddic mythology.

[333] See below p.180. It is possible that the name Thor is derived from the same root thor– denoting the ejaculation of semen which is noted in the epithet 'thoreni' applied to Aphrodite as sprung of Zeus' seed in the Derveni Orphic writings (see M.L. West, *Orphic Poems*, p.91). If so, this would approximate Thor to Ninurta and Skanda (jet of semen), son of Siva/Enlil/Wotan(see below p.239).

[334] See Tacitus, *Germania*, Sec.2.

ousted the indigenous Celts were the Tungri, whose other name, Germani, was used for all the tribes.[335] The chief god of the Germans is said to be the creator god Tuisto [from Tvastr/Tartarus/Tvoreshtar].[336]

The collective name 'Edda' for the sacred poems of the Germans is itself clearly related to the Indo-Āryan 'Veda', rather more than to the Iranian 'Avesta', just as Tuisto is more closely related to the Indic Tvastr than to the Iranian Tvoreshtar. The name of the Germanic Tree of Life, Yggdrasil, also possibly derives from the Āryan deity Indra who was adored in this form.[337] However, it must be noted that in the *Prose Edda*, "The Deluding of Gylfi", the end of the universe, Ragnarök, is heralded by a long winter exactly as in the Yima story of the Vendidad.[338] Also, we have seen that Wotan is derived from the wind-god Wata who is more prominently mentioned in the Iranian sacred literature than in the Indic.[339] This may suggest that the Germanic tribes derived their cosmological information from the Anatolian region at a date before the separation of the Indic from the Iranian Āryans. Further, a trace of the transmission of the early religion to the north through the Armenoid Sumerians and their Anatolian neighbours may perhaps be found in the name of the Eddic Ocean-god Aegir, which resembles the Sumerian Enki (Okeanos).[340]

---

[335] In this context, it is interesting to note that one of Hammurabi's inscriptions (C.J. Gadd and L. Legrain, *Ur Excavations: Texts, Vol. I: Royal Inscriptions*, London, 1928, Nr. 146, Pl.Q) refers to the "Elamites, Guti, Subartu and Tukriš" together as being peoples whose "mountains are distant and language complicated" (see A Ungnad, *op.cit.*, pp.48f.). It is not certain if the Tukriš were the same as Tacitus' Tungri, and, if so, where they were first situated.

[336] Tacitus, *Ibid.*

[337] See below Ch.XIII.

[338] See below p.77.

[339] See below p.214n.

[340] See below p.230.

SYNOPSIS

After creating and sustaining the cosmos for an entire Cosmic Age (kalpa), the Lord "sleeps" during his long "night". During this night, the cosmos is dissolved into its original subtle constituents in a flood called Naimittika Pralaya. In the second Cosmic Age following the divine night, our universe and its sun are gradually recreated. This process of universal regeneration serves as the basis of the divine mythology of the ancients.

At the end of the first cosmic age, the supreme Soul (Ātman/Shiva), desirous of creation, assumes an ideal, and androgynous, form (Vishnu) as a macroanthropos (Purusha/Ptah). From the nostrils of this macroanthropos emerges the wind-form of the deity, Vāyu (in the form of a Boar) which recovers the Earth sunk at the bottom of the cosmic ocean during the flood that brought the first cosmic age to a close. The boar/Vāyu then impregnates and spreads Earth, producing as a result extended Earth (Prithvi) and its "cover" primal Heaven (Dyaus) in a closely united complex.

However, the temporal concomitant of the rapidly moving Wind-form of the supreme deity, Shiva/Kala/Chronos, divides the united Heaven and Earth by castrating the Purusha. The semen that falls from the castrated phallus of Heaven impregnates the Purusha itself with the Cosmic Egg, which contains now Heaven in a state of utter concentration as Nun (the Mind), the element of Earth in a state of utter Darkness, as well as the desire of the supreme soul as Eros/Phanes/Brahman (the so-called Ogdoad of the Egyptians). The blood from the castration serves as the source of the incipient divine Consciousness (Hu, intellect, and Sia, perspicacity, the latter also serving as the magical source of the cosmic Light, Heka/Brahmanaspati). From this Egg then emerges the manifest cosmos, Earth, in the form of a lotus crowned with the Heaven of divine Light and Consciousness, Brahman.

This ideal Light (Horus the Elder/Osiris) is, however, shattered by the stormy aspect (Seth, "son" of Nut and Geb) of the light itself and forced to descend into the nether regions of the "lotus". Seth/Zeus/Ganesha, however, is virtually identifiable with the magical force of Brahmanaspati and preserves the castrated phallus of the ideal Man (containing the life of our yet unmanifested universe) by swallowing it.

In the underworld, where the light force lies moribund, the stormy and vital aspect of the solar force (Marduk) destroys the serpent of material resistance (Tiamat), and divides its body into the heaven and earth of our own universe so that the divine phallus may emerge between these regions in the Mid-region of our universe. The entire universe – which is informed by the vital force of Soma – is now shaped in the form of a "tree" [an analogue of the phallus itself] whose roots are in the underworld, branches in the mid-region and peak in heaven. Though the moon containing the animal life of the universe, Soma, is formed first in the Mid-region between earth and heaven, another obstruction to the emergence of the solar force persist in the early, and unruly, avian form of the sun represented by the monstrous bird Anzu. When this latter is also dompted by the stormy aspect of the solar force, and the Tree of Life has been purified of all its chthonic elements, the life and light of the Ideal Man are finally free to emerge in our universe as the sun.

I: PRALAYA

THE END OF THE FIRST COSMIC AGE (KALPA) AND THE BEGINNING OF
THE SECOND: THE FLOOD

T he story of the Deluge which we have used as an anthropological
aid in the previous chapter is indeed a popular representation of
the cosmic flood which ushers in the recreation of the material
universe after the collapse of the cosmos at the end of the first cosmic age.
The prehistory of the cosmos is presented in greatest detail in the Indic
Purānic literature.[341] In the *BP* III,xi,18-22, a day of the supreme Lord
is calculated as equalling 1000 Chaturyugas, each Chaturyuga[342] being
12,000 divine years long (that is, years as prevalent in the realm of the
gods),[343] or 4,380,000,000 terrestrial years.[344] After creating and sustaining
the cosmos for this extraordinarily vast period of time (kalpa), comes the
night in which the Lord "sleeps". This night is equally as long as the day of
the Lord and is the period when the cosmos is dissolved into its original
subtle constituents in the flood called Naimittika Pralaya (*BP* XII,4,3). The
first Kalpa was called Brahmakalpa (*BP* III,11,33ff.), since it was marked
by the perfect light of Brahma, and the second, after the cosmic cataclysm,
is the present one, called Padmakalpa (the age of the lotus), in which the

---

[341] Portions of the Purānas may indeed have been composed earlier than the Vedas, since
the *BrdP* I,i,1,40-41 maintains that they were heard by Brahman before the Vedas. The Flood
stories are to be found also in the Tamil 'Purānams', which copy the encyclopaedic genre of
the Sanskrit models.

[342] A chaturyuga is made up of four ages, Krita, Treta, Dvapara and Kali, corresponding to
a Golden, Silver, Bronze and Iron Age, in the course of which the divine virtue is gradually
diminished. We now live in the fourth, degenerate, age (Kaliyuga) of the second Kalpa called
Padmakalpa.

[343] A divine day is as long as a terrestrial year.

[344] In the *BrdP* III,iv,229f., the night, which is equal to the day of Brahma is said to be
4,328,980,000 years long. The difference in reckoning between the various Puranas is thus
slight.

divine light is transferred to the material universe.[345] Each kalpa is divided into fourteen "manvantaras" or ages of Manu, a Manu being the type of enlightened mankind.[346]

In the *BrdP*, the first form of the deity is that of the supreme Soul, Ātman: "This entire dark world was pervaded by his Ātman" (I,i,3,12), with its three essential energies, Tamas, Rajas, and Sattva, maintained in perfect balance. This unmanifest deity begins to be gradually manifested when one of the energies begins to predominate over the others. The first and highest, sattvic, form of the deity is as Vishnu, the ideal macroanthropos, while the rajasic is Brahman, who creates the material universe, and the tāmasic is Rudra, who destroys the universe at the end of a cosmic age. The transformation of Vishnu into Brahman, the self-conscious, enlightened form of the supreme deity, is accomplished by virtue of intense yogic meditation (I,i,5,6). The first act of the macroanthropos is to recover Earth through the force of his "breath" which emerges from his nostrils in the form of the wind-god Vāyu assuming the shape of a "Boar". This is followed by the intelligible creation beginning with the lower tāmasic and proceeding to the sattvic, the creation of the gods, of the "sages" who are intellectual creations of the deity, and, finally, of human life (I,i,5). Then Brahman manifests himself materially as the light of the universe. This light is formed within the Cosmic Egg which develops in the ideal macroanthropos, Purusha. The first cosmic age must have witnessed the creation of a universe as well, since the Naimittika Pralaya begins with a conflagration due to the "sun". However, it is possible that there was no human life in it, since that is mentioned only in the second cosmic age (Padmakalpa), whose seventh Manu, Manu Vaivaswata, is responsible for the transmission of the seeds of life to earth as well as for the mortality of the forms that spring from these seeds.[347] The first cosmic age was, according to *BrdP* I,ii,6, followed by the natural destruction of the cosmos and the intermediate period (pratisandhi) between two kalpas. During this intermediary period, the deity returned anew to his task of creation but this time proceeded farther in his material manifestation than in the previous cosmic age.

[345] Current astrophysical theories suggest that the cosmos is roughly 14 billion years old whereas, according to the BP, the cosmos is approximately 13,140,000,000 years old (the first day and night of the Lord plus half of the second day). The latter is likely to be more accurate since it is not based on fallible empirical observation but on spiritual intuition.

[346] Each manvantara lasts for 71 odd Chaturyugas, or 310,980,000 years (*BP* III,11,24). The names of the first six Manus of this Kalpa are Swāyambhuva, Svarochisha, Uttama, Tāmasa, Raivata, Chakshusha (*BP* VIII,1), and those of the Manus following ours (Shrāddhadeva/ Vaivasvata) will be Savarni, Dakshasavarni, Brahmasavarni, Dharmasavarni, Rudrasavarni, Devasavarni, and Indrasavarni (*BP* VIII,13).

[347] See below p.88, p.313.

We shall first consider the Naimittika Pralaya which occurred at the end of the first cosmic age. This cataclysm begins with a drought in which the sun burns everything up with his "seven rays", while the "Samvartaka" fire[348] burns the four worlds of Earth, the Mid-Region, Heaven and "Mahar" (the supracelestial realm). This conflagration is followed by torrential rains in which everything mobile and immobile is dissolved into one undifferentiated ocean of water in which the supreme deity Brahman "sleeps" during his long "night". In the *BrdP* III,iv,132, the destruction of the universe is said to begin with a drought during which the "samvartaka" fire burns "wood and fuel along with water … Seven rays of the sun that blazes in the sky sucking water, drink water from the great ocean. Being illuminated with that intake, seven suns are evolved. Then those rays that have become suns, burn the four worlds in the four directions. Those fires burn up the entire universe". The Earth is thus enveloped in flames until the seven suns merge into one and then the samvartaka fire burns up the underworld, Rasatala, as well (153). The three worlds as well as the superior, Maharloka, are thus burnt up entirely and the universe "assumes the form of a huge block of iron and shines thus" (159).

All the creatures of the universe are reduced to the state of the "mahābhutas" (principal elements) (231). Brahman himself as the sustainer of the creation gets merged into the Mahat (the principle of manifestation),[349] which in turn becomes Avyakta (the unmanifest) and the three gunas (Sattva, Rajas, Tamas) are restored to their initial perfect balance. Thereafter rise Samvartaka "clouds" which also "group themselves in seven, indentifying themselves with the suns" and these clouds succeed in extinguishing the fire when they shower as torrential rains. It is in this universal water (ambhas) called Ekarnava, Salila or Naras (174-8) that Brahma assumes the form of the macroanthropos. This Brahman is also called Kāla (185ff.) who, at the end of the divine "night" is impelled to recreate the universe. We shall see that Kāla/Cronos/Kumarbi, representing Time, features prominently in the Hurrian-Greek cosmogonies as the producer of the cosmic egg and its light.[350]

In the *PP* I,39,48ff., Vishnu (the form of the supreme lord as macroanthropos) is said to have taken four forms in the process of destroying the universe. First, he appears as the sun with which he "dried up the oceans" and at the same time removes the sense of "sight" itself, the

---

[348] The burning of the universe at the end of a cosmic age is called "kalpadaha" in *BrdP* I,i,5,122.

[349] See *BrdP* III,iv,2,115: "The manifest part evolving out of the unmanifest one is gross and it is called Mahan (Mahat)".

[350] See below Ch.VIII.

sun being traditionally associated with sight in India as well as in Egypt and Mesopotamia. Already at this point, he dives into the Abyss to search out Earth, the embryonic new universe which lies hidden there. Vishnu next appears as a gale (wind) which "convulsed the entire world" and at the same time destroyed "inspiration, expiration and all the forms of breath". The third form he assumes is that of fire, which reduces the universe to ashes, and finally he assumes the nature of water as a "hundred dark whirling clouds" which "gratified the Earth with ghee-like divine water".[351] This impregnation causes "the subtle world [i.e. of the senses of sight and breath], with the sun, wind and the sky" to be enclosed in the Earth that has been recovered from the abyss.[352]

In the *Vishnu Purana*, it is stated that "Vishnu assumes the form of Rudra [Shiva/Kāla] and inclines towards destruction in order to withdraw the entire creation into himself".[353] Rudra is not only the same as Time but also "the flame of Time" which "turns into the blasting breath of Shesa [the serpent]".[354] The serpent is thus clearly an aspect of Shiva.[355] In the Egyptian *Book of the Dead*, Ch.175, too, Atum declares:

> in the end I will destroy everything that I have created,
> the earth will become again part of the Primeval Ocean,
> like the Abyss of waters in their original state.
> Then I will be what will remain, just I and Osiris,
> when I will have changed myself back into the Old Serpent
> who knew no man and saw no god.[356]

The deluge that Atum threatens to overwhelm the universe with will mark the dissolution of the material universe into its original state in the Abyss Nun and the flood Hehu.[357]

---

[351]   See S. Shastri, *The Flood Legend in Sanskrit Literature*, Delhi: S. Chand and Co., 1950, p.34f.

[352]   We have noted the ancient Scythian and Vedic custom of filling the corpse with ghee (above p.60). This may be a ritual to ensure the resurrection of the dead body similar to the Egyptian, since the impregnation of Aditi by Dyaus (with ghee-like fluid) results in the birth of the fire-god, Agni (see below p.84).

[353]   See S. Shastri, *op.cit.*, p.48.

[354]   *Ibid.*, p.49.

[355]   As Hedammu no doubt is a form of Kumarbi in the Hurrian "Kingship of Heaven" myth (see below p.56).

[356]   See R.T. Rundle Clark, *op.cit.*, pp.140f.

[357]   See K. Sethe, *Amun und die acht Urgötter von Hermopolis* (*Abhandlungen der preussischen Akademie der Wissenschaften*, 1929, Nr.4), p.64.

In the *SP*, the endless ocean into which the universe is dissolved at the end of the process of cosmic destruction is called also Mahādeva, that is, Shiva himself.[358] A little earlier the same ocean is called the "ocean of mundane existence".[359] This is the Abyss itself, in which the supreme lord Vishnu rests on the back of the serpent Sesha, which represents the tremendous power of illusion, Māya, of the supreme soul (Shiva), whence the phenomenal cosmos will arise.

The destruction of the universe at the end of a cosmic age is recounted also in the 'Ragnarök' of the Germanic Edda.[360] The Edda however adheres to the Iranian Vendidad account of the flood[361] in beginning with a "winter" called Fimbulvetr (Terrible Winter). This is followed by the swallowing of the sun, the moon and the stars by "wolves" and a cataclysmic earthquake. Then occurs the flood and the poisoning of the universe by the Midgard 'serpent'. Finally, Surt, the god of Muspell, burns the entire universe with his fire. The congealing of the cosmos that precedes the conflagration seems to be peculiar to the Iranian and Germanic accounts of the apocalypse.

～

For an account of the stages which mark the new creation after the destruction of the previous cosmos, we may turn again to the *BP*. The flood at the end of the first cosmic age entails the total collapse of the cosmos, constituted of Heaven, Earth and the Mid-region, into the endless waters of the Abyss. During the flood, the Lord withdraws into this cosmic Ocean, within whose depths he reposes on the serpent Anantasesha (the eternal Sesha). Gradually waking, he begins to recreate the cosmos, first extracting, in the form of a Cosmic Boar, the universe, Earth, which lies sunken in the Ocean. The emergence of the light of the universe, which is called Protogonos in the Orphic theogonies, occurs in the first manvantara of the second kalpa, since Protogonos' Indic counterpart, Priyavrata, is said to be the son of the very first Manu, Swāyambhuva Manu.[362] This manvantara is also marked by the emergence of Earth and its division into seven islands (called continents in the Iranian literature) which represent various galactic formations (*BP* V,1,30ff.). Like Protogonos/Mitra, it was

---

[358] See S. Shastri, *op.cit.*, p.91.

[359] *Ibid.*, p.66.

[360] See 'Voluspa', st.31ff. The term "Ragnarök" means "the fate of the gods".

[361] See below p.93.

[362] The emergence of the first solar light in the universe is calculated by modern astrophysicists at around 100,000,000 years after the "Big Bang" (see below p.137), which is during the first manvantara.

Priyavrata who created the divisions of Earth by riding around Mt. Meru in his chariot.[363] Of the seven islands, the one we inhabit is the central one and called Jambudweepa (*BP* V,16,5ff.), which itself is divided into nine Varshas, of which one, Bharatvarsha, is the region which humans inhabit after the cosmic flood (*BP* V,19.9ff.).

The supreme Lord incarnates himself in various forms throughout the developing life of the cosmos in order to elevate the creation spiritually. Apart from the Boar, other incarnations of the supreme Lord are those of Prithu, who extracts the life-giving qualities from Earth when it has assumed the form of a Cow (in the sixth manvantara) (*BP* IV,18; *BrdP* I,ii,36,110ff.), the man-lion, Narasimha, the tortoise Kūrma (which helps bear the mountain Mandāra[364] on its back while the latter is being used as a ladle to churn the cosmic ocean with for the elicitation of the nectar of immortality), the seductress Mohini, and the dwarf Vamana, who is also the last of the solar Adityas who appear early in the present manvantara – the seventh – called Vaivasvata Manvantara (*BP* VII,8; VIII,7,12,18). The incarnation of the Lord as the Fish which transfers the son of the sun, the first man of the universe, Shraddhādeva (or Vaivasvata) Manu, from his celestial origin to Earth occurs relatively late since Shraddhādeva Manu[365] is but the seventh Manu of our kalpa (*BP* VIII,13,1), there being fourteen Manus in all in each kalpa.

At the end of the present cosmic age, there will be another flood called a 'Prākrita Pralaya' which will dissolve not just the gross form of the universe but even the subtle elements of Nature (Prakriti). The two Kalpas, along with the cataclysmic nights following them, constitute the entire lifetime (Dviparardha) of the creating deity (*BP* III,11,33ff.). Since this is the end of one complete cycle of creation, the second flood will be immediately followed by an 'Ātyantika Pralaya' which will destroy also the final crucial knot of Egoity (Ahamkara) that prevents individual consciousness in the cosmos from realising its complete identity with the Divine (*BP* XII,4,4ff.).

It is the cosmic flood which occurs during the creation of the sun at the beginning of our kalpa that serves as the basis of the flood stories

---

[363] The seven islands of Earth are formed by Priyavrata, the son of the first Manu, Svāyambhuva Manu, when he rides in his chariot around Mt. Meru, which is at the very centre of Earth (*BP* V,16,5-7). This is reflected in the Hieronyman Orphic fragment (78) also, where Protogonos wheels round the world in his chariot to bring light to it (see M.L. West, *Orphic Poems*, p.214).

[364] The Mandāra mountain is one of the four mountains surrounding the central Mt. Meru, the other three being Merumandāra, Supārshva, and Kumuda (see *BP* V,16,11).

[365] The name Shrāddhadeva is possibly etymologically related to Zarath-ustra and Zius-udra.

noted in the popular literature of the ancients. If we consider the evidence of Egypt first, we will note that, as Usener once pointed out,[366] the solar aspect of the flood is pointedly evident in the account of the sailing of Amun-Ra on the back of the cow, called Mehet Ouret (Great Flood) – a form of Hathor/Nut[367] – holding on to her "horns". We will encounter this bovine image of the goddess of the primeval waters and of the dawn also in the Indic sacred literature. The hymn to Amun-Ra in the Darius temple to this deity declares that the original seat of Amun-Ra was the high ground of Hermopolis Magna, where the "eight gods" of the Ogdoad were worshipped. Amun-Ra is said to have left this oasis and appeared in the moist, hidden egg along with the goddess Amente. Then he takes his place on the Great Flood. At that time, "there were no plants. They began when … the water rose to the mountain".[368] We note that the "great flood" in Egypt comes after the formation of the egg from which the divine light emerges, and long ages indeed separate the moment of the appearance of the divine light of Brahman from the emergence of the sun in our system.

In the *Book of the Heavenly Cow,* the eye of Re, which is equated with Hathor, is said to be the instrument of the punishment of degenerate "mankind".[369] Re embarks on this course of punishment in conjunction with the lord of the Abyss, Nun. A part of "humanity" is destroyed by the flood, but the remainder are saved by the sun-god's decision to stop Hathor's work of devastation by causing her to become drunk on blood-red beer. The sun then rises to the heavens on the back of the celestial cow.[370] The reference to beer is significant, since we shall note below that inebriation by beer is in fact characteristic of Seth, the counterpart of the Vedic Indra, who also raises the sun into the heavens infused with the force of Soma.

If we turn to the Egyptian king-lists, we will note that, in common with the Sumerian king-list, they begin with the reign of the gods, proceed to the demi-gods and spirits of the dead, and then, finally, to the human dynasties. Unlike in the Sumerian king-list, however, there is no mention of a "deluge" after the reign of the gods. The Egyptian gods mentioned at the head of the Manetho list are Hephaistos (Ptah), Helios (Re), Kronos (Geb), Osiris, Typhon (Seth), and Oros (Horus the Younger). Hephaistos is said to have "discovered fire for the Egyptians", which equates him with

---

[366] See H. Usener, *Die Sintfluthsagen,* Bonn: Friedrich Cohen, 1899, p.260.

[367] See PT 829 d/e; cf. R.T. Rundle Clark, *op.cit.,* p.184.

[368] *Ibid.*

[369] By "mankind" is probably meant a manifestation of quasi-human life anterior to our own.

[370] Cf. E. Hornung, *op.cit.,* p.149.

the Vedic Prajapati, whose son is Agni (Helios). Osiris and Typhon are the two aspects, solar and stormy, of the divine light, while Oros is clearly the nascent sun, Surya. We shall see that the sun is the last god in both the Sumerian and the Egyptian king-lists. As Manu is the ruler at the time of the Deluge and, indeed, of the incipient universe (corresponding to Ziusudra,[371] the son of the divine Ubar-tutu(k) of Shuruppak),[372] so the first "human" king – from Thinis, near Abydos, sacred to Osiris – in the Egyptian list (after some anonymous "kings" also from Thinis), is recorded under the name of Menes, which may be a cognate of Manu.[373] Menes therefore corresponds to Manu, the ancestor of mankind and ruler, originally, not of Egypt, or Sumer, or India, but indeed of the entire material universe.

In a related list supplied by Syncellus, we note again, at the head, Hephaistos and his son Helios, followed by Agathodaimon (probably Shu),[374] Kronos and Osiris and, then, after a lacuna, Typhon and the 'demi-god' Horus.[375] According to Malalas' list, however, Hermes (Thoth) arrived in Egypt from Italy [sic] and found Mestraim, of the family of Kham (as in the Hebrew biblical account) ruling there. On Mestraim's death, Hermes became ruler and, after him, Hephaistos (Ptah). Hephaistos' son, Helios, was the next ruler, and he in turn was followed by his son Sosis (Shu) and the latter by his son Osiris. Then come Horus and Thoulis[376] (who may be a counterpart of Typhon/Seth). The inclusion of the historical figure of Mestraim at the head of the list by Malalas seems not to have any cosmological significance, but rather seems to point to the Hamitic constitution of the earliest Egyptians. The reference to Hermes/Thoth entering Egypt from Italy may point to the northern invasion of a people devoted to Thoth/Tauith, that is, most probably, Hurrian Anatolians/ Trojans/proto-Italics, who worshipped the Bull-god Taurith. So the worshippers of Hermes who came from the north must have included Hurrians of the proto-Hititte branch.

---

[371]   See W.G. Lambert and A.R. Millard, *Atrahasis: The Babylonian Story of the Flood*, Oxford: Clarendon Press, 1969, p.19.

[372]   See T. Jacobsen, *The Sumerian King-List*, p.75.

[373]   The Germans too considered Mannus as the ancestor of the race (see above p.68). The Hebrew name, Noah, is also possibly a corruption of Ma-nu.

[374]   Philo of Byblos maintains that Agathodaimon, in the ancient Egyptian cosmology, is the serpent that encircles the middle of the cosmos (see Philo of Byblos, *The Phoenician History*, tr. H.W. Attridge and R.A. Oden Jr., Washington, D.C.: The Catholic Biblical Association of America, 1981, p.67). Shu is the cosmic wind and, for the characterisation of the Cosmic Egg as a "wind-egg", see below p.155n.

[375]   See *Berossus and Manetho.*, p.176.

[376]   *Ibid.*, p.153.

The fact that the solar significance of the flood is most directly apparent in Egypt highlights the Egyptians' exclusive concentration on the solar aspect of the original religion. On the other hand, the Sumerians seem not to have left a cosmogonical version of the flood in Mesopotamia but only a popular transformation of it into a human deluge story. In the antediluvian section of the Sumerian king-list, we find that the first mentioned cities are all representative of the various manifestations of the developing solar force in the underworld. The first mentioned is Eridu, the seat of Enki, the primeval deity of the Abyss who rules the underworld after the attack on An by his stormy aspect, Enlil.[377] Bad-tibirra, the second antediluvian city, was sacred to Dumuzi, the "son of the abyss", and Larak, the third, was the centre of a Pabilsag (Ninurta) cult.[378] The kings of Bad-tibirra and Larak are elsewhere identified with Dumuzi,[379] who is himself a form of the solar god, An. Thus En-men-lu-Anna, En-me-lu-Anna – who precede Dumuzi himself – in Bad-tibirra are said to be the same as Dumuzi in AO 4346.1-2 and CT 24, 9. The first king of Larak, En-sipa(d)-zi(d)-Anna is equally identified with Dumuzi (CT 24.9).[380] Ninurta, the god of Larak as Pabilsag, is thus identical to Dumuzi, the solar force. Sippar, the fourth antediluvian city, was the centre of Utu (sun) worship, and finally, Shuruppak was the home of Ziusudra, who, as we shall see, is the son of the sun. The *Epic of Gilgamesh* (XI) also states that, before the flood, the gods were at Shuruppak.

In the original Sumerian version of the Deluge, which may have served as the basis for the Babylonian *Atrahasis* flood story, we note again that the five antediluvian cities are directly ruled by gods:

> The first of those cities, Eridu, he gave to the leader Nudimmud,
> The second, Badtibira, he gave to the 'nugig',
> The third, Larag, he gave to Pabilsag [Ninurta],
> The fourth, Sippar, he gave to the hero Utu,
> The fifth, Suruppak, he gave to Sud [Ziusudra?].[381]

---

[377] See above p.52.

[378] *RLA* VI:495 (cf. F.R. Kraus, "Nippur und Isin nach altbabylonischen Rechtskunden", *JCS* 3 (1949), 78-80). Pabilsag may have originally been spelled Pabilhursag (see Poebel, *Historical and Grammatical Texts*, pl.i, p.51; cf. S. Smith, *op.cit.*, p.24).

[379] See W. Lambert and A.R. Millard, *Atrahasis*, pp.26f.; cf. H. Zimmern, "Religion und Sprache" in E. Schrader, *Die Keilinschriften und das Alte Testament*, Berlin: Reuther und Reichard, 1903, II:530ff.

[380] See Lambert, *ibid*. It should be noted that Dumuzi is listed also in the postdiluvian section as a king of Kuara (near Eridu) in the Uruk dynasty, after Enmerkar and Lugalbanda. It is possible that this is an unidentified king deified as Dumuzi.

[381] Lambert, *op.cit.*, p.141.

We see therefore that, both in the king-list and in the Sumerian Deluge myth, the order of the first cities follows the order of manifestation of the solar force in the underworld, beginning with Enki, the lord of the underworld, followed by Dumuzi/Marduk/Ninurta, the solar energy, and ending with the sun, Utu and his "son", Ziusudra.[382] It may be noted that an Early Dynastic fragment from around 2500 B.C. replaces Ziusudra with UR.AS (Earth)[383] reminding us that the process of the manifestation of the solar force that finds itself in the underworld is similar to that which signalled the rise of the primal light of An, who also, in the "An-Anum" list, is preceded by Uras.IB.[384] The UR.AS in the ED fragment may be an abbreviation of Ninuras,[385] who is synonymous with Ninurta. Then, even Manu/Ziusudra may represent a form of the powerful Ninurta, who, as we shall see, is responsible for the transmission of the divine life and light to the universe.

It is important to note that, in the *Atrahasis* epic as well as in *Gilgamesh* (Tablet XI), it is Enlil (Shiva) who causes the flood. And we shall see that it is Enlil (or his son) who attacks the divine light An and forces it down into the underworld and into our universe.[386] In the *SP*, Shiva is aided in his task of universal inundation by Indra,[387] the martial aspect of Shiva/Enlil. In the Babylonian epic of Erra, Marduk, the counterpart of the solar force, Ninurta/Muruga,[388] takes the place of his father Enlil in causing the flood:

> I got angry long ago: I rose from my seat and contrived the deluge,
> I rose from my seat, and the government of heaven and earth dissolved.
> And the sky, lo! shook: the stations of the stars in the sky were altered, and I did not bring [them] back to their [former]

---

[382] Yima, the survivor of the flood in the Iranian literature, is also called the son of the sun, Vivanghvant (see below p.93).

[383] See *Atrahasis*, p.19.

[384] See R. Litke,

[385] It could also mean Enki, Lord of Earth, since Ninurta, like Marduk, is identical to him (see below p.242).

[386] See below p.156. Enlil is also fearfully supplicated in the introductory hymn to Marduk in the Babylonian Akitu rituals, since his "anutu" or "anu–hood" is considered as a source of divine wrath (see H. Wohlstein, *The Sky-god An-Anu*, Jericho, NY: Paul A. Stroock, 1976, p.96).

[387] See below p.83.

[388] For Marduk as one of the epithets of Ninurta, see Tallquist, *op.cit.*, p.422. Ninurta is also called Madanu, one of the epithets of Marduk (*ibid.*).

positions.

....

The offspring of the living diminished, and I did not restore them
Until, like a farmer, I should take their seed in my hand.

....

I changed the place of the *mesu* tree and of the *elmesu* ...[389]

In his stormy nature, Marduk is very similar to Seth, Teshup, Zeus, who, as
we shall see, are both the storm-force and the solar force at the same time.[390]
    In the *SP*, the flood is caused by Shiva (Enlil) at the end of a cosmic
age.[391] When Shiva begins his task of cosmic destruction, he splits "asunder
these seven worlds,[392] and breaks the [golden cosmic] egg higher than the
highest". We note that, just as in the Egyptian account, the flood follows the
formation of the cosmic egg. Shiva is said to be "robed in Indra's thunderbolts"[393] as he goes about his task of cosmic devastation.[394]
    Shiva, however, is given a major creative role in the Dravidian
versions of the flood story, though, he is also the destructive aspect of the
supreme deity in the Puranas,[395] and corresponds to Enlil, who causes the
flood in the Sumerian flood story. This dual aspect of the power of Shiva
is observed also in the Egyptian representations of the serpent (sometimes
called Mehen, the "World-encircler",[396] sometimes Nehaher, "the one
with the fearful face"), which first holds together the corpse of Osiris and
then accompanies the emergence of his son, the incipient sun, Horus the

---

[389] Tr. L. Cagni, *The Poem of Erra*, Malibu, CA: Undena Publications, 1977, p.32. For
Muruga's similar destruction of the cosmic "mango" tree in the Tamil *Kantapurānam*, see
below p.204.

[390] Marduk's solar role is highlighted by the fact that he is considered "the one inside
Shamash" (VAT 8917 rev. l.5; see A. Livingstone, *op.cit.*, p.82f).

[391] In the Hebrew bible, too, the deluge is caused by the rise of the waters of Tehom, who
represents the same primeval waters as Tiamat in *Enuma Elish* (see A.J. Wensinck, "The
Ocean in the Literature of theWestern Semites", *Verhandelingen der Koninklijke Akademie
van Wetenschappen*, No.XIX (1919), p.2).

[392] That is, the seven "continents", the material matrices of the galactic formations of the
universe; see below p.164.

[393] See S. Shastri, *op.cit.*, p.88. In the *VP* too, it is Indra who releases the doomsday clouds
which destroys all the "cows". The latter are finally saved by Vishnu (*ibid.*, pp.43–6).

[394] This identifies Shiva with Varuna in the Dravidian account mentioned below (p.91f.),
since Varuna is but a later manifestation of Shiva in the underworld).

[395] See below p.88.

[396] Mehen also surrounds the rising universe envisaged as a primordial hill, Tatenen (see
R.T. Rundle Clark, *op.cit.*, p.171; cf. below p.169).

Younger.[397] Thus, when Osiris dies and descends into the underworld, his decaying corpse (represented as a mummy) is depicted as being held together by Nehaher.[398] We will see also, further below, that this serpent of the Abyss is the one which serves as a rope between the boat and the horn of the piscine form of the supreme deity that saves Manu during the flood in the *MP*.[399]

In the fragmentary Hedammu epic of the Hurrians, Kumarbi produces a dragon Hedammu (resembling the flood Narmada and Hathor) to destroy mankind.[400] The fact that, in the Hurrian epic of 'the Kingship in Heaven', Anu's seed (as well as his phallus) is contained in the belly of Kumarbi (Chronos/Kala/Shiva) also suggests that the creative waters of the flood caused by Shiva serve as the amniotic fluid of the universe. In Greece, too, Chronos is represented as a serpent twined around the cosmic axis of Ananke, Necessity.[401] This confirms the identity of Shiva/Chronos/Kumarbi with the serpent, especially in its creative role, since, as we shall see, Shiva represents Time as well as the aspect of Egoity which informs the universe.[402]

The serpent, however, also represents the resistant force of matter which must be overcome to allow the light of the sun to emerge in our universe. Hence the rise of the solar energy is typically preceded by a batttle of a heroic god representing the storm-force of the incipient sun against a serpent of restriction. This contrast between the two aspects of the serpent is highlighted in the last scene of the Egyptian *Book of Caverns,* which depicts a serpent within a mound of earth that helps regenerate Osiris as Horus the Younger along with another serpent encircling the solar beetle (Khepry) that is cut into pieces.[403] In the *Amduat* too, while Apop is destroyed in the seventh hour, in the eleventh and twelfth hours the emergent sun itself appears within the bounds of the serpent called "World encircler".[404] It may be noted, in passing, that the "hours" of the Egyptian books of the underworld certainly do not refer to our terrestrial hours[405]

---

[397]   See E. Hornung, pp.33ff; cf. R.T. Rundle Clark, *op.cit.*, pp.167ff.

[398]   See *The Book of Caverns* (cf. R.T.Rundle Clark, *ibid.*, p.169).

[399]   See below p.87.

[400]   See J. Siegelova, "Appu Märchen und Hedammu-Mythus", *Studien zu den Bogazköy-Texten* 14; cf. G. Wilhelm, *op.cit.*, p.84.

[401]   See below p.146.

[402]   See below Ch.VIII.

[403]   See E. Hornung, *op.cit.*, p.90.

[404]   *Ibid.*, pp.33ff.

[405]   It is unfortunate that Egyptologists still refer to the "nightly" and "daily" journey of the

but, rather, to divine ones. We have seen that, according to the *BP*, a divine day is as long as a terrestrial year,[406] which is the period taken by the sun to revolve through the twelve constellations of the zodiac (*BP* III,11,13; V,22,5). It is possible that the sun's yearly revolution as well as its diurnal passage may have been considered in Egypt to be repeated rehearsals of the agony of its original creation. The original night in which the sun was formed, however, is that of the supreme Lord, which, we have seen, lasts 4,380,000,000 terrestrial years.[407]

It is interesting to note that, in the *Skanda Purāna*, the fig tree (which symbolizes the entire emergent universe) at the centre of the cosmic streams is said to be unshaken by the "doomsday hurricane".[408] In the Nordic Edda too, the Yggdrasil which is destroyed at Ragnarök will inevitably revive the creation after this destruction since it contains within its trunk all the seeds of life.[409]

It may be noted that, although the Vedas contain no specific reference to a flood *per se*, the veiled reference at *RV* VII,88,3-5 where the sage Vasishta (one of the "seven sages")[410] declares that he embarked on a boat with the aid of Varuna and, riding over "ridges of waters" entered the latter's "lofty home" may be related to the deluge which precedes the emergence of the sun.[411]

In the *SP*, too, when the sage Mārkandeya – who substitutes for Manu – appeals to the Lord for a refuge in the boundless ocean, "the ocean of mundane existence", the Lord points out to him the holy heavenly river Narmada (a form of Parvathi, Shiva's consort), along the banks of which Mārkandeya as well as the other sages practise penance. Narmada also represents the flood which bears the sun. Narmada assumes for this solar birth the form of a cow with golden horns, a shape we have encountered in the representation of the flood Mehet Ouret, or Hathor, as the bearer of Horus, the sun, between her horns.[412] At the same time, Narmada represents

sun, as if such a momentous event as the felling of the Heavenly Light (Horus-Osiris) and its transformation into the sun (Horus the Younger) could occur every evening (see below Chs. VIII-IX).

[406] See above p.73.

[407] See above p.73.

[408] See S. Shastri, *op.cit.*, p.65.

[409] See "Voluspa"; cf. R. Cook, *The Tree of Life: Symbol of the Centre*, London: Thames and Hudson, 1974, p.12.

[410] See below pp.88ff.

[411] See S. Shastri, *op.cit.*, p.viii.

[412] See above p.79.

Earth, the material universe, itself. This is in consonance with her role as the consort of Shiva, who is the counterpart of Geb/Chronos/Time.[413] The transformation of the elemental universal matter of Earth into a Cow that yields nourishment to the various forms of life in the manifest universe is indeed related in the *BP* IV,17ff. This transformation is a repetition of that which occurred within the Cosmic Egg itself at the moment of the impregnation of the cosmic streams with the seed of the supreme deity which we shall notice in greater detail below.[414]

Mārkandeya is saved from the cataclysm by seeking refuge in Narmada's "flanks", for this cow's milk is said to be "ambrosial", just as Aditi's is, since it contains the divine "soma" [seed]. The result of Mārkandeya's imbibing of Narmada's milk is that "Divine vital energy" … "streamed through [him]" so that Mārkandeya "was able to breast the raging sea". There is, as we shall see below, an intimate connection between Hathor and the Tree of Life, which springs up from the waters of the abyss, just as there is between Aditi and Indra in the Vedas, and Narmada is a form of Aditi as well as Parvathi. Both Hathor and Aditi represent the basis of universal creation after the periodic destruction of the cosmos, and the Tree of Life is, as we shall see, the form of the material universe itself which arises from the abyss through the divine seed represented by Indra/Ninurta/Marduk. We see now that Mārkandeya is indeed a form of the sun-god himself, and we may conclude that Manu, whom he replaces, is, as the "son" of the sun, equally one.[415] Both Manu and Mārkandeya are solar forces directed to our universe and mankind and are thus considered ancestors of the race. As he is dragged along by the cow, whose "tail" he holds, for thousands of ages, Mārkandeya catches a glimpse of the Purusha "asleep"[416] in the cosmic ocean.

In the *SB*, Manu is described as offering a sacrifice after the flood recedes, and from this sacrifice arises, first, a "daughter" Idā [a variant of Ilā],[417] from whom is derived the human race. In the *SP*, Idā is called the "potency of Shankara [Shiva]",[418] that is, a reincarnation of his consort

---

[413] See below p.143.

[414] See below Ch.X.

[415] We have already seen that Ziusudra is substituted with Uras, representing Ninurta, above p.82.

[416] Or moribund, in Osirian mythological terms.

[417] Ilā and Idā are interchangeable in the *BP* (Ilā: IX,16,22) and other Purānas (Idā: *BrdP* III,60,11, *VP* 85,7) In *SP* (Vaishnava Khanda), it is a name of Narmada, the mighty river (and consort) of Shiva (see S. Shastri, *op.cit*, p.72). The second offspring of Manu is a male called Ikshvāku (see above p.53).

[418] See S. Shastri, *op.cit.*, p.72.

Parvathi herself, and is identified with Narmada "who destroys sin and delivers (mankind) from transmigration".[419] Narmada is, as we have seen, the power of the Flood itself which has borne aloft the incipient sun and the life of the newly formed universe.[420] While Idā is the "potency" of Shiva, Manu must be a form of Brahman.[421]

The fortunes of the first man, Manu,[422] himself during the deluge are recounted in detail in the Vedic *SB*. In *SB* I,viii,1, Manu is considered the son of Vivasvant.[423] Though Manu is differentiated in *RV* from Yama, who is considered to be another son of Vivasvant,[424] Yama bears the same epithet of "Shrāddhadeva"[425] which Manu also does in *BP*. So it is likely that we are dealing with the same figure, especially since the flood hero of the Avesta is also called Yima.[426] Manu is warned of the deluge by a fish (representing Prajapati in his piscine incarnation). *BP* VIII,24 further informs us that Manu is also called Shrāddhadeva (Lord of Faith),[427] while *BP* VIII,13 declares that this Manu begins the seventh 'Manvantara', our own. Since each manvantara has a duration of around 317,000,000 years (*BP* III,11,24), life on earth must have begun more than 1,902,000,000 years after the inception of the second cosmic age.

Manu saves himself in a ship which is tied to the "horn" of the fish[428] and is borne by the latter to the heights of "the northern mountain", which, not being specified as a Himalayan one, may well be an Armenian

---

[419]   Narmada may also be related to the Sumerian Nammu (see below p.104).

[420]   See above p.97; cf. S. Shastri, *op.cit.*, p.81.

[421]   See below p.88.

[422]   We have seen above (p.68) that Mannus was considered to be the first man also by the ancient Germans.

[423]   In *KYV* VI,5,6, Vivasvant is called an Āditya whose offspring are men and the one born after the first four Ādityas. In the *SB* III,1,3,3 Vivasvant is identified with Mārtānda, the eighth Aditya, who is at first unformed but later moulded into a man who generates the creatures of Earth. In the Avestan Hom Yast IX, Vivanghavant is called quite simply the "first of men".

[424]   In *RV* X, 10ff, Vivasvant engenders the first "man", Yama, as well as Yama's twin sister and wife, Yami, by mating with a daughter of Tvastr (see below p.125n).

[425]   See *The HW* II:615.

[426]   See below p.93.

[427]   The fact that Manu is also called Satyavrata, King of Dravida, in the *BP* VIII,24, has already been noticed above p.22.

[428]   See *SB* I,viii,1,5. It is hard to determine what the "horn" of the fish might be, unless it were a sword-fish. On the other hand, we may recall the image of Re emerging as the sun by holding on to the horns of the Cow Mehet-Ouret (see above p.79). The Indic imagery may be a transformation of the Egyptian. This is reinforced by the fact that Manu's daughter, Ida, who in *SB* I,viii,1,11-12 is said to characterise "cattle", is, in *TS* I,7,1 and II,6,7, represented

one. It is important to note that Manu is the divine ancestor of the race that is to inhabit the universe. Manu's "half-brother" (or *alter ego*), Yama (counterpart of the Avestan flood hero Yima) is indeed ruler of the lower heavens, according to *RV* I,35,6, and the sun and moon themselves are located in the mid-region between Heaven and Earth.

In the *MBh*, the divine identity of the fish is revealed to be that of Prajapati/Brahman (the name of the supreme god in his luminous, creative aspect), since the fish declares to the "seven sages" – who, unlike in the *SB* version of the story, accompany Manu in the ship – "I am Brahma, lord of progeny [Prajāpati] … I in the form of a fish have delivered you from this peril".[429] The fish goes on to state that Manu should create all creatures including "gods, asuras, and men and all the worlds and what moves and what does not move [i.e. animal and vegetable life]."

The *MBh* also includes the crucial detail missing in *SB*, that Manu was instructed to carry on board the boat "seed of every sort". That the seed that is preserved during the cosmic deluge is indeed the divine seed which informs all life in the universe is made clear in the Dravidian accounts of the flood, which state that Shiva instructed Brahman/Prajapati to safeguard in a golden pot (a substitute for the boat) the Vedas and other scriptures along with the seed of creation.[430] After the flood, the pot comes to rest at a sacred spot and Shiva reappears to release the contents of the pot and thus renew the terrestrial creation.[431]

At this point, we may briefly consider the "seven sages" who accompany Manu in the *MBh* version.[432] These seven sages are found also

as a cow produced by Mitra-Varuna. We have seen above (p.86f) that Ida is the same as Narmada.

[429] *Mbh* II, 187, 2ff. (tr. S. Shastri, *op.cit.*, p.9); cf. H. Usener, *op.cit.*, p.28ff.

[430] The common Vedic notion that the Vedas precede the actual creation of the universe is copied in the Hebrew rabbinical literature which maintains that there are seven things created before the world: "the Tora, conversion, the Garden of Eden, Gehenna, the divine Throne, the Sanctuary, the name of the Messiah" (see A. Wensinck, *The Ideas of the Western Semites concerning the Navel of the Earth*, Amsterdam: Johannes Mueller, 1916, p.17). This confirms the cohabitation of Indic and Hebrew peoples in the Near East and dates back perhaps to the contacts in the 17th c. B.C. between the Hurrian-Mitanni and the Habiru who served as their mercenaries (see B. Landsberger in J. Bottero, *op.cit.*, p.160; cf. M. Salvini, "Un royaume hourrite en Mésopotamie du Nord à l'époque de Hattušili I", in M. Lebeau (ed.), *About Subartu: Studies devoted to Upper Mesopotamia* (Subartu IV,1), Turnhout: Brepols, 1998, p.307).

[431] D. Shulman, "The Tamil Flood Myths", p.304.

[432] In the *BrdP* I,i,5,70 there are nine sages, Bhrgu, Angiras, Marīci, Pulastya, Pulaha, Kratu, Daksha, Atri, and Vasishta. In *BrdP* I,ii,32,96-7 Manu is included after Kratu to make a total of ten sages. In BrdP II,iii,1,21 there are only eight sages, Bhrgu, Angiras, Marīci, Pulastya, Pulaha, Kratu, Atri and Vasishta. In *BrdP* II,iii,1,7f. there are seven, whose names are

in the Sumerian accounts of the flood. In the tablet W 20030,[433] we find that each of the antediluvian kings (or, rather, gods) is accompanied by an extraordinary being called "apkallu"and, since this tablet lists only seven such kings, there are seven "apkallu" in all. The apkallu are the sages who arise from the Abyss to reveal science, art and civilisation to mankind.[434] The names of these apkallu are u-an, u-an-du-ga, en-me-du-ga, en-me-galam-ma, en-me-bulug-ga, an-en-lil-da and u-tu-abzu,[435] and their respective appearances are in the reigns of "a-a-lu", "a-la-al-gar lugal", "am-me-gal-an-na lugal", "e[n-m]e-usumgal-an-na lugal", "dumu-zi sipa lugal", and "en-me-dur-an-ki lugal".[436] From WB 1923,444 and W 20030,7, it is apparent that these kings ruled in Eridu, Bad-tibira, Larak, and Zimbir respectively, which establishes that the "apkallu" appeared during the development of the solar force in the underworld.[437] The first of these apkallu, U-An (identifiable with Adapa),[438] is characterised in Berossus' list by a piscine form which may correspond to the Matsya incarnation of the supreme Lord during the flood at the beginning of our present manvantara.

In Egypt too it is most probable that there was a tradition of seven sages who preceded the establishment of monarchy after the "deluge". The Palermo Stone, for instance, contains the names of nine kings of

---

given at II,iii,1,50 as Bhrgu, Angiras, Marīci, Atri, Pulastya, Pulaha, and Vasishta. In *BrdP* I,ii,38,26-33 again there is reference to the incarnations of merely seven sages in the present manvantara (the names of these being Visvāmitra, Jamadagni, Bhradvāja, Saradvan, Atri, Vasuman, and Vatsara). Given the relative frequency of seven as the number of the sages in the Puranas, the *Mahābhārata*, in Sumerian literature, as well as in Indian astronomy, we may assume that this was the original number, which was later amplified by the addition of such figures as Manu himself as a sage.

[433] See J. van Dijk, "Die Inschriftenfunde: II. Die Tontafeln aus dem res-Heiligtum" in *XVIII. vorläufiger Bericht über die von dem Deutschen Archaeologischen Institut und der Deutschen Orient-Gesellschaft aus Mitteln der Deutschen Forschungsgemeinschaft unternommenen Ausgrabungen in Uruk-Warka (1959/1960)*, Berlin: Heinrich J. Lenzen, 1962, pp.44ff.

[434] The apkallu are indeed the prototypes of the patriarchs before Noah in the Hebrew Bible (see H. Zimmern, "Biblische und babylonische Urgeschichte", *Der Alte Orient*, II (1901), pp.26ff.). In Indian astronomy, the "seven sages" are represented by the Pleiades. These apkallu are complemented in the postdiluvian section of this list by the "ummannu", or the scholars who aided the several postdiluvian kings in their respective reigns.

[435] See J. van Dijk, *op.cit.*, p.44.

[436] *Ibid.* In WB 1923, 444, the names are "a-lu-lim" and "a-lal-gar" reigning in Eridu, "en-me-en-lu-an-na", "en-me-en-gal-an-na" and "dumu-zi sipa" in Bad-tibira, "sipa-zi-an-na" in Larak, and "en-me-en-dur-an-na" in Zimbir. In W 20030,7 the names are given as "a-a-lu", "a-la-al-gar", "am-me-lu-an-na", "am-me-gal-an-na", "enme-usumgal-an-na", "dumu-zi sipa" and "en-me-dur-an-ki" respectively (*ibid.*, p.46).

[437] See above p.81.

[438] *Ibid.*, p.48.

Lower Egypt, while the Cairo fragment which may have formed part of the former contains a list of "kings" who clearly precede the kings of the Palermo dynastic list.[439] Of these kings seven bear wear the double crown of Upper and Lower Egypt.[440] Since these "kings" precede Menes (who represents Manu himself), we may reasonably conclude that these "kings" are indeed the same as the seven sages who ruled heaven and earth, which are represented in this list as Upper and Lower Egypt.

In *BrdP* I and *BP* VI, the sages are the "intellectual progeny"[441] of Brahma who antedate the Ādityas, the twelve suns of the manifest universe. In the *BrdP* III,iv,2,29, the sages of the family of Angiras are said to be located in the Bhuvarloka, which is the Mid-region between Earth and Heaven.[442] At *BrdP* III,iv,2,49ff., however, all the sages including Angiras are said to originally reside in Janarloka, the fifth world, which holds the seeds of mankind.

In the *MP*, the fish that saves Manu is again said to be a form of the supreme lord, Janārdana (Vishnu), while the rope that Manu ties between the fish's "horn" and the boat is the serpent, Vasuki, identifiable with the serpent of the Abyss, Sesha.[443] We note here a similarity also between the Ship of Life and the Tree of Life since both bear the serpent at one end, except that the Ship of Life merely bears the seeds of universal life, whereas the Tree also bears the sun itself atop its branches.[444] However, we have noted that the first man is a form of the solar deity himself.[445] Besides, the Ship of Life containing the seeds of life of the universe comes to rest atop a mountain, and it is on just such an elevation that the sun too appears.

From the identity of the fish, we may equate the underworld Vishnu/Janārdana with Prajapati/Brahma. Since the lord of the abyss in Sumer, Egypt, as well as in the Vedas is traditionally Enki/Osiris/Varuna, Vishnu must be the same as Varuna himself as the reviving solar energy. Varuna's association with Vishnu (as well as with Mitra, the "sun-god")[446]

---

[439] Breasted thought that the Cairo fragments must also have originally contained a set of kings of Upper Egypt who followed those of Lower Egypt (see Mercer, *ibid.*). If this were indeed the case, it is likely that the most ancient dynasties were founded in Lower Egypt.

[440] See S. Mercer, *op.cit*, p.16. The set of seven "kings" of a united Upper and Lower Egypt is followed by the kings of Lower Egypt (in the Palermo Stone)

[441] See below p.208n.

[442] See below p.315.

[443] See S. Shastri, *op.cit.*, p.28.

[444] See below Ch.XXIII

[445] See above p.87.

[446] In Sumer Gishnu (a corruption of Uishnu/Vishnu) is a name of the sun-god Utu (see K. Tallquist, *Neubabylonisches Namenbuch*, pp.12, 279).

is confirmed by the Egyptian identity of Osiris as Lord of the Abyss (abdu/ Abydos) and the Underworld, who is at the same time the brother, or rather, vital aspect, of Horus the Elder, and father of the sun-god Horus the Younger. This also explains Vishnu's other name Nārāyana, Lord of the Waters, which is typical of Varuna/Enki/Osiris. We have seen that Vishnu is represented in the Puranas as Anantasesha-sayee, the Lord who reposes on the serpent Ananta. This corresponds to Osiris in the underworld surrounded by the serpent Nehaher.[447] Vishnu/Varuna's trance-like sleep in the Purānas is thus the same as the "death" of Osiris caused by his *alter ego* Seth. The descent of the perfect light of Osiris-Horus the Elder/Brahman into the Abyss thus precedes its rise again as the light of our universe.

In the Dravidian *Cikalittala Purānam* of Arunāchalakkavirayar, we get further glimpses into the nature of the ship of life. The divine personages who survive the flood are said to be Siva himself and his wife Uma. The boat which saves Siva and his wife are considered as symbolic of the sacred sound "Om" itself, while the resting place of the boat is a "shrine" which stands as firm as "Dharma".[448] We may remember also that Ziusudra is blessed, at the end of the deluge, with immortality in the sacred land of "Dilmun".[449] The original form of Dilmun may well have been "Dharman" and represented the perfect holiness that this concept signifies in Vedic religion. Dilmun, as we have seen, is identified with the sacred "mountain" from which the light of the universe arises and which is the terrestrial source of the "me's".[450] It is unlikely that Dilmun originally had anything to do with the little island of Bahrain which later came to be identified with it.

David Shulman has pointed out that the creation stories in the Dravidian versions emphasise the importance of the shrine as the centre of the universe and seat of the renewed creation after the deluge.[451] Shiva interestingly names this shrine "the root of the universe", which is situated on a hill rather like the primordial hill from which the light of the cosmos arises in Egypt. The shrine therefore is the foundation of the universe itself. In the related Dravidian accounts of the deluge which engulfed the sacred city of Madurai, the latter city serves as an analogue of the shrine whence the universe emerges. In these stories, the flood is said to have been

---

[447] See below p.83.

[448] See D. Shulman, *op.cit.*, p.297.

[449] We have here a reminder of the divine nature of the first man (see above p.86f).

[450] See Y. Rosengarten, *Sumer et le sacré*, Paris: Editions E. de Broccard, 1977, p.56. The epithet "great "mountain" of the pure me's" is applied to other sacred Mesopotamian lands, such as Aratta and Sumer, as well (*ibid.*, pp.54ff.). 'Mey' is also the Tamil word for "just" (see K. Mutturayan, *op.cit.*, p.51).

[451] See D. Shulman, *op.cit.*, 27.

caused by Varuna [Enki] at the instigation of Indra.[452] The flood caused by Varuna, Lord of the Underworld, precedes the formation of the new sun. Shiva is the god who protects the city Madurai from the flood, no doubt that it may serve as the sacred foundation of our universe. The shrine atop the mountain is secure (as also is the sacred city of Madurai) from any destructive flood which may well up from the netherworld, Pātāla.[453] The mountain atop which the boat comes to rest may be considered as situated at the centre or navel of the universe. For the concept that the sanctuary is to be found atop a mountain at the navel or centre of the universe is to be found in Jewish (and later Muslim) theologians as well,[454] who no doubt derived it from Babylon. The mountain and navel clearly represent the phallic deity Shiva and his consort Parvathi (representing the cosmic vulva), so that they together constitute the entire emergent universe.

A close reflection of the crucial reference to the shrine in the Dravidian Indian accounts of the Deluge is to be noticed in the reference to the original of the shrine, which is the Abyss itself, in the Babylonian and Iranian flood stories. In the Babylonian epic, *Atrahasis*, Enki particularly advises Atrahasis to "roof [the ark] over like the Apsu/ So that the sun shall not see inside it", which indicates that the vehicle which contains the seed of all animals is, like the Abyss, completely dark.

The curious passage in *Atrahasis*, III,20, where Ea speaks to the "reed wall" of Atrahasis' dwelling may also be explained by the frequent Indian references to the lake of "reeds" in which the golden seed of Siva is dropped after being infused with his fiery form, Agni.[455] In a Sumerian magical text, Urn.49, the holy reed is said to rise from the swamps of Engur=Abzu.[456] The "reed" thus is an analogue of the ship of Life itself, since both contain the seeds of the incipient universe as well as its light. Thus it is not surprising to find that the boat of Ziusudra is also made of "reed".

[452] See the *Tiruvilai* of Paranjoti, 12, 18, 19 (D. Shulman, *op.cit.*, pp.311ff).

[453] The spire (gopurum) of the Hindu temple represents this mountain while the sanctum is dark and mysterious as the Apsu whence the universe and its light emerge. The waters of the Abyss are also symbolically remembered in the controlled water of the Dravidian temple tank, which has the same purifying and fertilising power as the "sweet waters" of Enki/ Varuna.

[454] See A. Wensinck, *Ideas*, pp.15f, 19ff, 40.

[455] See *RV* X, 51-3; *SB* 6, 3.1.31; *RV* X, 32.6; cf. W.D. O'Flaherty, *Asceticism and Eroticism in the Mythology of Śiva*, pp.92f., 159, 285. The "golden" seed is obviously related to the golden cosmic womb, "hiranyagarbha" as well as to the sun which is produced from it.

[456] See H. Steible, *Die altsumerischen Bau-und Weihinschriften*, Wiesbaden: F. Steiner, 1982 (*FAOS* 5) I:110.

If we turn to the Iranian Vendidad, we find that Yima the son of Vivanghvant (the sun)[457] is warned by Ahura Mazda of a "snow storm" which will turn into a flood on melting.[458] In the Avesta, as in the Purānas, Yima (Manu) is mentioned in connection with the seventh incarnation of Verethraghna (Vishnu).[459] In order to escape the cataclysm, Yima is asked to construct a "vara" [ark] which will bear the best examples of men, animals, and plants, and especially the "cows" which are on the mountains as well as in the valleys in "closed stalls".[460] Special reference is made to the fact that the "window which lets in the sunlight" be closed. That the Iranian version closely follows the Babylonian in this detail (which is perhaps found also in the original Sumerian though lost in its present fragmentary state), while at the same time leaving out the crucial reference to the Abyss, suggests that the Āryan flood stories as well as the Mesopotamian are based on an older proto-Dravidian/Hurrian original.

At the end of the Iranian Vendidad account of the deluge, Ahura Mazda explains that "the lights which shone in the vara" were "natural and human lights. All eternal lights shine from above, all human lights shine below in the inside (of the vara). Along with them one sees the stars, moon and sun shining in space". It is clear that the "human lights" are souls and that the vara, or the Ship of Life contains the light of the manifest universe, including the stars of the Mid-region. In the Vedas (RV I, 35,6) the realm ruled by Yama is said to be the lower Heavens adjoining Earth.[461]

The fact that the ship of life represents the entire universe is suggested also by the similar detail in the Ugaritic texts relating to Baal and the construction of his "palace" by his craftsman Kothar-and-Hasis. There Baal specifically objects to the inclusion of any windows in his "palace", since Mot (who represents Mortality) would enter through such an aperture. Unfortunately for Baal, Kothar-and-Hasis disobeys him and thus allows

---

[457]   In Iranian mythology the twins Yama and Yima represent death and life. Yima is called the first king and the founder of civilisation and his fabulous dwelling is in Airyanem Vaego, corresponding mythologically to the Indian Yamasadanam and etymologically to Āryavarta, the name applied to the Indo-Gangetic Plain settled by the later Indo-Āryans. Yima is to be distinguished from Gayomaretan (Purusha), who is the Cosmic Man killed by Angra Mainyu and whose seed is purified in the sun so that human life might arise on earth (see below p.116). However, Gayomaretan too is considered to be the founder of the Āryan race, or the chosen mankind (Farvardin Yast, 24). This suggests that Yima is but a reincarnation of Gayomaretan.

[458]   The "snow storm" is a reference to the icy state of the incipient universe that prevents the manifestation of the solar energy (see Ch.XXIV below).

[459]   See below p.222.

[460]   See H. Usener, *Die Sintfluthsagen*, p.208ff.

[461]   The two heavens above it are directly ruled by the solar force, Vivasvant; see below p.318.

Mot to enter in, whereupon Baal is killed and thereby rendered subject to his rule. It is only after Baal's consort, Anath's destruction of Mot that Baal is resurrected (no doubt as the sun), in a manner resembling Osiris' resurrection as Horus the Younger.

II: ĀTMAN

THE SUPREME SOUL: ĀTMAN/HARI, AMUN/RE

Then Flood story recounts in quasi-fictional form the process of the emergence of the sun in our universe, along with its life. But the entire cosmic creation after the destruction of the previous cosmos is an extremely long and complicated saga marked by several distinct stages that precede the moment of the arrival of the life-bearing "ship" manned by Manu, the son of the sun, on earth. We shall now focus more closely on the cosmoerotic transformations of the divine Soul and its Fiery Desire, Kāma/ Agni, during these dramatic stages of the new creation, from the first, ideal Light of the cosmos to its final physical manifestations as the light of earth, the light of heaven and the light of the Mid-region between heaven and earth.

To discern the first unmanifest state of the supreme deity, we may consider the cosmogonical scheme in the Vedas, *RV* X,129,1, where the first hypostasis (Ātman/Hari of *BP*) is called the One, which "breathless, breathed by its own nature: apart from it was nothing whatsoever". Although it is the only Existent, it is nevertheless surrounded by what is called a "Chaos" [Abyss] of dark and indistinct "water" (st.3), which, from the logic of the verse, must be still unformed.[462] This One corresponds to the Egyptian Amun (who is also called Atmu, Soul)[463] and is the sole living

---

[462] These primal entities correspond to the Egyptian Amun-Amunet, Nun-Nunet, Huh-Huhet, Kuk-Kuket and the Hesiodic Eros, Chaos, Earth and Tartarus (see below p.150f).

[463] Hu-Nefer papyrus, (see E.A.W. Budge, *op.cit.*, II:10,15). If the Egyptian Amun indeed represents a corruption of the Sanskritic 'ātman', then it must indicate the presence of an Indic priestly tradition in Egypt at a very early date, from at least the fifth dynasty, ca. 2500 B.C., when the worship of Amun is first attested. The Vedas do not give evidence of the worship of a god called, simply, Ātman. The concentration on the Ātman is peculiar, rather, to the Upanishads, and the Purānas, which latter are more comprehensive in their cosmogony than the Vedas.

Being, that which alone "breathes", in the earliest stages of the cosmos, just as Amun is the foundation of the Nun/Apsu.

RV X,129,1 goes on to state that from the One (Amun) arose Desire (Kāma), the "primal seed and germ of Spirit [Mind/Light/Horus/An/Brahman]". In *AV* III,21,4, Desire is used as an appellation of Agni, showing that Agni/Kāma is originally the desire of the One and the source of the ideal universe. That is why Agni is identifiable with Ātman as the very first form of the deity (Shiva). In *AV* XIX,52,1-3, the first hypostasis is said to be Desire (Kāma) itself, and it is said to have created Mind. Mind is the same as Prajāpati/Dyaus.[464] In *RV* X,90, further, it is stated: "Fervour [Tapas] creates Rta (the Sacred Order), and Truth"[465] and from these are produced first Night,[466] and then the Waters.[467] From the passage in the *Subala Upanishad* below we may infer that it is Mind that undertakes the austerities which produce Night and the Waters. The Waters are ever moving and infused with Rta, so they are also ever striving for Truth.[468] Indeed, their name (apā) itself means "action or movement", so that in the *Nighantu*, it is given as a synonym of "karma".[469]

It must be noted that other, slightly different, accounts of the primal elements of the cosmos are also to be found in the Vedas. In *RV* X,72 the first element (corresponding to the One, Amun) is called Non-Existence, which gives birth to Existence or Being, which must correspond, as in Greek philosophy, to the Mind, and from this, through the force of the "Productive Power" [Desire/Agni], Earth and the regions came into being.

---

[464]   See below p.140.

[465]   We may compare the mention of Amun-Amunet, Nun-Nunet, Atum-Routy, Shu-Tefnut in PT 301, pyr. 446-7 (K. Sethe, *Amun*, p.34f.; cf. S. Bickel, *La Cosmogonie Egyptienne avant le Nouvel Empire*, Fribourg: Editions Universitaires, 1994, p.28n). This is not an ogdoad but, rather, an order of generations, whereby Amun is represented as the source of Nun, who fathers Atum, etc. Atum's consort Routy is perhaps linguistically cognate with Sanskrit Rta. Routy is represented as a pair of lionesses and identified also with Atum's children Shu and Tefnut in PT 447 (see 'Ruti' in *LÄ* V:321). It is not surprising therefore that Tefnut is regularly identified with Maat, the sacred order (for Routy's relation to Tefnut see S. Bickel, *op.cit.*, p.190). Following the Vedic passage, Shu may particularly symbolise Truth, even as Tefnut symbolises Maat.

[466]   In Hesiod's theogony, Night and Erebus are born of Chaos (Nun, Apsu). Night is also said to be the wife of An in Sumerian cosmology (Ebeling KAR I no.38, 9-23), which makes An the same as the Light of Dyaus and Night an aspect of the primal Earth, Prithvi/Ki/Antum.

[467]   These Waters are not the formless cosmic streams of the Abyss/Chaos, but must refer to the substance of Heaven, which is, in an Assyrian exegetical text, said to be constituted of waters ('ša me') (see below p.150n).

[468]   See U. Choudhuri, *op.cit.*, p.156.

[469]   We have here an explanation of the identification of Rta (arta) with the later Hindu concepts of "karma" and "dharma".

Indeed, in the *SB* X,vi,5, Non-Existence is called Death and is the first entity in the cosmos, from which Mind[470] is created. That Death is the same as the supreme Lord in his unmanifest form is made clear by *Subala Upanishad* VII,1, where the ultimate essence of the lord of the Abyss, Nārāyana, is called "the Unmanifest", "the Imperishable" and "Death". The divine Mind produces through its own austerities (Tapas, i.e. fervent Desire) the Waters, which constitute the substance of Heaven. And, as we shall see, the Waters are not really formed into the primal elements of Earth and Heaven until the Desire of the One (Agni) impregnates the waters.[471]

A similar view of the development of the primordial divine energy is offered by the cosmogonical accounts in the Purānas. In the *BP* II,5, the [new] universe begins with the sole, ineffable divine Spirit, Ātman, called Hari (the transcendent form of the solar deity Vishnu/Atum). The cosmic streams (Apā, Nāra) are formed by the Lord (Nara) for his habitation and he reposes in the universal ocean for aeons as Nārāyana ('the Lord who rests in the waters').

In Egypt, Re is the equivalent of the solar force which informs the cosmos. However, the Lord of the Cosmos is called variously Amun-Ptah-Atum and it is his first form Amun which is, as we shall see, philosophically the most important of all. According to the Ramesside theologians, which incorporates the doctrines of Hermopolis, Memphis and Heliopolis in a unified scheme, Amun's first form is considered to be the primeval elements of the "Eight", his next [Ptah] Tatenen, the leader of the Eight, and then the Bull of Heaven [Atum].[472] The supreme god Amun/Osiris/Re thus has a threefold aspect as Soul (Amun), Body (Ptah), and Face (Atum).[473] In

---

[470] This reference to the Mind is clearly not to the Brahman which illumines the cosmos with ideal light and intellect, but rather to the consciousness of the lord of the Abyss as he acquires macroanthropomorphic form.

[471] See below p.138.

[472] See J. Assmann, *Egyptian Solar Religion in the New Kingdom: Re, Amun and the Crisis of Polytheism*, tr. A. Alcock, London: Kegan Paul International, 1995, p.159.

[473] The identity of Ātman with the universal soul and with Brahman (Āditya/Mitra) is indeed the central theme of the Upanishads. It is interesting to observe that the earlier form of Amun, Min is often represented with the head of a goat, just as Pan his Greek counterpart was. Pan is indeed often equated with Phanes, Dionysus, and Attis (see A.B. Cook, *Zeus*, II:349,296,1051). And we may also remember Heraclitus' dictum "ἐν τὸ πᾶν", "The All [Pan] is One [the One]". Amun is also represented with horns in his incarnation as Khnum, or Ptah/Prajāpati/Brahman (see *LÄ* I:239; cf. p.206n below).

It is interesting that the goat's horns on Amun are those of an Asiatic species and not of an indigenous one, like those of the goat symbol of Khnum (see K. Sethe, *op.cit.*, p.24). Sethe suggested that this indicates an Asiatic origin of the deity. It is unlikely that Amun alone was an Asiatic deity while his later form Khnum was an indigenous Egyptian one. Both must indeed have originally been Asiatic, proto-Hurrian gods.

Ch.300 of Pap. Leiden I 350, it is explained that Amun, the Sun [Re] and Ptah [the deities of Thebes, Heliopolis and Memphis] are all aspects of one another: "[The supreme deity's] identity is hidden in Amun, his is the Sun as face, his body is Ptah".[474] According to Macrobius' *Saturnalia*, too, Re is "Helios, ruler of the universe, breath of the cosmos [Ptah-Shu/Vāyu], energy of the cosmos [Amun-Agni], light of the cosmos [Re-Āditya]".[475]

Amun is the Lord of the Abyss in his most spiritual state as the divine Soul. Amun bears the typical epithet of "the Hidden One", since he is the original form of the deity as the Soul of the cosmos, which finally emerges as the ethereal light of Atum/Horus. Worshipped as the supreme god in Thebes,[476] Amun is a later form of a southern ithyphallic god, Min or Amin,[477] whose iconographic form represents the macroanthropos whose seed produces the Cosmic Egg. Amun is also replaced sometimes in the Ogdoad by Tenemu, meaning Invisibility.[478] Amun is also called "nj3w", which means "the Non-existent", exactly as in the Vedic passage quoted above.[479] He is thus the same as "the One" of the Vedas. In the Papyrus Leiden I 350, Ch.200, Amun is hymned as the supreme transcendent reality who is "secret of development" and, while he is identical in his "glittering" forms (body) to "the Great One in Heliopolis", to Ptah Tatenen, not even

---

[474]   See J.P. Allen, *Genesis in Egypt: The Philosophy of Ancient Egyptian Creation Accounts*, New Haven, CT: Yale University Press, 1988, p.54.

[475]   See Macrobius, *Saturnalia*, I, xxiii, 31.

[476]   The original god of Thebes was Montu who was worshipped in the form of a falcon, the symbol of Horus the Elder, and as a "strong Bull". Montu is also called "Amun the Elder" who, with his spouse Rattawy, creates Horus the Younger. Montu is thus a form of Osiris-Horus the Elder. This is also made clear from the fact that Montu is described as the god with "four faces" (K. Sethe, *op.cit.*, p.9f.), a typical appellation of the embryonic Brahman in the Cosmic Egg (cf. *BrdP* I,i,4,17: "The self-born deity [Swāyambhuva] has three states: He has four faces as Brahma; as Kāla he is Bhava the destroyer, as [Vishnu] he is the Purusha with thousand heads"). Montu, like Amun, may also be related to the ithyphallic Min, since the latter is also identified with Horus (see K. Sethe, *op.cit.*, p.20; cf. C.J. Bleeker, *Geburt*, p.11; Plutarch, *De Iside*, Ch.56). Amun himself is described in the hymn to Amon-Re of Hibis as the Bull "whose aspects consist of four faces on a single neck, 778 ears, millions upon millions of eyes and hundreds of thousands of horns" (A. Barucq and F. Daumas, *op.cit.*, p.328). The multi-faceted appearance of Marduk/Muruga may have been derived from the original adoration of the creative and solar aspect (Brahman) of the Soul (Ātman) in this manner.

[477]   Amun was, according to Sethe, originally a member of the Hermopolitan Ogdoad (Amun-Amunet) and later raised by the Thebans to a supreme god. This is unlikely considering that Amun is also related to the very ancient ithyphallic god of fertility, Min (see C.J. Bleeker, *Geburt*, pp.20ff.).

[478]   See K. Sethe, *op.cit.*, p.73.

[479]   See above p.96.

the gods know "his true appearance ... He is too secret to uncover his awesomeness, he is too great to investigate, too powerful to know".[480] Amun precedes the "bodily" aspect of the deity denoted by Ptah, while the "facial" aspect of the deity is represented by Re/Atum, with its two eyes, the moon and the sun within the solar system.

Amun is a counterpart of the Vedic Agni as Ātman, a primordial aspect of the divine Fire which is not emphasized in the Vedas so much as in the related Upanishads and Purānas. The name Amen may itself be related to the Sanskritic Ātman, Soul (Amun is called 'Soul' in a hymn to Amun-Ra, and also 'Atmu').[481] However, just as in the Vedas, the supreme Soul is often identified with its fiery aspect, and a variant of Amun spelled as 'grh', which appears sometimes as the fourth element of the Ogdoad,[482] may be related to the name of the Sumerian god of fire, Girra (Agni).

In the Shu texts of the First Intermediate Period, the original state of the supreme deity is described entirely in negative terms as being immersed in "the infinity, the nothingness, the nowhere and the dark".[483] We notice that these elements are the same as those which later produce the Cosmic Egg – Huh (the infinite cosmic streams, or "flood"), Amun (the ineffable divine soul), Nun (the still waters of the Abyss), and Kuk (the pitch darkness of the embryonic cosmos).[484] In CT 714 we are offered a glimpse of the first form of Amun in the waters of the Abyss:

The most ancient form in which I came into existence was as a drowned one.
I was [also] he who came into existence as a circle,
He who was the dweller in his egg.
....
First Hahu[485] emerged from me
And then I began to move.
I created my limbs in my "glory".[486]

[480] See J.P. Allen, op.cit., p.52.

[481] See A. Mariette, Les papyrus égyptiennes du Musée de Boulaq, pl.11–13, in E.A.W. Budge, op.cit., II, 10.

[482] See K. Sethe, op.cit., p.67.

[483] See R.T. Rundle Clark, op.cit., p.54f.

[484] See below p.151.

[485] Hahu is a form of Shu (see R.T. Rundle Clark, op.cit., p.74).

[486] CT 714 (see R.T. Rundle Clark, ibid.).

The latter half of this verse relates to the development of the supreme soul as a macroanthropos which we shall study further below. We note that Amun is said to dwell in his egg, though, as we shall see, the cosmic "egg" proper is not formed until much later.[487] In the stelophore Copenhagen A 72, Amun is also described in a way that immediately recalls the Vedic Agni:[488]

> Lord of Maat [Rta] without equal
> The one who begat his begetter
> Who created his mother and brought forth his hand.[489]

Amun, like Agni, is both son and consort of the waters. And we have seen that the Fervour of the supreme deity in *RV* X,190, creates the Waters, along with Rta, Truth, and Night.

We know from the Hermopolitan theology that the waters Nunet are created by Nun.[490] So Nun must represent an aspect of Amun himself. In fact, Nun represents the sattvic supraconsciousness of the deity in his ideal state.[491] It has generally been thought that Nun is equivalent to the waters of the Abyss since he is represented hieroglyphically with a wavy sign, which denotes water. But it is important to note that Nun represents still, rather than flowing, waters.[492] This inert aqueous state is best understood as the perfect undisturbed repose of the Divine Mind. Indeed, the Greeks rendered Nun as Noūv, the philosophical hypostasis of Mind.[493] It is not surprising that the deep sleep of human beings, as well as death, is supposed in ancient Egypt to be a descent into Nun.[494]

However, Nun also represents the erotic aspect of the deity (Kāma/Desire/Eros), for Nun is sometimes called the god who creates what he "desires",[495] and Nun is the realm of "sweet" waters, or seminal streams which constitute the blissful substance of Heaven.

---

[487] See below Chs.VIII-IX.

[488] See below p.137.

[489] J. Assmann, *op.cit.*, p.118. The phrase "brought forth his hand" refers to the autoerotic creative act which produces the cosmos.

[490] See below p.138.

[491] See below p.151.

[492] See K. Sethe, *op.cit.*, Art.145.

[493] See K. Sethe, *op.cit.*, p.35. It must be noted that Nun-Abzu (CT 24,14,26) is also one of the names of Enki, as Lord of the Abyss. It is possible that the Sumerian "Nun" ('Prince') (see below p.103) was used metonymously by the Egyptians to indicate the Abyss itself.

[494] See A. de Buck, "De godsdienstige opvatting van de slaap inszonderheid in het oude Egypte", *MVEOL* 4 (1939) (cf. "Nun", *LÄ* IV:534).

[495] CT 317 IV,114i (see S. Bickel, *op.cit.*, p.29); cf. CT 75, where he creates "in his heart" (see

In Hesiod's theogony, Eros represents the desire-filled Soul of the supreme deity, Amun.[496] However, the Egyptian Amun is also identified with Zeus as Zeus Ammonus.[497] This may be a primal form of Zeus distinct from the storm-god.[498]

R.T. Rundle Clark, *op.cit.*, p.83).

[496] This elemental Desire is that which arises later as Eros-Phanes/Brahman (see below p.155).

[497] See A.B. Cook, *Zeus* I:351. The earliest pictographic evidence of a Zeus Ammonus is from a 6th c. B.C. coin at Kyrene. Herodotus (*Histories* II:42,29,83) also equates Zeus with Amun.

[498] See below Ch.XIV.

III: NĀRĀYANA

THE LORD OF THE WATERS: APSU, VARUNA, NUN, OSIRIS

The Abyss/Chasm/Chaos is a representation of the Māya (the power of Illusion) of the supreme lord as he begins the creative process. In scientific terms it corresponds to the quantum "black hole"[499] which possibly initiated the cosmos according to the "superstring theory", a theory which also interestingly understands the four space-time dimensions of the familiar world as an illusion.[500] The first cosmic element that is formed by the lord of the Abyss to fill it is the cosmic streams called Apāh[501] in the Vedas and Purānas. These waters are the basis of the entire cosmos, and this is borne out also by the scientific fact that heavy hydrogen nuclei are formed early in the primordial stage of the cosmos and followed quicky after by helium nuclei (Agni).[502]

In Sumer, the primeval Enki, who is, not accidentally, also called Nun-[abzu], Prince of the Abyss,[503] is the same as the primal Osiris in Egypt, and Varuna in the Vedas. Enki, or Ea (in Akkadian) is therefore the supreme lord of the cosmic waters. The Akkadian name Ea indeed gives us a more accurate idea of the vital nature of the primal form of this deity than

---

[499] Black holes are the depths into which the earliest stars that exploded fell and which serve henceforth as the gravitational anchors of the emergent galaxies (see T. Folger, "The real Big Bang", *Discover*, Dec. 2002, p.45).

[500] See "Cosmos" in *EB*, Macropedia, 16:794.

[501] This term is clearly related to the Apsu/Abzu of the Akkadians and Sumerians, to the Egyptian Abdu (the basis of the name of the city of Osiris, Abydos) and also to Apop, the dragon of the cosmic seas (see below p.213ff). There is also a reference to the benign "abdu-fish" in several hymns to Re (e.g. AeHG no.19, no.30). The basic word from which these names are derived seems to be the Sanskritic "ap" (Sumerian "a") for water.

[502] See F.H. Shu, "The Cosmos", in *EB*, Macropedia, 16:792,4.

[503] See A. Deimel, *Pantheon Babylonicum*, p.194.

the Sumerian Enki, since it is related to the Semitic 'ha.a' meaning 'life'[504] as also to the possible root of the Egyptian Osiris[505] and to the Dravidian 'Usir'/'Uyir', signifying 'life'.[506]

The primeval watery form of the cosmos is represented with considerable elaboration in the Sumerian An=Anum god-list, which starts with three names of the mistress of the gods, Ishtar/Nammu: Sim.bi.zi, Nin.i.li, Nin.sar (BAR), and continues with the names of Nammu (which is the Emesal form of the Sumerian Imma):[507] Ama.u.tu.an.ki (Mother who gave birth to Heaven and Earth), SAL.agrig.zi, Nammu, Nin.ur.SAL.la (the female counterpart of En-uru-ulla/Enki)[508] and Nin.i.li,[509] who, being the consort of Alala (Enki), is the same as Damkina.

In the same god-list, the eight names of Nammu are followed by 21 ancestors of the god of heavenly light, An, and his consort Ki. These fathers and mothers are, unlike the Nammu elements, both male and female, since they represent a combination of earthly and heavenly material as undifferentiated Heaven-Earth (dA-nu-um u An-tum).[510] The first[511] of these ten pairs is En-uru-ulla-Nin-uru-ulla (the lord and lady of the primeval dwelling), whereas in the Old Babylonian list, Urash is the first. Then come two pairs related to Alala who most probably denotes Enki[512] in the form of the Cosmic Man.

According to the Old Bablyonian god-list, Nammu as the "Mother who gave birth to Heaven and Earth" (An/Antum) is a personification

---

[504] See H.D. Galter, *Der Gott Ea/Enki in der akkadischen Überlieferung* (Dissertationen der Karl-Franzens-Universität Graz, Graz, 1983, p.4ff.

[505] See J.G. Griffiths, *The Origins of Osiris*, p.94, for the suggestion that the name might be related to the word "might", which probably has the same connotation as the Latin 'virtus', itself derived from 'vir' (cf. fn. below).

[506] See *DED*, p.62. The term 'uyir' is also used for the male genitalia and it is possible that this is the source of the Sanskrit and Latin 'vir' as well. The Sumerian Enki meaning Lord of Earth is an appellation that this primal deity acquires only after he, as the light of the cosmos (An), is deposed from his kingship and sent down to Earth, which he then rules (see below Ch.XVII).

[507] See W.G. Lambert, "Cosmogony" in *RLA* VI:220.

[508] See below p.139.

[509] See W. Lambert, *op.cit.*, p.54. The Hieronyman Orphic theogony, according to Damascius, begins with water [the substance of Heaven] and mud [Earth] as the first manifestations of the universe (see M.L.West, *The Orphic Poems*, p.178).

[510] The 11th pair is represented as a single unit, Anki, constituted of a closely united An and Ki.

[511] The section relating to the "fathers and mothers" of An is to be read from bottom to top.

[512] In the Assyrian ritual text AO 17626 (RA 41 31), rev., Alala is equated with Enki (see A. Livingstone, *op.cit.*, p.199).

of the cosmic waters in which the Ideal Macroanthropos rests. Nammu is followed by Urash (Earth/Enki) and Anshargal (the great circle of heaven).[513] According to the Babylonian epic *Enuma Elish,* the original state of the cosmos is represented by a watery chaos, Tiamat (Nunet), who is the consort of Apsu (Nun).

If we turn to the treaties of the Hittites, we find a list of primeval Hurrian deities, usually twelve in number, representing the Anunnaki.[514] The Anunnaki are considered the guardians of the life-giving water ('me balati') of the underworld.[515] However they are also primeval deities since they include forms of the supreme deity that precede even Alalu, who, as we shall see, probably represents the Ideal Man. The names of these deities are Nara, Namsara,[516] Minki, Ammunki, Ammezzadu, Tuhusi and these are followed by Alalu, Anu,[517] Antu, Apantu,[518] Enlil[519] and Ninlil. In the Mitanni treaty of the Hittite kings, too, we find a list of Hurrian "primeval gods" who seem partly derived from the Sumerian.[520] These include Nara, Nampsara; Minki, Ammuki, Tuhusi, Ammizzadu and Alalu, who are then followed by Anu, Antu, Enlil, Ninlil/Ninurta, and Ningal (consort of Nannar, the moon-god).[521] Since the list ends with the moon, we may assume that all the deities before the sun of our system itself are considered as "primeval". The Anunnaki are comparable to the Vedic Asuras. That is why also Marduk, the force within the sun and counterpart of Horus the Younger, is king of the Igigi, while Anshar is the chief of the Anunnaki. In the Sumerian poem "Enki and the World-Order", Enki, or Ea as lord

---

[513] W. Lambert, "The Cosmology of Sumer and Babylon", p.52. The Middle Babylonian god-list "An=Anum" begins with Urash. But we may assume that the list beginning with Nammu is more complete.

[514] See A. Archi, "The Names of the Primeval Gods", *Orientalia* 59 (1990), p.114ff.

[515] V R 51, 37b ff. (cf. A. Jeremias, *Leben nach dem Tode*, p.73). The life-giving water is, however, equally present in the heavens (see H. Zimmern, *op.cit.*, p.452).

[516] The consort of Nara, Napsara (or Nampsara), bears a remarkable resemblance to Skt. 'apsara' meaning water sprite.

[517] The inclusion of An as a "primeval" god among the Hurrians confirms that the name belongs originally to the primal Heaven which forms the body of the supreme deity as Ideal Man (see below Ch.VII).

[518] Archi (*op.cit.*, p.116) conjectures that Apantu is "a name created in association with Antu".

[519] Enlil is the "counsellor" of the Anunnaki in *Atrahasis*, I,8.

[520] CTH 136; cf. the gods listed in Kbo XVII 94,26ff. and Kbo XVII 95 III 12-18 (E. Laroche, "Les dénominations des dieux 'antiques' dans les texts hittites", in *Anatolian Studies presented to Hans Gustav Güterbock on the Occasion of his 65th Birthday*, Istanbul: Nederlands Historisch-Archaeologisch Instituut in Het Nabije Oosten, 1975, pp.180,182).

[521] See D. Yoshida, *op.cit.*, p.16.

of the underworld, is called the "lord of the Anunna gods" (1.8)[522] while his son/solar aspect, Ninurta is called the chamberlain of the Anunnaki in *Atrahasis*, I, 9.

Since the word "nāra" is present also in Sanskrit[523] signifying "waters", it is possible that the first two names in the Hurrian lists are deifications of the waters of the cosmic streams or ocean. It is significant that the lord of the Abyss in the Purānas is called similarly Nārayana.[524] In the Kumarbi fragments, Nara Napshara is called the "brother" of Enki,[525] though the name seems to be a dual one including a male deity and his consort. It is possible thus Napsara correspond to the Sumerian Nammu as well as to the Babylonian Tiamat. Gurney thinks that Minki and Ammunki may be distortions of Enki-Ninki, the lord and lady of the Abyss.[526] Then Minki-Ammunki may correspond to En-uru-ulla-Nin-uru-ulla of the Sumerian list.[527] The significance of Tuhusi and Ammizzadu is obscure, though the next name, Alala, may well be a counterpart of Purusha as the primal Macroanthropos.

The proem to Hurrian poem of "The Kingship in Heaven" also lists ten primeval deities as N[ara, Napsara, Mink]i, Ammunki, Ammezzadu, [?[528]....] the father (and) mother of [...], [?[529] (and) ?[530]]u, the father and mother of Ishara, Enlil (and) Ninlil.[531]

In the Babylonian epic, *Enuma Elish*,[532] the first elements of the universe are Apsu (the Abyss/Nun) and his consort Tiamat, who correspond to Nun-Naunet in Egypt, and they represent the primal cosmic streams in which the Lord rests as the Ideal Man. Apsu and Tiamat produce Lahmu-

---

[522] For the unity of An-Enlil-Enki see below p.162.

[523] This is another instance where it is hard to distinguish Hurrian from Mitanni.

[524] See, for instance, *VP* I,3,24.

[525] See H. Güterbock, *Kumarbi*, Text Ic.

[526] O.R. Gurney, *Some Aspects of Hittite Religion*, Oxford: Oxford University Press, 1977, p.15.

[527] See above p.104.

[528] Archi conjectures that the broken name here might be Tuhusi.

[529] Archi conjectures that the broken name here might be Enlil, though it is more likely to have been Anu.

[530] Archi conjectures that the broken name here might be Apantu, though it is more likely to have been Antu.

[531] See A. Archi, *op.cit.*, p.114.

[532] *EE* I,121. Tiamat is also represented in the form of a 'monster' (*EE* IV, 95ff; cf. CT 13,33 I in L.W. King, *op.cit.*, p.117).

Lahamu[533] and Anshar-Kishar,[534] who represents the united Heaven and Earth. These primal deities are followed by An (Horus the Elder) and his brother Ea (Osiris), and, finally, Ea's son, Marduk (Horus the Younger).[535] The Ea/Enki who follows An as his "brother" is clearly not the original Lord of the Apsu, but the manifestation of Enki/Osiris as Lord of Earth, or the "underworld". Marduk is a late evolute of Enlil/Shu as "the force within the sun [or the light of the universe]", and is considered the son, or final manifestation of Enki. We see therefore that the order of the gods is reversed in the process of cosmic manifestation. In the primeval stage, the primal Enki is followed by Enlil and then An. In our universe An descends into the underworld as Enlil,[536] lies moribund in it as his "brother" Enki, and then rises again as Enki's solar son, Marduk.[537]

In the Egyptian *Book of the Dead* II,39, Osiris is indeed called "the ba (soul, pneumatic form) of the sun [that is, the light of the universe], by means of which he [Amun-Re] copulates himself".[538] Osiris thus may be considered the soul of the cosmic light (Horus the Elder), just as his son Horus the Younger (Marduk) is the force of the sun.

In Hermopolis, the Mind of the Abyss, Nun, is said to have "created [Nunet] as the first Existent and let the Flood [Huh] arise".[539] This is the substance of Heaven, and Nunet is substantially related to Nut and to Hathor, who develop from her.

---

[533] Lahmu is probably the boar-form of Vāyu (see below p.134). In a Babylonian magic text we find three antecedents of An: Alala-Belili [corresponding to the Ideal Macroanthropos], Lahmu-Lahamu [corresponding to Vāyu] and Duri-Dari [Kāla/Time] (see W. Lambert, "The Cosmologies of Sumer and Babylon", in *Ancient Cosmologies*, p.53). Anshar-Kishar thus are synchronous with Time/Kāla, an effect of the wind-god, Vāyu/Enlil (see below Chs. VIII,X).

[534] This stage in the cosmos is represented in the Hurrian "Kingship in Heaven" by Kumarbi/Chronos/Duri-Dari.

[535] The identification of Marduk with Horus the Younger is confirmed by his name, meaning 'sun calf', Horus the Elder/Atum-Re being the "Bull of Heaven".

[536] See below p.200.

[537] See the final title of Marduk as "Ea" in *EE* VII,120.

[538] The bennu (phoenix) bird identified with Osiris is also called the "ba" of the sun (see A. Piankoff, *Le "Coeur" dans les Textes Egyptiens*, Paris: Librairie orientaliste Paul Geuthner, 1930, p.56; cf. S. Quirke, *The Cult of Ra*, London: Thames and Hudson, 2001, pp.28-30). The phoenix is especially associated with the soul, pneuma, and breath (see 'Phoenix' in *LÄ* IV: 1033ff). The association of the "ba of the sun" with Osiris-Re's masturbation suggests that it is the seed of Osiris that forms the substance of the sun.

[539] See K. Sethe, *op.cit.*, p.75. cf. the quote from *BD* above, where Osiris is the "soul" of the sun.

The flood of Huh (or Hehu), also called Mehet-Ouret, is the third element in the Hermopolitan Ogdoad[540] and the substance of Earth. It is also the source of the flood that we have discussed above in connection with the popular deluge story. In the *Book of the Dead*, 175, Atum threatens universal destruction whereafter Earth will return to Nun and Hehu.[541] Nun is said to be "in Hehu and vice-versa".[542] Hehu is "the river of the lord of the universe [Atum] when he was in the floods of Hehu and in Nun in a state of inertia".[543] Hehu is the flood from which Earth and the Cosmic Egg develop. It therefore represents the rājasic aspect of the supreme deity.[544]

In the *BP*, Nārāyana is the name of the lord in the waters and, generally, in the cosmologies of the Purānas, Hari/Vishnu (Atum-Re, the solar energy) is represented in his later form as a macroanthropos reposing on the giant snake Adi-Sesa that floats upon the primeval ocean.

In the *BAU* III,9,16, Varuna is equated with macroanthropomorphic Nārāyana/Vishnu of the *BP*, that "Person [Purusha] whose abode is water, whose world is the heart, whose light is Mind, who is the ultimate resort of every soul." Like the Sumerian Enki, the Vedic Varuna is mostly worshipped in his later manifestation as the Lord of the underworld as well as of the waters. At the same time, Varuna, like Enki, is particularly the "lord of the sweet waters" and the primal Varuna is directly related to the Kāma(Desire)/Agni[545] of the supreme deity, representing as he does a state of bliss and immortal life. This is made clear in *BU* III,ix,22, where it is stated that Varuna is based on water, which is based on semen, which is based on the heart (22).

---

[540]   See below p.151f.

[541]   See K. Sethe, *op.cit.*, p.64.

[542]   See S. Bickel, *op.cit.*, p.24.

[543]   *Ibid.* Atum is the same as Amun, the latter being the "hidden" Soul of the deity (see Pap. Boulaq pl.11-13; cf. E.A.W. Budge, *op.cit.*, II:10).

[544]   See below p.110.

[545]   Hence the identification of Varuna and Agni in *RV* VII,88,2 (see below p.306n).

IV: PURUSHA

THE IDEAL MAN – ALALU, PTAH

T he Lord of the Abyss gradually assumes a macroanthropomorphic form as the Ideal cosmic Man. The process of this primal, and entirely ideal, manifestation of the Lord (Hari) is recounted in the *BP* II,5. The Lord, desirous of creation arouses, out of his own power of illusion, Māya – aided by Time (Kāla-Shiva) – the three forms of divine energy – Sattva, Rajas, and Tamas. We see already that Shiva, though representative of the destructive aspect of the deity, is indeed one of the primal agents of cosmic creation, as Time, and, as we shall see, especially as the cosmic Ego.[546] The aim of the cosmic creation is not only the harmonious order of the physical universe but also its rise to self-consciousness (Brahman).[547]

When the divine energies are differentiated, the supreme soul assumes three forms, the sattvic aspect being represented by the macroanthromorphic Vishnu, the rājasic by the luminous Brahma, and the tāmasic by the Shiva who will destroy the cosmos at the end of its cycle (*BrdP* I,i,4,5f.). This is a trinity that is "mutually interdependent; these do not become separated even for a moment" (*BrdP* I,i,4,11).

The first result of the disturbance of the equilibrium of the three divine energies during the earliest moments of the cosmic creation is the emergence of Mahatattva or Nature (Prakritī/Pārvatī, consort of Shiva), combined of Rajas and Tamas. It is from Mahatattva or Prakriti that

---

[546] We note the creative aspect of Chronos also in the Orphic theogonies, and in the proto-Stoic cosmogony of Pherecydes (see below p.145).

[547] That is why the demon Vrtra that Indra famously battles in the Vedas is at once the demon of material restriction as well as of the unconscious (see J.Miller, *op.cit.*, pp.62,95,178). V.G. Rele, *The Vedic Gods as Figures of Biology*, Bombay: D.B. Taraporevala Sons, 1931, pp.56, 103, observes the same contest between the unconscious and consciousness within the human microcosm.

Ahamkāra (Cosmic Egoity), dominated entirely by Tamas, arises. In the *BrdP* III,iv,4,37 Ahamkāra is said to evolve from Mahat, and from the Ahamkāra arise the Bhūtas (elements) and the Indriyas (senses). The entire material universe is a result of the dull egoistic element of Ahamkāra. From the Lord's power of imagination (illusion, Māyā) is formed first his heart, or spirit.[548] The heart gives rise to the Ego (ruled by Rudra-Shiva, III,6,24f), the Mind (which will be ruled by the Moon, II,10,30), and the Intellect (to be ruled by Brahman).

Manas (Mind), whose presiding deity is the Moon, arises from the highest form of Egoity, that related to the sattvic level of energy,[549] as also do the other gods who preside over the ten organs of knowledge and action. Manas is a characteristic of the Moon (*BP* III,6,24) and represents the emotional reservoir of the deity (*BP* II,10,32). It is thus located in the heart itself of the supreme deity.

From the rājasic level of Egoity of the supreme deity, on the other hand, arises Buddhi (Intellect) which is ruled by Brahman (*BP* III,6,23). From the 'space within his heart' arise the [ideal] faculties of sense, discernment and the physique. From the last three is formed the divine life-force or breath (Prāna). The five senses are related to the organs of knowledge – ears, tactile organ, nose, eyes, tongue – and the five forms of action to the organs responsible for speech, holding, walking, excreting and generating. The gods Dik [ears], Vāyu [nose], Sūrya [eyes], Varuna [tongue], and the Ashwins [skin] control the organs of knowledge, while Agni [speech], Indra [arms], Upendra (Vishnu) [legs], Mitra [excretion], and Prajāpati [generation] control the organs of action.

From the tāmasic Egoity, the dullest level of divine energy, emerges the prime matter of the universe, first as Ākāsha (Space) and its property Sound. From Ākāsha arises Vāyu (Wind), with Touch as its specific property, though, as an evolute, it contains also the properties of its preceding category, in this case, Sound. Vāyu then turns into Prāna (Life-breath). From Vāyu also arises Tejas (Fire) with its special property, form. From Tejas comes Ambhah (Water), with taste as its special property, and from Water, finally, Prithvī (Earth), with smell as its characteristic.

The deity develops organs as a macroanthropos in order to give the gods, or the presiding geniuses of all knowledge and action, who have

---

[548] The heart is the seat of the supreme deity's Māyā (Ātmamāyā; see *BP* II,10,30). We shall encounter the significance of the heart (Horus) and tongue (Thoth) of the deity also in the Heliopolitan cosmogony (see below p.115).

[549] This may be one reason why the moon is called Gishnugal, the Great Light, in Sumer and Egypt (see below p.255). This level of divine energy corresponds to Nun as well as to Thoth (see below p.121).

already been created, domains of personal influence (III,6,10).[550] From the incipient hunger and thirst of the materialising deity is formed the face, with the mouth forming first ruled by Agni. Vahni/Agni particularly rules the faculty of speech.[551] The principal organ of the mouth, the tongue, is presided over by Varuna (who, as we shall see, is the orginal form of Hari/Vishnu himself and counterpart of Enki/Osiris). Similarly are formed the nose, controlled by Vāyu (Wind), the eyes controlled by Sūrya (the Sun) the ears presided over by Dik, the skin ruled by Oshadhi [the Ashwins], the arms ruled by Indra, the generative organs ruled by Prajāpati, the excretory faculty ruled by Mitra, and the navel (the organ of transmigration) ruled by Yama (death) (II,10,15ff.). The organs of locomotion, the legs, are ruled by Vishnu, the most athletic solar force (III, 6,22).

In the *BP*, the macrocosmic manifestation of the primal lord, Vishnu/Brahma, is described in terms related to the passions. We may note that the tāmasic aspect of the supreme Lord is represented in the Abyss as well as in the Egyptian Ogdoad by the pitch Darkness, Kuk, that characterises the incipient cosmos until the rise of the divine Light (Atum/An/Brahman). From his own shadow (Night, related to the tāmasic quality mentioned above), Brahma [i.e. Nārāyana] is said to create Anger, Despair, Ignorance, Carnality and Concupiscence (III,20,18), while, from his bright form (Day, related to the sattvic quality), he creates the gods (22). The Manu's (prototypes of man in the several cosmic ages) arise from his Mind (49).[552] From his hips (related to the rājasic quality) arise the Asuras, marked by sexual desire (23), and then, from various other parts of his physical form, the Gandharvas, Apsaras, and demi-gods. The emergence of the "gross" form of the Lord follows that of his "subtle" form, constituted of the various orders of gods, Prajāpatis, Manus, Devas, Asuras, etc. (II,10,37ff.).

The formation of the deity as Purusha/Vishnu, the Ideal Man, is the result of the promptings of the divine 'heart' or spirit. This ideal Man, is, however, as we shall see, actually androgynous, since it is in his stomach that the Cosmic Egg develops which carries our manifest universe. In this second stage of creation, the Supreme Lord activates these basic categories of Sattva, Rajas and Tamas, through his Maya, into the macrocosmic and

---

[550] For an interesting study of the operation of the Vedic deities within the central nervous system of the human microcosm see V.G. Rele, *op.cit.* For a more metaphysical understanding of the various gods, see Aurobindo Ghose, *The Secret of the Veda*, Sri Aurobindo Birth Centenary Library, vol.10, Pondicherry: Sri Aurobindo Ashram, 1971.

[551] In *RV* X,125 (Vāk Sūkta), Vāk, like Agni, is said to be born in the waters, and is the supreme lord who creates, and sustains the universe.

[552] This points once again to the priority of the moon, the presiding deity of Manas, to the sun, whose son is the seventh Manu, Vaivasvata.

microcosmic organisms of the universe. This results, macrocosmically, in the Cosmic Egg or womb from which the lord manifests himself as the Divine Light and Consciousness, Brahman.

Turning briefly to the *Paingala Upanishad* I,4ff., we find that the process of creation is delineated somewhat more simply than in the *BP*. The tāmasic consciousness produces Vishnu as the Cosmic Person who sustains the material universe. We note again that the macroanthropos (Vishnu) is identified with the lowest state of the manifestation of the deity since the cosmos arises from his body. The rājasic consciousness (associated with the creator, Brahman) results in the Hiranyagarbha, which is partly spiritual and partly material. The entirely spiritual Sattvic consciousness of the divinity is said to constitute the "seed of the universe" [rather like the Desire of Ātman].

In the *BP*, the divine Mind, which is the most spiritual aspect of the manifesting deity since it represents the highest level of divine energy, Sattva, is ruled by the Moon. The second aspect of the deity, his rājasic, is said to be dominated by Brahman, the creator of the manifest universe and the light that emerge from the Cosmic Egg.

In the more simplified cosmogonical scheme of the *Laws of Manu*, Ch.I – which are said to have been instituted by the same Manu (Vaivasvata Manu, the seventh Manu of our Kalpa) whom we have encountered in the Flood story above – the supreme deity is called the Self-existent (Swāyambhu), and he creates the waters and places in them the germ of life which develops into a golden egg. The egg is then divided by the Lord into two halves which become Heaven and Earth with a Mid-region between them. From himself the Lord then draws forth Mind [Brahman] and from the latter Egoity (which also possesses Self-Consciousness), the Soul and the five sense organs. We note that the ideal forms of the deity are represented as appearing from the Cosmic Egg in the *Laws of Manu* whereas in the *BP* these elements are already present in the earliest stage of the divine consciousness.

In *KYV* IV,6,2, the ideal cosmos formed by the creator, Vishvakarman, or Prajāpati, is described as a macroanthropos:

> Then did the sky and earth extend
> With eyes on every side, with a face on every side,
> With hands on every side, with feet on every side

From the Egyptian gloss which we shall note below we may assume that these "eyes", "face", "hands" and "feet" stand for gods,[553] who rule over the

---

[553]   Though, in later Brahmanism, they are equated with the four castes as well; see

intellectual faculties of macrocosmic and microcosmic man. The sky and earth mentioned in the first line are not to be understood as our sky and earth but as ideal Heaven and Earth informed by the gods.[554]

The Lord as a Cosmic Man, Purusha, is of colossal proportions as is evident from the dimensions provided in *BP* II,6,36ff. There it is stated that our universe merely spans the distance between the heart and the waist of Purusha. From his hip downwards extend the underworlds of Earth and from his chest upwards the four divine worlds, Maharloka, Janaloka, Tapoloka and Satyaloka. In the *BP* III,6,26 it is stated that the head of the Purusha is Heaven, the feet Earth and the navel the Mid-region.

Purusha is considered as the ideal or intelligible form of the entire physical cosmos as well (*SB* XIV, 5,5,18). This ideal Purusha that is formed from the desire of the Lord is supposed to have issued from the Waters, Virāj (*AV* XIX, 6,9).[555] In the *RV* X,90 ('Purushasūkta'), however, while Purusha is said to have been born of Virāj, the latter too is born of the former. Thus Purusha too is a form of Agni, who emerges from the waters and from whom the waters emerge. In the *Shvetāsvatara Upanishad*, the Cosmic Man is called "the omnipresent Shiva" (III,11), that is Shiva (Ātman) as Vishnu. That Purusha is replete with divine life is made clear by the identification of the birth of the gods with this early stage in the cosmic evolution. Prajāpati as primal creator is equally said to be the generator of the gods (Devas), the Vasus, the Rudras, as well as the Ādityas and all the worlds (*RV* X,121). Thus Prajāpati is the name of the creative aspect of Purusha as Brahman.

The Cosmic Egg which develops in the womb of the supreme deity bears the Intellectual Light (Brahman) of the universe which represents also the Self-Consciousness of the deity. In the Purānas, Purusha [i.e. as Brahman] is indeed called the mirror of divine self-consciousness, the coming to consciousness of the supreme Self (*BP* VI,5,17).[556] We have noted

---

Manusmriti, I,31.

[554] Cf. the Egyptian Tura hymn below p.117, where the primordial Man emerges before heaven and earth.

[555] We have already in the previous chapter considered these waters as the counterpart of the Egyptian Nunet, the original substance of Heaven.

[556] This is also the real significance of the obtuse biblical rendering of the same idea in *Genesis* I:27 as God creating "man" in "his own image". Adam, meaning "man" in Hebrew, is linguistically the same as Purusha. The god who creates Adam is El and not Yahweh (see p.144). However, since El is Chronos, and the "man" that he creates is the anthropomorphic Brahman/Phanes (Chapter XII below), Adam is indeed the later manifestation of the deity as the First Man rather than as the Cosmic Man. In the Hebrew genesis, Adam and Eve (who correspond to Manu Swāyambhuva and his female counterpart Shatarūpa) are confused with the first humans of the Iranian *Bundahishn*, Mashye and Mashyane, who are related to the seventh Manu/Yima (see below p.312).

already that, in Egypt, Nun is the source of the growing self-consciousness of the primal deity as Re/Atum.[557] The intelligible universe of the gods is followed by the perfect Light of the divine Mind, Brahman.

The first fully conscious form of the supreme deity in our universe is as the divine Light, Brahman, who emerges from the lotus-formed universe that arises from the navel of the Lord (which, as we have seen above, represents the Mid-region). It is Brahma who divides this lotus (*BP* III,10,8) into three worlds (heaven, earth and its mid-region) to serve as the region in which the souls transmigrate for the enjoyment of the fruits of their action (karma).

Since the intelligible being of the Purusha is constituted of the gods, he is sometimes equated with Indra, the chief of the gods – who is also virtually identical to Shiva.[558] Indeed, Indra, like Shiva, is considered (X,119) the supreme Self (Ātman) itself as well as the spirit within the sun.[559] In the *Aitareya Āranyaka* III,12; II,4, the metaphysical counterpart of Purusha is called Ātman (Soul), who is identifiable with Indra. Thus Indra represents the divine Self, and the self of the cosmos. Indra is equated in *RV* VI,47,18 with the primal Varuna himself, since it is declared that Indra assumes multifarious forms through his Māya, or power of illusion. In *SB* VI,i,1,1-14, Indra, who is the Self of the deity, kindles the vital airs to form, indeed, seven cosmic men, purushas, who then combine into one. In *SB* V,iii,5,28, Varuna is said to have ordained Indra as the Prajāpati and lord of all. This suggests that Indra is more precisely the First Man, rather than the Ideal Man, since he, like the First Man, is androgynous.[560]

---

[557] See below p.174.

[558] See below p.186f. It has been suggested (for instance, by P. Kretschmer, "Indra und der hethitische Gott Indra", *Kleinasiatische Forschungen* I (1930), p.307) that the name Indra and the Iranian "andra" (see below p.139n) may be related to the Greek "aner"/man (the Vedic word for man, "nar" is clearly the original to which the Greek has added an initial euphonic "a"). However, Indra's name is more closely related to Vedic "ina" and "indriya" meaning strength as well as manliness (see V. Machek, *op.cit.*, pp.146ff.). Hittite has a counterpart to this Vedic word in "innarawanza" (XVII 20 II 3, Bo 84 I 25) and its plural "innarawant" (IX 31 I 36 II 6=HT 1 I 29) (see E. Laroche, "Recherches sur les noms divins hittites", *RHA* VII, Fasc.45 (1946-7), p.74). J. Przyluski ("Inara et Indra", *RHA* V, Fasc.36 (1939), pp.142-46) also suggested that Inara, the Hittite counterpart of Indra (see below p.134), may derive from a root "nar" ("man"). V. Machek ("Name und Herkunft des Gottes Indra", *AO* 12 (1941), p.146) objected that it is not certain that "nar" could be an abbreviated form of "inar". However, the Vedic "ina" may have given the name Inara, just as the Vedic "indriya" may be related to Indra.

[559] See *KYV* XIX,80-9, *RV* VIII,46,14.

[560] See below p.181.

In the Sumerian god-list "An=Anum", the macroanthropomorphic form of the deity may have been represented by Alala,[561] who precedes Lahmu-Lahamu, Duri-Dari, and the four sets of deities who go before Anki, united Heaven and Earth,[562] and An, the divine light corresponding to the Indic Brahman In a Babylonian list of the ancestry of An,[563] we find first Alala, then Lahmu-Lahamu (probably Vāyu the Boar), followed by Duri-Dari (Eternal Time, associated with Chronos/Kumarbi/Shiva/Enki). Alala (=Hurr. Alalu), may indeed mean 'Man (=Lord) of the waters', since "ālu" is the Dravidian for "man" (related to the Akkadian "awilu") and "ā" is the Dravidian as well as Sumerian term for "waters".

The Egyptian counterpart of Purusha is Ptah, who is, in texts from the New Kingdom (Pap. Berlin 3048), described as a macroanthropos dwelling in the sky. Ptah is represented as spanning heaven and earth:

> Your feet are on the earth, your head [in] the distant heaven,
> …
> You raise the work that you have accomplished
> By leaning on yourself with your own strength
> By raising yourself by virtue of the solidity of your arms.
> …
> It is your strength which raises the waters towards the distant heaven
> The saliva which is in your mouth is the cloud of rain
> The breath of your nose is the hurricane
> And the water which you spread is on the mountains
> The right eye of Ptah is the sun and his left the moon.[564]

Ptah is said to have Horus the Elder as his "heart" [i.e. Spirit] and Thoth as his "tongue" [i.e. Intellect]. Ptah is thus the "heart and tongue" of Atum "planning and governing everything he wishes".[565] The heart of Ptah is that element of the cosmic man which shines as the Light of the Cosmos (Atum/Brahman), while the tongue will form the vital moon (Thoth). The moon, as we shall see, is the repository of the seed of all animal life (represented by

[561] See R. Litke, *A Reconstruction of the Assyro-Babylonian God-list An:ᵈA-nu-um and An: anu šá amēli*, New Haven, CT: Yale Babylonian Collection, 1998, p.22, as well as the Hurrian gods mentioned above, p.105.

[562] These four pairs may constitute the Sumerian counterpart of the Egyptian Ogdoad (see below p.151ff).

[563] See W. Lambert, "Cosmology", in *op.cit.*, p.53.

[564] See A. Barucq and F. Daumas, *op.cit.*, p.396.

[565] Memphite Theology, 9 (Shabaka stone) in J.P. Allen, *op.cit.*, p.43.

the slaughtered Bull in the Avesta) while the sun preserves the seed of the enlightened species of mankind (represented by the slaughtered first Man, Gayomaretan).

The importance of the heart as the source of intellection is evidenced in the Vedas (*RV* I,105,15), too, in the reference to Varuna's opening out his thought by means of his heart. The heart is also the seat of Rta, the universal order, which itself is born of tapas, the heat of spiritual contemplation (*RV* X,129,3).[566] In Egypt too (CT 1130 VII 464g) ,we find that the gods are said to have emerged through the "sweat" of the supreme deity,[567] which in India as well symbolised the intense spiritual fervour which initiates the divine creation.

The Shabaka text mentioned above reveals the final identity of Ptah with Horus the Elder/Atum, since the latter is but the "face" (with its two luminous eyes) of the supreme deity [Amun] whose body (constituted of the gods) is called Ptah. Ptah is particularly identified with the ithyphallic Amun of Luxor in a Saitic sepulchral text on the coffin of Princess Ankhnesneferibre,[568] since he is the same as Amun, whose "body" he represents. In a Ptolemaic inscription in the temple of Ptah in Karnak, Ptah-Tatenen is identified with Amun "who arose in the beginning and created the sky, the earth, the water, and the two sun-mountains".[569]

Ptah is also represented by his vital force, Shu, who typically represents the rising sun:[570] Ptah is thus said to rise "[as the sun] in the heavens"[571] and guide the sun along the body of the sky-goddess, Nut, in his daily journey and ward off the sun's enemies along the way.[572] Ptah's consort is normally Sekhmet, who is identified with Mut, Tefnut (Maat), and this highlights his particular association with Shu, consort of Tefnut.

---

[566] See J. Miller, *The Vision of Cosmic Order in the Vedas*, London: Routledge and Kegan Paul, 1985, *passim*.

[567] See S. Bickel, *op.cit.*, p.120.

[568] See M.S. Holmberg, *op.cit.*, p.103.

[569] *Ibid.*, p.166. This reference to sky, earth, water seems to be related to the Vedic reference to the three three cosmic regions in which Agni is born, from the heavens, from earth and from the waters (see above p.20). This cosmogonical sequence may also be evident in the appeal to "Mitra [Brahman, the Light of Heaven],Varuna [Lord of Earth], Indra [Lord of the Mid–Region] Nāsatiyas [the equestrian solar twins]" in the Mitanni treaty (see above p.62).

[570] We will note that Enlil too is regarded as the rising sun in Sumer (see below p.309).

[571] *Ibid.*, p.67.; cf. Pap. Berlin 3048, pl.5, 2ff: "He [the sun] rises on thine head and sets on thine arms" (*ibid.*, p.58).

[572] See A. Barucq and F. Daumas, *op.cit.*, p.404.

Hathor is also said to have been present with Ptah when the latter performed his act of creation.[573] Hathor is, however, more accurately called the "daughter" of Ptah,[574] since she is the consort of the divine Light, Horus the Elder, who first appears from the Cosmic Egg, constituted of the Ogdoad who are, indeed, Ptah's "children".[575]

In the Heliopolitan Tura hymn, we get a description of an anthropomorphic deity as the first animate form of the universe:

> He came forth as self-created
> All his limbs speaking to him
> He formed himself before heaven and earth came into being
> The earth being in the primeval waters in the midst of the "weary flood".[576]

In this verse, the "limbs" stand for the gods. We note again that the macroanthropomorphic Ptah is posited at the stage of Shu, before the formation of Earth, which is still in the depths of the waters. In the "Memphite Theology" of the Shabaka stone, the gods are said to enter "every kind of wood, every kind of mineral, every kind of frit, everything that grows all over [Ptah]".[577] In CT 75 the primal god is said to contain in himself the totality of gods, their million "ka"s, or spirits.[578]

Amun is represented as speaking to his limbs, the gods, in the process of creating them. In the hymn to Amun from the 19th century,[579] Amun as Ptah is said to be "the venerable howler", an epithet also given to Rudra-Shiva in the Indic literature,[580] and this "howling" is related to Ptah's utterance of the divine words which create the gods:

> He made his cry resonate, he the venerable howler
> On coming to the earth which he had created when he was alone
> He articulated the [creative] words in the midst of silence
> ...

---

[573]   See C.J. Bleeker, *Hathor and Thoth: Two Key Figures of the Ancient Egyptian Religion*, Leiden: E.J. Brill, 1973, p.66.

[574]   *Ibid.*, p.192f.

[575]   See below p.119.

[576]   See J. Assman, *op.cit.*, p.161.

[577]   See J.P. Allen, *op.cit.*, p.44.

[578]   *Ibid.*, pp.15ff.

[579]   See A. Barucq and F. Daumas, *op.cit.*, p.234.

[580]   See *ShP* 12,30.

He began to howl when the earth was silent

His bellowing resonated when there was no one else but he

What he had engendered he caused to live".[581]

In CT 312 IV 74g-75f, the gods are born as "spirits of light" from the "root of the eye" of Atum and constitute his "flesh".[582]

Ptah is also the dispenser of the ka's (characters) and the ba's (souls) of the gods as well as of men during the creation.[583] The ba's can be assigned to Osiris[584] (or Thoth, the 'tongue', and corporealising agent of Ptah) and the ka's to Horus (the 'mind', and photogenetic agent of Ptah), respectively. Though Ptah may have originally been considered a son of Atum, in the Shabaka Ptah text, Ptah is rightly extolled above Atum. The seed and the hands of Atum used in the creative act (usually identified with Shu and Tefnut) are considered the "teeth and lips" of the mouth of Ptah.[585] The "mouth" of the supreme deity represents the power of annunciation: "I am Annunciation in (the Sole Lord's) mouth and Perception in his belly".[586] We notice therefore that this is a pristine, intellectual stage of creation, with the "Desire" of the creator manifest as intellection and intuition. The gods are indeed frequently adored as having been created of the mouth of Amun (that is, through his creative word, Hu).[587]

Hu, intellectual expression, and his consort, Sia, intuition, are the creative powers with which Amun-Atum vivify the inherent forces of the Cosmic Egg and "create the gods". Hu and Sia are said in a New Kingdom commentary on the *Book of the Dead* to be "the blood which fell from the phallus of Re, when he was going to mutilate himself".[588] Since the castration of Re corresponds to the castration of Anu in the Hurrian epic of the Kingship in Heaven, and the castration of Prajāpati by Shiva, we may

---

[581] See A. Barucq and F. Daumas, *op.cit.*, p.222; cf. J.P. Allen, *op.cit.*, p.51.

[582] See S. Bickel, *op.cit.*, p.119.

[583] This aspect of Ptah is represented by Heka (see S. Bickel, *op.cit.*, p.152ff.). Heka is also said to have brought the Ennead to life (*ibid.*, p.153). Tefnut, or Maat, who is closely associated with Sia and Heka (probably as their mother; see below p.206), is equally represented as the one who vivifies the Ennead, (*ibid.*, p.170). And, as we shall see, Re-Atum too is admired as the ultimate life of the Ennead (see below p.174).

[584] Cf. *BD* II,39: "It is Osiris... It is the ba of the sun, by means of which he copulates himself", referring particularly to the form of the bennu phoenix that Osiris assumes in emerging as the sun.

[585] See M.S.–Holmberg, *op.cit.*, p.122.

[586] CT 647, in J.P. Allen, *op.cit.*, p.39. Annunciation and Perception refer to Hu and Sia.

[587] See S. Bickel, *op.cit.*, p.140.

[588] See M.S.-Holmberg, *op.cit.*, p.42.

assume that this event precedes the formation of the Cosmic Egg which, in the Purānas arises, from the seed of Prajāpati/Shiva.

It has been noted that the Cosmic Egg is formed by Amun himself.[589] Ptah (Amun's "body") is the name particularly of the materialising agent or the efficient force of Amun.[590] In the relatively late Ramesside theogony of Memphis, Ptah is considered to be the demiurgic creator of the Cosmic Egg.[591] Ptah is considered the creator of the gods, the "goldsmith" who first forms the eight gods in his workshop in Nun.[592] It is stated, for instance, that "the toes of his [Ptah's] body are the Hermopolitans".[593] The eight formed gods of the Ogdoad are thus considered the "children" of Ptah.[594] Ptah is also revered as the moulder of all living beings,[595] no doubt on account of his "tongue", Thoth/Tvoreshtar/Tvashtr, who represents the formative aspect of the supreme deity.[596]

Ptah is sometimes addressed as the Venerable Nun[597] and even considered to be the same as Nun-Naunet, the "father-mother" of the Heliopolitan Atum.[598] We have seen that Nun represents the original spiritual form of the lord of the Abyss which in Egypt is associated with primal Consciousness. This suggests that the intellectual efficiency of

---

[589] "[Amun] Who formed his own egg" (J. Assmann, *op.cit.*, p.138); cf. p.150 below.

[590] See the Suty-Hor hymn (in J. Assmann, *op.cit.*, p,94f.):

   "You [Amun-Re] are a Ptah, you cast your body from gold,
   One who gives birth,
   But is not born".

[591] Ptah is represented as fashioning the Cosmic Egg on a potter's wheel (see E.O. James, *The Tree of Life: An Archaeological Study*, Leiden: E.J. Brill, 1966, p.132; cf. S. Marakhanova, "A Version of the Origins of the World in Egyptian, Orphic and Gnostic Cosmogonies", in *Ancient Egypt and Kush*, Moscow, 1993, p.279).

[592] See K. Sethe, *op.cit.*, p.51.

[593] Pap. Leiden I, 350, Ch.90 (see J.P. Allen, *op.cit.*, p.51). In the hymn to Amun from the 19th Dynasty, Ptah is considered a form of Amun whose "toes" are the Ogdoad (A. Barucq and F. Daumas, *op.cit.*, p.222).

[594] "The children of Ptah-Tatenen who arose from his body" (Theb. T. 87b); see K. Sethe, *op.cit.*, p.41,43.

[595] The Ptah priests are called "supreme leaders of handicrafts" (M.S. Holmberg, *op.cit.*, p.50).

[596] See below Ch.V.

[597] Berlin Pap. 3048 (see A. Barucq and F. Daumas, *op.cit.*, p.400).

[598] See J. Zandee, "The Birth-Giving Gods in Ancient Egypt", in *Studies in Pharaonic Religion and Society in Honour of J. Gwyn Griffiths*, London: Egypt Exploration Society, 1992, p.180; cf. M.S. Holmberg, *op.cit.*, p. 20.

Amun (the Soul) in forming the gods[599] is derived from the Abyss. Thoth representing his tongue is the aspect of Ptah that is particularly associated with Nun.[600] Ptah himself is considered to be the formulator of the divine language, and he, like Thoth, is worshipped as the god of hieroglyphs.[601]

In Heliopolis, Re, although strictly signifying the solar energy of the primal deity, is also adored as the consort of the waters. In the papyrus text entitled "The Book of knowing the evolutions of Re, and of overthrowing Apepi" (Pap. 10,188, BM) dated around 312 B.C., in which Re announces his various manifestations, Re declares that he first manifested himself in the form of Khepera (who is represented as a sun-bearing scarab beetle),[602] and existed alone in the material basis of Nun.[603] Re-Atum-Khepera is said to have laid a foundation in Maat (here Nunet) and made the forms of life. We note that Nunet, representing the waters of the Abyss, is already identified with Maat/Rta. However, Tefnut, Re's daughter is, also considered an embodiment of Maat, just as Re is identified with Khepera, a form of his son Shu.[604] But that is because Re is both the son and consort of the waters. And the entire cosmos is virtually brought forth by Re through an act of masturbation:

[Re] made the universe when he joined with his fist in pleasure.[605]

In another almost identical version of the same story, however, Re-Kephera is replaced as creator by Osiris, the Lord in, and of, the Waters, showing that Osiris is equivalent to the first form of the supreme deity in the sweet waters of the Abyss. That Osiris is a creator god like the Hermopolitan Amun or the Heliopolitan Re is suggested also by the fact that the original Hermopolitan cosmogony seems to have been constituted of a Pentad, rather than an Ogdoad, and the chief of this Pentad may have been Osiris.[606]

---

[599] See CT 647 VI 267b-j (cf. S. Bickel, *op.cit.*, p.137ff).

[600] See below p.122.

[601] See J. Assmann, *op.cit.*, p.173; cf. p.123 below.

[602] See J.P. Allen, *op.cit.*, p.19f.

[603] In the 'Seventy Five Praises of Ra' which are inscribed on the walls of royal tombs of the XIXth and XXth dynasties at Thebes, Khepera, like Amun, is further called "the hidden support of Anpu" (see E.A.W. Budge, *op.cit.*, I:339ff).

[604] See below p.311.

[605] CT 321 IV 147d-e (see S. Bickel, *op.cit.*, p.73).

[606] See K. Sethe, *op.cit.*, p.40.

V: TVASHTR

THE MIND OF PTAH:
"LORD OF THE BA'S", HU, THOTH/OSIRIS, TVORESHTAR

We may pause here to consider in greater detail the crucial "tongue" of the macroanthropos. We may recall that the process of the idealisation of the supreme god detailed in the Purānas entailed the rise of the Heart from the imagination (illusion) of the deity. From the Heart arise the Mind ruled by the Moon (*BP* II,10,30), the Ego ruled by Rudra-Shiva, and the Intellect ruled by Brahman (III,6,24f.). The Mind, Ego, and Intellect are thus emanations of the "heart" of the deity.

However, the *BP* (II,10,17ff.) also declares that the Mind is first formed as the mouth (speech) and tongue (taste) of the supreme deity (the former ruled by Agni and the latter by Varuna), just as the Ego as life-breath (Vāyu) is focussed in the nose, and Intellect (Brahman) in the sight. The mouth and tongue of the macroanthropos thus express the first manifestation of the Mind (Manas) presided over by the Moon.

Hence it is not surprising that, in Egypt, Thoth reappears as the moon. The relationship between the conceptional power of the "heart" and the shaping power of the tongue ("speech") is clarified in the Egyptian Shabaka "logos doctrine" text, 56: "For it is the (the heart) which causes all conceptions to emerge, and it is the tongue which repeats what has been thought by the heart",[607] and 57: "For every divine word came into being through what the heart thought and the tongue ordered".[608] In another Edfu text related to Thoth, he is called the "heart (ib) of Re, tongue of [Ptah-] Tatanen, and gullet of Imn-rn-f".[609] We note here the same association

---

[607] In the Orphic fragment 168.32 too, the creation is said to issue from Zeus' heart after swallowing Phanes (see M.L. West, *Orphic Poems*, p.257).

[608] See A. Piankoff, *op.cit.*, p.97.

[609] See M. de Rochemonteix, *Le Temple d'Edfou*, Caire: Institut français d'archaeologie

between the Mind, heart and tongue which we have observed in the *BP*. Thoth's word is indeed the agency whereby all the forms of the universe emerge.

In LD IV 29b, Amun, Amunet and Ptah (the vital force) are grouped together in a triad while Nun, Naunet, and Thoth (the intellectual force) are in another,[610] showing the close relatedness of Thoth to Nun/Enki, a relationship which we will recover in the Vedas between Varuna and Tvashtr.

Thoth, or Tauith, is often adored in the form of a bull.[611] Thoth's role as a primal creator god is confirmed in the Shabaka text.[612] Thoth is indeed a duplicate of the primal Osiris and Amun as creator god, since he is but an aspect of them. The Hermopolitan theogony indeed begins sometimes not with Amun but with Thoth (called the self-begotten Mind),[613] who lays the Cosmic Egg on the waters. This is because Thoth/Tvoreshtar/Spenta Mainyu is the creative aspect of the primal deity as macroanthropos. It should be remembered that Osiris and Thoth are both called the first of the Ogdoad or the Pentad of Heliopolis.[614]

Thoth's importance as a creator god emerges especially in the New Kingdom.[615] In an Edfu Heliopolitan text, the creator of Shu himself is called Tauith, rather than Amun or Atum, showing that Thoth is the efficient force or form of the supreme deity: "Thoth, thou has ejected Shu from thy mouth

---

orientale du Caire, 1897, I, p.273.

[610] See K. Sethe, *op.cit.*, p.77.

[611] See E.A.W. Budge, *op.cit.*, II,6. In the *Bundahishn*, the primordial Bull is particularly associated with the moon which stores its seed – representing all the animal life of the universe – after it is killed by Angra Mainyu (see below p.188f). The worship of the primal god as a Bull is attested from Anatolia to Sumer and the Indus Valley. This may account for the similarity of the name of the Egyptian Tauith and the tauromorphic Hurrian god Taurit. Taurit is the most ancient god of Anatolia (see V. Haas, *Geschichte der hethitischen Religion*, p.322). The bull, like the ram, symbolises virility (*SB* XII,vii,1,10-12; V,ii,3,8; cf. W. O'Flaherty, *op.cit.*, p.134).

[612] See K. Sethe, *Dramatische Texte zu altägyptischen Mysterienspielen*, Hildesheim: G. Olms, 1964, pp.50ff. G. Maspero believed that Thoth was indeed the first god worshipped as a creative power by the ancient Egyptians and that Re was an aspect of him which assumed a religious predominance later (see, for instance, *Histoire ancienne des peuples de l'Orient classique*, I, 147ff., *Etudes de Mythologies et d'archealogie égyptienne*, II, 259).

[613] Thoth's appellation as "Mind" clearly associates him with the primal deity, Nun, just as Tartarus is a "region" or aspect of Earth (the waters) ruled by Eros in Hesiod's theogony. We will note (see below p.143) that the creator Prajāpati too is, in the Vedas (*KYV* II,6,6), called "as it were the Mind".

[614] See A. Barucq and F. Daumas, *op.cit.*, p.88, and K. Sethe, *op.cit.*, p.37.

[615] See S. Bickel, *op.cit.*, p.54.

– he emerged from thy spit – thy lips ejected him".[616] Shu's son, Geb, too is said to be "glorious", that is, formed, owing to "what has arisen in thine [Thoth's] body".[617]

Since Hu is considered as the agent whereby Shu was created,[618] Thoth must be closely associated with Hu, the expressive power of the deity. Since Shu, created by Hu, is, as we shall see, prior to Sia/Heka, we may assume that Thoth, who is related to Hu, is equally prior to Shu and to Sia/Heka.[619] This confirms the order of appearance of the primal forms of the deity as 1.Ptah/Purusha, 2.Thoth/Hu, 3.Vāyu/Enlil/Shu, 4.Brahmanaspati/Sia-Heka.

Thoth's word is indeed the foundation of "maat", the cosmic law.[620] Since Maat is identified with Tefnut, the consort of Shu, Thoth's role as the "foundation" of maat reveals his close relation to Shu.[621] Thoth is indeed the "lord of the laws" and the guardian of the truth: "I, Thoth, am the eminent writer… the writer of the truth, whose horror is the lie".[622] As the repository of wisdom, Thoth is also considered the inventor of the hieroglyphs, while the "books of Thoth"[623] are the most sacred.

We have seen that the mind (Manas), which represents the highest form of Egoity of the supreme deity according to the Purānas, is ruled by the moon.[624] Thoth also represents the moon, which precedes the birth of the sun, since he is also the moon-god born of Horus the Younger's seed on Seth's forehead.[625] Thoth's manifestation in the cosmos as the moon is not surprising since the moon, in the Iranian *Bundahishn*,[626] stores all the seeds of animal life in the universe and Thoth is the lord of all life-forms. The

---

[616] H.K. Brugsch, *Religion und Mythologie der alten Ägypter,* Leipzig: J. Hinrich, 1891, p.429.

[617] Pap. Berlin 3048, pl.5, 6ff; see M.S. Holmberg, *op.cit.*, p.58.

[618] See below p.206.

[619] Thoth, as an aspect of Ptah, is indeed the father of Heka/Sia (see below p.206), as Tvashtr is of Brahmanaspati (see below p.208).

[620] That "maat" is the same as 'rta' (and its later form 'dharma') is made clear by the social and political aspects of this universal law in Egypt, which resemble the bases of the Indian caste system. Thoth, for instance, ensures that "every guild fulfils its obligations, the countries know their frontiers and the fields their appurtenances" (C.J. Bleeker, *Hathor and Thoth*, p.140).

[621] As we have noted above, sometimes Thoth is even identified with Shu, and his consort Sekhet with Tefnut (see E.A.W. Budge, *op.cit.*, I:517).

[622] See C.J. Bleeker, *op.cit.*, p.136.

[623] Thoth is also the original of "Hermes Trismegestes", the composer of the Hermetic Corpus.

[624] See above p.110.

[625] See below p.259.

[626] See below p.258.

figure of Soma, also representing the moon in the Āryan cosmogony, gives us a further insight into the life-giving virtue of Thoth, since Soma, the formative life-force is said to be originally found in the dwelling of Tvashtr (Thoth), where it is imbibed by Indra.[627] Since Thoth's role is essentially a life-giving one,[628] just as Horus' is a light-giving, it is not surprising that it is Thoth who reappears as the moon and Horus as the sun.

Thoth as the source of all forms is thus to be associated with the "ba"s, which represent the immaterial forms (or souls) of the various entities in the universe. Thoth is thus the natural counterpart to the more solar Heka/ Horus, which deities have dominion, rather, over the "ka"s,[629] the very essence (spirit) and character of a person.[630] According to the BD Ch.134, Thoth is also called "the son of the Stone who emerged from the egg",[631] which may signify his relation as the moon to Osiris, who appears as the solar phoenix bennu from the benben stone.

Thoth is also called the "eldest son of Re",[632] which may be understood of the lunar form which precedes the solar in our universe. Thoth as the moon is indeed the "messenger" of the Spirit of Horus. Hence he is associated with Hermes the messenger-god as well as with the moon, the herald of the sun.

In the Vedas, the demiurgic creator god who forms Agni (who later appears as the lord of speech) is Tvashtr, a name that may be related to the Egyptian Tauith (and the Hittite Taurit) and is certainly cognate with the Avestan Tvoreshtar, Greek Tartarus, and German Tuisto. Tvashtr's particular association with intelligible Form approximates him to the Platonic and Aristotelean Demiurgus. Like Thoth, Tvashtr is described, in KYV I,5,8, as the force that forms the seed (Soma): "as many modifications of seed when poured as Tvashtr makes, in so many shapes does it become fruitful". Tvashtr is again called the "maker of the forms of pairings of animals; verily he places form in animals", just as Agni, whom he also forms,

---

[627] See below p.277.

[628] This formative aspect of Thoth may be related to Khnum (see below p.205n).

[629] See below p.206.

[630] See LA, "ka", "ba". Cf. also A. Piankoff, op.cit., p.56, which refers to a religious text of the Middle Empire which distinguishes the two psychological entities thus : "Le cœur (ib) [representing the ka] de ton âme (ba) se souvient de ton corps".

[631] See E. Hornung, Das Totenbuch der Ägypter, Düsseldorf: Artemis and Winkler, 1990, p.260 (cf. 'Thot', in LÄ, VI:499).

[632] See A. Klasens, A Magical Statue Base (Socle Behague) in the Museum of Antiquities at Leiden, 1952, p.57. cf. A. Barucq and F. Daumas, op.cit., p.463; and J. Zandee, op.cit., p.170, where Thoth, as well as Shu, is called the "eldest son" of Atum.

is the "impregnator of seed", that is, the creative force.[633] In *RV* X,184,1 Tvashtr is said to shape the embryonic forms in the womb that are moulded by Vishnu. In *RV* I,95,2, the birth of Agni (that is, first, as the god of the underworld)[634] is said to be due to a sacrificial kindling by Tvashtr. Thus "the [Vedic] sacrificer" too assumes the role of "the divine Tvashtr", since, by kindling and adoring the fire, he recreates and sustains the universe in its original life-giving forms.[635]

Since Tvashtr is responsible for the formation of Soma in *KYV* I,5,8, he is particularly related to the moon, which stores the universal seeds of animal life. Tvashtr is said in the Vedas (*RV* II,23,17) to have created Brahmanaspati (Heka) as well.[636] In the *BP* VI,6,38, Tvashtr reappears as one of the twelve Ādityas, or suns, along with Vivasvān, Aryaman, Pushan, Savita, Bhaga, Dhata, Vidhata, Varuna, Mitra, Sakra and Urukrama. Tvashtr has a particular affiliation with Varuna since his primary creative role is not shared by the other Ādityas, except Varuna-Mitra as forms of Agni.

In the Avesta, Tvashtr is called Tvoreshtar, or Spenta Mainyu.[637] Tvoreshtar is the one who fashions the starry mantle for Ahura Mazda (Farvardin Yasht XIII,3) and builds the chariot for Mithra (Mihir Yasht X,67).[638] There is also a deity called the "Protector", who is coupled with

---

[633]   According to *RV* X,17 (cf. also Sāyana's commentary on *RV*, I,117,1-2), Tvashtr's daughter is called Saranyū and is given in marriage to Vivasvān (cf. *RV* X,10, where Yama and Yami are described as the children of the Sun and the Lady of the Waters (Saranyū); cf. also *RV* X,14). In *RV* VIII,26,21, it is interesting to note, Vāyu is equally called the son-in-law of Tvashtr, but it is not clear if his wife is Saranyū or another daughter of Tvashtr's.

[634]   See below Ch.XX.

[635]   See *RV* IV,58,10f:

> Bear to the gods the sacrifice we offer; the streams of oil flow pure and full of sweetness.
> The universe depends upon thy power and might within the sea, within the heart, within all life.

Cf. J. Miller, *op.cit.*, Ch.12.

[636]   Cf. H.-P. Schmidt, *Brhaspati und Indra*, Wiesbaden: Otto Harrassowitz, 1968, p.109. Tvashtr is said to create with his fingers, just as the Egyptian Atum is represented as creating the earliest divine Ennead through his fingers, toes, and seed (see J. Assmann, *op.cit.*, p.172); Atum here takes on the role of Amun in his form as Ptah (see above p.85, and A. Barucq and F. Daumas, *op.cit.*, p.293).

[637]   For the identity of Tvoreshtar with Spenta Mainyu, see Yasna 44,7, where Ahura Mazda is addressed as "creator of everything by means of Spenta Mainyu" (see W.M. Malandra, *op.cit.*, pp.36,43).

[638]   This recalls the construction of the palace of Baal by Kothar-and-Hasis in the Ugaritic texts of Canaan (see C.H. Gordon, "Canaanite Mythology", in S. Kramer, *Mythologies of the Ancient World*, pp.203ff.). Kothar is called, in one text, "son of Yamm", the sea-god (*ibid.*, p.209), which may mean that he is an aspect of Yamm/Enki.

Tvoreshtar, the Creator, in Yasna 57, i, 2, as the twin deities who "created all things in the creation". In *KYV* IV,6,2, Vishvakarman (i.e. Prajāpati/Tvashtr) is said to have formed "Indra the protector", the term 'protector' being identical to the Avestan "payu". This suggests that the Avestan "Protector" was indeed originally Indra, though in the later Zoroastrian religion, Indra is a fiend in spite of his oblique identification with the Iranian dragon-slayer, Verethraghna (whose several incarnations identify him with the solar force Vishnu in his Vāyu form).[639]

In Hesiod, Tartarus corresponds to Tvashtr/Tvoreshtar, but the formative aspect of the latter deities seems to be lost in the Greek theogony, which considers the constituents of the Cosmic Egg in a simple spatial manner and Tartarus as the pitch dark region of Earth (l.119) in the Chaos/Chasm or Abyss. It is clear, however, that the four primal elements of the cosmos in Hesiod are not to be understood as spatially different from one another but as different constituent forces of the Abyss. The relation between Tartarus and the darkness of the Egyptian Kuk is also self-evident.[640]

The German counterpart of Thoth/Tvashtr/Tartarus is Tuisto, who is described in Tacitus as "earth-born",[641] just as Tartarus is considered a "region" of earth.

Just as the divine Light, Atum, emerges from the darkness of the Cosmic Egg, Tartarus/Tvashtr/Thoth is the mental source from which the divine Light and Intellect emerge. And when the divine Light is submerged in the underworld (as the Lord of Earth), this inward strength of the supreme deity is the power that both provides the weapon for the destruction of the serpent that hinders the emergence of the solar force and itself rises as the moon which bears the animal life of the entire universe.[642]

---

[639] See below p.224.

[640] See above p.95n, below p.152.

[641] See Tacitus, *Germania*, Sec.2.

[642] See below p.190.

VI: VĀYU

THE BREATH OF THE DEITY: SHU, ENLIL

The first temporal movement in the cosmos is initiated by the breath of the Lord, who is worshipped in India as the wind-god Vāyu. That Vāyu, or his Sumerian counterpart Enlil, was the chief deity among the peoples of the ancient Near East is made clear from the passage in the Sumerian epic of "Enmerkar and the Lord of Aratta" quoted above. [643] In the *SP*, when the resting god awakens, he begins to agitate the cosmic streams. Then, assuming the form of a boar (which, as we shall soon see, is a typical aspect of the wind-god),[644] he plunges into the Abyss, where, with his tusk, he extracts the substance of the previous cosmos, Earth, which had been dissolved by the cataclysm which ended the previous cosmic age (kalpa). Directly after the recovery of Earth, Vishnu begins the task of cosmic recreation starting with the gods, fire, the moon and the sun. This "wind" which emerges as the breath of the Purusha and works on the primal waters is noted also by modern astrophysicists as the first gaseous agent of the formation of solar light in a hitherto darkened universe.[645]

    KYV V,6,4, relates that Prajāpati generated the earth in the form of a wind, Vāyu, which moved on the waters (Aditi) and implanted the fire

---

[643] Vāyu is called Buriaš (from Skt. pūrvia, "the first" [-born]; cf. Gk. boreas) by the Kassites (see G. Dumézil, "Dieux cassites et védiques à propos d'un bronze du Louristan", *RHA* 52 (1950).

[644] The first incarnation of Vishnu as a boar corresponds to the first incarnation of Verethraghna in the Avesta. Among the Germans, the boar was sacred to Freyr, the ithyphallic god of the Vanir. Freyr is a son of Njordr, who may be related to the earth-godddess Nerthus mentioned by Tacitus (*Germania*, Sec.40). Freyr may be a Vanir version of the primal deity in his macroanthropomorphic form. In the oath "So help me Freyr and Njordr and the almighty god" (see *DNM*, p.92) it is likely that Freyr represents Heaven as Njordr Earth and the "almighty god" the solar deity.

[645] This is evident in the description of the first light of the universe offered by modern astrophysicists (see T. Folger, "The Real Big Bang", *Discover*, Dec.2002, p.43).

in them. *KYV* VII,1,4 continues the account of Prajāpati's moving on the waters as wind, which represents the first incarnation of Vishnu (i.e. the supreme lord called by his ultimate solar name), in the first manvantara, as Vāyu:

> This was in the beginning the waters, the ocean. In it Prajāpati become the wind moved. He saw her, and becoming a boar he seized her. Her, become Vishvakarma, he wiped. She extended, she became the earth, and hence the earth is called the earth [lit. the extended].

The cosmic wind thus represents also the extensive power of the divine spirit.[646] Vishvakarma is the expanded or fertilised Earth as daughter and consort of Vishvakarman/Tvashtr, who, as we have seen, is the supreme Lord in his fabricative and formative aspect. Vāyu is thus an aspect of Tvashtr. The primal cosmic matter is also polymorphous and dark. Vishvakarma as an early form of Earth is indeed represented as a Cow.

That Vāyu the spiritual force or wind working on the waters is a form of Ātman/Agni is made clear in *RV* III,29,11, where Agni is said to be the same as Mātarisvan (Vāyu): when he is "formed in his Mother; he hath, in his course, become the rapid flight of wind". The luminous quality of Vāyu is attested in the later manifestation of Vāyu in our incipient universe as the light of the Mid-region, just as Agni is the light of Earth and Āditya of Heaven (*SB* VIII,iii,2,1). Further, in *KS* XIX,8 (9,16f.), Vāyu is called the "glow of the fire". Vāyu is also, much like Agni, called "apām raso", the essence of the waters (*VS* IX,3; *SB* V,i,2,7) in which it was born. And finally, Vāyu is generically identified with the microcosmic breath in *SB* I,i,3,2.

We have seen that, in the Purānas, the Lord is represented as reposing in deep sleep in the waters of the Abyss as the supreme Purusha (Male). This sleep is in fact a cosmic yogic trance, which, in the *VP,* is called "the product of [Vishnu's] own illusion [Māya]" as he contemplates his own spirit.[647] Since the "sleep" of the Purusha is a creative trance, it gradually causes a churning of the waters of the cosmic ocean, which results in a small hole bubbling out of it. From this hole (which may correspond to that phenomenon called a "black hole" in modern astrophysics) blows out a tremendous gale (air), which is the wind-form of the deity (Enlil/Vāyu), and, from the turbulence of this gale on the waters, is created fire, which

---

[646] Cf. the notion of the extension of the sacrifice p.187 below.

[647] The "sleep" of the Purusha is similar to that of Osiris in the underworld. Osiris' mummy is revived by the spirit of Re, with which it is, after a period of darkness (in the sixth hour of *Amduat*), united (see below p.219).

dries up the cosmic deluge and allows the appearance of our universe in the Mid-region between Earth and Heaven and, finally, of its ruler, the sun.[648] We note here a systematic deployment of the elements in the creative process that resembles the process of destruction itself.[649] The fact that Vāyu turns into fire confirms the essentially fiery nature of this wind. We will see that after the separation of Heaven and Earth, it is Vāyu who holds Heaven and Earth apart.

In the *BrdP* I,ii,7, the supreme Lord asleep in the cosmic ocean assumes the form of wind and searches for the submerged Earth in the form of a boar. So too, in the *BP* III,13,18, Vāyu emerges from Brahma's nostril as a cosmic boar which recovers Earth from the bottom of the cosmic ocean. The reference to the emergence of the boar from Brahma's "nostril"confirms the identity of Vāyu to the Heliopolitan Shu, who is also "sneezed" out by Amun-Re.[650]

In the Avestan Mihir Yasht (127) the boar, which is the fifth form of Verethraghna,[651] is said to be the form of "the wise man". Vayu is himself the first incarnation of Verethraghna. We may note that Wotan too is called "Fjölsrið" or "the Very Wise One" in the Germanic Edda.[652]

In the *Bundahishn*, the primal elements of the Cosmic Egg are Heaven and Earth.[653] Between the two is the Void, which is also called "Vay" (3).[654] "Vay" is clearly related to the wind-god Vāyu who typically spans the distance between separated Heaven and Earth. The *Bundahishn* however does not ascribe the extension of the primal waters into Earth to Vay itself. Rather, the earth is merely said to have been formed of water (22-3).

In Egypt, Shu is said in CT 75 to arise within the self-developing god, Atum, and on being exhaled into manifestation by Atum, to work upon the waters. The result is the extended earth of Geb who constitutes, along with Nut, the prime element of the Cosmic Egg. Although the raising of the Earth submerged in the course of the dissolution of the cosmos is not

---

[648] See S. Shastri, *op.cit.*, p.42.

[649] See above p.75f.

[650] See below p.130.

[651] See below p.222n.

[652] See "Gylfaginning", in *The Prose Edda*, p.49; cf. below p.210.

[653] See below p.156f.

[654] See R.C.Zaehner, *op.cit.*, p.35. The concept of the Vay as the Void is retained in the "vavohu" or "bahu" of the Hebrew *Genesis* 1:2, which couples it with "tohu" (Tehom/ Tiamat), formlessness. We may also note that, in the Epicurean cosmogony, the Cosmic Egg is encircled by a serpent of wind (see below p.154). In the Talmudic Hagiga 12a, Tohu is referred to as the source of darkness (=resistance to light; cf. below p.292) and encircling the earth (see A.J. Wensinck, "The Ocean", p.41).

ascribed to Shu in Egyptian records, the *Book of the Dead* (Spell 175) does mention that Earth, after it was created, disappeared beneath the primal waters,[655] while the Edfu inscriptions describe its later rise in the form of a lotus.[656]

Shu is the form of the supreme deity which creates the Mid-region, the Void, the space between Heaven and Earth: "It is in his feet that I have grown/ in his arms that I have developed/ in his limbs that I have made a void" (CT 75).[657] In fact the name Shu may well be derived from the verb šw meaning "to be void".[658] We have noted above that Vay is the one who is associated with the Void in the *Bundahishn* too.

In CT 75 Shu declares that Atum-Re "created me in his heart ... he exhaled me from his nose", so that he himself is "exhale-like in form".[659] We have noted above that the divine breath is formed from the "space within the heart" of the supreme deity in the *BP* as well.[660] Shu is described as ʿnh "life" and nhh "endless time",[661] and the "heart" of Atum.[662] In CT II,39bff., Shu is called "Lord of years, living for ever, Lord of eternity".[663]

Shu (life) and Tefnut (maat, the sacred order), who, according to the *Book of the Evolutions of Re*, were enclosed in Nun for several aeons, are said to be begotten of Atum by means of sneezing and spitting (the Egyptian words for these actions closely resembling the sounds of the names, Shu and Tefnut):[664]

> When I surveyed in my heart by myself, the developments of developments
> became many
>
> ...
>
> I copulated with my hand
>
> ...

---

[655] See E.A.E. Reymond, *op.cit.*, p.127.

[656] See below p.168.

[657] See J.P. Allen, *op.cit.*, p.16.

[658] See S. Bickel, *op.cit.*, p.85.

[659] See J.P. Allen, *op.cit.*, p.15.

[660] See above p.110.

[661] CT spells 75-80 (see J. Assmann, *op.cit.*, p.80).

[662] CT 80 II 34g-35h (see S. Bickel, *op.cit.*, p.48).

[663] *Ibid.*, p.85.

[664] The material difference between the emissions resulting from the two actions may also be indicative of the subtler nature of Shu compared to that of Tefnut.

I sneezed Shu and spat Tefnut.[665]
It is my father, the "Waters", that tended them
...

When I developed into this world,
Shu and Tefnut grew excited in the inert waters in which they
were and brought me my eye after them.[666]

In a 19th Dynasty hymn to Amun, Shu is called the "ba" (subtle body, soul) of Amun, just as Tefnut (Maat, the divine law) is his "ka" (character, spirit).[667] Shu and Tefnut, who arise from Atum, are also forces by which Atum rises to cosmic life and consciousness. We see also in the passage quoted above that Shu and Tefnut are responsible ultimately for the birth of the solar light.

Shu continues the role of Amun in being a god of vital air and is related to Amun as breath to soul. Shu is represented by the North Wind,[668] symbol of the life-breath.[669] That Shu represents the life-breath also is made clear from line 48 of the same text: "My clothes are the wind of life". It is Shu who later enlivens the embryonic light in the Cosmic Egg as well: "[Shu] has learned to enliven the one in the egg" (CT 80).[670] Indeed, Shu is the life of the light of the sun as well. In CT 76, for instance, Shu declares: "I am the one who made it possible for [the Sole Eye of Atum] to give brilliance to the Darkness".[671] Indeed, like Vāyu and Enlil, Shu is not only the primal wind but also a fiery and luminous phenomenon, as is evident especially in the Shu theology of CT 75-80.[672]

Shu, we have noted, is himself a specific form of Amun, the original lord of the Cosmic Egg. Amun-Re is, in a hymn to Amun of Cairo (Pap. Boulaq 17),[673] called "Lord of Maat [i.e. Tefnut]", exactly as if he were the

[665]   The references to "sneeze" and "spit" are due to the sound-associations between the names of Shu (šw) and Tefnut (tfnt), and the words jšš (sneeze) and tf (spit) (see J.P. Allen, op.cit., p.14).

[666]   Pap. Bremner-Rhind, 17ff. in J.P. Allen, op.cit., p.28; cf. PT 527, pyr.1248a-d (S. Bickel, op.cit., p.73). The "eye" is the sun.

[667]   See A. Barucq and F. Daumas, op.cit., p.227.

[668]   So too is Enlil's son Ninurta/Adad (see A. Livingstone, op.cit., p.75; cf. below p.192n).

[669]   See S. Bickel, op.cit., p.130.

[670]   See J.P. Allen, op.cit., p.22.

[671]   See J.P. Allen, op.cit., p.19; cf. Enlil as the rising sun (below p.224). Shu/Enlil is thus the source of the solar force of Marduk, "the one inside Šamaš" (see below p.267) .

[672]   See J. Assmann, Re und Amun: Die Krise der polytheistischen Weltbilds im Ägypten der 18.20. Dynastie, Freiburg: Universitätsverlag, 1983, pp.116f.

[673]   See A. Barucq and F. Daumas, op.cit., p.193.

same deity as Shu, and also "creator of gods,/ who raises the heavens and distances the earth". Shu is also traditionally the one who sustains Heaven and Earth after their separation. In a text to be found on the walls of the tombs of Seti I and Rameses IV at Thebes, Shu is also called "he whose forms are hidden", exactly like Amun, while Tefnut is called "the guide of Ra to his members".[674] We see therefore that Shu continues the mysterious nature of his progenitor Amun as the hidden support of the universe.

Ptah, the name of the supreme deity as macroanthropos, is also used as a synonym of Shu/Vāyu/Enlil, the wind-like force which extends Geb, the earth. In the Middle Kingdom, Ptah was considered a son of Atum, and thus the equivalent of Shu. Ptah is indeed hymned as the one "who raised the sky and made all that is",[675] just as Shu is the deity who holds heaven and earth apart after their separation by Osiris. In Pap. Berlin 3048, Ptah-Tatenen is identified with Shu as the one who "raised the sky for [the sun] and stretched out the earth for [the sun] and who moves [the sun] on the belly of Nut and who guides [the sun] on secret ways".[676] We may note the reference to the "stretching" out of the earth which we have encountered in the Indic literature as well.[677] Ptah's relation to Shu as the vital breath and life-force is made clear by the reference in Pap.Harris I to Ptah Tatenen as the one "who lets the throat breathe and gives air to every nose".[678] In an inscription on a sculpture of a Hathor cow from the New Kingdom, Ptah is called "the Lord of Semen Maat",[679] which identifies him again with Shu.

The different "generations" of Heliopolitan gods are indeed the same as the primal cosmic divinity Amun-Re at various evolutionary stages. Thus also is Agni the essential fiery substance of all the primal gods in the Indic cosmogony. We shall see below that Nunet, Tefnut, Nut, Hathor and Isis are different stages of the same primordial watery element. Amun, Nun, Shu, Horus the Elder and Osiris are equally continuous stages of the life-giving solar force.[680] In fact, in CT 78, Shu declares that "his 'identity' [name]

---

[674] See E.A.W. Budge, op.cit., I:340f. The divine "members" represent the various gods (see above p.117).

[675] See S. Morenz, Aegyptische Religion, Stuttgart: W. Kohlhammer, 1960, p.183.

[676] See M.S. Holmberg, op.cit., p.153.

[677] See above p.128.

[678] Ibid., p.41; cf. Pap. Berlin 3048, 3, 10: "He who made the wind ... and refreshes the throat with the breath which comes [from his mouth]" (ibid., p.105f.).

[679] Ibid., p.191.

[680] See the hymn of Chapter 50 of the BD, where it is stated that, at the rising of Re, "Naunet makes the 'nini' reverence to your face/ Maat holds you in embrace day and night" (A. Barucq and F. Daumas, op.cit., p.173) showing that Re is present at all stages of the cosmic development, first as Nun, the consort of Naunet, and then as Shu, consort of Tefnut/Maat.

became Osiris, son of Geb".[681] This identification of Shu with Osiris, son of Geb, again suggests that Osiris-Horus represent a later, more vital stage of the original creator-god Osiris, resultant on the manifestation of the phallic force of Shu.

Shu is indeed the life-force of Re himself and represents the male principle and life, which is "eternal recurrence", whereas Tefnut is the female principle and 'maat', the cosmic law, which is "eternal sameness".[682] Shu as the life-force is also responsible for the restoration of Isis after her decapitation by Horus the Younger, and the revivification of Osiris in the underworld:

> I will fix the head of Isis on her neck[683] and assemble Osiris's bones.
> I will make firm his flesh every day and make fresh his parts every day.[684]

The emergent sun (Osiris revived as Horus the Younger) is also an effect of Shu, just as Osiris, son of Geb, is himself infused with the life-force of Shu.

Tefnut, the consort of Shu, like Pārvatī/Ninhursag, represents a cosmic 'vulva', just as Shu, like Shiva/Enlil represents a 'phallus' (the two forces which unite in the creation of the universe constituted of Nut and Geb).[685] Hathor is also called "mistress of the vulva",[686] since she is a later form of Tefnut. Hathor is further associated with Re's hand (also a symbol of Tefnut and called Nebet-Hetepet), when Re "copulated" with his phallus (Shu) during his auto-erotic creative act.[687] Both Tefnut and Hathor are, significantly, identified with Maat,[688] the Law of the Universe.[689]

---

[681] See J.P. Allen, *op.cit.*, p.23.

[682] See CT 78; cf. J.P. Allen, *op.cit.*, p.21. Tefnut is regularly identified with Maat, the goddess of the Divine Order of the universe, who is called a "daughter" of Re, or Amun-Re.

[683] That is, after Horus cut off her head and replaced it with a cow's head, see below p.264.

[684] CT 80 (see J.P. Allen, *op.cit.*, p.24).

[685] See J. Zandee, *op.cit.*, p.169.

[686] *WAS* III:195.

[687] See C.J. Bleeker, *Hathor and Toth*, p.68.

[688] See A. Mairette, *Dendérah: Description générale du grand temple de cette ville*, Paris : A. Franck, 1870-75, II, 62a.

[689] Similarly, Ishtar/Innini proclaims:
"I am the word of the lord (Marduk), over its evil power I preside
At his word the heavens above are stilled of themselves, his is a word of majesty"
(see S. Langdon, *Tammuz and Ishtar*, Oxford: Clarendon Press, 1914, p.112).

In the Babylonian *EE*, the first of the three pairs of gods who are created by Tiamat and Apsu, Lahmu and Lahamu,[690] may correspond to the "boar" form assumed by the wind Vāyu which emerges from the nostrils of the ideal macroanthropos, since Lahmu probably has a monstrous form.[691]

The Sumerian counterpart of Shu is, more clearly, Enlil, Lord of Wind. Enlil is called Diru (Dur-an-ki), the bond between Heaven and Earth, since it is he who, like the Egyptian Shu and the Bundahishn Vay, sustains heaven and earth after their separation,[692] with the pervasive force of air. Enlil, like Vāyu, is associated, in SBH 22, vs. ll.17-8, with life-breath as well as with the creation of men (UP V no.1 I l.12; KARI4, ll.22ff.).

It must be noted that Enlil, again like Vāyu, is to be considered a fiery phenomenon. Enlil's 'me', or power of destiny, is described as one "which does not manifest as light" because he is the god of fire as spirit, as one whose "divine (presence) cannot be seen". The me's are sometimes said to be bestowed by Enlil on his 'younger brother' Enki, 'lord of Earth'.[693] It is also reported that Enki then gives the me's directly to Enlil's son, Ninurta, or, sometimes, to Ninurta's wife, Inanna or Ishtar (STVC 34, 1,15 and SRT I,23).[694] Ninurta's wife is Inanna because Ninurta, son of Enki/Enlil, is the same as his solar father, Enki/Osiris-Horus the Elder, the cosmic light that is forced into the underworld. While Enki is considered the "dispenser of fate for nature and people", Enlil is the one who "confirms this fate". This is indeed corroborated in Egypt by the appellation of Shu's consort as Maat, the divine laws.

---

[690]   It is interesting to note that Sennacherib substituted Ea and Marduk with Lahmu and Assur in his Assyrian version of the Babylonian epic (see F.M.T. de Liagre Boehl, "Die Religion der Babylonier und Assyrier" in *Christus und die Religionen der Erde*, II, p.456). This does not however necessarily equate Marduk with Assur, since Assur/Anshar is represented in the fragmentary 'Ordeal of Marduk' as being responsible for Marduk's torments (see below p.267). Assur is also, clearly, the "Assyrian Enlil" (see below p.160). This means that the Enlil who acts as the hero of Sennacherib's epic is the son of the primal Ea, since the wind is indeed his breath.

[691]   W. Lambert points out that these names denote "some kind of sea-monster" (W. Lambert, "The Cosmology of Sumer and Babylon", in C. Blacker and M. Loewe (ed.), *Ancient Cosmologies*, London: George Allen and Unwin, 1975, p.53. Lahmu is represented in the An=Anum god-list as one of the two doorkeepers of Eridu (see *RLA* V:431).

[692]   In the myth of "The Creation of the Hoe" (see H. de Genouillac, *Textes religieux sumériens du Louvre*, no.72; cf. T. Jacobsen, *Treasures*, p.103), Enlil is represented as separating heaven and earth.

[693]   See the Hymn to Enki in A. Falkenstein and W. von Soden, *Sumerische Hymnen*, Zürich: Artemis Verlag, 1953, p.109. his is not the primal Ea but Enki/Osiris in the underworld.

[694]   See Y. Rosengarten, *op.cit.*, pp.79, 81.

According to the Phoenician cosmogony of Sankuniathon[695] that was edited by Philo of Byblos, the original state of the cosmos was characterised by a "dark and windy gas (αέρ), or a stream of dark gas, and turbid, gloomy chaos".[696] The chaos is the same as the Chasm, or Abyss. The wind "lusted after its own sources" producing a mixture called Desire (πόθος) and then Mot, which represents a primordial slime typifying the underworld and death.[697] We see again that the wind-form of the deity is responsible for the manifestation of Earth, which in its underworld regions is considered the realm of death.[698]

---

[695] According to Philo of Byblos, Sankuniathon himself based his cosmogony on that of Thoth, who ruled the kingdom of Egypt (see Philo of Byblos, op.cit., pp.29,59). However, Philo considers Thoth to have been, originally, a Phoenician (ibid., p.99; cf. Malalas' account of Thoth, p.80 above).

[696] See Philo of Byblos, op.cit., p.37.

[697] Ibid., p.37, and p.77, fn.29. The cosmic Wind which we have studied in this chapter is the cosmological original of the Platonic and Neoplatonic philosophical hypostasis of Ψυχή.

[698] See Ch.XVII below.

VII: DYAUS–PRITHVĪ

THE IDEAL HEAVEN AND EARTH: OURANOS-GAIA

In *KYV* V,5,4 the process whereby Vāyu stretches Earth is described as one through which Agni produces Earth: "Agni longed for [the waters], he had union with them, his seed fell away, it became this [earth]." The Sanskrit word for Earth ('prithvī') literally means 'the extended'.[699] In *RV* II,35,7, the "teeming Milch-Cow" (Earth) is said to be in the "mansion of Agni". In *KYV* V,5,4, Agni is said to have generated Earth and Heaven autoerotically – like the Egyptian Re – when dwelling in the waters, when his lust for the chthonic waters (his mother or mothers) caused him to spill his seed. Agni in the waters is the same as the primal Enki/Osiris, and Enki's predilection for creative masturbation has already been noticed. Heaven, the hyper-cosmos, is called Svarāj, while Earth is Virāj. As we shall see, the extended Earth emerges later from the Cosmic Egg in the form of a lotus atop which Brahman, the Intellectual Light of Heaven rests.

Thus the impregnation of Aditi by the Lord of the Abyss is both the luminous Heaven called Dyaus (from Skt.'div'=to shine) and Earth. At *RV* I,95,7 Agni, when he unites with the waters, draws forth from his Mothers a fiery vesture. This vesture may be the heavenly body of the primal Man. It should be noted here, also, that the light of Dyaus is not yet manifest, and this hidden heavenly glow may indeed correspond to the halo observable in the dark matter of the universe 100 million years after the "big bang".[700]

Agni is both the consort and child of Aditi. At *RV* X,5,3, Agni is said

---

[699] Earth is said, like the waters, to be based on the Truth (synonymous with Rta) and therefore the first of the worlds (*SB* VII,iv,1).

[700] See T. Folger, *op.cit.*, p.43.

to be the child of Dyaus and Aditi, though he is equally Aditi's consort.[701] Similarly, as we shall see, the waters in the underworld are said in *KYV* V,5,4 to be Varuna's "wives". At *RV* I,95,4, the waters are called the "mothers" of Agni, who is typically called the "child of the waters" (apām napāt). However, the child Agni is also said to have "by his own nature brought forth his Mothers".

In the Vedas, the product of the union of Dyaus/Daksha with Aditi is said to include also the the entire set of Ādityas (*RV* X,72), whose leaders are Mitra-Varuna (*RV* VII,66).[702] The Ādityas correspond to the Titan sons of Ouranos and Ge in Hesiod (l.133). The Titans include Chronos and Hyperion, who are but aspects of Ouranos himself. The Ādityas, are later, in the seventh Manvantara, manifested as the suns of the several universes.[703]

In the Purānas, the primal sky is produced by the fire which emerges after the wind which, as we have noted above, issues through a cleft in the waters.[704] This fire, called the Vaishvānara, dries up the waters, and the cleft in the ocean itself now appears as the sky (*PP* I,39,140ff.) This may correspond to the formation of Heaven by Earth as a cover for herself in Hesiod. In the *PP* I,39,146, the wind is said to emerge in the primal cosmos from the sky and, in I,39,153f., the supreme lord is said to next produce the "lotus"-formed Earth (Geb/Ge) from his navel.

Amun is sometimes represented as a Km-3.t-f serpent which emerges from Nun and creates Heaven (Nut). Heaven then creates an Egg, from which a second serpent arises that is identical to Ptah-Tatenen (Geb),[705] who constitutes the material matrix of our universe called earth.[706] In another version, Nun is said to have first created Nunet (the waters of Heaven) and it is Nunet who then forms heaven, Nut.[707] This suggests that Nunet is rather closely related to Tefnut, who produces Nut as well as Geb. So we may assume that the order of primal creation is Amun-Nun, Nunet, Nut and Geb.

---

[701] In Egypt too Re is said to have created himself, and also created his mother and consort (his procreative "hand"; see A. Barucq and F. Daumas, *op.cit.*, p.157; cf. above p.100).

[702] See p.231n below.

[703] See p.231n below.

[704] See above p.128.

[705] See below Ch.XI.

[706] See K. Sethe, *op.cit.*, p.63. This earth is to be distinguished from primal Earth.

[707] *Ibid.*, p.74f. It is interesting that, in an Assyrian exegetical text on Sumerian theology (see A. Livingstone, op.cit., p.33), the heavens are explained as being "of water" ("ša me").

The Old Babylonian Sumerian god-list, which begins with Nammu as "Ama.tu.an.ki", the mother of Heaven and Earth, continues with Earth (Urash) followed by En-uru-ulla, meaning "the Lord of the primeval dwelling". Urash and En-uru-ulla may be forms of Enki.[708] It is possible also that Enki himself is identifiable with Antum, the earthly consort of An, since they both have the symbolic number 40.[709]
In the votive inscription of Lugalkisalsis of Uruk, Nammu's consort is said to be An.[710] This reveals that An is not only the manifest divine light that will emerge later from the Cosmic Egg, but also the counterpart of the primal deity Dyaus (Heaven) of the Vedas. Indeed then the Sumerian term "Dingir" used most characteristically of An (though, by extension, equally of all gods) may be related to Skt."div" (=to shine) which gives "Dyaus".[711]

In the Hurrian epic of the Kingship in Heaven, Alalu is combatted by the primal heaven Anu[712] and forced to flee to Earth, where he becomes Lord of Earth (Enki). The Anu who overthrows Alalu, whom we have identified with the Ideal Man, Purusha, in the cosmic waters, must be the fiery form which the deity assumes after the appearance of Vāyu. This form apparently already consigns the macroanthropomorphic deity into the realm of Earth, though Kumarbi, who later attacks Anu, is indeed a form of Enki, Lord of Earth.[713]

According to the proto-Stoic Pherecydes,[714] Zas (Dyaus/Agni) himself turns Chthonie (who corresponds to the Earth recovered by Vāyu) into Ge (Earth, called Prithvī, 'the extended', in the Vedas) by giving the former a robe symbolically decorated with Ge and Okeanos.[715] The

---

[708] See W. Lambert, "The Cosmology of Sumer and Babylon", in *Ancient Cosmologies*, p.52. Since En-uru-ulla follows Urash, just as Belet-ili does Nammu, it is quite likely that this name indeed refers to Enki rather than to Anshargal, who follows.

[709] See M. Rutten, "Les Religions Asianiques", p.39.

[710] See H. Wohlstein, *op.cit.*, p.27.

[711] An itself is used as a name of both Shiva and Vishnu in the *MBh* (see S. Sörensen, *An Index to the Names in the Mahabharata*, London: Williams and Norgate, 1904, p.42).

[712] See J.S. Cooper, *Presargonic Inscriptions*, New Haven, CT: American Oriental Society, 1986, p.103. This Anu is not the same as the manifest light, An, who follows Anshar and Anki in the Sumerian god-list An=Anum (see below Ch.XII).

[713] See below p.142.

[714] According to Philo of Byblos, Pherecydes owed his cosmological learning to the Phoenicians (see Philo of Byblos, *op.cit.*, p.67).

[715] See M.L. West, *The Orphic Poems*, p.11; cf. M.L. West, *Early Greek Philosophy and the Orient*, p.54. Okeanos is clearly derived from the Sumerian Enki. See also the Emperor Julian's Hymn to King Helios, which declares that "Helios is Oceanus, the lord of two-fold substance" (Julian, *Works*, III, tr. C.Wright, London: W. Heinemann, 1913, p.403). Okeanos, or Enki as the Lord of Earth, is also the "ocean" which surrounds the manifest universe. M.L.

assumption of the role of Enlil/Vāyu[716] as impregnator of Earth by Zas shows that Dyaus/Zas is manifest along with Vāyu.

In Hesiod, Earth is prior to Heaven since it is Earth (Gaia) who draws out Ouranos (Heaven) to cover her, "Equal [in expanse] to herself, to cover her on every side, and to be an ever-sure abiding-place for the blessed gods" (*Theogony*, ll.126-9). We have seen that the first gods are deities who preside over the several intellectual and physical faculties of the Ideal Man, and we may assume that Heaven is the substance in which these faculties operate.[717] Ouranos or Heaven is thus the constitution of the Purusha himself. After Earth draws Heaven about herself, she mates with him so as to create a host of Titans including Chronos and Hyperion – who gives birth to the sun and moon. The children of Ouranos are hidden by their father in a "secret place of Earth" since he fears their extraordinary strength (ll.156ff.). These primal creations of the Purusha/Ouranos which are prevented from manifesting themselves may be considered as intelligible productions of the divine Subconscious, since the deity does not acquire Consciousness until the emergence of Atum as the divine Light.

According to Cicero (*De Natura Deorum*, 62), the father of the first Zeus is called Caelus, who must be the same as Ouranos, since he is said to have been "mutilated by his son". This son is Chronos, who is, as we shall see, the same as Zeus Aitherios.[718]

In the Phoenician cosmology of Sankuniathon, Ouranos is the son of the Most High, Elioun, and his sister is Ge.[719]

West suggests that the name of Okeanos' consort, Tethys, may also be derived from Tiamat (see M.L. West, *The East Face of Helicon*, p.147). But it is equally likely that both these names are derived from the Vedic Aditi.

[716]   See above p.128.

[717]   We may note that Earth is said, in ll.160-2, to constitute the "seat of the gods", since it serves as the substance of the gods. We shall see below (p.207) that the Sumerian 'mešu' tree [of life], whose trunk represents "earth", is similarly considered as the "flesh of the gods".

[718]   See below p.146.

[719]   See Philo of Byblos, *op.cit.*, p.47.

VIII: KĀLA

ETERNAL TIME:

DURI-DARI, ENKI, CHRONOS, KUMARBI, SHIVA, ZURVAN, GEB

The elements of Earth and Heaven close united in the Ideal Man are separated by the temporal aspect of the Ideal Man himself called Time (Chronos/Kumarbi/Enki). Since the breath of the Ideal Man arises in the form of a "rapidly moving wind", we may assume that the movement of the Wind-God is also responsible for the appearance of Time. Time may be considered to have not properly emerged until after the infusion of the divine breath/fire into the prime matter of Earth. That is why Chronos is considered a "son" of Ouranos. We must also remember that Chronos/Time operates on an entirely subconscious level since the Ideal Man has not yet achieved consciousness, the divine light of Brahman.

The separation of Heaven and Earth by Time entails the castration of Heaven's phallus, but this mutilation, as we shall see, is indeed a "self-sacrifice". The castration of the divine phallus causes its seed to impregnate the Cosmic Man himself resulting in the formation within his stomach of the egg from which the material matrix of the universe, Earth emerges in the form of a lotus suffused by the divine light of Brahman/An.

In the Sumerian god-lists, Time or Eternity, Duri-Dari, is preceded by two pairs,[720] the first of which, Ekur-Gara, perhaps refers to "the Mountain dwelling" of Enlil.[721] Next comes Lahmu-Lahama, whom we have identified

---

[720] See An-Anum, Tablet I (in R. Litke, *op.cit.*, p.22); cf. W. Lambert, "The Cosmology of Sumer and Akkad", p.53.

[721] The mountain perhaps refers to the universe which emerges as the "primeval hill" in Heliopolis, from which the sun-god (Osiris) emerges as a phoenix. Since Atum/Osiris are said to arise particularly from that part of Nun called the Flood of Hehu, we may associate Ekur with this Hermopolitan element, as well as with the Earth of Hesiod which is a part of the Abyss.

with the "boar" form of Enlil/Vāyu.[722] Duri-Dari, Eternity,[723] which follows, no doubt corresponds to the Eternal Time represented by Kronos/Kāla/ Zurvan/ Kumarbi.

Berossus, in his *Babyloniaca,* identifies Enki with Kronos [Kumarbi].[724] We have seen that Enki has the symbolic number 40, which is also that of An's "consort", Antum,[725] who represents Earth as well as the cosmic waters [Okeanos] which surround Earth.[726] This suggests that the primal Ideal Man, Alalu, who has been deposed by Anu and forced into the realm of Earth, where he becomes the Lord of Earth (Enki) is identifiable with Kumarbi/Chronos who attacks Anu.[727]

In the Hurrian epic of the Kingship in Heaven, Kumarbi is considered Anu's son,[728] and he destroys his father Anu so as to assume the rule of the primal cosmos. Kumarbi (Chronos) indeed castrates Anu (Heaven/the ideal Cosmic Man) while dragging him down from Heaven. However, Anu succeeds later in fleeing to his natural abode, that is, Heaven. The manner of Kumarbi's castration of Anu is reminiscent of Chronos' in Hesiod:[729]

> After [Anu] Kumarbi rushed,
> and seized him, Anu, by his feet
> and pulled him down from the sky.
> He bit his loins[730]

In the *AV* we find that Kāla is indeed posited as a primal element of creation, though this is slightly anachronistic since the primal Soul itself is quite undifferentiated spatially as well as temporally until it begins to breathe as the cosmic wind.[731] According to *AV* XIX,53,8-9, both Prajāpati (here the

---

[722] See above p.134.

[723] So in the An=Anum list.

[724] See W. Lambert and A.R. Millard, *Atrahasis*, p.135.

[725] See M. Rutten, "Les Religions Asianiques", p.39.

[726] We have seen how the name Enki was transformed into Okeanos by the Greeks to indicate the waters surrounding the manifest universe (see above p.139n).

[727] Ea, Enki's 'Akkadian' name, reflects his virtue as the lord of life, whereas the Sumerian name Enki itself is appropriate to him as Lord of Earth, or the underworld.

[728] Kumār, in India, is the name of Shiva's solar son, Skanda/Muruga, who is the ninth form of Agni, the first form being Rudra/Shiva himself (see p.214 below).

[729] See Hesiod, *Thegony*, ll.173ff.

[730] See H.G. Güterbock, "Hittite Mythology" in S. Kramer, *op.cit.*, p.156.

[731] The priority attributed to Kāla in the *AV* is to be found also in the *Bundahishn*, which

creative form of the supreme deity, identical to Brahman who is "as it were the Mind", *KYV* II,6,6) and Fervour (Desire/Agni) are said to be generated by Kāla, Time. Desire and the Mind are then said to have created Heaven. In the same text (*AV* XIX,54), Time is further represented as the generator of the waters[732] along with Brahman (Mind/Prajāpati), the Mind's Fervour (or Desire/Agni), and the quarters (or Space). But *RV* X,190, as we have seen above,[733] posits Fervour as the creator of the waters. Kāla is typically an epithet of Shiva, whose consort is called Kāli. Shiva/Enki as Time is thus closely allied to the Desire (Agni) of the supreme lord which serves as the prime motive force in the manifestation of the Deity. The erotic, as well as spiritual and ascetic, aspect of Shiva/Kāla is indeed clearly emphasised in the Shaivite mythologies.[734]

In the Sassanian Pahlavi texts, Zurvan (Time) is considered the creator of both the twin forces of good and evil, Ahura Mazda and Angra Mainyu, who dwell in Heaven (the Boundless Light) and Earth (Darkness) respectively.[735] Since Heaven and Earth are the basic constituents of the Cosmic Egg, the creative aspects attributed to Zurvan are akin to those of Kāla in the *AV* passages quoted above, as well as to those of Chronos in the Orphic cosmogonies.[736] In the *Bundahishn* Ch.I, Zurvan (Time) is indeed an aspect of Ahura Mazda, since he inhabits eternally the region of infinite space called Light. Indeed, Ahura Mazda is also considered the father of the solar force, Mithra, as well as of Atar, who corresponds to Brahmanaspati, Ganesha/Seth.[737] As such he corresponds to Geb/Chronos/Zurvan himself.

In Egypt, Time is posited at the stage of the appearance of Shu [Enlil]: "[the Command of the supreme god] created Time – when Shu was there to raise the sky" (*CT* IV,325).[738] However, Plutarch (*De Iside et Osiride*, Ch.12), rightly considers Geb and Nut to be identical to Chronos and Rhea.[739] If so, Chronos must have absorbed the chthonic substance of his mother, Gaia, while his consort Rhea inherits the heavenly nature of his father, Ouranos.

---

reveals the Iranian affiliations of the *AV*.

[732] The text omits mention of the Intellectual Order (Rta) of the universe as a concomitant phenomenon at this stage in the evolution of the cosmos (see above p.96).

[733] See above p.96.

[734] See W. O'Flaherty, *op.cit.*, Chs.IVff.

[735] See R.C. Zaehner, *op.cit.*, p.10.

[736] See below p.145.

[737] See below p.208.

[738] See R.T. Rundle Clark, *op.cit.*, p.76.

[739] It should be noted that the male Geb, in Egyptian mythology, represents earth rather than heaven, as in Greek and Sumerian and Indian mythology.

In Egypt, the counterpart of the episode of Prajāpati's seduction of his daughter is Re's impregnation of the cow Nut as the Bull of Heaven,[740] who, here, stands for Geb/Chronos, consort of Nut, Heaven.[741] Once again we see that Chronos and Ouranos are but the same deity.[742] Like the sacrifice of Purusha which is commonly understood as a suicide in Vedic religion, the mutilation of Re is also represented as a self-castration of Re in Egypt.[743]

There are also references in the Egyptian literature to the "separation of Heaven from Earth and from the Abyss (Nun)".[744] Geb and Nut are sustained by the force of Shu after their separation by the latter.[745] Amun, who is closely related to Shu, is also represented as a serpent who creates heaven and earth, the serpent being the most pneumatic of all creatures.[746] In the *Amduat* the gigantic serpent called the "World-encircler" through whose coils the solar journey is undertaken in the underworld similarly represents Time.[747] We shall see that the wind-egg in Epicurus is represented as encircled by a serpent of wind.[748] The serpent is also the form taken by Enki/Okeanos surrounding Earth, showing once again the identity between Enlil and Enki. We have seen that Chronos too is represented as a serpent.

According to the Phoenician mythology ascribed by Philo of Byblos to Sankhuniathon, the Phoenician counterpart of Chronos was El, son of Ouranos and Ge.[749] This El is the same senior god whom the Hebrews too once worshipped in their originally polytheistic pantheon before they transferred their sole allegiance to his son, Jahve, under the tutelage of Abraham.[750] El is the same as Kronos and battles Ouranos over a long

---

[740] See E.O. James, *op.cit.*, p.177. Another cognate appellation is "Bull of his Mother [i.e. Heaven]" which is applied to Horus, Amun and Min (see J.G. Griffiths, *op.cit.*, p.91, C.J. Bleeker, *op.cit.*, p.101; A. Barucq and F. Daumas, *op.cit.*, p.367). We note here once again the identification of Re-Horus with Min-Amun (see below p.173f).

[741] See E.A.W. Budge, *op.cit.*, I:100.

[742] Since the Bull of Heaven is also an epithet of Atum, the son of Geb and Nut (see above p.68), Atum too is a continuance of the substance of his father Geb.

[743] See below p.205.

[744] PT 627 pyr 1778 a-b (cf. S. Bickel, *op.cit.*, p.184).

[745] See p.132 above.

[746] See K. Sethe, *op.cit.*, p.26f.

[747] See below p.218.

[748] See below p.154.

[749] See Philo of Byblos, *op.cit.*, p.49; cf. H.G. Güterbock, "Hittite Mythology" in S. Kramer, *Mythologies*, p.160.

[750] Jahve is the counterpart of Seth/Zeus (see below Ch.XIV) but robbed of his original cosmological significance by the Hebrews following Abraham (see above p.16). The original polytheistic form of Yahwism is detectable in 2 *Samuel* 7:1f, where Yahweh is associated

period of time in order to avenge his mother, Ge, who had been violated by Ouranos.[751] Kronos succeeds in ousting Ouranos from his kingdom and captures Ouranos' mistress, who is given by Kronos in marriage to his brother, Dagon, from which union is born Demarous, or Zeus Adados.[752] Kronos' three brothers (counterparts of the Titans) are Baetylos, Dagon and Atlas, which last, as we shall see, is identifiable with Uppelluri and the Cosmic Egg.[753]

The supercession of the original Heaven is reflected in the early Greek cosomologies, as in the Hurrian, as a castration of Ouranos (Dyaus) by Chronos. Chronos' attack on Ouranos is an indication of an extremely violent nature that recurs in the character of his stormy son Zeus (Seth/Ganesha). The Hesiodic Chronos is the daring son of Earth and Heaven who responds to his mother's desire to thwart his father's habit of hiding his offspring and not allowing them to become manifest. It is significant that Ouranos' hiding of his children is particularly described as "evil-doing" in Hesiod's *Theogony*, l.158, since Chronos is not the only villainous figure in the early drama of the cosmos. To aid his mother in her distress, Chronos undertakes to castrate Ouranos, whose anthropomorphic form in the Hesiodic account clearly identifies him with the Purusha himself.

In the Orphic cosmogonies, the Cosmic Egg is said to be formed by Chronos out of Aither and the Chasm.[754] Chronos particularly forms Protogonos, or Phanes in the Cosmic Egg.[755] The proto-Stoic cosmogony of Pherecydes, on the other hand, begins with Chronos [Time], Chthonie, and Zas.[756] Chronos is said to "generate" fire, wind and water[757] in the five matrices of the gods from Chthonie and Zas.[758] Zas must therefore be

---

with the Canaanite temple of Obed-Edom, i.e. of the priest of the goddess Edom, who is identifiable with Asherah, consort of El.

[751] See Philo of Byblos, *op.cit.*, p.50f.

[752] *Ibid.*, p.51.

[753] See below p.154.

[754] See M.L. West, *The Orphic Poems*, p.70.

[755] *Ibid.*, p.178.

[756] H. Diels, *Doxographi Graeci*, Berlin, 1879, p.654; cf. Probus, *In Verg. Ecl.*6. Pherecydes calls 'Zas' Aither.

[757] Cf. the Assyrian exegetical text RA 62 52 17-8:

Girra: Anu: fire.
Primeval: Ea: water.
East wind: Enlil: wind.

(see A. Livingstone, *op.cit.*, p.74).

[758] The gods are called the fivefold race in the Vedas (*AV* VII,6,1) as well.

identical to Aither and Chthonie to the Chasm. Euripides (*Chrys.*)[759] too refers to the "Earth and the Aither of Zeus", but this Zeus is the same as Zeus Aitherios or Chronos. Cicero (*De Natura Deorum*, III,53) indeed refers to Aither (i.e. Zeus Aitherios) as a father of Zeus.[760] At the same time, we have seen that Chronos is closely associated with Geb as well. This suggests that Chronos, though aethereal, partakes especially of the Chthonic aspect of his mother. In the Orphic theogonies, Chronos, who is also identified with Herakles (Vishnu),[761] is traditionally represented as a serpent united with the cosmic axis, Ananke or Adrastea or Nemesis.[762] The serpentine form of Chronos associates him also with that of Okeanos/Enki.[763]

---

[759] Fr. 839 Nauck.

[760] This will be confirmed in the case of Dionysus below p.180.

[761] See p.251 below.

[762] Cf. p.76 above, where Vishnu is the archetypal macroanthropos, whose tāmasic aspect is embodied in the serpent Sesha (see below p.291). Shiva/Chronos/Time is thus the Illusion/Māyā of the Purusha/Vishnu.

[763] See below p.218.

IX: BRAHMĀNDA

THE COSMIC EGG

The result of the castration of the Heavenly body of the Ideal Man is the formation within his own body of a Cosmic Egg which bears our own universe. We must remember here that this body is now dominated by Kāla/Chronos. In *RV* X,121, Daksha is said to impregnate Aditi with the germ of the golden egg, and Daksha may be identified with the potency (Agni) of Dyaus.[764] Aditi we may understand as the cosmic streams which provide the prime matter of Earth. Daksha is also called "dakshapati", the lord of daksha, at *RV* I,95,6.[765] In *RV* II,35,13, the golden germ, Hiranyagarbha, is said to have been engendered in the waters by Agni the Bull, since Kāla/Angra Manyu are forms of Agni himself. We have seen that Chronos is credited with the formation of the cosmic light in Orphic and proto-Stoic cosmogonies.[766] In the Purānas and the *MBh* as well, Shiva is called the Lord of Hiranyagarbha.[767]

In *SB* VI,i,1,1-14, Prajāpati is said to enter into union with extended Earth and this union already engenders the Cosmic Egg. Prajāpati is here identifiable with Vāyu and Dyaus, who is indeed the product of Vāyu's union with Earth. In other words, the creation of the egg is due to the initial embrace of Vāyu and Earth. Prajāpati is called Hiranyagarbha at *SB* VI,6,6,5: "Hiranyagarbha is Prajāpati and Prajāpati is Agni". At *RV* X,121, too, Hiranyagarbha is identified with Prajāpati. Since it is indeed Vāyu who impregnates Earth, and the particular form in which the egg is engendered

---

[764] See above p.148.

[765] Daksha is also typically associated with "the Sacrifice", since he is Prajāpati's *alter ego*.

[766] See above p.145, and below p.155.

[767] See, for instance, *LP* I,20,80-6.

is related to the breath or wind that emerges from the Purusha, it is not surprising that the egg, in the Greek accounts too, is called a "wind-egg".[768]

In the *SP*, our entire universe is said to exist in the "belly-like 'Egg of Brahma' [Brahmānda]".[769] At *SB* III,i,3,26, the "entire universe" is said to be constituted essentially of Heaven and Earth. All the worlds of the universe are thus formed from the "maternal body" of the Earth[770] impregnated by the spiritual force of Daksha (Agni), who must be the same as Dyaus (Heaven). According to the Purānas, from the Egg, and through Vishnu's navel (representing the womb of the universe/[771]Tefnut), arises the lotus of Earth upon which sits Brahman/Āditya (the divine Light/Osiris-Horus).[772] According to *BrdP* I,i,3,26, Brahma is four-faced[773] and begins to fill the worlds with his creation. His first creations (prajās) are marked by Ignorance (Tamas) and the later by Sattva (*BrdP* I,i,5,29ff). These creations are followed by the birth of Rudra and the nine sages his "mental sons".[774]

In the *BP* III,11,40, we learn also that the Cosmic Egg which contains our universe is not the only one in the cosmos but that there are innumerable others like it:

> This Brahmānda which consists of the eight special modifications and sixteen effects of Prakriti ... is surrounded without by the layers of the five elements, the layer of each element being ten times the dimension of the internal dimension of the preceding shell. All this is only like an atomic particle in [Lord] Hari. In Him there are countless other shells like this, all of which together even is like a few atomic particles for Him.

Heaven and Earth are the major contents of the formed Cosmic Egg, since they represent the constitution of the Cosmic Man. In the Vedas (*RV*

---

[768]   See below p.154.

[769]   See S. Shastri, *op.cit.*, p.67.

[770]   Cf. *SB* VII,iv,1,12 where Earth is called the "foundation" of all.

[771]   See W.D. O'Flaherty, *op.cit.*, p.159. That the Purānas reflect the sources of the most ancient Vedic cosmogonical notions is established by the similar reference, in *RV* X,82,6, to the "Unborn's navel" on which the golden egg rests.

[772]   That Brahman is the same as Horus the Elder is made clear by the fact that the latter too is represented at Dendera as a child (or a serpent) resting on a lotus that rises above the water (see C.J. Bleeker, *Hathor and Thoth*, p.63).

[773]   In Egypt, in the sun-temple of Medinet Habu, Atum too is represented as four-faced, or a "Ba with four heads", the ba's being those of Osiris (water), Geb (earth), Shu (wind) and Khepera (light/fire) (see J. Assmann, *Re und Amun*, p.263).

[774]   See below p.208n.

X,149), for instance, it is stated that Heaven (Dyaus) and Earth (Prithvī)
emerged from the primal waters or the watery substratum of the universe.
AV IX,5,20 describes Earth as the waters' breast and Heaven as the waters'
back, showing that the two realms are surrounded by the waters. In the *BrdP*
I,i,3,32ff. and the *VP* 84a, the Egg is said to be surrounded by seven sheaths,
the innermost being constituted of water, and the other of fire, wind, ether,
egoity (ahamkāra, bhutādi), Mahat (the subtle element of Nature) and,
finally, the Pradhāna (the principle of Nature itself).

That this universe which emerges from the Egg will be withdrawn
and then re-emitted by the deity after uncountable ages in a sort of divine
inhalation and exhalation is suggested by *MBh* 12,36:

> I am Hiranyagarbha, the god ... becoming manifest I am
> perpetually standing in the sky, then, at the end of a thousand
> mundane periods [yugas] I shall draw together the world again;
> having made the beings, the stationary as well as the movable,
> [reside] in myself, I shall ... drive [them] asunder and make here
> the whole world again.[775]

In *LP* I,20,80-6, the seed arises from Agni/Shiva's phallus[776] and is said to
have been placed in the womb [navel] of Vishnu [the macroanthropos, who
is the tāmasic form of the supreme deity and lies in the cosmic streams which
develop into Earth][777] and that golden seed became an egg which floated in
the waters for a thousand celestial years. Just as, in the Orphic cosmogony,
the Egg is split by the wind-serpent which surrounds it,[778] here the Egg is split
by a wind (Vāyu/Enlil) into two, the top half becoming the sky [Heaven] and
the lower half the Earth, while the yolk turns into a golden mountain (from
which the sun will emerge into the Mid-region of our universe). Finally, at
sunset [the hour of Atum, the perfected sun-disk], the Lord of Hiranyagarbha
is born.[779] Since sunset is the moment of the descent of the sun into the
underworld [Earth] in Egypt, we may assume that this form marks the first
birth of the solar force, Agni, as Varuna/Osiris, the sun of Earth.[780]

---

[775] Cf. *BP* III,11,22-32.

[776] We remember that Chronos is considered to have produced the Cosmic Egg in the Greek cosmogonies.

[777] Enki is similarly identified with Antum (see above p.142).

[778] See below p.147.

[779] See above p.108.

[780] See below Ch.XVII.

In the *KB* VI,1-9, however, the seed of Prajāpati is said to develop into a creature with a thousand eyes and feet, that is, a macroanthropos. But this macroanthropos is Brahman and not the primal Ideal Man, Purusha. Indeed, we find a similar conception of the cosmic light in anthropomorphic form in the Orphic Phanes. The depiction of Brahman as a child atop the Tree of Life[781] shares in the same imagery.

In Egypt, the Cosmic Egg is sometimes said to be formed by Geb and Nut themselves,[782] for, as we have seen, Geb is himself identified with Kronos by Plutarch.[783]

In the Heliopolitan theology, Atum as a primal god impregnates Earth (Mehet Ouret, the Great Flood) who comes into existence "in order that [Atum] might rest upon her" (CT 79 II24f-25e).[784] Mehet Ouret is thus the same as Huhet who represents the "flood" in the Ogdoad. The form in which Atum rests on Earth is as the Cosmic Egg which consists of the eight primal elements of the Abyss, since he declares that "my egg is solid on the vertebrae of Mehet-ouret" (CT 647 VI 267f-g).[785] The Cosmic Egg is said to be formed particularly in the Isle of Flames.[786]

That Atum here is another name for Amun is made clear from the fact that Amun is depicted as uniting with the waters which surround him and thereby producing a Cosmic Egg constituted of the elements of our universe.[787] The "seed of the eight primeval gods" of the Ogdoad is the potency of Amun himself,[788] who is said to have formed his own egg, "knit his fluid together with his body to bring about his egg in isolation".[789] The eight, or rather four dual-, gods who represent the essential constitutents of the Egg are Nun-Nunet, the Abyss itself with its heavenly waters;[790]

---

[781] See below p.171.

[782] See E.A.W. Budge, *op.cit.*, I:95.

[783] See above p.143.

[784] See S. Bickel, *op.cit.*, p.65.

[785] *Ibid.*, p.66.

[786] See K. Sethe, *op.cit.*, p.49; cf. the development of Skanda/Ninurta in the lake of reeds atop the 'white mountain' in the Purānas (see below p.240).

[787] That is why the Egg is said to arise from the waters of Nun (see K. Sethe, *op.cit.*, p.62).

[788] 'Hymn to Amun', Pap. Harris, in K. Sethe, *op.cit.*, p.80.

[789] Pap. Leiden I 350 (Ch.40), in J.P. Allen, *op.cit.*, p.49.

[790] Nun-Nunet, the primeval waters of the Abyss, are related to the waters of the underworld (see K. Sethe, *op. cit.*, p.64) as well as of Heaven. Cf. the Assyrian exegesis of "heaven" as being constituted of "waters" ('ša me') in K 170+Rm 520 rev. l.6 (see A. Livingstone, *op.cit.*, pp.30ff.). Nun is the lord of the Chaos/Chasm of Hesiod's *Theogony*, ll.116ff.

Huh-Huhet, representing the flood which forms Earth;[791] Kuk-Kuket, representing Darkness,[792] and Amun-Amunet, representing the essential Soul as well as the Light of Atum.[793] These prime elements are indeed the same as the original constituents of the Abyss but now concentrated in the seed which springs from the phallus of the primal macroanthropos to produce the Egg.

The eight constituents of the Ogdoad are coagulated into the Cosmic Egg as a result of the impregnation of the "flood" by the fiery seed of Amun. Since the Egg is knit together by Amun as Ptah, the Ogdoad which constitute it are called the children of Ptah-Tatenen "who arose from his body" (Theb. T 87b),[794] though the inclusion of the epithet Tatenen is meant only to suggest the product of Ptah's fertilisation of the Egg rather than its cause.

Of the eight gods of the Hermopolitan Ogdoad, the highest aspect of the supreme deity, Nun, must correspond to the sattvic, most concentrated state of the supraconscious Lord, Amun. Thus it is Nun who addresses the first discourse to Atum that allows the latter to obtain self-consciousness.[795] This is no doubt the basis of the adoration of Enki (Osiris) as a god of wisdom. Also Nun, Nunet, and Thoth are sometimes grouped together as a triad, just as Amun, Amunet and Ptah are.[796] Thoth, as we have seen, is the formative aspect of Nun and closely associated with wisdom.

In Heliopolis, Nunet is indeed the watery substance of Heaven[797] and the solar force Atum develops therein. The soul (ba) of Nun is said to be Re, who arises from Nun.[798] In a Coffin Text, Atum too is said to be "floating" in the waters as a seed in its egg.[799] Atum (An/Brahman/Mitra) is also described in CT 80 as "being alone with the waters" at the beginning of the creation.[800] When it arises, the solar force rests on Mehet-ouret (the great Flood), who is a development of the second constituent of the

---

[791] See above p.108.

[792] Kuk and Kuket are the equivalent of Tartarus in Hesiod's *Theogony*, 119,721.

[793] Amun-Amunet are sometimes substituted with Kerh-Kerhet (see E.A.W. Budge, *op.cit.*, I, Ch.VII).

[794] See K. Sethe, *op.cit.*, p.43.

[795] See S. Bickel, *op.cit.*, p.30.

[796] See K. Sethe, *op. cit.*, p.77.

[797] See above p.107.

[798] *Ibid.*, p.36n.

[799] See J.P. Allen, *op. cit.*, p.14; cf. *BD*, Ch.15, and CT 714 VI 343 j-l, where he is referred to as "the one who is in his egg" (see S. Bickel, *op.cit.*, p.58).

[800] CT 80 (see J.P. Allen, *ibid.*, p.22).

Ogdoad, Huhu (the Flood), which forms Earth. Thus the sun is said to arise "on the back of Earth in the Lake of the Two Knives".[801]

Atum, the sun, rises out of the pitch darkness of Kuk, and the latter is indeed said to have made "light (i.e. the sunrise) and the sunset",[802] while his consort Kuket is the one who made "Night and Day".[803]

Amun indeed provides the light and life which vivify these primordial powers of the golden Cosmic Egg, as the Theban stela of Satepihu to Onuris, with attributes typical of Amun-Re makes clear:

> his radiance causes there to be light for his Ennead,
> they come to life when they see through him[804]

Indeed, the eight primeval gods are themselves a form of Amun, as we note in the inscription in the Mut temple in Karnak: "[his first form] was the eight primeval gods, until he realized himself as one of the eight gods through [his] determination when he reappeared in the primordial beginning [that is, as the divine light]".[805] In the Ramesside Amun theology, too, which syncretizes elements of the Heliopolitan, Memphite and Hermopolitan/Theban theologies,[806] the constituents of the Cosmic Egg are considered to be the eight primeval gods of Hermopolis.[807] We have seen that Amun as vivifier of the eight gods is called Tatenen (Ptah),[808] the god worshipped especially in Memphis. Later Amun emerges as the solar light Atum (the Bull of Heaven or the Bull of his Mother), which finally manifests itself as the sun.[809]

The solar god is said to be formed through the unification of the four male deities, Nun, Huh, Kuk, and Amun into a black Bull, while the four female deities merge into the form of a black Cow (Hathor). The Bull is the personification of the "spirit of life" which impregnates the Cow (extended

---

[801] See K. Sethe, *op. cit.*, p.80.

[802] See K. Sethe, *op. cit.*, p.76.

[803] *Ibid.* The soul (ba) of Kuk is said to be "Night" (see K. Sethe, *op.cit.*, p.36n). In one instance, Nun and Nunet are represented with the same sign denoting Night that Kuk and Kuket also are (*ibid.*, p.66n).

[804] See J. Assmann, *op.cit.*, p.103.

[805] See K. Sethe, *op. cit.*, p.81.

[806] See J. Assmann, *op.cit.*, p.160

[807] *Ibid.*

[808] E.A.W. Budge, *op.cit.*, II, 7.

[809] Pap. Leiden I, 350, Ch.80, in J.P. Allen, *op.cit.*, p.50.

Earth) in "the waters in the Lake"[810] to create the solar god, variously represented as a scarab (Khepera) or Osiris-Horus (Varuna-Mitra). In Heliopolis, similarly, Re is also called "the Bull of the body of the [Great] Ennead, who generates himself within the egg" [811]

The cosmic aim of the creator-god is not merely to create the cosmos but also to form the light of the cosmos. The eight gods of the Ogdoad are thus called the "Fathers and Mothers" of light,[812] just as the ancestry of An, the god of the light of the heavens, is constituted of "21 fathers and mothers" in the Babylonian god-list 'An=Anum'.[813] The fact that Dyaus/ Anshar, though signifying Heaven, is prior to the Cosmic Egg makes it clear that the primal Heaven is not manifest light like Āditya/An. Apart from the essential Darkness (Kuk) which characterises the egg, we find certain Theban texts which refer to the "invisible egg"[814] reaching the Isle of Flames (or the primordial Hill) which is found in the Lake of the Two Knives to create light there.[815] They are also said to let the sun-god appear from a lotus (Geb) in the waters.[816] From our knowledge of Purānic cosmogony, we will realise that the "sun" here is the same as Brahman, the Light of the cosmos, rather than the sun of our system. Also, the 'Lake of the Two Knives' with its fiery island or primordial hill is related to the fiery golden seed of Agni/ Shiva in the Indic literature, since it is this which produces both a "white mountain" (*MBh* III,218,27-30)[817] and a lake of golden lotuses (*MP* 158,27- 50; *PP* V,41,118-42). The lotus itself represents Earth, the material matrix of a universe (there being innumerable other universes that arise from the supreme deity).

In Mesopotamia, there is little reference to a Cosmic Egg, though the deities called Enshar-Ninshar (lord and lady of the 'Circle') in the An-Anum god-list may possibly refer to an embryonic formation of the light of the universe. In the An-Anum god-list, the set of gods, Duri-Dari, is in

[810] See K. Sethe, *op.cit.*, p.85.

[811] See J.Assmann, *op.cit.*, 114.

[812] Theb. T95c, 96g.

[813] The Sumerian god of the cosmic light, An-Girra, is clearly a solar god like Atum-Re and not a mere sky-god, as his name seems to suggest.

[814] See K. Sethe, *op.cit.*, p.79.

[815] *Ibid.*, p.50, p.80. One is reminded of the Purānic account of the lake surrounded by fire in the *AB* (see below p.239).

[816] *Ibid.*, p.50. Atum is said to rise from a lotus in the abyss before heaven and earth were formed in PT 1587a-d. Re is represented with a lotus at his nostrils called the "soul of Re" (see R.T. Rundle Clark, *op.cit.*, p.67), that is, the universe itself that is animated by the divine soul.

[817] Cf. *SP* I,2,29,81-210.

fact followed by three pairs, beginning with the Enshar (lord) and Ninshar (lady) of the Circle,[818] and continuing with the Circles of Heaven (Anshar) and Earth (Kishar).

The Cosmic Egg is a feature apparently lacking also in the Hurrian epic of the Kingship in Heaven. However, in the epic, Kumarbi is impregnated with the seed of Anu.[819] The fact that Teshup and his brothers develop in the belly of Kumarbi suggests that the latter serves as the androgynous matrix of the emergent cosmos. This is the same as the impregnation of the Purusha in the Purānas, since, as we have seen, Kumarbi/Chronos is the same as Alalu deposed to Earth. The result of the impregnation of Kumarbi is that Teshup, the Weather-god (Zeus/Seth), along with the other gods of the Mid-region including Tashmishu (Suwalliyat, the sun-god/Horus the Elder), and Marduk are formed in the belly of Kumarbi.[820]

The mythological representative of the Cosmic Egg itself in the Hurrian epic may be the figure of Uppelluri (a product of Kumarbi corresponding to the Greek Atlas). Uppelluri, who bears on his shoulders Heaven and Earth as well as, later, Ullikummi, the phallic stone representing the starry Mid-region, may indeed be a personification of the Cosmic Egg, which also bears Heaven and Earth in itself. This possibility is reinforced by the fact that in RV X,121,1, Hiranyagarbha is apostrophised in a quasi-anthropomorphic way as one who "holdeth up this earth and heaven".

In Hesiod (*Theogony*, ll.459ff), the impregnation of Chronos is suggested in the ruse devised by his consort Rhea to prevent him from swallowing his children. She forces a "stone" into her husband which he mistakes for his child and this saves the life of the infant Zeus.[821] But this stone is none other than the castrated phallus of Ouranos itself.

In the Orphic theogonies, the Cosmic Egg is formed by Chronos out of Aither (Dyaus) and the Chasm (the Abyss).[822] The egg is surrounded by a serpent which breaks it by squeezing. In Epiphanius' account of Epicurus' cosmology, the serpent encircling the egg is itself constituted of wind.[823] The association of the egg with wind is also made clear in the description of Chronos' giving birth to "Eros and all the winds" in an Orphic poem

---

[818]   See the similar appellation of Amun as the "Circle" in the Egg, above p.99.

[819]   See H.G. Güterbock, "Hittite Mythology" in S. Kramer, *op.cit.* .

[820]   Teshup, Tashmishu, and Marduk correspond, as we shall see, to the Egyptian Seth, Horus the Elder and Horus the Younger.

[821]   See below p.211.

[822]   See M.L. West, *op.cit.*, p.70.

[823]   *Ibid.*, p.202.

quoted by Apollonius Rhodius.[824] In the cosmogonies of Hieronymus and Hellanicus, Chronos, who springs from the waters, produces the egg.[825] Again, though there is no reference to the formation of the divine light in a Cosmic Egg in Hesiod, in the Orphic account of Protogonos, Phanes is represented as being born of an egg.[826]

Since the eight elements, or Ogdoad, which constitute the Cosmic Egg in Egypt are also the first elements of the cosmos itself, they correspond to the first elements of Hesiod's cosmogony as well.[827] Thus, the Hesiodic Chasm (or the Abyss, the Babylonian Apsu), Earth, the darkness of Tartarus, which is loosely understood as a region of Earth, and Eros (Desire/Agni-Varuna/Enki) correspond to the four Hermopolitan ones, Nun-Nunet (Heaven), Huh-Huhet (Earth), Kuk-Kuket (Darkness) and Amun-Amunet (Light/Atum). We see that Eros' identity with Amun and equally with Phanes is a further explanation of the typical Upanishadic identification of Ātman with Brahman.

We have observed in *RV* X,129 that Kāma (Desire) is a primal element in Vedic cosmology identified with the fiery Agni which finally results in the heavenly light (Atum, An, Brahman). This confirms that the first creative impulse of the Lord of the Abyss (Enki) is Desire and his fullest manifestation is as the Light of the Cosmos (An). Eros must be the same also as Heraclitus' Fire and the 'constructive Fire' of the Stoics.[828] It must be the fiery agent too which infuses the matter of the Chasm/Abyss as wind to engender the cosmos.

In the Orphic cosmogony,[829] Eros is used as a name of Phanes, or Protogonos, himself, so that the desiring god of creation, Amun-Re/Nun-Osiris/Enki/Varuna, is identified with his luminous manifestation. Phanes is said to generate all the gods auto-erotically and, mating with his daughter Night, produces our heaven and earth, which emerge from the Cosmic Egg.[830]

---

[824]   *Ibid.*, p.200. Eros is the same as Phanes/Brahman (see below Ch.XII).

[825]   See *ER* IV,126.

[826]   See M.L. West, *Orphic Poems*, p.70; cf. fn below for the reference to the birth of Eros from a "wind-egg" in Aristophanes.

[827]   See Hesiod, *Theogony*, ll.116ff.

[828]   See A.B. Cook, *Zeus*, I, p.28f.

[829]   Laitos (784 F2, 4-6) states that Orpheus himself derived his theology from Sanchuniathon of Beirut (see M.L. West, *Orphic Poems*, p.177), just as Pherecydes obtained his from the Phoenicians (see above p.139n).

[830]   In the mock-cosmogony of Aristophanes' *Birds* (693ff.), Eros (Phanes), born of the "wind-egg", mates with "winged Chaos" [=Chasm, Nun] to produce the gods (see M.L. West, *op.cit.*, p.111). The gods created by Phanes must be the same as those created by Brahman

The supreme lord of the Zoroastrians is Ahura Mazda, who is the creator of the Heaven and Earth[831] that informs the Cosmic Egg. The interpretation given to the term 'ahura' by the ancient Persians was, according to Herodotus (I,131), "the circle of heaven",[832] which seems to follow the Sumerian "Anshar". It may be assumed that by 'ahura' is meant 'Ahura Mazda'. The "Circle of Heaven" (Anshar) itself is the "Boundless Light" in which he dwells.

In the *Bundahishn*, Ch.I, the original dwelling of Ahura Mazda is called the Boundless Light. The opposite of this is the Darkness in which Ahriman (Angra Mainyu) resides.[833] In the Avesta (Yasna XXX,3), Spenta Mainyu (who is Ahura Mazda's creative aspect) and Angra Mainyu, who is his antagonist,[834] are said to be two primordial spirits of good and evil, who are both created by Zurvan (Chronos/Time).[835] In the Avestan Farvardin Yasht 2 and 28 we learn that Heaven is formed by Ahura Mazda's creative aspect, Spenta Mainyu, who is identical to Tvoreshtar, the creative aspect of Purusha, the macroanthropos. Ahura Mazda is the ruler of Heaven just as his counterpart Angra Mainyu is that of Earth.

In the *Bundahishn*, heaven, or the "sky", within the Cosmic Egg is described in the following manner:

> First [Ahura Mazda] created the sky, bright and manifest, its ends exceeding far apart, in the form of an egg, of shining metal that is the substance of steel, male. The top of it reached to the Endless Light;[836] and all creation was created within the sky … The vault of the sky's width is equal to its length, its length to its height, and

---

(see below p.172). However, we have seen that the ideal sense-faculties and organs of the Cosmic Man are also considered to be "gods" (see above p.100).

[831]   Inscription of Darius (Dna 1-12,30-35,47-60; cf. W.M. Malandra, *op.cit.*, p.50).

[832]   The objection of linguists to the derivation of the Skt. "asura" from "aššur" based on the phonetic transformation involved (so, for instance, H. Sköld, "Were the Asuras Assyrians?", *JRAS*, April 1924, p.266, and W.E. Hale, *Asura in Early Vedic Religion*, Delhi: Motilal Banarsidass, 1986, p.37) is resolved by I. Gelb's evidence of the change of š to s in the term "šubaru": "in the old Akkadian and old Babylonian period … while the Assyrians keep to š … the Babylonians from the Kassite period on begin to spell the name of the Subarians with s" (*Hurrians and Subarians*, Chicago: University of Chicago Press, 1944, p.30). J. Przyluski, "Devas et asuras", *Rocznik Orjentalistyczny* 8 (1931–2), p.26, too maintained the derivation of "asura" from "aššur".

[833]   See R.C. Zaehner, *op.cit.*, pp.34f.

[834]   See W.M. Malandra, *op.cit.*, p.19.

[835]   See above p.143.

[836]   The dwelling of Ahura Mazda.

its height to its depth ... Like a husbandman the Spirit of the Sky is possessesed of thought and speech and deeds, knows, produces much, discerns... And to help the sky [Ahura Mazda] gave it joy, for he fashioned joy for its sake.[837]

The sky, which is male, produces water and, from water, earth.

In the Avesta, Earth is regarded as a Cow created for the "husbandman and the herdsman", through a "manthra (sacred prayer/brāhman) of butter and milk". The Cow itself is said to have been first gained by Zarathusthra, along with the Word, Obedience to the Word, and Dominion (Farvardin Yasht XIII,88). It is likely that Zarathustra, "the first priest, the first warrior, the first agriculturist" (*ibid.*),[838] is indeed the same as Ziusudra, another "first man", or Manu, but one appearing at the deluge that precedes the emergence of the sun in our system. Ziusudra is, as we have seen, identifiable with Ninurta, the solar force.[839] And the Cow obtained by him may be understood as the material universe to be peopled by the seed which he preserves during the deluge and allows to be purified in the sun.

In the *Bundahishn*, Ch.I, Earth is said to be particularly metallic in constitution (23-4), which bears a resemblance to Ninurta's formation of earth with metallic elements in *Lugal e.*[840] After the formation of the sky (Heaven/Dyaus), water is created and then earth, plants, cattle (represented by the seed of the Bull of Heaven), mankind (represented by the seed if the First Man, Gayomaretan),[841] and finally fire (18,19).

In the Avesta, Vāyu is celebrated in the Ram Yast, XI, 43, as the deity who "goes through (vyemi) the two worlds, the one which the Good Spirit [Spenta Mainyu/Ahura Mazda] has made (i.e. the Boundless Light) and the one which the Evil Spirit [i.e. Angra Mainyu/Ahriman] had made (i.e. Darkness)". The Zoroastrian conception of the wind-god as a warrior god who battles the devas (gods). Ram Yast (XI) is indeed diametrically opposed to the Vedic understanding of Indra, the leader of the gods, as a friend of Vāyu. On the other hand, it may be close to the Sumerian account of Enlil's opposition to the gods in *Atrahasis.*[842]

---

[837] See R.C. Zaehner, *op.cit.*, p.39.

[838] These represent the three ancient Iranian "castes".

[839] See above p.82

[840] See below p.298.

[841] Gayomaretan is called the first Aryan as well, though he is to be distinguished from Yima (see below p.313).

[842] See below p.161.

In the Edda ('The Deluding of Gylfi', 'Voluspa'), the first of the regions to be formed from the Abyss, or Ginnunga-gap, is Muspell, which is called a "southern" region of burning fire and ruled by Surt (a name that may be related to Asura). This may correspond to Heaven. It may have been considered to be "southern" only because the deity's navel from which the Cosmic Egg emerges is to be considered to be at a higher level than the Egg itself. We will note that the Tree of the universe is also considered to be upside down, with its roots in heaven and its branches in the Mid-region.[843] That Muspell is in fact Heaven is made clear by a later reference to it, in the same work, as the realm of the Aesir, the gods, "in the sky", where the third root of the Yggdrasil ash rests.[844]

The second region to be formed of the Ginnungagap is called Niflheim, which is the counterpart of the lower levels of Earth, the underworld.[845] It is considered to be a lifeless region characterised by ice and frost, and not yet illuminated by any solar force.

The Mid-region is the Ginnunga-gap itself, since, as we have seen from the Iranian evidence, it is still void.

---

[843] See below p.273.

[844] See *The Prose Edda*, p.43.

[845] See "The Deluding of Gylfi", in *The Prose Edda*, p.31.

X: ASURA

THE EXPANDING COSMOS: ANSHAR-KISHAR, ANSHARGAL-KISHARGAL

In the An=Anum god-list, after the reference to Enshar and Ninshar, come the circles of Heaven (Anshar) and of Earth (Kishar), and the great circles of Heaven (Anshargal) and of Earth (Kishargal). The fact that Anshargal follows Anshar suggests that the Cosmic Egg is now in a process of expansion. Anshargal-Kishargal are followed by UrashIB and NinIB, representing Earth, and a final phase of united Heaven and Earth called Anki.[846] for all these stages are composed of Heaven and Earth (An+Antum=Heaven+Earth).[847] These circles of Heaven and Earth within the Cosmic Egg are, of course, to be distinguished from the primal Heaven and Earth which constitute the substance of the macroanthropos. These five sets of deities after Duri-Dari correspond to the Heaven and Earth which are said to be the principal elements of the Cosmic Egg in the Vedic literature.[848] Also, as we have seen, Heaven and Earth are the major components of the egg in the Iranian *Bundahishn*.[849]

In the Old Babylonian Sumerian god-list, the chthonic epithets of the primal Enki, Urash and En-uru-ulla, are followed by Anshargal, the Great Circle of Heaven[850] and, then, by the light of the universe, An.

---

[846] See W. Lambert, *op.cit.*, p.54.

[847] Cf. CT 24.1,8; 19 Col.I, 4; 20, 6a: An-sar: A-nu-um u Antum. Anshar, the circle of Heaven, may be distinguished from the term for the universe itself, Esara, the house of the universe (K 3445+R 396; CT XIII, 24f.), since the latter includes its own heaven, earth, and mid-region.

[848] See above p.148f.

[849] See above p.156f.

[850] Anshargal, the great circle of Heaven, corresponds to the great circle of the cosmos after its expansion by Enlil.

In the Babylonian ritual text A.O. 17626 (rev.), we find Enki followed by Anshar (Enlil).[851] That the "circle of heaven" represented by Anshar along with his consort Kishar (Damascius' Assoros and Kissare) is a stage of the cosmos governed by the god of Wind, Enlil, is made clear from the identification of the two in CT 24,49,76.[852] In the Old Babylonian and Middle Babylonian god-lists, Enlil himself is derived from a primordial cosmic pair, Enki-Ninki.[853] We have already noted the Greek references to the "wind-egg".

In the Babylonian *Enma Elish,* Anshar is the father of both An (the divine light) (I,14) and Enki (lord of Earth) (II,8).

The Assyrians used Anshar as a glorificatory title of their principal god, Assur, and the equation of Assur with Enlil is evident from the fact that Assur's consort is indeed the same as Enlil's, Ninlil. Assur is indeed called the Assyrian Enlil.[854] In the Assyrian 'Annals of Salmanassar II', Assur is equated to Anshar, "the great lord of the totality of the great gods," and then followed by Anu, "the king of the Igigi and the Anunnaki".[855] Anshar, however, is clearly an earlier stage of the cosmic light An himself at a time when the heavenly element is not separated from the earthly (Anum u Antum). The deity that rules this stage of cosmological evolution is Enlil/Vāyu. Assur's persecution and trial of Marduk are depicted in the fragments relating to "Marduk's Ordeal".[856] Assur is representative of the Anunnaki of the *Atrahasis* episode mentioned above, as Marduk is of the Igigi, so the conflict between Assur and Marduk may betoken that between the Vedic Asuras and the Devas (gods).

---

[851]   See A. Livingstone, *op.cit.*, p.198f..

[852]   See A. Deimel, *Pantheon*, p.65.

[853]   See W. Lambert, *op.cit.*, p.51. Lambert's explanation of this Enki as different from the customary Enki is right insofar as Enki is different from Ea, though the two are indeed different forms of each other.

[854]   Sidney Smith attempted to connect Assur with Osiris as well as with Marduk (see S. Smith, "The Relation of Marduk, Ashur, and Osiris", *JEA*, 8 (!922), 41-44). "Ausares", which may have been the original Egyptian form of Osiris, may be related to the primal god, Varuna/Enki, but only indirectly to Enlil as an aspect of Enki. The identification of Marduk with Enki is made in the *EE* VII,120. The Eridu god, Asarluhi, who becomes identified with the Babylonian Marduk, may also have been a son of Enki whose name may have been derived from a lost epithet of Enki as 'Asar'/Ausares.

[855]   J. Hehn, *Die biblische und babylonische Gottesidee*, Leipzig: J.C. Hinrichs, 1913, p.92. Enlil is called "the father of the gods", since it is he who vivifies the constituents of the Cosmic Egg and sustains the universe which emerges from it. Anu, the divine Light, is considered to be one of the (heavenly) Anunnaki also in *Atrahasis* (see below p.136n); hence his appellation here as king of both the Igigi and the Anunnaki.

[856]   See A. Livingstone, *op.cit.*, Ch.VI.

In the Babylonian flood story, *Atrahasis,* I, Enlil is represented as the counsellor of the seven great Anunnaki (Vedic Asuras), against whom the oppressed gods (Devas) revolt. The Anunnaki are, especially in Assyrian times, associated with the underworld (Earth) and may have been consigned to it by An, the lord of heaven.[857] As underworld deities, the Anunnaki come to possess a chthonic or matter-related character and will be typically associated with Nergal, the sun of Earth. A similar phenomenon is observable in the case of the Vedic Asuras who were denigrated to the status of demons. The Devas, or gods, ruled by Indra and led by Shiva's martial and solar son, Skanda (Muruga/Marduk),[858] are the equivalents of the Igigi.

It is possible that in Sumer itself there was originally an equal reverence for both the Igigi and the Anunnaki as gods of our heaven and earth.[859] In Zoroastrianism, on the other hand, only the Ahuras are deemed worthy of worship, while the daivas are considered demoniacal forces. The Zoroastrian reform, as we have seen, is less interested in cosmology than in a stark dualistic ethics represented as a long battle between good and evil, the forces of Spenta Mainyu and Angra Mainyu, the Ahuras and the Daevas.[860]

We have seen, however, that Enlil governs the Anshar-Kishar stage of cosmic evolution. So it seems that Enlil (strictly the breath of the Cosmic Man, Alala and the impregnator of Earth) is still a powerful aspect of the deity at this early stage of the cosmic evolution. And since, as we have seen from the Greek evidence, Aither (the Heavenly constitution of the Primal Man) and Chronos (Kāla/Enki)[861] are related to each other, the three deities Enki, Enlil and An form an integral trinity.[862]

In the Vedas, the epithet Asura is used for the Ādityas (sons of Aditi)[863] as well as the Dānavas (sons of Danu),[864] and comes to mean, generally, the forces of the primeval cosmic realm that are superseded by the "Devas", the younger `gods', who convey the fiery power of Brahman to

---

[857] See the division of the cosmos in the fragment relating to the *EE* below p.319, where the Anunnaki rule lower Earth and the Igigi middle Heaven, while An rules upper Heaven.

[858] See below Ch.XIX.

[859] See the Etana Epic; also Maqlu II 138ff.

[860] See below p.189.

[861] See above p.145.

[862] See above p.109.

[863] The Ādityas are also the suns of the several galaxies which fill the mid-region between the heaven and earth of our universe (see below p.171n).

[864] See below p.292

the Mid-Region of our universe as well as to human beings.[865] Of the two types of Asuras, the Dānavas may correspond to the underworld Anunnaki and the Ādityas to the heavenly.[866]

The revolt of the leader of the gods, Indra, against the Asuras, as well as against the Asura Varuna[867] is no doubt undertaken to allow the solar energy to emerge through the interstices between the heavenly and the earthly elements. As a result of this conflict, the term "Asura" comes to have a pejorative connotation in India in opposition to "Deva". In Hesiod (*Theogony*, 630ff.) a similar contest between gods and Titans takes place which culminates in the victory of Zeus, chief of the gods.

The Asuras are represented as having been conquered by the gods and their leader, Indra. In *RV* X,157, for instance, the gods are said to have destroyed the Asuras and "brought the sun hitherward with mighty powers", the feat especially attributed to the chief of the gods, Indra. Indra's role as leader of the 'Devas' or gods may suggest a supercession of the Asuras' supremacy in the universe, just as Marduk is installed as leader of the Igigi (who correspond to the Devas) as distinct from the Annunaki (Asuras).

---

[865]   H. Zimmern (*op.cit.*, p.486) conjectured – erroneously – that the "daivas" in Zoroastrianism may correspond to the "Anunnaki" (typically underworld deities) of Sumerian myth, while the "Amesha spentas" are the counterpart of the "Igigi". The Amesha Spentas are in fact similar to the Indic Ādityas (see below p.232n).

[866]   See above p.105.

[867]   Indra particularly seems to supersede the primal Varuna in *RV* X,124,4; cf. below p.187.

XI: PADMA

THE MATERIAL MATRIX OF THE COSMOS: URASH/PTAH-TATENEN/GEB

The principal product of the Cosmic Egg is Brahman, the light of the cosmos. This light arises atop the material matrix called Earth which emerges from the Cosmic Egg in the form of a "lotus". In Egypt, the material matrix of the universe is considered to arise in the form of primeval "hill". This primeval hill which rises from the divine embryonic complex represents the phallic force [of Amun as Shu][868] and the core of the incipient physical universe. The hill is said to emerge particularly from the "navel" of the Lord.[869] The "primordial hill" and the "navel" represent the phallus and the womb of the supreme deity as macroanthropos. In Sumer, Enlil, who is commonly called the "great mountain" (signifying the 'divine phallus') is accompanied by a consort, Ninlil, or Ninmah, who is later called Ninhursag, "Lady of the Base of the Mountain".[870] This suggests that Enlil and his consort are, like Shiva and Pārvati, the basis of the manifest universe which emerges in the form of a mountain.

In the Purānas, the lotus formation of Earth contains *in potentia* all the 'jivas' (lives) of the universe. The division of Earth into seven "islands" is due to the whirling action of the first form of the Divine Light, Priyavrata.[871] It is atop the lotus that the Lord finally manifests himself as Brahman, the

---

[868]   The phallic role of Shu is shared by the Sumerian Enlil, who is typically called 'the great mountain' (see p.227 below).

[869]   We note that the "navel" and "mountains" are equally regarded by Hebrew commentators as having been created before the heaven and earth and light (see A.J. Wensinck, *Ideas*, pp.17ff.). The rabbis, however, with typical Hebrew anthropo- and geocentricism, consider the 'mountains' as terrestrial forms, rather than as forms of the incipient universe.

[870]   See *Lugal e*, ll.394-5 (cf. J. van Dijk, *op.cit.*, II:101). In India, many phallic stones are represented erect in a base which represents the vulva.

[871]   See below p.172.

light of the Mid-region (III,20,14ff.). In the *PP* I,39,153-4, the lotus is said to be blazing like fire and equal to the "goddess earth" (I,40,4). Its "filaments" are said to be the mountains on the lotus-formed Earth, the central one of these mountains being Mt. Meru (*BP* V,16,7) which is situated at the very centre of the innermost "dweepa" or island of Earth called Jambudweepa.[872] *BrdP* I,ii,15,18 declares that "it originated from the umbilical cord of Brahma [i.e. Purusha]", The sun arises from and is invisibly anchored to this mountain (*BP* V,21,7ff.; V,16,2).[873]

In *BP* III,10-12, the creation of the manifest universe is depicted in considerable detail. The "lotus" on which Brahman is born is violently agitated by winds (Vāyu). He therefore subdues the wind and swallows the water around the lotus, whereupon his lotus-seat fills the entire sky (III,10,7). At this stage he decides to divide the lotus into the heaven, earth and mid-region of our universe. The material grid of the entire universe is described in *BP* V,16, which details the "seven oceans" as well as "seven islands" of 'Earth' which constitute the galactic formations of the universe.[874] In *BP* V,17,11 Bhāratvarsha, the outermost region of the central island, Jambudweepa, is referred to as the only region in which lives may obtain merit or demerit through their karma.[875]

In the *RV*, the navel is also called the place of the "sacrifice", and the womb of Rta [Maat].[876] The Vedic sacrificial altar is thus considered as the womb of the entire universe which is ritually created and sustained by the Vedic priests. The navel of the universe is also the "sanctuary" of the original Abyss, and Eridu[877] may have been considered the earthly representative of the navel of the universe in much the same way that, much later, Jerusalem was considered the sacred sanctuary of Israel,[878] and Madurai of the Indic

---

[872] Cf. below p.316. In the *Bundahishn*, Ch.XII, Mt. Albûrz is described in the same cosmic terms as Mt. Meru, since it is said to be "around this earth and is connected with the sky" (3).

[873] In the *BrdP* I,ii,15,15ff., Mt. Meru is also called "Sumeru", which may well be the same as the Akkadian (hence proto-Dravidian) name for the land of Sumer, Šumeru.

[874] In the Avesta (for instance, Mihir Yasht [10], IV,15), the seven islands are termed "continents" and are called Arezahi, Sawahi, Fradadhafshu, Widadhafshu, Wouru.bareshti, Wouru.jareshti, and Xwaniratha. In the Babylonian map of the universe dating from the eigth or seventh century (see W. Horowitz, *Iraq*, 50 (1988), 147-66), the manifest universe is depicted as a land mass including all the known near eastern regions of Babylonia, Assyria, Elam, Urartu, and the Zagros, and surrounded by a river called "marattum", the "Bitter", which is probably the same as Okeanos surrounding Ge.

[875] The capacity of world-renunciation that informs the phallic symbolism of the ancient Indo-European religions is thus invested in man alone (see below p.302).

[876] See *RV* II,3,7; *RV* IX,72,7; *RV* IX,82,3; *RV* IX, 86,8.

[877] The original form of Eridu may have been Uru-du, meaning "good city".

[878] See A. Wensinck, *op.cit.*, p.15. Mt. Sion especially was considered the centre of the navel

Dravidian lands.[879] In the Sumerian myth of "Enki's Journey to Nippur", too, Enki is represented as raising the "city" from the Abyss as a mountain above the waters,[880] which is clearly symbolic of the first emergence of the universe. The sanctuary, the 'navel' of the macroanthropos, is associated with a high mountain that cannot be touched by the deluge and thus survives it. The ancient temple structures of India, Sumer and Egypt embodied the navel and the primeval hill in their shrine and tower respectively. Together they represent the entire universe.

In the Hebrew rabbinical tradition derived from the Babylonian/ Egyptian, the sanctuary (mountain) which we have discussed above is considered to be the seat of the First Man as well.[881] In the Kabbalah, for instance, the navel of the universe is considered the "throne" of the cosmic man, Adam Kadmon. We know that the mountain is but the core of the "lotus" formation of Earth which arises from the Cosmic Egg formed within the Ideal Man (who is different from the divine Light which emerges, also in anthropomorphic form, from him). That the kabbalistic "throne" is related to the phallic "mountain" represented by Enlil in Sumer is made clear by Sumerian enthronement rituals. During these rituals, the king receives the "me"s from Enki in Eridu, the crown from Sin in Ur,[882] the "princely clothing" from Inanna in Uruk and the throne from Enlil in Nippur.[883] The phallic mountain or "throne" of Enlil thus represents the first form of Earth itself.

In the Heliopolitan cosmology, Geb and Nut, who represent Earth and Heaven, are the first physical constituents of the Cosmic Egg, which, as we have seen, is formed by Geb himself. In the Egyptian *Book of Nut*, it is not Geb (Kronos) who swallows his offspring,[884] the "stars", but his consort the sky, Nut. Shu intervenes to allow the stars to be reborn in the Mid-region between Heaven and Earth.[885] The sun (that is, the solar

---

by the Hebrews. Some Moslem theologians transferred this centre to Mecca, though others continued to consider Jerusalem as the source of the creation, especially the Holy Rock, under which arises all the "sweet water" of the world (*ibid.*, p.33). The concept of "sweet" waters is clearly derived from the Enki/Varuna theology of Eridu (see above p.108).

[879]   See D. Shulman, *The Tamil Flood Myths*, pp.311ff.

[880]   See S. Kramer, *Sumerian Mythology*, 61ff.; E.O. James, *op.cit.*, p.139.

[881]   See A. Wensinck, *op.cit.*, p.21.

[882]   In the Babylonian astronomical text *Mul-apin*, the constellation Aldebaran, "the jaw-bone of the Bull", is identified with "the Crown of Anu" (see H. Wohlstein, *op.cit.*, p.94), which points to a lunar association of this constellation.

[883]   See J. Renger, *RLA* 5:129; cf. A. Annus, *op.cit.*, p.xx.

[884]   As in Hesiod, ll.459ff.

[885]   See E. Hornung, *Ancient Egyptian Books of the Afterlife*, p.116.

force, Re/Agni) is thus free to move in the heavenly substance of Nut. We note here that the separation of Earth from Heaven is here attributed to Shu.[886] However, Osiris is equally credited with the separation of Nut and Geb,[887] since Osiris is the solar form of Shu.[888] Osiris is also the god of Maat (Sum. me's), just as Shu is.[889] Atum too is sometimes associated with the separation of Heaven from Earth, since he is but the same as Horus the Elder-Osiris.[890]

Geb emerges as the rising Earth from which the material universe is formed. This is the same as the primordial hill from which the sun emerges, and this hill is encircled by the serpent Nehaher[891] (representing perhaps the wind-god Enlil)[892] surrounding Earth in serpentine form. Geb is called the leader of the Ennead, that is, of all the gods.[893] Just as in the Purānic and Iranian cosmologies, in Egypt, Earth, or the material universe, is represented as an island (covered with reeds) that emerges from the primeval waters. This is most clearly evident in the records of the temple of Edfu, which also refer to the island or mound as a "lotus" formation in much the same manner as the Purānas do.[894] This island is supposedly produced by the insemination of the embryonic material called 'bnnt' by the "seed of Nun".[895] The first occurrence after the emergence of the island is the creation of form, d̠t, and the spiritual essences, 'ka's.[896] However, it is possible that the deities called "Sages" preceded the formation of the island

---

[886] See S. Bickel, op.cit., p. 197f.; cf. E. Hornung, ibid.

[887] See E.A.W. Budge, op.cit., II:100.

[888] It is interesting to note that Tushratta in his letter to the Egyptian Pharaoh (Kn 27, l.87, see H.-P. Adler, Das akkadische des Königs Tushratta, p.221), calls on Amun and Teshup (Zeus/Seth) at the same time, indicating thereby the similarity of these two gods as well, since Seth is but the stormy aspect of Osiris (see below p.193) and Osiris is a form of Shu/Amun.

[889] This is another confirmation of the henotheism or pluriform monotheism of the Egyptian pantheon (see above p.17).

[890] See S. Bickel, op.cit., pp.182ff; see also Ch.XII below.

[891] See R.T. Rundle Clark, op.cit., p.171.

[892] We have noted above (p.154) the description of the serpent surrounding the Cosmic Egg as being constituted of wind.

[893] See J.G. Griffiths, op.cit., p.175.

[894] See E.A.E. Reymond, op.cit., pp.56ff.

[895] Ibid., p.64. The primordial constituents of the Egg from which Earth emerges are clearly the same as the Ogdoad of Hermopolis (ibid., p.70, p.76ff.).

[896] For a detailed account of the various stages of the formation of Earth and of the deities presiding over these see E.A.E. Reymond, op.cit., Chs.2-11.

itself.[897] These sages assume the form of falcons in the waters ("wāᶜret") and foretell the creation of the cosmos.[898]

As in the Indic records, Earth emerges in the form of a Lotus, "the Great Lotus that issued from the pool in the Island of the Two Flames,[899] the "Province of the Beginning which initiated light".[900] The island is also called the Island of the Combat,[901] perhaps referring to the impending attack on the divine light Atum/Brahman by the storm-force Seth/Ganesha.[902] This combat also seems to have entailed the submersion of Earth beneath the primeval waters so that it henceforth forms the Underworld.[903] This may be the reason why the place called "the Beginning of the Earth" was at the same time a burial place for Osiris.[904]

In the Heliopolitan theology, the island of Earth is represented rather as a mound that emerged from the primeval waters.[905] However, in the Edfu myth about "the Island of the Egg", it is revealed that the creation of the mound is a secondary creative act.[906] It is said to have been created by the deities called "shebtiw".[907] The Edfu records also refer to several "pāy" lands which emerge after the initial mound.[908] These may correspond to the the islands or continents encircling the central one in the Indic and Iranian cosmologies. There are also allusions to secondary "pāy" lands, which may represent the newly formed Earth after its initial submersion beneath the waters, since the defeat of the snake is necessary before the gods can occupy these lands.[909]

---

[897] *Ibid.*, p.66 (cf. above p.88f).

[898] *Ibid.*, p.96.

[899] The Island of the Two Flames is also to be found in the Hermopolitan theology (see K. Sethe, *op.cit.*, p.49). From the Edfu records we discover that the two "flames" are the source of the two blazing eyes of Atum/Brahman (see E.A.E. Reymond, *op.cit.*, p.83).

[900] *Ibid.*, p.68.

[901] *Ibid.*, p.107.

[902] See below Ch.XIV.

[903] *Ibid.*, p.127.

[904] *Ibid.*, p.117; cf. *BD* Spell 175, which refers to the disappearance of Earth under the waters after its first creation.

[905] *Ibid.*, p.59.

[906] *Ibid.*, p.93.

[907] *Ibid.*, p.139.

[908] *Ibid.*, pp.151ff.

[909] *Ibid.*, pp.194-6.

In CT 80 Geb is called the "lotus" on which Atum could find a seat.[910] The Edfu texts also confirm that the lotus serves as the throne of the solar god.[911] The Edfu description of the original island is also very close to the Hermopolitan since both call it the "island of the two flames".[912] The Edfu texts also associate the "island of the two flames" with the creation of light.[913] The Egyptian Geb/Tatenen (Earth) is, especially in *The Book of the Earth*, depicted in the depths of the Abyss receiving the incipient sun before it is ejected from the waters of Nun.[914]

The sun, or solar force, is indeed said to be born thrice, from Heaven as well as from Earth and from the Waters. Nut, the consort of Geb, is the first generatrix of the sun. In the *Book of the Day,* the sun is depicted as being born from the vulva of Nut and travelling towards her head where it is swallowed by the mouth of the sky-goddess.[915] In the CT 'Book of the Two Ways', however, it appears that the course of the sun born of the Heavens is one that takes it into the Earth, that is, the "underworld". Rosetau, for instance, is described as being "at the boundary of the sky" and contains the corpse of Osiris "locked in darkness and surrounded by fire",[916] Osiris' corpse being typically in the netherworld.

The god who rules Earth itself is called Ptah-Tatenen.[917] Tatenen is an aspect of Ptah as the "rising universe"[918] as well as as creator of gods and men.[919] In a hymn to Amun, the supreme god is described as having first assumed the form of the Hermopolitan Ogdoad and then that of Tatenen in order to bring forth the primeval gods.[920] Tatenen is identified also with

---

[910] See J.P. Allen, *op.cit.*, p.22.

[911] See E.A.E. Reymond, *op.cit.*, p.84.

[912] See K. Sethe, *op.cit.*, p.49; E.A.E. Reymond, *op.cit.*, p.70. Like the Purānic division of the lotus into seven islands, the Edfu records too mention several "pꜥy" lands which arise after the central island (iw) around it (see E.A.E. Reymond, *op.cit.*, p.171).

[913] See E.A.E. Reymond, *op.cit.*, p.68.

[914] See E. Hornung, *op.cit.*, p.102.

[915] *Ibid.*, p.117.

[916] *Ibid.*, p.11.

[917] See E.A.E. Reymond, *op.cit.*, p.63.

[918] Cf. H.A. Schloegl, *Der Gott Tatenen*, Freiburg: Universitätsverlag Freiburg Schweiz, 1980, p.71.

[919] See W. Helck, *Urkunden der 18. Dynastie, Übersetzungen zu den Heften 17-22,* 284 (cf. H.A. Schloegl, *op.cit.*, p.39).

[920] See J. Assmann, *Ägyptische Hymnen und Gebete*, Zürich: Artemis Verlag, 1975, p.315 (cf. H.A. Schloegl, *ibid.*, pp.75ff).

Geb in the "Book of Gates" (scene 51), and with Osiris,[921] since the universe which rises from the underworld is indeed the restored phallic force (Shu) of Osiris.[922] In the "Book of Earth" the identification of Tatenen and Geb with Osiris is glossed with the explanation that, while Geb is the name of the God of Earth itself, Tatenen is that of the god as hidden in the serpent,[923] that is, as the nascent universe.

The frequent epithet of Ptah, Tatenen, signifying "the rising earth" is a reference to the emergence of the extended universe as the "primordial hill" associated with Shu. In a Theban hymn from the time of Rameses II (Pap. Leyden I, 350), Amun is said to have transformed himself into Ptah-Tatenen "in order to give birth to the Primordial gods".[924] In the early dynastic 'Shabaka' text, it is stated that Tatenen is a name of Horus [the Elder] as the uniter of the two lands of Egypt,[925] that is, of heaven and earth,[926] an office equally attributed to Shu.

In the An=Anum list, after the Anshar/Anshargal (Enlil) deities, appears a pair representing the Earth (Urash IB),[927] which must represent the emergent universe. This is followed by the last cosmic stage in which Earth and Heaven are closely united within the Egg, Anki.[928]

[921] See J. Assmann, op.cit., p.146 (cf. H.A. Schloegl, op.cit., p.35).

[922] See below p.219.

[923] Tatenen, along with Geb, is closely associated with the snake which guards the solar force within its coils in the underworld (cf. E. Hornung, op.cit., p.100; H.A. Schloegl, op.cit., p.96). Tatenen is an aspect of Osiris, lord of the underworld, and helps bring forth the sun, Horus the Younger (see H.A. Schloegl, op.cit., pp.84ff., p.117).

[924] See M.S.-Holmberg, op.cit., p.168.

[925] Ibid., p.19; cf. also Pap. Berlin 3048,6,4ff (ibid., p.106), where the sun and moon are considered the two eyes of Ptah exactly as if he were Brahman (Prajāpati)/Horus the Elder himself.

[926] See below p.233.

[927] Urash is the Emesal dialectal form signifying Earth. Urash IB must be distinguished from Urash in the Old Babylonian god-list mentioned above p.100.

[928] See below p.181.

XII: BRAHMAN

THE DIVINE LIGHT AND INTELLECT:

RE-ATUM, HORUS THE ELDER, PRIYAVRATA, SUWALLIYAT, AN, PHANES

The final product of the Cosmic Egg is the perfect Light and Intellect of the deity called Brahman, who, like Atum, is said, in the Purāṇas, to be situated above the lotus growing from the navel of the Lord.[929] The current astrophysical investigations posit the first appearance of solar light at around 100 million years after the "big bang".[930] This primal light results from the coalescence of hydrogen gas clouds around the densest regions of dark matter which produces a nascent fireball about 200 times larger than our sun. This light is at first occluded by the hydrogen fog which still surrounds it, though it succeeds in burning it away through its intense radiation.[931] What modern scientists cannot know is that this dazzling effulgence born of the golden egg is also the Intellect, or Consciousness, of the cosmos.

In the *BP* XII,9,21, as well as in the *PP* I,39,103 Brahman (An/Mitra) appears as a child atop a fig-tree,[932] the Light being typically represented in ancient Near Eastern literature and art as arising from the branches of a tree.[933] The infant shape which the Lord assumes in these Purāṇas is said to be "the self of all", that is, of the universe, since he is but the manifest consciousness and brilliance of the Purusha.

---

[929] See below p.176.

[930] The "big bang" theory posits a primeval "fireball" which encompassed the entire universe in a state of utmost concentration before it exploded into the myriads of continuously "expanding" galaxies that constitute our universe. This fireball corresponds to the golden Cosmic Egg of the ancient mythologies.

[931] See T. Folger, *op.cit.*, p.42; cf. the references to Phanes being at first visible only to Night, and to Eros dispelling the darkness (below p.179).

[932] See S. Shastri, *op.cit.*, p.39; p.62.

[933] See below p.282.

Brahman/Mitra as the Lord of Creation is called Prajāpati, who is thus said to be produced within the golden cosmic womb, "Hiranyagarbha" (*RV* II,35,13).[934] In *KYV* VII,1,4, Prajāpati is used as a name of the primal Mitra/Vishnu, since he is said to have mated with his "mother" Aditi and thus created the world of the gods and the Ādityas. In *AV* XIX,53,8, Prajāpati, like Brahman, is called the son of Kāla (Chronos/ Shiva/Agni), since it is Shiva's castration of Varuna/Dyaus which produces the Cosmic Egg.

According to the *Manusmrithi*, when the Lord manifests himself as Brahman (also as a macroanthropos) from the egg, he creates the gods, the sacred sacrificial rite, the Vedas, the various qualities, and the castes. At this point, He divides his cosmic Self into male and female and creates the material phenomena of the universe.[935] In order to create beings, he first produces ten great Sages, as well as the seven Manus, the gods, and all the other lower forms of being.[936] The process of the creation of the physical universe is the same as that we have seen as emerging from the tāmasic Egoity of the deity in the *BP*. The divine Mind is said here to create "by modifying itself" (I,75) and its first product is the Ether (corresponding to Space), with Sound as its particular quality. From Ether modifying itself arises Wind, with its quality of Touch. From Wind arises Light, with its characteristic Colour, and from Light Water, with its quality of Taste, and finally, from Water, Earth, with its quality of Smell.

In the *BP* (V,1), the earliest form of the emergent light is represented by Priyavrata, the son of the first Manu, Swāyambhuva Manu. This Manu and his female half, Shatarūpā, join together sexually and from this very first sexual union is born Priyavrata (Protogonos, Phanes) and his siblings. It is Priyavrata who divides Earth into seven islands by riding around Mt. Meru in his chariot. Priyavrata is indeed the same as Dionysus.[937]

In the Egyptian Ramesside theology, the tremendous brilliance which emerges on the separation of Earth and Heaven is considered the "face" of the supreme deity, called, Atum, or, more precisely, Re (Aton), the full-fledged (noonday) sun. The term Atum ("the perfected") refers particularly to the perfected sun-disk at sunset, but it signifies more than the sun itself, being as it is the light of the cosmos. That Atum is not merely the sun is made clear by the fact that he is adored in the Edfu Temple as the "majestic

---

[934]   cf. *RV* X,121.

[935]   See *Manusmrithi*, I,i,32.

[936]   It is important to note that, in the *BP*, the sages precede the Manu's, since they are purely intellectual ("mind-born") creations of the supreme deity (cf. below p.208n).

[937]   See below p.181.

God who constantly shines with his two eyes [i.e. the sun and moon]",[938] which he acquires later, after the formation of the universe. Like the Orphic Phanes or Protogonos, Atum is also adored, especially in the New Kingdom and after, as the "boy in the heavens",[939] showing that Atum is the same as the manifest Heavenly Light, An, Brahman. Amun is addressed, also in the Berlin Papyrus 3055, 20,6/7, as "the divine boy from Hermopolis". This juvenile Amun is, more accurately, the "face" (Atum) of the supreme deity, the solar energy which manifests itself as Horus/Phanes/Brahman.

That Atum is utlmately the same as Amun, as well, is made clear by the fact that Atum is also called, much like Amun, "the God whose name is hidden"[940] and Soul.[941] It is interesting to note that Shamash too, in Babylon, sometimes bears the name "Amna",[942] which may be related to Amun. In the Heliopolitan cosmogony, Atum is, like the Hermopolitan Amun/Shu, worshipped as the creator of the entire universe since it is he who creates seed itself.[943] (Re, the other name of the solar force, is also adored as "the lord of Maat [Tefnut]"[944] just as if he were Shu) As creator of Earth, Atum is called "the great Bull" (Sarg CG 61032).[945] Also, just as Amun, Atum too is said to be the one whose "primordial liquid" created the egg.[946] As the head of the Heliopolitan Ennead, he is also the "creator of Heaven",[947] or of "the two heavens",[948] as well as "creator of heaven and earth" (Pap. Harris I, 25,5 and 27,5).

Amun, who represents soul, breath, and wind, is thus the spiritual source of the solar force Re, with whom he is often associated as Amun-Re. We may remember that the sky-god Horus the Elder (Mitra/An) was also

---

[938]   K. Mysliwiec, *Studien zum Gott Atum*, Hildesternberg: Gersternberg Verlag, 1979, II:191.

[939]   *Ibid.*, p.147.

[940]   Pap. Greenfield, in K. Mysliwiec, *op.cit.*, p.194.

[941]   *Ibid.*, p.201. It is clearly a lack of cosmological insight which prompted the peremptory substitution of Amun with Aton in the reign of Akhenaton (see S. Quirke, *op.cit.*, pp.167-9).

[942]   See A. Deimel, *op.cit.*, p.252. In Sippar, the city of the sun-god, too, we find the divine name "amnanu"; see H. Zimmern, "Religion und Sprache", p.487.

[943]   CT 306 IV 60e-f (see S. Bickel, *op.cit.*, p.38).

[944]   Pap. Boulaq 17; see A. Barucq and F. Daumas, *op.cit.*, p.193.

[945]   See K. Mysliwiec, *op.cit.*, II:180. Interestingly Atum is also called the "creator of Sound (=Earth)" (*ibid.*), which recalls Agni's appellation as Vāk, Sound or Speech, in the Vedas (see below p.231). The faculty of speech in the Ideal Man is also ruled by Agni (see above p.110).

[946]   CT 648 VI 270m-n (see S. Bickel, *op.cit.*, p.234). This identifies him with the Amun-Shu/Enlil stage of the cosmic evolution.

[947]   See K. Mysliwiec, *op.cit.* pp.143ff.

[948]   *Ibid.*, p.144.

identified quite early with the southern god Min,[949] who was a precursor of Amun. The entire cosmic odyssey is indeed a self-development of Amun into Atum as the light of the universe (Prajāpati/Brahman/Mitra/Āditya).

Atum is said in CT 76 to develop "out of the Flood (Hehu), out of the Waters (Nun), out of the Darkness (Kuk), out of the Invisible (Tenemu)",[950] which are the same as the Ogdoad of Hermopolis and the first elements of Hesiod. The last element in this Coffin Text is the supreme Soul of Amun himself. Sometimes Atum is said to arise from the floods of Hehu, Night (Kuk) and Trouble,[951] the significance of the last item being unclear. It is possible that the desire (Kāma/Eros) of the lord of the Abyss which produces Māyā (illusion) is understood here as a disturbance of the perfect repose of non-manifestation.

Atum is often described as being alone in Nun (CT 80II 33 e-f, CT 312 IV 75, B6c, CT 261 III 383 c-d).[952] In Sarg CG 41002 of the Bubastidic-Saitic group, Atum is said to "repose in Nun in the arms of his mother Nut [Nunet]".[953] Atum is also represented as "resting" on the back of the heavens in the form of Mehet-ouret,[954] whose son is said to be Horus.[955]

Atum emerges from a lotus [Earth/the material universe of Geb] in the watery abyss, Nun. In the Edfu texts (III,186,4) we have a striking reference to the birth of the divine light from the lotus, "This august god who came into being in the Great Pool and was led forth from Nun within the lotus".[956] We remember the rise of Brahman from the lotus which grows from the navel of Vishnu, the supreme lord, in the Purānas. In STG no.69 III, there is a reference to the "living fire that came forth from Nun, who makes light for the heavenly people [the gods]".[957]

Atum's "birth" is also understood as a rise to consciousness (that is, to the eminence of Mind) of Re, the original name of the solar deity who lies inert in Nun until Nun speaks to him.[958] This elevation is due primarily to Heka (Brahmanaspati, lord of the Mind/Brahman/Mitra) as the "spirit of

[949] See above p.98n; cf. S. Mercer, op.cit., p.98.

[950] See J.P. Allen, op.cit., p.18; cf. K. Sethe, op.cit., p.72f.; cf. S. Bickel, op.cit., pp.46f.

[951] CT 76 II, 4c-d; see S. Bickel, op.cit., p.26.; cf. S. Morenz and F. Schubert, Der Gott auf der Blume, Berlin, 1953.

[952] See S. Bickel, op.cit., p.36f.

[953] See K. Mysliwiec, op.cit., p.143.

[954] See S. Bickel, op.cit., p.66.

[955] See A. Barucq and F. Daumas, op.cit., p.139.

[956] See E.A.E. Reymond, op.cit., p.82.

[957] See J. Assmann, Egyptian Solar Religion, p.104.

[958] See S. Bickel, op.cit., pp.30,36,46; cf. p.151 above.

light" inherent in the waters of Nun,[959] and allows the emergence of Atum-Re as the energy of the sun. From a hymn in the Darius temple it Amun-Re himself finally rises as the light to the heavens since he is said to "rise from the Abyss in the region of Hermopolis Magna" and is given the dominion of Heaven and Earth by Nut (Heaven).[960]

In Heliopolis, the principal sons of Geb (Chronos) and Nut are called Horus the Elder and Osiris. These are the twin aspects of the primal deity as the solar light, the former (Suwalliyat/Tashmishu/Shamash) being the first pure light, and the latter the moribund. Horus the Elder is generally understood as a sky-god, and his name has been understood to mean "face" (of the supreme deity) or "heaven".[961] It is more likely that the name is related to Iranian Hvare and Skt. Svarya /Sūrya ("the shining one", "the golden"), which denote the solar force. This is corroborated by the fact that the name Horus is sometimes coupled with the sign for "gold", which can also be read as "of the city of Ombos" (whose chief god was Seth, who represents his stormy aspect). After the 12th Dynasty, the customary interpretation of the name was as "the golden Horus".[962]

The resemblance of Horus to the Sumerian An is strengthened by the fact that, like the term "dingir" for An, the name Horus came to stand as a general determinative for god. The description of Re in the Suty-Hor hymn is also evocative of An's divine virtue as the light of the universe: "The brilliance of heaven is like your brilliance,/ Your colour shines more brilliantly than its skin".[963] Horus may thus be understood as the aethereal brilliance of Re.

Horus the Elder is the consort and son of Hathor.[964] Hathor's consort is particularly Horus of Edfu. Hathor is derived from Nut (who is the actual "mother" of Horus the Elder) and is said to be "the Great who lives in the seed in her name of Nut [the sky]" (Theb. T.283b,5).[965] This indicates that Nut is the same substance which turns into Hathor at the stage of the emergence of the divine Light, Atum. In fact, Hathor herself is a goddess

---

[959] *Ibid.*, p.90.

[960] See H. Usener, *op.cit.*, p.260.

[961] See S. Mercer, *op.cit.*, pp.96f.

[962] *Ibid.*, pp.77f.

[963] See J. Assmann, *op.cit.*, p.95.

[964] See S.Mercer, *op.cit.*, p.89. The Vedic and Purānic Vishnu too is considered to be at once the consort and son of Aditi (see below p.231f).

[965] The "seed" is that which first flows out from Amun (the Soul) and is the basis of the Cosmic Egg which is constituted of heaven (Nut) and earth (Geb) (see K. Sethe, *op.cit.*, p.177). It is possible that Hathor is related to the Vedic Aditi even linguistically, and its common interpretation as 'the house of Horus' a later imposed Egyptian one.

of the "sky" and both Nut the sky-goddess and Hathor are represented as a cow, though she symbolises the heavenly part of the Cosmic Egg, whereas Hathor represents the primordial matter of our universe.[966]

Hathor is characterised as golden, "the gold of the gods",[967] since the Cosmic Egg from which the Light emerges is a "golden egg" and she is the consort of the brilliant Horus the Elder. Since Nut is in turn a derivative of Nunet, the consort of Nun, Horus the Elder must be essentially the same as Nun (Osiris/Enki/Varuna), the husband of Nunet, but in his manifestation as the cosmic light (Brahman/Mitra/Vishnu). Hathor is thus also associated with (and probably a consort of) Min, the ithyphallic god of the south, the predecessor of Amun who was identified with Horus the Elder.[968] After the descent of the divine light into the underworld, Hathor becomes the mother of the sun, Horus the Younger, at which time she is identifiable with Isis, consort of Osiris and goddess of Dawn. Indeed Hathor's name could also mean "house of Horus".[969]

Exactly like Brahman in the Purānas, and Atum, Horus the Elder too is represented at Dendera as a child (or a serpent) resting on a lotus that rises above the water.[970] Like Osiris, Horus represents a later manifestation of the primal creator god Osiris/Enki infused with the life-force of Shu/Vāyu/Enlil.[971] Re is thus adored as the soul of Shu in his form as Horus the Elder. Re is also described as "He who raised heaven on high for the circuit of his two eyes", that is as Amun-Shu.[972]

At first, Horus the Elder is called "the Sightless", since the sun is formed in the firmament after the sacrifice of Osiris.[973] Later, he is called 'the two-eyed',[974] when the mature (Aton) and dying (Atum) phases of the sun of our system serve as his right and left eyes.[975] Sometimes his two eyes are

---

[966]   See M.E. Lefebure, *Le Tombeau de Seti* I, 1886, IV:XVff (cf. C.J. Bleeker, *Hathor and Thoth*, p.48).

[967]   See A. Barucq and F. Daumas, *op.cit.*, pp. 445ff.

[968]   See C.J. Bleeker, *Geburt*, p. 67; see above p.25.

[969]   See J.G. Griffiths, *The Conflict of Horus and Seth*, Liverpool: Liverpool University Press, 1960, p.13.

[970]   See C.J. Bleeker, *Hathor and Thoth*, p.63.

[971]   In an inscription on the walls of the temple at Ombos, he is identified with Shu; see E.AW. Budge, *op.cit.*, I:468.

[972]   AeHG no. 44 (see J. Assmann, *op.cit.*, p.77).

[973]   Pap. Bremner-Rhind (see R.T. Rundle Clark, *op.cit.*, p.92).

[974]   Pap. Bremner-Rhind, 34 (see J.P. Allen, *op.cit.*, p.28; cf. S. Mercer, *op.cit.*, p.125).

[975]   See below p.177.

represented by the sun and moon.[976] Though Horus the Elder is considered a brother of Osiris, the two are, in fact, one god. For, Osiris too is called the sky in a lament for Osiris, where Seth is said to have "felled the sky to the ground".[977] We shall see that Osiris is a son of Geb/Enki/Kumarbi/Kronos, who is overcome by Seth/Teshup/Zeus, another son of the same parent.

Horus the Elder is also called "the youth who emerges from the phallus"[978] which must be a reference to the phallus which produces the Cosmic Egg and emerges as the primordial hill, Geb. Horus' first appearance from the waters of Nun is indeed "on the high ground",[979] or the primeval hill representing the phallic force of Shu which holds the heavens and earth apart.[980] Then the sun rests on the Cow (called 'Mh.t-wr.t', the Great Flood) by holding on to its horns and swimming, as it were between them.[981] That the Cow is related to the Earth is made clear by the Hymn in the temple of the Great Oasis which states that the sun "appeared on the back of the Earth".[982]

Horus the Younger is, as we shall see, a rejuvenated form of Horus the Elder-Osiris, after the felling of the sky by Seth. However, he is often addressed in close association with Horus the Elder, since they are both forms of Shu:

> His magnificent image is the 'form of the god of the horizon' [Horus the Younger]
> ...
> Lord of the two divine eyes [Horus the Elder]
> In front of whom are the sun and the moon,
> His right eye and his left eye are Aten [the mature sun] and Atem [the setting sun].[983]

Ptah is equally identified with the light of heaven, just as Prajāpati is used as a name of Mitra/Brahman as the creator god. Though Ptah is typically the "body", of the supreme deity, he is also adored as the face of the deity. Thus in Pap. Berlin 3048, 6,4ff. it is said that Ptah's "right eye is the disc of

---

[976] See below p.260.

[977] Pap. Bremner-Rhind, 5,7,8 (see H. Te Velde, *Seth*, p.85).

[978] See A. Barucq and F. Daumas, *op.cit.* p.137.

[979] CT 335 (=*Book of the Dead*), 17, in J.P. Allen, *op.cit.*, p.32.

[980] See K. Sethe, *op.cit.*, p.79.

[981] *Ibid.*

[982] *Ibid.*, p.80.

[983] See A. Barucq and F. Daumas, *op.cit.*, p.167.

the sun, and thy left eye is the moon".[984] Similarly, Ptah is identified with Osiris and in texts of the New Kingdom he appears as the ruler of the underworld.[985] In a Coffin Text from the 21st dynasty, a falcon god is called Ptah-Sokaris, "great god, eldest son of Osiris",[986] showing that Horus the Younger, the solar offspring of Osiris, is equally a form of Ptah.

In the Hurrian poem of Ullikummi, Teshup is constantly seen in the company of his "pure brother" Tashmishu, the Hurrian form of Suwalliyat, the Hittite-Hurrian Sūrya.[987] Tashmishu and his stormy brother, Teshup, are the two gods of Heaven that are the Hittite counterparts of Horus the Elder/ Osiris and Seth. As in Egypt, Tashmishu (Horus the Elder), Saushga/Ishtar (Isis), and Teshup (Seth) are represented as going in search of the stone Ullikummi,[988] which is symbolic of the phallus of An castrated by their parent Kumarbi/Chronos.[989] The vital power of the phallus is that of Enlil, the wind-god, whose Emesal name 'Mullil' gives the divine phallus its name Ullikummi (Mullil of Kummiya).[990]

In the Sumerian cosmogony, An, the light of the heavens, is clearly the great light of the cosmos. Just as Mitra and Varuna are considered as forms of Agni,[991] so too, in an Assyrian exegetical text, An is identified with Girra, the fire-god.[992] In the Akkadian Akitu ritual too, the 'star' An is called "furious Gibil".[993] In the Late Babylonian period, the quality of An is described, in a temple hymn (A.O. 6494 and BRM. IV:8), as a "fearsome radiance" which may be identifiable with Mitra/Xvarenah of the contemporary Persians.[994] As the Mind or Intelligible Light, corresponding to the Vedic Brahman, however, An retains the power of the "word" and he is called the "word" of deities such as Enki and Sin, who are particularly identifiable with wisdom.[995]

---

[984] See M.S. Holmberg, *op.cit.*, p.106.

[985] *Ibid.*, p.100.

[986] *Ibid.*, p.133.

[987] See H.G. Güterbock, "The god Suwaliyat reconsidered", *RHA* 19 (1961), p.12.

[988] See H.G. Güterbock, "Hittite Mythology", in S. Kramer, *Mythologies*, p.168.

[989] See below Ch.XVI.

[990] Kummiya was the city sacred to Teshup. 'Kummi' is used in Tamil to designate a phallic-shaped grinding stone.

[991] See below p.306.

[992] See above p.145n.

[993] See F. Thureau-Dangin, *Rituels Accadiens*, Paris: Leroux, 1921, p.138f.

[994] H. Wohlstein, *op.cit.*, p.123.

[995] See H. Wohlstein, *op.cit.*, p.70.

In Assyria, Anu is called Essarhadon, "The First-born",[996] and this is the same as Protogonos, or Phanes, the first light of the cosmos.

Tammuz too is identifiable with the Osirian aspect of An since he is said to be destroyed by a "flood" and forced into the underworld.[997] Tammuz, who is normally one of the gatekeepers of heaven, thus bears the same solar force as Anu.[998]

We have seen that, in Greece, Chronos too was worshipped as Zeus Aitherios. Although it is strictly the "second Zeus", Dionysus, who constitutes the light of the cosmos,[999] the aethereal Zeus too is called "sun-eyed" in the Orphic hymns, as well as in Euripides, Aristophanes and Sophocles.[1000]

In the Orphic theogonies, the tremendous light of the ideal universe which is born of the Cosmic Egg and is adored as the lord of the universe is called Protogonos, or Phanes. He is, according to the Hieronyman theogony, at first visible only to Night and only after the two mate do Earth and Heaven emerge as manifest entities.[1001] In the pseudo-Lucianic *Amores,* Eros, who is the same as the Orphic Phanes, is apostrophised in the following manner:

> thou from obscure and disordered formlessness gavest form to everything. So from the whole world thou didst remove, as it were, a universal shroud of death, the Chaos which lay about it, and banished it to the furthest recesses of Tartarus.[1002]

We have seen that the initial obscuring of the light is also attested by modern cosmological research.[1003] This is reflected in the Hieronyman Orphic fragment (78) also, where Protogonos wheels round the world in his chariot to bring light to it.[1004]

In the Phoenician cosmogony of Sankuniathon, Aeon and Protogonos are produced by the wind Colpia and his wife Baau.[1005] These winds may be a reference to the wind-egg from which the light emerges.

---

[996] *Ibid.,* p.269.

[997] See below p.267.

[998] See O 175, l.9 (RA XVI, p.145) (see H. Wohlstein, *op.cit.,* p.100).

[999] See below p.180.

[1000] Orphic, Frag, 123, 6 (Abel); Euripides, Frag., Nauck, p.531; Aristophanes, Nub. 285f.; Sophocles, *Antigonae,* 102f. (see A.B. Cook, *op.cit.,* p.196f.).

[1001] See M.L. West, *Orphic Poems,* p.208f.

[1002] *Ibid.,* p.255.

[1003] See above p.171.

[1004] See M.L. West, *Orphic Poems,* p.214.

[1005] See Philo of Byblos, *The Phoenician History,* p.40f. Baau is clearly related to the "vavohu"

Like Phanes, the Thracian god Dionysus is also represented as a golden child.[1006] Dionysus is indeed considered to be a son of Zeus Aitherios and Semele. If we refer to Cicero's ennumeration of the different Zeus',[1007] we may consider Zeus Aitherios as the "first" Zeus and identical to Chronos. This Zeus marries Rhea and engenders Demeter.[1008] Then he consorts with his daughter Demeter (*Theogony* l.912) to produce Persephone. Zeus Aitherios also consorts with Semele to produce Dionysus (l.940), whom we have identified as the divine light, Horus the Elder/Brahman/An. Dionysus, according to Nonnos, is the "second Zeus".[1009]

The name Dionysus is derived from the name of the Thracian sky-god Dios, corresponding to the primal sky-god Zas[1010] (who, as we have seen, is the counterpart of Dyaus, the heavenly form of the Cosmic Man).[1011] And his name, when broken up as Dios Nysos, could mean 'God the son'.[1012] Dionysus is also commonly called "ὁ παῖς", the son.

Dionysus is another representative of the Osirian aspect of solar cosmology especially in his dramatic dismemberment and resurrection. Dionysus' destruction corresponds to the felling of Horus the Elder-Osiris, who is forced to descend into the underworld before he is resurrected.[1013] Phanes, as we shall see, is swallowed by Zeus Adados/Teshup/Seth. It is not surprising that Herodotus (II, 156) identifies Dionysus with Osiris. Plutarch (*De Iside et Isiride*, 364d) too expressly identifies Osiris with Dionysus. In a late Hellenistic Orphic hymn to Helios (fr.237), Dionysus is called the one who "first came to light, and was named Dionyus/ because

---

or "bahu" of the Hebrew Genesis 1:2 (see p.129n above).

[1006] Diodorus quotes an Orphic hymn to Helios in which Phanes and Dionysus are identified (see M.L. West, *Orphic Poems*, p.206).

[1007] *See Cicero, De Natura Deorum*, III,21.

[1008] See "Hymn to Demeter", 460ff.

[1009] See Nonnos, *Dionysiaca*, 10, 298. The third Zeus mentioned in Cicero, the Cretan Zeus, is the same as Dionysus (Osiris), since he is said to be the son of Chronos. Our sun, however, is the son of Hyperion (l.371) who is a Titan "brother" of Chronos (and consort of Theia).

[1010] See A.B. Cook, *op.cit.*, II, 277ff. The Hesiodic Zeus is a stormy solar deity distinct from Zas his forbear, who is the primal Heaven/Dyaus (see above p.139). The Hesiodic Zeus, as the son of the Titan Chronos, is the counterpart of Ganesha, son of Shiva, while his "uncle", the Titan Hyperion, father of Helios, Eos and Selene, approximates more to the figure of Brahman. Helios may be the same as Suwalliyat/Sūrya (bearing in mind that Greek always substitutes 'h' for Sanksritic 's').

[1011] See above p.137.

[1012] See A.B. Cook, *ibid.*, II, 288; there is in fact evidence that Pappas and Attis were Phrygian terms used for a god who, like Osiris, was reborn as his son (*ibid.*, 292ff.).

[1013] See below Ch.XVII.

he whirls (dyneitai) through infinite Olympus".[1014] This reminds us again of Priyavrata/Protogonos.

The Androgynous Prajāpati

We have noticed that the final stage in the An=Anum god-list before the rise of the divine Light, An, is the Cosmic Man as an androgynous unity of Heaven and Earth, Anki. Once manifest as the divine Light, however, An/Prajāpati, divides himself into two halves, male and female.

This is especially revealed in the Indic Purānas and the *Manusmriti*.[1015] In the *BrdP* I,ii,9, as well as in the *BP* III,12,49ff, after the creation of the seven sages, Brahma divides himself into the first Manu, Swāyambhuva, and Shatarūpā.[1016] Since androgyny is a quality of Shiva as Ardanarishvara as well, it is clear that the first Manu is the same as the Ātman, Shiva. In the *BrvP* IV,35,39, the male half of the androgynous Purusha or Shiva is called Kāma, which explains the erotic "unruliness" of the Hurrian KAL.[1017]

The resemblance of Indra/Inara to the androgynous Hurrian deity [d]KAL was noticed by P. Kretschmer.[1018] J. Przyluski too suggested that the Hittite deity Inara[1019] may indeed be a female version of the Indic Indra.[1020] It is possible that Inara was an androgynous deity, since the other form of this deity, [d]KAL, bears, in one Hittite tablet, the epithet 'innarawanza' alongside a [d]KAL 'lulimi', signifying that this deity is both male and female.[1021] The Indraic association of Inara is strengthened by its relation to the Hittite word "innarawant",[1022] which is the counterpart of the Sanskrit "indriya" (strength, the Greek equivalent being 'ανδρεία).[1023] This suggests that Indra

---

[1014]   See M.L. West, *Orphic Poems*, p.253.

[1015]   See above p.126. We may note also that Re in his solar aspect is typically represented by a beetle, which, according to the ancients, was androgynous since the male and female resembled each other so closely (see E.A.W. Budge, *op.cit.*, I, 356; cf. Porphyry, *De Abstinentia*, iv, 9).

[1016]   This act is reflected vaguely in the Hebrew Bible, which recounts the creation of woman out of the "rib" of the first man (*Genesis* 2:21-2).

[1017]   See below.

[1018]   See P. Kretschmer, *op.cit.*

[1019]   It is interesting that Inara seems to have been a Hattic (that is, proto–Dravidian/Hurrian) deity rather than a Hurrian or Hittite. See E. Laroche (*op.cit.*, p.83).

[1020]   See J. Przyluski, "Inara et Indra".

[1021]   See P. Kretschmer, *op.cit.*, p.300

[1022]   See p.114n above.

[1023]   See V. Machek, *op.cit.*, p.146. "Ina" means "strong" in Vedic.

is the same as the first Manu who is the same as the Purusha after he has divided himself into male and female. If so, his role as Angra Manyu,[1024] the fury which destroys both the male and female form of Brahman/Prajāpati, is a further evidence that the sacrifice of the First Man is, like that of the Purusha, a self-sacrifice.

This androgyny of the earliest cosmos is to be noticed also in the mythology of the Hurrians. Although the epic of the Kingship in Heaven recounts only the violence of Kumarbi, there is to be found, in another fragmentary Hurrian poem, another cosmic deity called, logographically, KAL, who is represented as an androgynous deity,[1025] although "kal" in Sumerian means "strong man, hero".[1026] Although this designation was mostly used for guardian spirits, it is possible that their original significance was a loftier one such as that of the first gods.

In the Germanic Edda, the First Man, or "giant", Ymir is killed by his great-grandson Wotan, who is the counterpart of the Iranian Wata/Vayu.[1027] The macroanthropomorphic Ymir[1028] who develops in the Mid-region, Ginnunga-gap, is the counterpart of the Prajāpati/Brahman, while his female partner Shatarūpa is represented in the form of a cow Audhumla, who feeds Ymir with her milk. Ymir and Audhumla thus are the Germanic forms of the First Man, Gayomaretan, and the Bull of Heaven, of the Iranian *Bundahishn*. This cow also produces, by licking the "ice-blocks", a man called Buri, whose grandson is said to be Odin (Wotan), the wind-god. We have seen that the Kassites called Vāyu Buriaš (Boreas).[1029] So we may assume that the Germanic Buri is the name of the first form of the wind-god, Vāyu, whereas Wotan/Wata is that of the same force that, much like Shu, later sustains our universe within the Mid-region between heaven and earth.

In the *Bundahishn*, the Bull of Heaven, which is the counterpart of the Germanic Audhumla, and representative of the pure animal life of the first creation, and the First Man (Gayomaretan), the counterpart of

---

[1024]   See below Ch.XIII.

[1025]   The logogram KAL may be read as either Lamma or Alad (See *RLA* VI:447f.). Under Tuthaliya IV, the oath-god ᵈKAL was worshipped as a male and provided with a wife, Ala (CTH 625; see D. Yoshida, *op.cit.*, p.327).

[1026]   See P. Kretschmer, *op.cit.*, p.303.

[1027]   See below p.214n.

[1028]   See S. Sturlusson, *The Prose Edda*, 'Gylfaginning'; cf. *The Poetic Edda*, "Grimnismol", 40-1. This Ymir represents the first Manu, Swāyambhuva, rather than the seventh who is called Yima/Manu in the Āryan tradition.

[1029]   See above p.127n.

Ymir, are both located "in the middle of the earth", in Airanvezh, which is considered as "the land of the Āryans".[1030]

___

[1030] See R.C. Zaehner, *op.cit.*, p.40. Thus Gayomaretan is also the first of the Aryas (Farvardin Yasht 87). The "land of the Aryas" refers to the Mid-region between heaven and earth as well as to the native lands of the Āryans.

XIII: ANGRA MANYU

THE PERSISTENCE OF THE VIOLENCE OF CHRONOS

The creator god who has newly split into male and female halves is attacked by one of his own offspring in just the same way as Ouranos was by Chronos. The violent story of the castration of Ouranos by Chronos is continued in the new cosmos by the stormy son of Chronos, Zeus. The rage of the storm-god is represented in the Indo-Iranian literature as a divine mania called Angra Manyu/Mainyu. In the Hurrian fragment discussed above, KAL is described as being "unruly" and finally deposed from his kingship of heaven by Enki with a punishment following this defeat involving mutilation.[1031] KAL is the same as Prajāpati/Brahman, and the Enki who is considered to have "deposed" KAL in the Hurrian fragments is seen to be related to the Kumarbi/Chronos who assaults Anu/Ouranos.[1032]

In the later Assyrian festival calendar V.A.T. 9947 from the time of Sennacherib, Anu is depicted as being subjugated by Enlil, and on the 24th day Enlil even "cuts off Anu's neck".[1033] Enlil is then enthroned in the temple-tower which is designated as the "grave of Anu (ki-mak sa d.An-im)".[1034] Enlil is also fearfully supplicated in the introductory hymn to Marduk in the Babylonian Akitu rituals, since his "anutu" or "anu-hood" is considered as a source of divine wrath, akin to the Indo-Iranian "manyu".[1035] We see here that Enki/Kumarbi is identical to Enlil, and the mutilation of KAL must correspond to the swallowing of the phallus of Heaven by Zeus.

[1031] See H.G. Güterbock, "Hittite Mythology", pp.162ff.

[1032] See above p.142.

[1033] Marduk, who becomes identified with Enlil, is similarly represented as cutting off Anu's neck (VAT 9947 obv., l.11; see A. Livingstone, *op.cit.*, p.127).

[1034] See H. Wohlstein, *op.cit.*, p.137.

[1035] *Ibid.*, p.96.

However, Zeus is indeed a counterpart of Teshup, the son of Kumarbi, so Teshup/Seth/Zeus too are related to Enlil. We see also why Enlil is frequently adored as a phallic force, or "kur (mountain)".

In the Babylonian flood story, *Atrahasis* (I,223), the god called Wê-ilu[1036] is represented as being sacrificed by the Anunnaki (Asuras) when the gods revolted against the Anunnaki.[1037] It is Enlil, besides, who demands this sacrifice (I,173). We shall see below that Marduk too is forced by Anshar/Enlil to suffer tortures in the underworld.[1038] Since Marduk is the life of the sun, it is possible that the sacrifice of Wê-ilu is related to the sacrifice of Horus the Elder/An and the subsequent rise of the universe and its sun. We shall see also that Enki however succeeds in salvaging the divine substance of the sacrificed god and in creating semi-divine life out of it.[1039] This is similar to Osiris' regenerative function in the "underworld". Wê-ilu, therefore, must be generically related to that of KAL and Manu Swāyambhuva.

In the Vedic literature, Shiva-Rudra is characterised by the violent rage called Manyu (*SB* IX,i,1,6). According to *SB* VI,i,1,2, when Prajāpati/Brahman desired to have union with his daughter, Dawn (who is related to Aditi, the primal waters, since Usha is a later form of Aditi), Rudra/Shiva is instructed by the gods to avert this incestuous intercourse,[1040] whereupon Rudra pierces Prajāpati with an arrow.[1041] The myth of Shiva's attack on Prajāpati for his incestuous intercourse with his daughter Dawn is a repetition of the assault on Ouranos by Chronos in the Hesiodic theogony. However, the seed of Prajāpati forms the solar force, Skanda.[1042]

Although Indra is distinct, as we have seen, from Angra Manyu, he is identified with Angra Manyu in *RV* X,83, as well as in *AV* IV,31,5.[1043] We

---

[1036] The name perhaps gives the Akkadian word for man (awîlu), since this sacrifice results in the life of mankind (see J. Bottero, *Mesopotamia*, p.241).

[1037] An is included as one of the Anunnaki, but this must be the primal Dyaus/Ouranos that is attacked by Kāla/Chronos.

[1038] See below p.266f.

[1039] See below p.314.

[1040] Cf. *SB* I,vii,4. Since the punishment inflicted on Prajāpati/Brahman (An) in the Vedas is due to his incestuous intercourse with his daughter Usha (Inanna), we should not be surprised to note that, in Sumer, Inanna herself is both An's daughter and consort (see the hymn (A.O. 6458) where (ll.19-20) Inanna is declared An's legitimate consort (H. Wohlstein, *op.cit.*, p.111).

[1041] Cf. *SB* I,vii,4. This story is repeated in the Purānas with Brahma substituting Prajāpati (see, for instance, *SP* III,40,1-59; cf. W. O'Flaherty, *op.cit.*, p.126).

[1042] See below p.239.

[1043] See *ShP* III,15,39, where Indra remarks, "Śiva is no different from me" (cf. W. O'Flaherty,

have already noted the identity of Indra/Shiva to the androgynous Sumerian deity called KAL,[1044] so the sacrifice of the First Man is seen to be a self-sacrifice. Angra Manyu represents the divine rage of the original cosmic forces which, if uncontrolled, could serve as the source of all manner of disasters. This destructive rage which sometimes characterises Indra is identified directly with Varuna (Enki) as well.[1045] Sometimes, however, perhaps by analogical use of the epithet, even the adversaries of Indra (as in *RV* I,104,2; VI, 52,2; X, 152,2) are called Angra Manyu.

Indra is said to have "slain" his father: "What God, when by the foot thy Sire thou tookest and slewest, was at hand to give thee comfort?" (*RV* IV,18,12). Indra's father is said to be Dyaus in *RV* IV,17,5, and in *KYV* V,7,1, Indra is directly identified with Prajāpati, suggesting that he is not merely a son of Prajāpati but indeed an aspect of him (just as Chronos is an aspect of Ouranos/Aither).

In the Vedas, Prajāpati/Brahman is also called "Purusha". Since Indra is indeed the same as Purusha,[1046] the sacrifice of the latter is indeed a self-sacrifice. That the sacrifice of Prajāpati, or Purusha, is a self-sacrifice is clearly stressed in the Vedas. *KYV* IV,6,2, for instance, declares: "Do thou thyself [Vishvakarman =Prajāpati] sacrifice thyself to thyself, rejoicing".[1047] In *RV* X,90 ('Purushasūkta'), Purusha is offered as a sacrifice by the gods and out of him are formed the creatures.[1048] In *TS* V,2,5,1 the cosmic Purusha is called "the sacrifice". And all the gods are said to extend this sacrifice (*RV* X,10,9,5). Brahmanaspati in particular, as a Brāhmanical god, assumes the title of Lord of the Sacrifice.[1049] We shall see that Heka, the counterpart

---

op.cit., p.89). Indra is the same as Kāma/Agni since he is, in Indic mythology, typically the enemy of ascetics and even of his alter ego, the ascetic Shiva (*SP* V,3,150,7-35). In the *BrvP* IV,35,39, the male half of the androgynous Purusha or Shiva is called Kāma.

[1044] See above p.181.

[1045] In *RV* X,83, for instance, both Indra and Varuna share this identification with the divine Fury.

[1046] See above p.114.

[1047] This sacrifice of Purusha which initiates the creation of the universe is the basis of the oldest Indo-European human sacrifices attested especially in Iran, Germany and Gaul (see Bruce Lincoln, *Myth, Cosmos and Society: Indo-European Themes of Creation and Destruction*, Cambridge, MA: Harvard University Press, 1986), and, to a lesser degree, in India. The description of the Purushamedha in *SB* XIII,vi suggests that, in India, the human victims were not slaughtered, for, according to *SB* XIII,vi,2,12-13, "if thou wert to consummate [the victims], man would eat man. Accordingly, as soon as fire had been carried round them, [the sacrificer] set them free, and offered oblations to the same divinities, and thereby gratified those divinities".

[1048] This closely resembles the episode in the Babylonian *Atrahasis* mentioned above p.186.

[1049] Cf. *SB* I,vii,4,21-2.

of Brahmanaspati, is indeed identifiable with Sia, considered to be the "blood" which flows from the castration of Re's phallus.[1050] In *VS* II,13, Brahmanaspati is beseeched to "extend" the sacrifice, whereby is probably indicated the "formal" extension of the virtue of the castrated phallus.[1051]

In *RV* X,90, the sacrifice of Prajāpati/Purusha has the result that "three-fourths" of him remains in heaven as life eternal, whereas one fourth of him descends to the manifest universe as the creation (v.3). The creation itself involves the emergence of animal life, the Vedic hymns, and the castes of men. The moon arises from Purusha's Mind (v.13) and the sun from his eye, Indra and Agni from his mouth and Vāyu from his breath. From his head is formed the sky and from his feet, earth, while from his navel arises the mid-region (v.14). We see that the emergence of the entire universe is due to this original sacrifice.

The Zoroastrians who abhor Indra seem not to appreciate the Promethean significance of this cosmic phenomenon. Indeed, the Zoroastrian reform, like the Hebrew religion dependent on it, seems not to be based on comprehensive cosmological insight so much as on a moralistic obsession with the perfection of the ideal Heaven and the relative corruption of the material universe which will emerge from Earth after the violent separation of Heaven and Earth by Chronos.[1052]

In the *Bundahishn*, Ch.IV, Angra Mainyu attacks and draws part of the ethereal expanse of Heaven into the Mid-region, the Void, where the solar system ruled by the sun will be finally located. The text reports that Angra Mainyu attacked the sky in its ideal form [i.e. as Heaven] and "dragged it down into the Void", so that only "one third of the sky was above the station of the stars on the inner side". The Void thus becomes the region of the material universe.

In the *Bundahishn*, Ch.III, all of the primordial ideal creations are also attacked by Ahriman (Angra Mainyu) and corrupted or destroyed. Both primal beings, the First Man and the Bull, are killed by Ahriman/ Angra Mainyu. The seed of the slaughtered first Man is purified in the sun,

---

[1050]   See below p.205f.

[1051]   See below p.207. The notion of "extending" the sacrifice also betokens the expansion of the sacrificial symbols into their original cosmic form and force (below p.294).

[1052]   The rather negative view of the creation of our universe as a sinful one in the Avestan literature is perhaps the source of the story of the fall of man in the Hebrew Bible. The resemblance of the story of Adam and Eve and their sinful thoughts to that of the first twins Matro and Matroyao (who are born of the seed of the first Man, Gayomaretan), described in the *Bundahishn* Ch.XV (see below p.312), is too striking to be coincidental and reveals a Hebraic borrowing from Iranian sources. It is interesting to note also that only true cosmological understanding provides man with the higher idealistic and ascetic impulses that have become so highly developed in Indian thought.

whence it is transmitted to our earth, while the seed of the Bull is purified in the moon.

In the Avesta, too, Angra Mainyu destroys all the pure creations of Ahura Mazda and is considered to be a completely evil force that counteracts the splendid goodness of Ahura Mazda and his creative aspect, Spenta Mainyu.[1053] That is why the Daivas and their leader, Indra, are considered demons by the dualistic Zoroastrians.[1054] It is interesting to note that Indra[1055] is considered by the Zoroastrians not as identical to Angra Mainyu but as an evil *assistant* of this arch-fiend. This suggests that the resemblance noted between Indra and Shiva may be one due to their close association and not to an original identification. The other assistants of Angra Mainyu are Akomano (evil thought), who opposes Vohu-mano; Sauru (Vedic Sarva, a name of Rudra-Shiva),[1056] who opposes Kshatra Vairya; Naunhaithya (Skt. Nāsatyas,)[1057] who oppose Spenta Armaiti; Tarich and Zerich (*Bundahishn*, I,17). Angra Mainyu's injection of disease into all life[1058] requires the counteraction of Airyaman (Skt. Aryaman), who in Iran is particularly the god of health (Fargard XXII).[1059] Thus, apart from Mitra-Varuna and Aryaman, the other principal Vedic deities, Indra and the Nāsatyas are considered to be evil by the Zoroastrians. In the *Denkart* too Indra is called "kusitar", the killer.[1060]

We note also that the assistants of Angra Mainyu are akin to the Vedic Ādityas. We have seen that the Ādityas are both primal products of the union of Dyaus and Aditi, as well as, in our own manvantara, the suns of the several galaxies in our universe.

In the *Prose Edda* ("Gylfaginning"), the Mid-region (Ginnungagap) of our universe between Muspell (Heaven) and Niflheim (the underworld)

[1053] Angra Mainyu and his counterpart Spenta Mainyu may have been developed by the Zoroastrian reformers by analogy with the twins Yama and Yami, since they too are called "yema", twins, but created by Ahura Mazda himself.

[1054] Similarly was Lucifer, the light-bearer, turned into a devil by the Hebrew imitators of Zoroastrianism.

[1055] The Iranian forms of Indra include "Andra" (*Vend.*10,9; 19,43) as well as "Indra", the first of which may be the older Āryan form (see P. Kretschmer, *op.cit.*, p.313).

[1056] See V. Machek, *op.cit.*, p.144.

[1057] See below p.207n.

[1058] Manyu/Indra's association with disease is repeated in the baneful effects of Nergal/Agni (see M.K. Schretter, *Alter Orient und Hellas*, Innsbruck: AMOE, 1974, p.88ff. and F. Hrozny, "Un dieu Hittite", p.36).

[1059] See below p.232n.

[1060] See A.V.W. Jackson, *Grundriss der iranischen Philologie*, II:656.

is vitalised by the sacrifice of the First Man, or "giant", called Ymir.[1061] Ymir is sacrificed by Wotan (Enlil/Ganesha) and his brothers, Wili and We. Wotan himself seems to have been understood by the Nordic peoples as merely a Trojan prince, though he is clearly the god of Wind, Wāta/Vāyu/Enlil, who sustains our own universe.[1062] From the corpse of Ymir are fashioned the firmament (his skull) and earth (his flesh) and the surrounding ocean (his blood). The ocean represents the waters whence the sun of our system emerges, and corresponds to Okeanos surrounding Earth. The substance of the sacrificed Ymir thus constitutes the material universe of the Mid-region between primal Heaven (Muspell) and Earth (Niflheim).

[1061]   Unlike in the Vedas and the Avesta, where Yama/Yima is the seventh Manu, Ymir is used in the Germanic mythology as a name of the first Manu.

[1062]   See below p.201n.

XIV: GANESHA

THE STORM-FORCE: TESHUP, SETH, ZEUS

The violence of Kāla/Chronos/Kumarbi, who causes the castration of the Ideal Man, persists particularly in the turbulent nature (Angra Manyu) of his offspring, Ganesha/ Zeus/Teshup/Seth. This offspring is a storm-force that is said to have attacked the divine light (in the form of the First Man) and thereby forced this light into the underworld. Modern astronomers too speculate that the first gigantic fireball, as the source of all the suns of the incipient universe (Mid-region), collapsed after about 3 million years (as supernovas still tend to do) and thus created the seeds for all the future stars and solar systems of the universe.[1063] However, it must be noted that the storm-force also encourages the resurgence of the solar energy in the form of the incipient sun of our system.

In the Hurrian epic of the Kinsghip in Heaven, one of the products of Anu's seed formed in the belly of Kumarbi is Teshup, the Weather-god,[1064] along with the other gods of the Mid-region who include Tashmishu (Suwalliyat, the sun-god), and Marduk. These are the gods who correspond to Seth, Horus the Elder, and Horus the Younger in the Heliopolitan cosmogony. Teshup interestingly is not merely a son of Kumarbi (Enki), but also of An, since it is the latter's seed that is preserved in Kumarbi when Kumarbi bites off An's genitals. Teshup's mother is said to have been Earth (Text Ib9 of the epic) since Earth is the consort of Heaven, who is castrated by Kumarbi. Tashmishu[1065] is Teshup's "pure brother", and Tashmishu may be the Hurrian name of the Hittite Suwalliyat (Sūrya).[1066] Teshup is indeed

---

[1063] See T. Folger, *op.cit.*, p.45.

[1064] Teshup is a later Hurrian form of the earlier Hattian deity adored in the form of a bull, Taru, Taurit (see above p.87n, KG, p.134f.).

[1065] The Hurrian form hides the Akkadian name of the sun-god 'Shamash' within it.

[1066] See H.G. Güterbock, "The God Suwalliyat reconsidered", 1-18. Güterbock considers

regularly coupled with his "pure brother" Suwalliyat, just as Adad is with Shamash.

Just as Seth is represented in Egypt as dragging Osiris down, and Zeus swallows Phanes, or his genitals, their Hurrian counterpart uses a sickle (much like that used by Kumarbi to castrate An) to sever the phallus of Heaven, Ullikummi, from off the shoulders of the giant Uppelluri who bears Heaven and Earth.[1067] Since we have discerned the Cosmic Egg in the figure of Uppelluri, the severing of the "stone" Ullikummi from it clearly denotes his seizure of the phallus of An from it. From the Orphic evidence we may assume that Teshup finally swallows this phallus so that the universal life that it contains moves into his own body.[1068]

Just as Seth is given the dominion of heaven in Egypt,[1069] Teshup's rightful domain as the storm-god is, likewise, heaven. That Teshup is the equivalent of the Egyptian Seth is borne out by the cuneiform treaty of alliance between Hattusilis and Rameses II, where Shamash and Teshup are mentioned in the same way as Shamash and Adad in Assyria are.[1070] In the official state copy of the treaty itself, mention is made of Seth of Zippalanda and of Seth of Arinna,[1071] who are to be identified with Teshup, the consort of the Sun-goddess of Arinna.

The "vizier" [brother] of Teshup is said to be Ninurta, but we have seen that Ninurta himself is identified with Suwalliyat/Tashmishu.[1072] The sun-god and weather-god are therefore two aspects of the same deity and co-operate in the formation of the sun of our system. Thus the two are often considered as dual deities (Shamash-Adad).[1073]

---

these names to be indicative of Ninurta and he is right insofar as Ninurta is ultimately the same as his father Enki/Osiris-Horus the Elder, though he is properly the solar seed of his father.

[1067]   According to Text Ib of the Kingship in Heaven epic, the mother of Teshup seems to have been Earth (see H.G. Güterbock, *Kumarbi*, p.87), just as his father is clearly An. Kumarbi is himself a chthonic deity. and androgynous, since he gives birth to Teshup and his siblings. Plutarch too (*De Iside et Osiride*, Ch.12) considers Chronos to be identical to Geb (though Geb is clearly masculine in Egypt and Nut feminine).

[1068]   See below p.212.

[1069]   See below p.194.

[1070]   S. Langdon and A.H. Gardiner, "The treaty of alliance between Hattusili, king of the Hittites, and the pharaoh Rameses II of Egypt", *JEA* 6 (1920), 187.

[1071]   W.M. Mueller, "Der Bündnisvertrag Ramses' II und des Chetiterkönigs", *MVAG* 7 (1902), pl. I-XV.

[1072]   See below p.242.

[1073]   Ninurta and Adad are both equally governors of the North Wind (STT 400 rev. 37-40; see A. Livingstone, *op.cit.*, p.75).

The Egyptian counterpart of Teshup, Seth, is a son of Geb, and the stormy brother of Osiris. An Egyptian text declares that Seth felled Osiris the sky.[1074] This felling of the heavenly light is necessary for the emergence of the solar force in the mid-region, since it involves, crucially, the consumption of the heavenly phallus and its transference into the underworld. Osiris may have been killed by Seth in the form of a bull,[1075] which is also the form of Teshup/Taru.[1076] Osiris' resurrection is effected ritually through a mouth-opening ritual which requires the heart and the foreleg of a bull, the latter representing perhaps the foreleg (or phallus) of Seth.[1077] Thus, although Osiris is murdered by his "brother" Seth, he is later resurrected in the underworld as his son, Horus the Younger, the sun-god of the horizon.

Like Shiva (Rudra, the howler), whose assistant is Indra, Seth is called "the howling god" (PT 298, 326, 1150, etc.).[1078] Like them, too, Seth is clearly a phallic god, since the moon, Thoth, who is engendered by the homosexual union of Seth and Horus the Younger, itself needs the stimulation of Seth's phallus to become infused with light and sight.[1079] Thus, although Seth is often considered a hostile god since he kills Osiris, in a text in the Papyrus Jumilhac, Seth (also called Bata) is depicted as an Apis bull carrying the coffin of Osiris on his back.[1080] The "arm" of Seth is a weapon with which he vanquishes Apop,[1081] to secure the passage of the sun-barque.

The birth of the sun is indeed related to the tragic passion which Osiris undergoes whereby the light of Heaven is transformed into the principal light of our solar system. Seth is, however, merely the *alter ego* of

---

[1074] See above p.177.

[1075] See H. te Velde, *op.cit.*, p.86.

[1076] See above p.191f.

[1077] H. te Velde (*op.cit.*, p.89) thinks that the foreleg is Seth's, since, in "other texts", the foreleg of Seth is to be "strictly guarded by Isis and the sons of Horus". It is possible that the foreleg has a phallic significance as well since Zeus is supposed to have swallowed the phallus of Heaven (see below p.212). Seth is also represented in the mouth-opening ritual by his metal 'mshtyw', which is mentioned in the chant accompanying the ritual to open Osiris' mouth (*ibid.*, p.88).

[1078] See S. Mercer, *op.cit.*, p.66. According to Plutarch, the name of Seth means "the overpowering". According to a Leiden papyrus, his name represents the intoxicating power of beer (see H. te Velde, *op.cit.*, p.3ff.), which may be analogous to the soma-intoxicated and wine-intoxicated strength of Indra and Dionysus respectively.

[1079] See H. te Velde, *op.cit.*, p.49f.

[1080] *Ibid.*, p.97.

[1081] *Ibid.*, p.87.

Osiris.[1082] Seth, the stormy aspect of Osiris himself, is a god associated with intoxication, and especially the inebriating force of beer: "He confuses the heart to conquer the heart of the enemy".[1083] We see clearly the relationship between the death of Osiris at the hands of Seth and the death of the soul through the corrupting passions which it is the purpose of the funerary rites to overcome. Seth is occasionally also identified with Apop, the serpent that he combats,[1084] since the latter represents the gaseous wind which surrounds Earth. As Plutarch noted of the Greek hydra, "Typhon is the element of the soul which is passionate, akin to the Titans, without reason, and brutish, and the element of the coporeal which is subject to death, disease and confusion".[1085]

Seth also plagues the incipient sun Horus the Younger in several battles with the latter, according to 'The Contendings of Horus and Set'. These conflicts include the violation of Horus the Younger by Seth, the castration of Seth by Horus, the decapitation of Isis by Horus for the sympathy shown by her to Seth, and the cutting off of Horus' hands by Isis.[1086] It may be noted that castration is attributed to Seth as well,[1087] though the occurrence of self-mutilation in the rites of the Dionysiac religion as well as in those of the Phrygian god Attis, is probably due to an imitation of the fate of the sky-god, rather than that of his opponent.[1088]

However, these internecine conflicts are finally resolved and Horus and Seth unite in the rule of Heaven and Earth, or the two lands of Egypt. It is important to note that it is Seth who is given rule over Heaven since Osiris/Horus has already been dragged down from Heaven to the realm of

---

[1082]   That Seth is but Osiris' *alter ego* was brilliantly suggested by H. te Velde, *op.cit.*, p.95.

[1083]   Pap. Leiden I 348, rt.13,4; cf., H. Te Velde, *op.cit.*, p.7. As the god of fermented liquor, Seth is clearly a "Bacchic" god. We may note also the phallic role of Seth in inspiriting Horus the Younger as well as the moon, Thoth.

[1084]   See H. te Velde, *op.cit.*, p.104. Plutarch also considers Seth as the equivalent of Typhon (see *De Iside et Osiride*, 367).

[1085]   Plutarch, *De Iside et Osiride*, tr. J.G. Griffiths, University of Wales Press, 1970, p.197.

[1086]   *BD* Ch.113; see S. Mercer, *op.cit.*, p.74.

[1087]   See PT 1463e: "Before the sexual strength of Seth was made impotent" (cf. te Velde, *op.cit.*, pp.57ff. It is not necessary that this line in itself indicate castration, but Horus' stealing of Seth's seed (CT IV,237b) is transformed in the cult to an act of castration.

[1088]   Attis was said to have been castrated by Rhea (see Lucian, *De Dea Syria, The Syrian Goddess*, tr. H.W. Attridge and R.A. Oden, Missoula, MT; Scholars Press, 1976, p.23). According to A.B. Cook (*op.cit.*, 292ff.), Zeus, Pappas and Attis were Phrygian terms used for a god who, like Osiris, was reborn as his son. For the relation between Attis, Adonis and Osiris, see *De Dea Syria*, pp.13ff.

Earth,[1089] whereas Seth remains as a god of thunder and storm in the region above it, corresponding to the Hurrian "weather-god", Teshup and Zeus Adados.

Politically too, Seth and Horus form a single regal unity. The Egyptian queen is called the one "who sees Horus-Seth", that is, her husband the pharaoh, as a god of dual aspect. The Pyramid Texts too frequently represent the pharaoh as Horus-Seth.[1090] The Pharaoh Amenhotep is described as sitting on the throne of Horus as well as on the seat of Seth.[1091] That both are effects of Shu (Enlil/Vāyu) is made clear from the Merneptah stele which describes the pharaoh as one "who sits on the throne of Shu".[1092] That Seth and Horus are the stormy and solar aspect of the same deity is further demonstrated by the fact that in the 18th Dynasty the king is compared equally to the two and, according to Te Velde, "Ruling, the king is Horus, when he must use force he is Seth".[1093] Seth is thus related to the Indra form of Agni, whereas Horus is a product of the Mitraic.

The precise counterpart of the Egyptian and Near Eastern storm-god in India is Skanda's enigmatic "brother" Ganesha.[1094] It is interesting that, in the An=Anum list, Shamash the sun-god and his stormy counterpart dIM are represented as dSulaat and dHa.ni.is respectively.[1095] The latter may well be the same deity as Ganesha in the Indic religion. Ganesha is identified in the RV and the AB with Brahmanaspati, the power of light.[1096] We may remember that it is Seth's phallus that infuses the light into the eye of Horus and, as Hornung perceptively suggested, it is possible that Seth is closely allied to Heka.[1097]

Like Seth, Ganesha was apparently considered originally as a malevolent deity called Vināyaka who caused obstacles to men and inflicted

---

[1089] See H. te Velde, op.cit., p.61.

[1090] Although most Egyptian kings seem to have had only a "Horus name", in the second dynasty, Peribsen was the "Seth name" of a king whose "Horus name" was Sekhemib (see H. te Velde, op.cit., p. 72). This again suggests that the worship of Seth faded out early in Egypt.

[1091] See H. te Velde, op.cit., p.71.

[1092] The Pharaoh is also said to be seated on the throne of Amun (see LÄ I:238).

[1093] See H. te Velde, op.cit., p.71; This is much like the distinction between the sage Mitra and the aggressive Indra (see below p.221).

[1094] Just as Seth is coeval with Osiris as well as with Horus the Younger, his Indic counterpart Ganesha is equally so with Shiva and Skanda, since the latter is but the solar aspect of his "father".

[1095] Tablet III, No.269ff; see R. Litke, op.cit., p.145.

[1096] RV II,23,1; X,112,9; AB IV,4; I,21 (see S.L. Nagar, The Cult of Vinayaka, N.Delhi: Intellectual Publishing House, 1992, p.44).

[1097] See E. Hornung, Das Amduat, II:131; cf. p.207 below.

barrenness and delirium on them.[1098] The cruel aspect of the Sethian cults is reflected in some of the Ganesha cults in India too, which are given to worshipping an obscene image of the god in the course of drunken and sexually promiscuous revels.[1099] Significantly, in the *ShP*, Ganesha, who is delineated with sinister traits, attacks Brahma (Ouranos) himself after he attacks his father Shiva (Chronos). This is most probably a reference to the similar attack on Osiris by Seth. Also, like Zeus, who swallows the phallus of Ouranos/Chronos, Ganesha too is depicted with a "pot-belly" which contains the entire universe.[1100]

Further, Ganesha obstructs the sacrificial devotions of the gods (*BrP*) and hinders men from worshipping Soma (*SP*).[1101] In the *BrvP*, Ganesha is visited at birth by Sani (Saturn/Chronos, who is the same as Shiva himself),[1102] whose maleficious gaze causes Pārvatī's son to lose his head, which is then replaced by Vishnu with the head of an elephant,[1103] the form in which he is worshipped today in India. In the *ShP* and the *SP*, it is Shiva himself who beheads his son and then, on Pārvatī's pleading, finds an elephantine replacement for it.[1104] In the *BrP*, Ganesha is depicted, much like Seth, as the one who bears the moon (Thoth) on his forehead.

We have noted that Indra bears a close resemblance to Shiva and is an "assistant" of Angra Mainyu (Shiva) in the Avesta. Indra is particularly the tremendous force of solar energy and is characterised especially by his weapon, vajra, which allows the solar energy to emerge as the light of the universe. Thus he is closely related to Shiva's son Ganesha/Brahmanaspati/Seth, who aids the formation of the sun in the underworld. At the same time, Indra is also related to Skanda/Muruga/Marduk[1105] and therefore to Enlil's son, Ninurta or Inurta.[1106] The latter, however, is indeed the same as

---

[1098]   See the *Mānavagrihyasutra* and the *Vājapayagrihyasutra* (in S.L. Nagar, op.cit., p.45).

[1099]   See 'Ganesa' in *HW* 1:378.

[1100]   See S.L. Nagar, *op.cit.*, p.115.

[1101]   *Ibid.*, pp.16, 49, 52.

[1102]   See below p.214.

[1103]   *Ibid.*, p.12f.

[1104]   *Ibid.*, pp.8f.

[1105]   For the relationship of Indra to Skanda see below p.241.

[1106]   This variant spelling is attested in AKF II 12[8]. Among the Kassites, Ninurta is given as one of two Akkadian glosses to the name "Marattaš", which may stand for the leader of the Maruts (see G. Dumézil, *op.cit.*, p.27; cf. A. Deimel, *Pantheon*, "Nin-ib", p.210). It is possible also that it is to be read as Mitra (see below p.183n). Indra is called "marutvat", accompanied by Maruts, in *RV* I,100,1 (cf. *RV* III,4,6; III,47,1; III,50,1). Dumézil has suggested that the other gloss, Gi-dar, is also probably a corruption of Indar. At any rate, we note that Indra is identified with the solar son of Shiva, Skanda/Ninurta.

his stormy brother since he too – like his "brother" Teshup (Seth/Zeus) – is described as fighting the dragon and facilitating the development of the sun.

The birth of Indra, the chief of the gods, resembles that of Seth, who is said to have emerged "sideways from his mother".[1107] At RV IV,18,1-2 Indra is said to have issued sideways from his mother Aditi and, on his birth, his mother hid him (IV,18,5). Although this awkward manner of his birth associates Indra with Seth, as well as with Zeus, Seth represents Ganesha, the son of Shiva, rather than Indra himself. Once again we note a fusion of the force represented by Indra/Shiva with Shiva's violent son, Ganesha, who himself is inextricably related to his solar brother Skanda. Indra, who is closely associated with Shiva, is indeed split into the two forces (or "sons") which constitute the solar energy, Skanda and his storm-force Ganesha.

Indra is born in the waters of the Abyss and Tvashtr is referred to as his father (RV III,48,2). At RV IV,17,4 Indra is called the "son of Dyaus", of whom Tvashtr is but an aspect. Indra indeed represents the seminal solar force of Shiva which will form the sun. Indra's vital and heroic quality – that of Zeus/Teshup/Ganesha – is emphasised by his frequent epithet of divine 'Bull'.[1108] While Agni is described as a Bull who "sharpeneth his horns to pierce the Rakshas (demons)", Indra too, is regularly admired with the same epithet.[1109] The Bull is also a typical epithet of Teshup of the Hittites, who is a counterpart of Seth/Zeus Adados.[1110] Similarly, in Sumer, the term "Bull of Heaven" is used of Girra (Agni), and it also serves as an appellation of Enlil, (CT 24,5,41 and CT 24,41), as well as of Adad (CT XV, 3f.), that is, of the stormy wind-like stages of solar evolution which, finally, are of greater importance in the formation of the sun than the purely luminous element represented by the pure brother of Adad/Seth/Teshup/Ganesha.

Since Indra is associated with Angra Mainyu/Manyu, the Zoroastrians excoriate Indra as an evil 'deva', particularly in the Vendidad.

It is interesting to observe, in this context, that Wotan (Vāta/Vāyu), as god of Wind, is equally called Mercurius by Tacitus (Germania, Sec.9), showing the intimate relationship between Vāyu, Shiva and Indra and their offspring.

[1107] See Plutarch, De Iside et Osiride, Ch.12; cf. H. te Velde, Seth, God of Confusion, p.27.

[1108] The adoration of deities in the form of a bull may be traced back to Anatolia, where bovine altars are found in the ruins of Çatal Huyuk from the 7th millennium B.C. The founders of this most ancient culture may have been proto-Hurrians/Dravidians since the Subartu (=Hurrian) culture was widespread in the Near East from very early times (see A. Ungnad, Subartu, p.114) and the transmission of the bull-cult to Sumer may have been via Elam, where the temples, like the present-day South Indian ones, bore bull's horns on their tower (see W. Hinz, op.cit., p.56).

[1109] At AV IV,11,2, Indra is called a "draft ox".

[1110] See G. Wilhelm, op.cit., p.70.

The hostility towards Indra among the Iranians is matched by the later hostility towards Seth among the Egyptians.[1111] One reason for the animosity of the Zoroastrian reformers towards the devas and their leader may have been the fact that Indra, the leader of the gods, as the drinker of Soma may have also been worshipped as an orgiastic deity.[1112] This may have contributed to the Zoroastrian ostracism of his cult.[1113]

In the Vedas, Indra's arm or "fist" is represented as a drum (*RV* VI,47,30-1). At V,20,3 the vehemence of the ritual war-drum is called "Indra-like". In ancient Mesopotamia, too, the hide of an ox was used to make the ritual war-drum, and the sound of the drum is said to represent the voice of god. More importantly, the drum is also identified by the Assyrian exegetes with "Indagara", a name which probably represents Adad/ Ramman (CT 24,10,14), the storm-god, whose control of thunder-claps may account for the identification.[1114] As we shall note below, Ramman (Adad) is the storm-force of Ninurta, in his battle against monstrous creations such as Asakku. The celebrated fight of Indra against Vrtra in the Vedas is conducted with a special weapon called "vajra" which is forged by Tvashtr and this weapon is indeed the same as the "storm-flood" of Adad.[1115]

The Sumerian storm-god Adad is, among the Canaanites, called Hadad.[1116] In Babylon, the storm-god is attested as Rihamun (the howler).[1117] And Adad, Ramman, Rihamun are typically called the "Bull of Heaven".[1118] In the exegetical god-list, `Anu ša amēli', this god is described as representative of thunder, lightning, storm, etc., which evokes the peculiarly stormy nature of this cosmic god. Adad is called the stormy aspect of

---

[1111]   See H. te Velde, *op.cit.*, pp.61, 68, 121, 141.

[1112]   In RV VIII,81, Indra is called, exactly like Shiva, "the dancer" and "the lover of carouse". Indra in the MBh is called the god of the seed who is symbolised by "Indra poles" similar to the Shivalingam (see W. O'Flaherty, *op.cit.*, p.85).

[1113]   S.A. Cook (*op.cit.*, p.70) points out a related example of aversion to the orgiastic Dionysiac religion evidenced in a Nabatean/Palmyrene inscription on a seal in the British Museum, where the sky-god or "god of heaven" is called the one "who does not drink wine" as well as the "good and rewarding god".

[1114]   See A. Livingstone, *op.cit.*, pp.179,184. Nindagud, which is read 'Indagara', is identifiable with Adad (see A. Deimel, *op.cit.*, p.225). The phonetic resemblance of Indagara to Indra is indeed remarkable. It must be noted that Anu is also identified with the drum in BM 34035 (see A. Livingstone, *op. cit.*, pp.173,184). For Adad, see A.R.W. Green, *The Storm-God in the Ancient Near East*, Winona Lake, IN: Eisenbrauns, 2003, Ch.I.

[1115]   See below p.199.

[1116]   See A.R.W. Green, *op.cit.*, Ch.III.

[1117]   From the Babylonian "ramamu" = to howl, scream (see H. Zimmern, "Religion und Sprache", p.445).

[1118]   See P. Jensen, "Adad-Mythus" in *RLA* I:26.

Marduk also in CT 24,50,10b,[1119] Marduk being identical to Ninurta.[1120] In a boundary-stone of the Kassite king, Nazimaruttas II, Adad is designated as the son of An,[1121] who is identical to Enlil-Enki, the father of Ninurta/ Marduk.[1122]

The storm-force Seth, Adad is, not surprisingly, related to the birth of the sun.[1123] The force which fells the sky is equally that which produces the flood which bears the sun aloft into our universe. That the exact storm that Adad represents is identical to the flood which forms the sun is made clear in several sacred Sumerian texts, including the epic *Lugal e*. When Ninurta undertakes a mighty battle against certain mountainous "regions of resistance",[1124] Enki calls to Nin-ildu, "the great carpenter [or demiurgus] of Anu",[1125] who is, as we have seen, the counterpart of Tvashtr, to fashion the mighty mace of Ninurta. Ninurta's "arm", or weapon, is itself represented as a separate deity called Sarur. The stormy nature of this mace is revealed in Gudea's Cylinder B, where the mace of Ningirsu [Ninurta as lord of the flood] is described as being the "fiery stormwind". This fiery stormwind is indeed deified as the storm god Ri-ha-mun or Adad. Adad is also called "the most powerful of the Weapons" of the "rebel lands", that is, of the Anunnaki, who are typically based in the underworld.[1126]

[1119] "ilAdad=ilMarduk ša zu-un-nu".

[1120] See below p.299. Ninurta ("Lord of Earth") is indeed the name of the moribund solar force (Enki), while his Babylonian counterpart Marduk actually bears a name ("sun-calf") that is more suited to the incipient sun. Again, as in the case of the names "Enki" and "Ea" (see above p.103), the North preserves older forms of the most ancient religion than the innovating Sumerians do.

[1121] M.J. de Morgan, *Délégation en Perse*, Paris, 1900, II, Pl.16-19 (see H. Wohlstein, *op.cit.*, p.86). Similarly, Nannar too, the son of Enlil, is designated the "mighty offspring of An" (VAB I,p.188; RISA, p.272, Clay Cone A; see H. Wohlstein, *op.cit.*, p.37).

[1122] See, for instance, UET I,145, l.1; The Epic of Anzu, l.31.

[1123] In the Indian epic *Rāmāyana*, Rāma is the name of a princely scion of the *solar* dynasty of the Ikshvākus.

[1124] See J.V.Kinnier Wilson, *op.cit.*, p.51. Kinnier Wilson's interpretation of this battle in geological, rather than cosmological, terms is entirely unfortunate. The terms resistance and rebellion applied to the hostile forces which the gods combat are uniformly attested in the literature of Sumer, Egypt and India; cf., for example, the Egyptian references in AeHG no.30: "I beat the donkey. I punish the rebels/ I have destroyed Apophis in his attack"; and the hymn in the Medinet Habu sun-chapel: "... who drives off the rebel in his hour, and burns the enemies of Re" (Medinet Habu VI 421B). In the Vedas, the name of the serpent Vrtra itself suggests resistance (see A.K. Lahiri, *Vedic Vrtra*, Delhi: Motilal Banarsidass, 1984, Ch.2).

[1125] Ninildu is indeed an aspect of Enki's (as Nudimmud, the fabricator); see below p.225.

[1126] See A. Falkenstein, "Sumerische religiöse Texte", ZA 55 (1962), p.36; cf. J.V. Kinnier Wilson, *op.cit.*, p.62.

That the stormwind is related to a cosmic flood is suggested also by the Sumerian term 'amaru' for weapon, which may be interpreted as "flood", as a hymn to Nergal makes clear:

> So strong was his Weapon, its upward rising was unopposable,
> In its aspect as a storm, it was the great Flood which none could oppose;[1127]

From the reference to the floods which Soma engenders in *RV* IX,42,1 when liberating the sun,[1128] also, we may identify this flood as being the cosmic storm in which the incipient sun is formed and borne aloft.[1129] Ramman is, again, called "bel abubi", lord of the deluge.[1130]

Adad (the weapon of Ninurta) is also associated with Ninurta's father, Enlil, as an agent of the destruction of humanity during the Flood.[1131] The myth of Enlil's descent to the underworld as punishment for his rape of Ninlil relates a passion similar to Osiris'.[1132] Although the myth of Enlil and Ninlil depicts the underworld journey of Enlil himself, it is clear that he represents rather the storm force, after he has cut off An's neck. Enlil thus is the vital and stormy aspect of the solar force in his descent into the underworld, whereas Enki is the moribund solar force in the underworld.

The close association of the god of thunder with the sun (the god of justice) is evident also in the oaths and standards of the ancient Mesopotamians. Thus Adad and Nergal (Seth and Horus the Younger) are found together on standards of the Assyrian kings,[1133] one of whom

---

[1127] See Kinnier Wilson, *op.cit.*, p.53. Kinnier Wilson also suggests that the cause of the flood in *Atrahasis* may originally have been not the "noise" caused by man, but rather "the noise of the rebel gods, which will have disturbed [Enlil] – even as it disturbed Apsu in *EE* I,25ff" (*ibid.*, p.112). The rebel gods may be the Sumerian counterpart of the Iranian "daivas" and the Indic Asuras. In *BP* VIII,24,8, the reason for the flood at the end of the sixth Manvantara (which precedes the formation of the light in the seventh) is that the Asura Hayagreeva (much like the Anzu bird) stole the Vedas from Brahman.

[1128] See below p.295.

[1129] See above pp.78ff.

[1130] H. Zimmern, *op.cit.*, p.448; p.555.

[1131] See E. Ebeling in *RLA* I:26, for Adad's role in the Flood. We have seen how Shiva in the *SP* is robed in "Indra's thunderbolts" when he destroys the cosmos. Shiva is thus a counterpart of Enlil/Angra Mainyu, Indra of Ninurta, and the thunderbolts themselves of Adad.

[1132] See H. Behrens, *Enlil und Ninlil: Ein Mythos aus Nippur*, Rome: Biblical Institute Press, 1978, pp.220ff.; cf. S. Kramer, "The Mythology of Sumer and Akkad", pp.96ff.

[1133] See F.A.M. Wiggermann "*Nergal und Ereškigal*" in *RLA* IX:226. Adad and Nergal here must be the same as Seth and Horus the Younger, rulers of Heaven and Earth, in Egypt.

is even called Shamsi-Adad ('Adad is my Shamash').[1134] In the great god-list, 'An=Anum', Adad is listed alternately with Shamash as ᵈ(su.la.at) BAD and ᵈ(ha.ni.is)BAD. 'Sulaat' is clearly the same as the Hittite/Hurrian god Suwaliyatta, representing the sun,[1135] while "hanis", as we have noted above, may be related to the Indic Ganesha, as well as to the name of the kingdom of the Mitanni, Hanigalbat, whose chief god was Teshup.[1136] We have already seen that Seth and Horus the Younger are coupled together constantly in Egypt.

Just as Adad is an exceptionally stormy aspect of the primeval cosmic wind represented by Enlil, in the Avesta, Ram represents the same aspect of Vāyu.[1137] The Avestan 'Ram Yast', which is addressed to the same stormy deity as Adad/Ramman, is, significantly, about Vāyu. Vāyu is Indra's close companion in the Vedas, and Ramman is thus a continuation and intensification of the wind-force of Vāyu through which the sun is engendered. Ram must therefore be related to Angra Mainyu (Shiva/Indra) as well, who, in the *Bundahishn*, kills both the first Man and the Bull of Heaven. The Zoroastrian reform which makes Vayu combat Indra (Ninurta, whose mace is Ramman/Raman itself) is thus a confusion of the original cosmological qualities of the gods due to Zoroaster's moralistic aversion to Indra as an assistant of Angra Mainyu.

According to Philo of Byblos, the Phoenician theogony on which the Greeks based theirs began with Elos (Chronos), and Demarous (Adad). Demarous, the son of the union of Ouranos' wife Ge with her son Dagon,[1138] is the same as the Hesiodic Zeus (Teshup).

In Hesiod, the castration of Ouranos is followed by the reign of his enemy Chronos (who, we may add, witnesses the birth of the cosmic Light of Phanes from the Egg formed in the body of Ouranos, the Ideal Man). Unfortunately, Chronos has an alarming habit of swallowing his children, and thereby preventing them from becoming manifest. So, in order to

[1134] See S.A. Cook, *The Religion of Ancient Palestine*, p.131.

[1135] See H.G. Güterbock, "The god Suwaliyatta reconsidered". The Āryan form 'sūrya' (from suar=to shine) is also evidenced among the Kassites as Šurias̆.

[1136] Hanis may also be related to 'hnnw' which is determined with the Seth animal in Egypt and means 'tumult' and the opposite of 'maat', a typical association of Horus' (see J. Zandee, "Seth als Sturmgott", *ZÄS* 90 (1963), 144-56).

[1137] The Avesta (Yasht 14, Yasht 8) also uses the form Wata to denote the more corporeal form of the god of Wind Vayu (cf. *RV* X, 136,4 which refers to "the steed of Vāta, the friend of Vāyu"). The name Wata is also reflected in the Hittite divine name, Huwattassis, god of Wind (see E. Laroche,"Recherches", p.69). The Germanic Wotan/Odin is etymologically related to Otem/Atem (breath) and mythologically to Vāta/Vāyu.

[1138] See Philo of Byblos, *op.cit.*, p.51. Dagon is a corn-god, and the father of Demarous/Adad (see above p.145).

save the life of her baby Zeus, Chronos' consort Rhea, on the advice of her parents, Heaven and Earth, resorts to a special ruse.[1139] This involves the substitution of a stone for the baby so that Chronos swallows the stone and thereby allows the baby to be born. This stone, as we will see, is the same as the phallus of Ouranos/Phanes.[1140] In Homer, Zeus is recognizable as a storm-god, and, according to Diogenes of Apollonia, the Homeric Zeus is the "apotheosis of air [Vāyu]".[1141] Zeus is also identified by Herodotus with Teshup's Syrian counterpart, Adad, as Zeus Adados.[1142] Zeus Dolichaios is also represented as bearing the same axe and lightning in his hands as Ramman does.[1143]

Zeus as a storm-force destroys his father Chronos and then swallows the phallus of Ouranos/Phanes which had been stuffed into Chronos. He thus forces the life and light of Ouranos down into Earth from whence it will rise up into our universe as the sun. The fact that Phanes is swallowed by Zeus [Adados] renders more easy the identification of the divine pairs, Phanes and Zeus, Horus the Elder-Osiris and Seth, Tashmisu-Suwalliyat and Teshup, Ninurta and Adad, Skanda and Ganesha, for it is due to the absorption of the vital force of Heaven by the storm-god that the cosmic light is reborn as the sun of our system.

We have seen that the details of the birth of the Cretan Zeus, Zagreus,[1144] who was protected by the Kouretes and Korybantes clashing bronze shields and spears round the tree in which the cradle of the child-god was hung,[1145] resemble those of the birth of Shiva's son, Skanda. However, as we have noted, Zeus is more akin to Skanda's "brother" Ganesha than to Skanda himself. So the Greek Zeus combines in himself the two aspects of the solar force.

[1139] It may be useful to recall here the incident of the Egyptian Heaven, Nut, swallowing her children (see above p.165).

[1140] See below Ch.XVI.

[1141] See A.B. Cook, *Zeus*, I:351.

[1142] By the end of the second century B.C., Zeus comes to be identified quite commonly with Adad as Zeus Adados (see A.B. Cook, *op.cit.*, I:549).

[1143] See A.B. Cook, *op.cit.*, I:604ff. and H. Zimmern, 'Religion und Sprache' in E. Schrader, *op.cit.*, p.448.

[1144] Zagreus itself is an epithet which points to the Near Eastern origin of this god, since it is derived from the Zagros mountain range (see A.B. Cook, *Zeus*, I:.651). The Cretan Zeus was originally called Kouros (see M.L. West, *op.cit.*, p.131). This would be related to the term kur, "mountain", applied to Enlil as well as his son Ninurta.

[1145] See Hug. Fab.139 (cf. A.B. Cook, *Zeus*, I:530).

In the Germanic Eddas, the god who battles the serpent like Seth and Zeus is Thor, who is called "son of earth [Geb/Chronos]" in the Eddic "Lokasena", 58.

In the Ugaritic texts, the death of Baal at the hands of Mot (Death) in the underworld is followed by a brief reign of a son of El (counterpart of Kronos/Geb) and Asherah called Athtar the Terrible, who may well be a Canaanite counterpart of Atar, the Iranian fire-god.[1146] The Canaanite Athtar, who becomes ruler of the underworld,[1147] may be a counterpart of Seth, since, as we shall see, Atharvan[1148] is the epithet of Brahmanaspati, who is identifiable with Ganesha/Seth.

[1146] For the identity of Atar/Atharvan with Brahmanaspati/Ganesha/Seth, see below p.208.

[1147] See C.H. Gordon, "Canaanite Mythology", p.212.

[1148] That the Ugaritic mythology, dating from the 14th c. B.C., was influenced by the Āryan is made clear by the fact that there is a reference to Agni itself in text 52, sec. 4 (see C.Gordon, "Canaanite Mythology" in S.N. Kramer (ed.), *Mythologies*, p.186).

XV: BRAHMANASPATI

THE MAGICAL POWER OF PTAH: "LORD OF THE KA'S", HEKA, SIA

Although the stormy son of Chronos/Geb is rather destructive in nature, he also shares in the magical virtue of another product of the castration of Heaven by Chronos. This is the magical source of Light and Intellect itself called Heka. We have already noted the importance of Heka in the deity's rise to consciousness.[1149] In the Berlin "Hymn to Ptah", Ptah's magical force is called Heka, "Magic", and we shall see that this is the Egyptian equivalent of Brahmanaspati ("lord of Brahman"), the source of the light of Brahman/Mitra in the Vedas.[1150] Heka is also Ptah's creative word and is deified as a "son" of Ptah and Sachmet, or, in Esna, son of Khnum and Menhit.[1151] In the Heliopolitan cosmogony, the annunciation of the divine forms is effected through the mouth of Atum and is itself called Heka, Magic, which is thus the equivalent of the magical brahman prayer.

In a New Kingdom commentary on the *Book of the Dead* we find references to Hu and Sia, who represent the powers of utterance and understanding,[1152] the "ancestor gods" that were formed of "the blood which fell from the phallus of Re when he was going to mutilate himself",[1153] the castration referring to the self-sacrifice of Ptah/Purusha/Prajāpati. According to a Coffin Text which states that "Hu and Heka defeat the

---

[1149] See above p.174f.

[1150] See J.P. Allen, *op.cit.*, p.40.

[1151] Menhit is associated with the primal goddess Neith, who is herself the mother of the sun (see "Chnum" in *LÄ* I: 952; cf. A. Piankoff, *op.cit*, p.94). Khnum as a primal deity is indeed identifiable with Ptah (see "Chnum", *loc.cit.*). Khnum, who is represented as a potter-god, is closely connected to the fabricating aspect of Thoth/Tvashtr since he is said to form the embryo (see S. Bickel, *op.cit.*, p.202).

[1152] See M.S. Holmberg, *op.cit.*, p.43.

[1153] *Ibid.*, p.44.

malignant snake for me",[1154] it is possible that Heka is identifiable with Sia. In CT 261, too, Heka is mentioned in association with Hu.[1155] CT II,39c states that Atum created Shu by means of his Hu. Shu, further, claims: "I do not obey the Magician (Heka), since I came into being before him".[1156] This suggests the actual cosmological priority of Hu and Shu to Heka. Sometimes we see Heka represented alongside Maat/Tefnut, the consort of Shu.[1157] In the Vedas, Heka's counterpart, Brahmanaspati, is also called 'rtaprajāta' (son of Rta/Maat/Tefnut).[1158]

Sia, which may be translated as 'perspicacity', is in fact the spiritual insight which constitutes the magical power of the brahman prayers. Heka symbolizes the intelligible paradigm of all the gods of the cosmos. For instance, it is said of Heka: "I am the one whom the Sole Lord made … when something came from his mouth … All was mine before you developed, gods".[1159] Further, he is "the Eldest of the holy place of the primordial beginning".[1160] Heka's creative energy also manifests itself as Light,[1161] revealing Heka's close affiliation to Horus the Elder. Re, the solar deity, too as a creator god is, like Heka, called "Magician".[1162] The typical appellation, "magician", of Heka as creator god is related to the "ka" of created beings,[1163] which refers to their spirit/character, as opposed to the "ba", which refers to the soul (and is to be associated with Hu). Thus, in a Coffin text, Heka is called "Lord of the ka's".[1164]

Re also requires the help of Heka as well as of Isis in the seventh hour of Amduat in warding off the dragon Apopis, which associates him with the character of Seth.[1165] In the Vedas, we have seen that Brahmanaspati is identified with Ganesha[1166] and is also the constant companion of Indra in

---

[1154]   CT VII, 466b; cf. H. te Velde, *op.cit.*, p. 178.

[1155]   See J.P. Allen, *op.cit.*, p.38.

[1156]   CT I, 372b; cf. H. te Velde, "The God Heka in Egyptian Theology", *JEOL*, 21 (1970), p.183.

[1157]   Pap. Khonsumes (*Mythological Papyri*, pl.16) [pl. xxxii]; Pap. Greenfield, pl.108 [pl. xxviiia] ; cf. H. Te Velde, *op.cit.*, p.185.

[1158]   *RV* VII,23,15.

[1159]   CT 261; cf. J.P. Allen, *op.cit.*, p.37; cf. also CT III, 389.

[1160]   See H. Kees, in *ZAS* 65 (1930), 83.

[1161]   See E. Hornung, *Das Amduat*, I, 81, cf. II, 98; also H. Te Velde, *op.cit.*, p.177.

[1162]   Pap. Bremner-Rhind, 28, 22; cf. Te Velde, *op.cit.*, p.182.

[1163]   See C. Maystre, 'Le Livre de la Vache du Ciel', *BIFAO*, 40 (194), 104.

[1164]   See H. te Velde, *op.cit.*, p.179.

[1165]   See below p.206.

[1166]   See above p.195.

his battle against the Panis, who prevent the flow of the solar energy. Heka as the "Eldest Magician" is similarly associated with Seth in a passage of the Sphinx stela.[1167]

As in India, in Egypt too the magical prayers or spells of Heka are considered esoteric wisdom that is accessible only to the initiated.[1168] In the Vedas, the 'brāhman' prayers are employed by the Brāhmanical priests to magically recreate and control the macrocosmic forms of Agni/Ātman in their daily sacred rituals. Brahmanaspati, or Brihaspati, is generally regarded as the sacred power (brahman or mantra) of the gods (*TS* VI, 1,2,4.).[1169] Brahmanaspati is also said to be the creator of the gāyatrī metre (*TS* I,7,11,1), which is that of the first verses of the Rgveda. This points to his special significance as the creator of divine speech and to his close relationship with Agni, who rules the faculty of speech. Brahmanaspati is the Vedic counterpart of the deified Heka as Lord of the divine Word. As a counterpart of Heka, Brahmanaspati is clearly younger than Vāyu/ Enlil/Shu, since, as we have seen, Shu insists on his priority to Heka/Sia.[1170] However, like Heka, who is also regarded as the intelligible pattern of the cosmos, Brahmanaspati is indeed the totality of the divine Ideas which create the gods of the universe. Brahman is thus said to be superior to the gods since they owe their existence to him. In *RV* II,26,3, Brahmanaspati is called the "father of the gods", just as Prajāpati (the creative aspect of Brahman) normally is. But it should be borne in mind that Brahmanaspati's creative role, unlike Prajāpati's, is restricted to the intellectual formation of

---

[1167]   See te Velde, *op.cit.*, p.177.

[1168]   See "Zauber" in *LÄ* VI:1328.

[1169]   Brahmanaspati is further called the divine 'Brāhman' priest (*TS* III,2,7,1), the most important of the four types of Vedic priests – Hotr, Udgātr, Adhvaryu and Brāhman. Of the other priests, the hotr is associated with Mitra-Varuna (Agni) and the adhvaryu with the Ashvins or Nāsatyas (*VS* XXVIII,19). In *SB* XIII,v,4,24, the domain of the hotr is the eastern part of a kingdom, that of the udgātr the northern, that of the adhvaryu the western, and that of the brāhman the southern. We will note further below (p.317) that the revolution of the sun in *BP* V,21,7, is marked by Yama as its southernmost limit, Varuna as its western, Soma as its northern and Indra as its eastern. This suggests that the Hotr is associated with Indra, the Udgātr with Soma, the Adhvaryu with Varuna, and the Brāhman with Yama. Then Indra must be allied to Mitra-Varuna (Agni), the Ashvins to Varuna, and Yama to Brahmanaspati. The Veda associated with the Hotr priests is the Rg, just as the Sāma is with the Udgātr, the Yajur with the Adhvaryu and the Atharva with the Brāhman.

As regards the solar twins, the Ashvins, they are said to be begotten of Indra in *RV* II,12,7, and the goddess of Dawn, Usha, is their sister. Their name suggests their equestrian affiliation and they serve indeed as Usha's charioteers. They also bear some resemblance to the other companions of Indra/Shiva, the Maruts, who help Indra in his battle against the dragon Vrtra (see V. Machek, *op.cit.*, p.153n).

[1170]   See above p.206.

the universe; he is the creator of the intelligible stage of the universe rather than of the physical. Prajāpati, on the other hand, as the lord of the creation, engenders the worlds in Form (rūpa) as well as Name (nāma).

The emergence of Brahmanaspati is described mystically in the obscure first verses of *AV* IV,1:

> The brahman that was first born of old Vena[1171] [ ] hath unclosed from the well-shining edge; he enclosed the fundamental nearest shapes of it, the womb of the existent and the non-existent.

> He who was born forth the knowing relative of it speaks all the births of the gods; he bore up the brahman from the midst of the brahman; downward, upward, he set forth with the svadhas.

Just as Agni is said, in I,95,2, to have been formed as an infant by Tvashtr, in *RV* II, 23,17, Brahmanaspati too is said to have been created by Tvashtr (Thoth). Brahmanaspati thus is a form of Agni/Shiva. In *AV* IV,1,5-6, Brahmanaspati is called "the universal ruler" and "father Atharvan".[1172] Atar is also the Iranian name of the fire-god. Brahmanaspati is further called Angirasa, the chief of the sons of Angiras. Although Angiras is one of the seven sages who are said to be "created" by Brahman, they are considered also to be the sevenfold sons of Heaven and Dawn (*RV* IV,2,15; III,53,7; X,67,2; I,71,5).[1173] The Angirasas are associated with the brahman prayer

---

[1171]   Vena is identified by *SB* VII,iv,1,14, with Brahman, that is, Prajāpati; cf. the reference to the godhead as Swāyambhu, "the Self-born" in *Manusmriti,* I,5-13. In *BP* IV,13,18ff., however, Vena is represented as a tyrannical king, of whose body is formed Prithu (see above p.78). We recognize here the terrible aspect of Ouranos as Chronos/Kāla (see above Ch.VIII).

[1172]   The *AV* is also called Brahmaveda, indicating its dedication to Brahmanaspati, or Atharvan.

[1173]   The angirasas are engendered by Dyaus' impregnation of his "daughter" Usha, the Dawn. We shall note below (see p.88n) that one of the sons of Dyaus and Usha is Rudra-Shiva, who represents the force of the sun. Usha is sometimes called the "sister" of the Ādityas. Usha as the light which precedes the light of the sun is closely related to Aditi, both being called "cow" in the Vedic literature. In this they resemble Hathor and Isis in the Egyptian mythology.

The birth of the sages or angiras is described elaborately in the *BP* and *BrdP*. (For the differences in the number of the sages in the Purānas, see p.88n above). Brahma [that is, Vishnu, the Cosmic Man] embarks on the process of creation in nine stages (*BP* III,10,14ff.) starting with Mahāttattva or Prakriti (abstract Nature) and continuing with Ahamkara (Egoity), Tanmātras (subtle elements), the organs of knowledge and action, Mind and the deities who preside over the said organs, Ignorance, vegetable life, animals, and, finally, men. Ignorance is then multiplied fivefold and manifested in unruly spirits, the last of whom is Rudra-Shiva (III,12,6ff,). After this frustrating episode of the creatures of Ignorance, Brahma

itself (10,61,7). For, the assistance provided by the Angirases to Indra in his battle against the "Panis" is restricted to the chanting of magical prayers which loosen the bands of restriction caused by their enemy (I,62; I,121,1; IV,2,16).

Like Heka, Brahmanaspati, helps Indra in his fight with the Panis and his aid is constituted of the power of the magical 'brahman' prayer.[1174] In *RV* II,23,17, Brahmanaspati is called "the Lord of the Prayer, the avenger of sin, the retaliator of wrong, the murderer of the Lie, the sustainer of the great Truth".[1175] We see that Brahmanaspati continues the role of his "father" Thoth/Tvashtr/Tvoreshtar/Spenta Mainyu, who is but an aspect of the Zoroastrian Ahura Mazda, who also loves the Truth and abhors the Lie (Druj).

Brahmanaspati's employment of the magical brāhmanical power frees the "cows" from the chains of untruth after first opening the "three" doors of the vala. Brahmanaspati thus succeeds in driving out the "cows" and causing 'svar' ('the shining one', the sun) to appear (*RV* II,24,3). Thereby he is said to have discovered "the dawn, sun and fire" (X,68,9). Similarly, in *RV* III,31,15, Indra his companion is also said to have created the sun, dawn, the path of light and fire.[1176] In *RV* X,67,5, Brihaspati, as the assistant of Indra in the battle against the Panis, is again said to have discovered "the dawn, the sun, the cow and the lightning". The cow is related to the light of the dawn, which prepares the way for the sun of the heavens, or 'lightning'.[1177]

---

creates ten "mentally created sons", Marichi, Atri, Angiras, Pulastya, Pulaha, Kratu, Bhrigu, Vasishta, Daksha, and Nārada (III,12,21). We may locate the appearance of Brihaspati at this stage.

Similarly, in the *BrdP* I,ii,8 and 7, Vishnu/Brahma's creation after the recovery of Earth begins with the purely intellectual creation of Asuras (from his tāmasic aspect), Devas (gods) and Pitrs (ancestors) (from his sattvic aspect), and Manushyas (men, or their ideal forms) (from his rājasic aspect), as well as the types of lower forms of life. Other mental creations include five "Kartrs" (agents) Rudra, Dharma, Manas, Ruci and Akrti (I,ii,9,1) and nine "mentally created sons", Bhrgu, Angiras, Marici, Pulastya, Pulaha, Kratu, Daksha, Atri and Vasishta (I,ii,9,18-19).

[1174] Indra himself embodies the vital force of the kshatriya (see below p.222).

[1175] See H.-P. Schmidt, *op.cit.*, p.109.

[1176] In the Vedic sacrifice Indra's discovery of light is symbolic of the sacrificer's kindling of the divine flame hidden deep in his heart (see J. Miller, *op.cit.*, pp.232ff.)

[1177] Dawn (=cow) may be related to the moon as well (cf. the cow/s of Sin discussed below p.256) since both prepare the way for the sun of the heavens (=lightning). Dawn (Usha/Isis) is closely related to Aditi (Hathor) and Earth, since she is said to be a daughter of Dyaus' and incestuously impregnated by her father with the Angirasas, the sevenfold sons of Heaven and Dawn (*RV* IV,2,15; III,53,7; X,67,2; I,71,5). Usha is sometimes called the "sister" of the

XVI: LINGAM

THE DIVINE PHALLUS

We have seen that the stormy son, or aspect, of Chronos/Shiva/Enlil causes the destruction of the first luminous form of the universe. At the same time, this son, Zeus/Teshup/Ganesha is instrumental in preserving the vitality of the primal Heaven within himself and in conveying it to the Mid-region wherein our own universe will be situated. In the *Bundahishn*, Ch.I, the region created between the region of Endless Light wherein Ahura Mazda dwells and the Darkness ruled by Ahriman (Angra Mainyu) is called the Void, or "Vay"(3).[1178] This is the region which is now to be infused with the galaxies derived from the original light of Heaven. When Zeus, infused with the life of the universe represented by the divine phallus, emerges from the underworld, where he, along with his *alter ego*, the solar force, finds himself, he causes the universe (in the form of the phallic Tree of Life) to move into the Mid-region between Heaven and Earth.

The exact process whereby our universe manifests itself after the castration of Ouranos is depicted in the Greek Orphic myths. The phallus of An/Ouranos which is infused into Enki/Chronos[1179] is said to be consumed by a son of the latter. We have seen that the phallus of Ouranos is thrust into Chronos by Rhea in order to allow the survival of the infant Zeus. Later, Zeus causes Chronos to disengorge the stone and release his brothers who

---

Ādityas, who are sons of Aditi, consort of Dyaus. She is considered a sister of the Ashvins (sons of Indra) as well (see above p.207n).

[1178] See R.C.Zaehner, *op.cit.,* p.35.

[1179] We have seen that Chronos is himself an aspect of the Cosmic Man, or Heaven, in the matrix of Time and that the infusion of Ouranos' phallus into Chronos represents the impregnation of Purusha in the Purānas.

had been swallowed by their father. Then he destroys his father and his Titans and takes over the kingship of heaven along with the gods.[1180]

The stone which saves Zeus from Chronos' rapacity is the same as the phallus of Ouranos which Chronos had severed and represents the vital solar power which will vivify the Mid-region of our universe.[1181] Whereas in Hesiod (*Theogony*, ll.499f) Zeus sets up the stone as a cultic object, in the Orphic theogonies, Zeus devours the stone. Significantly, the commentator of the Derveni theogony explains that Zeus indeed swallowed "the sexual organ" (aidion).[1182] In the Orphic theogony, Phanes is said to be devoured by Zeus,[1183] thereby absorbing the original universal into himself, but we may assume that it is the phallus of Phanes that is thus consumed. As the Orphic rhapsodies proclaim:

> Because of this, together with him, everything came to be again inside Zeus,
>
> the broad air and the lofty splendour of heaven,
>
> the undraining sea and earth's glorious seat,
>
> great Oceanus and the lowest Tartara of the earth,
>
> rivers and boundless sea and everything else,
>
> and all the immortal blessed gods and goddesses,
>
> all that had existed and all that was to exist afterwards
>
> became one and grew together in the belly of Zeus.[1184]

The phallus of Phanes which is absorbed by Zeus is the same as that of Ouranos with which Cronos/Kumarbi/Geb was infused after he castrated Ouranos. Zeus' swallowing of Ouranos' or Phanes' genitals allows it to appear as the starry mid-region wherein the solar force will be manifest as the moon and sun. However, the heavenly life and light of Phanes, absorbed by Zeus, has to first descend to the depths of Earth (the underworld)

[1180] In Sumer, Ninurta is said to have superseded, or killed, his father Enlil ("Ninurta stood over Enlil and turned him to dust and ashes" (VAT 10099, 10; see A. Livingstone, *op.cit.*, p.119). This may correspond to the swallowing of Phanes, or his phallus, by Zeus.

[1181] Cf. the image of Ninurta the solar force as the semen of the mountain his father, p.242 below.

[1182] See M.L. West, *Orphic Poems*, p.85. It is not surprising therefore that Protogonos is called both Phanes and Priapus in the Orphic Hymn VI (*ibid.*, p.252).

[1183] See M.L. West, *op.cit.*, p88f.

[1184] *Ibid.*, p.89. The image of the entire universe contained in the belly of the Lord is found also in the Purānas (see *BP* III,8,10ff).

before rising up to the mid-region of the stars that shine for the benefit of mankind.

The phallic stone, which may be considered as belonging to Ouranos as well as to Phanes, is related to the monstrous stone Ullikummi in the Hurrian fragmentary poem, "The Song of Ullikummi". The stone grows on Upelluri's shoulder alongside Heaven and Earth and may represent the starry life of the universe which will occupy third region between Heaven and Earth, which is to be ruled by the sun, that is, by Teshup's brother Suwalliyat/Tashmisu.[1185] Ullikummi also grows rapidly through the cosmos, in a plainly phallic manner. Teshup's fight against Ullikummi, which may be a counterpart of Zeus' swallowing of Phanes or his genitals, results in. Teshup's cutting this stone from the shoulders of Upelluri, and, although the conclusion of the poem is lacking, one may assume that Teshup too absorbs Ullikummi.

We have noted above that it is Enki/Chronos/Kumarbi who castrates An, so Ullikummi represents the force of An thrust into Kumarbi and then absorbed by his son Teshup. The name Ullikummi itself is probably a corruption of 'Mullil [=Enlil/Shu/Vāyu] of Kummiya',[1186] so Enlil represents the vital force of An. Ullikummi is said in the Hurrian poem to be a creation of Kumarbi/Enki/Kāla/Shiva's for the purpose of destroying the latter's son, Teshup. This reveals the tremendous force of the phallus of Ouranos.

In India, as among the Hurrians, Shiva himself is the phallic force (lingam) which fills the universe with its fiery life, Agni. We have seen that Shiva is born of the union of Dyaus/Prajāpati, with his daughter Usha, the goddess of Dawn,[1187] whom we may recognize as a form of Earth.[1188] So the manic force (Angra Manyu) that castrates Dyaus is indeed that of Dyaus' own phallus. In the SB VI,i,3,8ff., the fiery force which vivifies the universe, Agni, is said to be identical to Shiva-Rudra, who is but the first of the nine manifest forms of Agni. The other forms are Sarva, Pashupati, Ugra, Asani, Bhāva, Mahādeva and Īshana,[1189] who are embodied in the waters,

---

[1185] A remarkable modern recurrence of the stone as a symbol of the starry region is to be found in Arthur C. Clarke's 2001: A Space Odyssey, where the mysterious phallic "monolith" is finally revealed to be a star-corridor.

[1186] Since he combats Teshup in his sacred town, Kummiya (see H.G. Güterbock, "Hittite Mythology", pp.166,170).

[1187] See SB VI,i,3,8ff.; cf. p.186 above.

[1188] See above p.209n.

[1189] If Ishana is related to the sun, it may be a name related to Hittite Istanu, the name of the sun-god (see O.R. Gurney, op.cit., p.10).

plants, Vāyu, lightning, Parjanya (the rain-god), the moon[1190] and the sun respectively. The final form of Agni, Kumāra, is the son of Shiva, Skanda/Muruga.

In the *BrdP* I,ii,10, the identification of the forms of Agni/Shiva with the universal phenomena is somewhat different. There, the first form of Shiva – who is the creation [or phallus] of Brahma – is Rudra, and is said to be embodied in the sun, the second, called Bhāva, in the waters, the third, called Sarva, in the earth, the fourth, called Īshana, in the wind (Vāyu), the fifth, called Pashupati, in the fire, the sixth, called Bhima (corresponding to Asani), in the ether, the seventh, called Ugra, in the initiated brāhman priest and the last, called Mahādeva, in the moon. The order of manifestations in the *SB* is more chronological than that of the *BrdP*, which represents them spatially in a series of concentric circles. For we note that the first and last forms, in the *BrdP* account, are constituted by the sun and moon respectively, the second and seventh by the waters and the Mind, the third and sixth by Earth and Heaven, the fourth and fifth by the Wind (Vāyu) and plantal life (Pashupati) – which latter is no doubt to be identified with Soma.

In *BrdP* I,ii,10,76ff, the corporeal form of Rudra is called Raudri and its son is the planet Saturn. Similarly, the body of Bhava is Apāh (the waters), and his son is Venus, the body of Sarva is Earth and his son is Mars, the body of Īshana is Wāta and his sons are Manojava ("rapid as the Mind") and Avignātagati ("of inscrutable movement"),[1191] the body of Pashupati is Agni (fire) and his son is Skanda, the body of Bhima is the Ether and his son is Heaven, the body of Ugra is the initiated Brāhman priest and his son is Santāna, the body of the Moon is Mahat and his son is Budha. The reference to the moon and the sun as forms of Shiva further identifies Shiva with Indra, who, as we shall see, represents the force within both the moon and the sun.[1192]

In the *SP* and *ShP*, Shiva is represented as once losing his phallus, when he is cursed by some sages for his lasciviousness. The phallus however

---

[1190] The term Mahādeva (the great god) for the lunar aspect of Shiva corresponds exactly to the Sumerian/Egyptian appellations of the moon as "the great light" (see above p.5, below p.245).

[1191] The inclusion of Wāta as the body of Vāyu (a form of Shiva in the manifest universe), in the Purānas is especially significant since this deity is more evident in the Avesta than in the Vedas. This indicates the greater antiquity of the Puranic cosmology compared to the Vedic. Besides, it is clear that Wata is identical to Wotan, since the latter's two "ravens", the one black the other white, are called, in "Grimnismal", Huginn (thought) and Muninn (memory), which must be corruptions of the Sanskritic names of the two "sons" of Wata in *BrdP*. The "ravens" of Wotan are said to "fly over the world each day".

[1192] See below pp.257f, p.306.

becomes an immense fiery pillar which pierces the three worlds until it is fixed in the vulva of Shiva's consort and worshipped as the "source of the universe".[1193] We may also consider in this context the severed phallus of Shiva in *LP*17ff,[1194] which is also installed ritually as a cultic object,[1195] and represents the universe. In the *BrdP* I,ii,27,23, it is Indra who loses his phallus when he is cursed by the sage Gautama for violating his wife Ahalyā. This incident reinforces the identification of Indra with Shiva.

It is interesting to note that, in the Vedas and Purānas, whereas Brahman (Atum-Re) creates mentally (as we have seen in the creation of the gods studied above), Shiva is the first to create sexually (*ShP* VII,1,12; VII,1,14; VII,1,17), since, as we have seen, he is identical to the first androgynous Manu, who copulates with his female counterpart Shatarūpā.[1196] Brahma creates "mind-born sons" (primarily the sages),[1197] whereas Shiva creates through his own phallic power combined with the power of his female aspect, Pārvatī, representing the cosmic vulva.[1198] Pārvatī is the daughter of the Himālaya mountain (Parvata),[1199] and we may assume that this mountain has the same universal significance as the primordial hill in Egypt, and the great 'kur' in Sumer. Shiva is therefore a deity particularly oriented to the material universe that emerges in the Mid-region between Heaven and Earth.

In Egypt, the luminous cosmos represented by Horus the Elder is felled by Seth and forced to descend into the underworld as Osiris who will be revived as a new sun in the waters. Since the passion of Osiris is reenacted carefully in the funerary rites of the kings of Egypt, we may assume that these rites were conducted for the revival of the soul as the sun or star – or, as the Upanishads express it, for the transformation of the individual ātman into the eternal Brahman. The light appears first from a stone called 'benben' atop the primordial hill that represents Earth rising from the waters of Nun. The stone, which is symbolic of the phallus of the

---

[1193] *ShP* XII:17ff. (see A. Daniélou, *Shiva and Dionysus*, tr. K.F. Hurry, London: East–West Publications, 1979, pp.62f.).

[1194] Cf. W. O'Flaherty, *op.cit.*, p.181; cf. below p.273.

[1195] Cf. M.L. West, *East Face*, p.280.

[1196] See above pp.172,181.

[1197] See above p.92.

[1198] The common interpretation of the references in the Rigveda to the "shishna" worshippers as indicative of an Aryan aversion to Dravidian phallic worship is absurd, considering the phallic nature of the Vedic Shiva/Indra.

[1199] The name Parvatha (Mountain) appears in the Vedas (*RV* VI,49,14; X,158,3) as the name of a deity, probably Vāyu (see below p.240n). The Indians associated the great mountain with their own high mountain range.

castrated sky-god, represents the life of the Mid-region between Earth and Heaven,[1200] though the hill is also a phallic symbol in itself. PT 1652 also declares: "Atum-Khepry, you grew tall as the Hill, you rose as the benben in the House of the Bennu in Heliopolis".[1201] The deity who emerges from the "benben" stone as the sun-bird or phoenix, bennu, is Osiris/Atum,[1202] as the sun of our universe.

[1200] See below p.219.

[1201] See *LÄ* I:694f.

[1202] See below p.311.

XVII: VARUNA

THE SOLAR FORCE IN THE UNDERWORLD: ENKI, OSIRIS, VARUNA

Τhe furious storm-wind of Seth/Adad/Teshup/Zeus Adados which forces the luminous Heaven into the nether regions of the cosmos also revives the solar force with the universal life that it contains within itself. In Egypt, Osiris, originally the vital force of the sky-god Horus, is killed by Seth and descends to the underworld, but after his resurrection by his wife Isis, he becomes ruler of the dead in the underworld. Osiris, as we have seen, is also the primal god as Ideal Man/Vishnu as well as the Cosmic Light. Similarly, the phoenix 'bennu', which is normally identified with Osiris is also identified with Atum in CT 76 II 3h-4c.[1203] Atum also is sometimes called "the one who is in the underworld" (Pap. BM 10541).[1204] In the *BD* Atum-Re is said to be adorned with the two feathers that also decorate the crown of Osiris.[1205]

In the Heliopolitan cosmology, Osiris is the Lord of the Abyss[1206] and is called the one who "dwellest within Abtu",[1207] or one "who drawest thy waters from the Abyss of heaven",[1208] that is Nun. Like Nun, Osiris is represented with a sign denoting waters, just as Enki and Varuna too are lords of the Waters. As the Lord of the Waters, and, like Enki and Varuna,

---

[1203] See S. Bickel, *op.cit.*, p.240.

[1204] See K. Mysliwiec, *op.cit.*, II:158.

[1205] *Ibid.*, p.196.

[1206] See K. Sethe, *op.cit.*, p.38f., p.77n. Osiris is identified by Herodotus (II,156) with Dionysus (An/Horus the Elder), as Isis is with Demeter (Earth) and Horus with Apollo (the sun). We may remember also that according to Megasthenes, "Dionysus" [=Brahman] was the civilisatory agent in most ancient India (see above p.64).

[1207] See 'Hymn to Osiris' from the *BD*, in E.A.W. Budge, *op.cit.*, II:153. Abtu is the source of the name of the city Abydos, which is thus the Egyptian counterpart of Eridu.

[1208] 'Hymn to Osiris', XVIII Dynasty (ca. 1500 B.C.), in E.A.W. Budge, *op.cit.*, II:148f.

Osiris is associated particularly with the pleasure-filled waters.[1209] Just as Enki is the lord of the "sweet waters" in Sumer, Osiris is the lord of "fresh water" (PT 589a).[1210] He is the deification of the Desire of the divine Soul (Amun).[1211] Osiris and Amun are thus closely linked as the Desire of the Lord and the Soul of the Lord, as the Hermopolitan theology makes clear.[1212]

The waters which Osiris rules are the source of all life and immortality. Like Ea, Osiris is the life-force whereby all things grow: "The gods live by me. I live and grow as Neper… I am not destroyed: (CT IV,168c-170b).[1213] He is also called the "Lord of Life, through whose forms one lives, without whom there would be no life".[1214]

That the underworld is also surrounded by waters is suggested by the proto-Stoic reference to the consignment of the dragon-serpent Ophioneus to Okeanos.[1215] Osiris even rules the Ocean which surrounds Earth in the form of a serpent, as an inscription on the sarcophagus of Sethos I makes clear: "This is Osiris; he encircles the underworld".[1216] That is no doubt why Enki, Osiris' Sumerian counterpart, is translated as Okeanos by the Greeks. And we may remember that Sesha, the serpent on which Vishnu sleeps, is the Māyā or illusory power of Shiva himself.[1217] We see that the sleep of the solar force in the underworld is a repetition of the original sleep of the Ideal Man in the cosmic waters. It may also be remarked that the serpentine form of Osiris around the underworld resembles that of the wind-serpent (Shu/Enlil) around the Cosmic Egg.[1218]

Interestingly, the waters reached by the sun in the second hour of the *Amduat* are called Wernes, which is reminiscent of the Vedic Varuna.[1219]

[1209] In fact, his name is written with the sign for flowing waters … Osiris, like Enki, is typically associated with life-giving water (he is once called "Fresh Water" (see J.G. Griffiths, *Origins*, p.156), or semen.

[1210] See S. Mercer, *op.cit.*, p.156.

[1211] The Egyptian term "ndmmt", pleasure, that is used for the pleasure of the creating god, Amun/Atum/Osiris in Heliopolis (CT 321 IV, 147d-e, PT 527; cf. S. Bickel, *op.cit.*, p.73) is remarkably similar, phonetically, to the Sumerian name of Enki, Nudimmud, which is glossed in Akkadian in the Anu-ša-amēli list as "ša nabnite" ("as the Moulder") (see R. Litke, *op.cit.*, p.238).

[1212] PT 446 (see K. Sethe, *op.cit.*, p.34).

[1213] See J.G. Griffiths, *op.cit.*, p.165.

[1214] A. Barucq and F. Daumas, *op.cit.*, p.89.

[1215] See below p.296f.

[1216] See J.G. Griffiths, *op.cit.*, p.155.

[1217] See above p.77.

[1218] See above p.154.

[1219] See E. Hornung, *Ancient Egyptian Books*, p.34.

The waters of Wernes are followed by those of Osiris in the third hour. In the fourth hour, however, the waters are replaced by the desert of Rosetau, or Sokar. In the sixth hour, that is, halfway through its passion, the sun of the underworld reaches the waters of Nun after leaving the desert of Sokar and lies in the waters as the corpse of Osiris. These waters are clearly regenerative, as the Tenth Hour of the *Amduat* makes clear.[1220] It is during the sixth hour that the corpse of Osiris is united with the spirit of Re. In *The Book of Caverns,* Osiris, who lies within the earth sphinx Aker at the centre of the underworld, becomes ithyphallic when the spirit of Re passes through the cavern. Since Osiris is but the underworld form of Horus the Elder/ Brahman/Ouranos who has been castrated by Time, we see that the sixth hour in the underworld marks the return of his sexual potency. According to the Pyramid Texts, too, Osiris in the underworld is assimilated to Re, the solar force, at midnight.[1221] Since it is Zeus/Teshup/Ganesha/Seth who preserves the divine phallus in himself we may also reasonably associate Re with Seth.[1222] Osiris as the solar force of the universe thus begins to rise from Earth, which is represented by a primeval mound, Tatenen (who is identical to Osiris' father, Geb), and surrounded by the serpent Nehaher, who is but another form of himself.[1223]

The Djed column, which we have studied above as a symbol of Geb is also a most ancient symbol of Osiris himself,[1224] since Osiris and Seth are but two aspects (sons) of Geb. The pillar is considered as the "backbone" of Osiris.[1225] R. Cook has suggested that the Djed has the form precisely of the sacrum, the lowest joint of the backbone, which is the seat of sexuality wherein the serpent Kundalini (of the Indian Yogic system)[1226] resides.[1227] And the aim of yogic discipline as well as of the cosmic evolution is to purify the passions in order to allow the spiritual light to emerge as the light of the universe. We have seen that, in *The Book of Caverns,* the dead Osiris at the centre of the underworld becomes ithyphallic when the spirit

[1220] *Ibid.*, pp.33ff.

[1221] See E. Hornung, *Conceptions of God in Ancient Egypt: the One and the Many,* tr. J. Baines, Ithaca: Cornell University Press, 1982, pp.93-6.

[1222] Cf. p.196 above for the resemblance between Seth and the Indra/Vishnu form of Agni, who is the Indic counterpart of Re (see Ch. XXII below).

[1223] See R.T. Rundle Clark, *op.cit.,*pp.169ff.

[1224] See E.O. James, *op.cit.,* p.38. Osiris is, like Enki/Ninurta/Varuna, the Lord of Earth.

[1225] See *LÄ* I:1100ff.

[1226] See below p.291.

[1227] See R. Cook, *op.cit.,* p.14. As V.G. Rele, *op.cit.,* p.104, suggests, Kundalini is probably the same as the Vedic Vrtra.

of Re passes through the cavern. This must represent the reviving light of the universe, as well as of the soul (Ātman), which is now in the process of being regenerated as the sun after the purging of the passionate element represented by Osiris' *alter ego* Seth.

Osiris' role as ruler of the underworld is, interestingly, also shared by Ptah (Pap. Berlin 3048, pl.8, 6),[1228] showing that it is the same macroanthropic deity who is now evident in his vital aspect as Osiris. Osiris acts as judge of the underworld, presiding over the Hall of Maati, wherein the dead are judged.[1229] And Maat is, as we have seen, virtually the same as Tefnut, the consort of Shu, and it is Shu who represents the vital aspect of Ptah.

In the Egyptian *Book of the Gates*, the solar journey is undertaken in a barque which is called the "barque of the Earth",[1230] since Earth is the region in which the sun is first manifest, just as it is also manifest in the Heavens and, finally, the Waters. In both this book and in the *Amduat*, the solar journey through Earth is undertaken within the coils of the World Encircler, the gigantic serpent representing Time.[1231]

In the Indic literature, the secret name of the Lord of the Waters, Varuna, Varana (from the Sanskrit term for "cover")[1232] may refer to the encirclement of Earth by Okeanos. In the *KB* 18,9, the sun is said to have entered the waters and there become Varuna. This is not just a reference to the setting sun but to the birth of the sun itself in the underworld. From the underworld the solar force rises to the realm of Soma (Mind/Moon/Nannar)[1233] and then emerges as the rising sun, Sūrya/Horus the Younger/Shamash. Varuna's location in the west in *BP* V,21,7[1234] corresponds to Osiris' typical appellation as the god of the setting sun and of the spirits of the west, or the "westerners". The western region ruled by Varuna is the

---

[1228] See M.S.–Holmberg, *op.cit.*, p.100.

[1229] See E.A.W. Budge, *op.cit.*, II, 159.

[1230] See E.T. Hornung, op.cit., p.60.

[1231] *Ibid.* In the *Enigmatic Book of the Underworld,* the *ouroboros* serpents represent the birth and end of time (*ibid.*, p.78). In the Nordic Eddas, the Midgard serpent is called the "encircler of Earth" ('Voluspa', 60). Since the "magur" boat in Sumer is identified with the moon (see below p.255), we see why Vrtra (the serpent corresponding to the Egyptian "world-encircler") is identified with the moon (see below p.259)

[1232] See *GB* I,i,7, where Varana is said to cover everything (cf. U. Chouduri, *Indra and Varuna*, p.95).

[1233] In the *BP* (V,22,8), the moon (Soma representing the nutritive and energetic force of the moon) is located above the sun ("in the north"), just as the twenty eight constellations are situated above the moon one above the other (V,22,11).

[1234] See below p.318.

entrance to the underworld, the realm of Osiris. Varuna in the underworld.
is the same as the Heavenly light Brahman/Mitra that has been shattered by
Angra Manyu.

Varuna is the lord of the waters, and, according to *RV* X,190,2,[1235]
from the waters arise the Year,[1235] denoting the entire physical universe, as
SB VIII,7,1,1 explains ("the Year is this universe").[1236] In the "year", or the
universe, arise the sun and moon, heaven and earth, the regions of the air,
and, light. Both the earth and the heavens are said in *AV* IV,16,3 to be the
domain of the Asura, Varuna: "This earth is King Varuna's property as well
as those high heavens, whose ends are far separated from one another; the
two oceans are his orifices". The association of Varuna with the 'seat' of the
universal light in *RV* VIII,41,9 is an indication that Varuna rules the Earth
atop which the light of the universe shines.

The close relationship between Indra/Shiva/Agni and Varuna (Osiris)
is borne out by more than one passage in the Vedas. In *RV* IV, 42, Indra
calls himself Varuna "I am King Varuna". However, Indra is not exactly
the same as Varuna but a form of him since, in *RV* VII, 82,5 we read that
"In peace and quiet Mitra waits on Varuna, the Other [Indra] awful, with
the Maruts seeks renown".[1237] In *RV* VI, 68, 2, Indra with the mace used

---

[1235] The Year (that is, the manifest universe) is also identifiable with the primordial Cow
since it is filled with its milk. *RV* X,87,17 declares that the Cow gives the "milk of the year".
(For the destruction of Vishvarūpa by Indra as the stormy aspect of the solar energy [Seth/
Teshup] see below p.293). As F.R. Schroeder first pointed out, the "year" may also be the
same as the deity worshipped as Hera by the ancient Greeks and having possible associations
with the "Cow" (cf. J. Haudry, *La religion cosmique des Indo-Europeans*, Milan, Paris: Arché,
1987, p.103). A.J. van Windekens' suggestion that Hera may represent a Cow (Glotta,
1958,p.309f.) may be glossed by the fragment of Euripides (Doxographi, 286; Vorsokratiker,
7,31, B,6 (I,311,14)) which calls Hera one of the four roots of all things and "the bearer of
life", a description which exactly matches that of the Cow in the Avesta (Yasna 37,1) and in
the Vedas. The three other roots mentioned by Euripides are, first, Zeus, and, after Hera,
Aidoneus and Nestis, who feeds mortals with his tears. These roots may be later forms of
the primordial (Lord of the) Abyss, Earth, Tartarus and Eros in Hesiod's theogony as well
as of Nun, Huh, Kuk and Amun in the Hermopolitan (see above Ch.IX). Aidoneus may be
the lord of the underworld, Hades. Nestis seems to be related to the Nāsatyas. The four roots
may also correspond to the deities of the divine formula 'Mitra-Varuna, Indra, Nāsatyas' (see
above p.116n) which evokes the process of the sun's formation.

[1236] Cf. *SB* VIII,2,1,17: "the year is these worlds".

[1237] According to the *BP* VI,18,10ff., the Maruts are the sons, not of Aditi, but of Diti, who,
like Aditi, is one of the thirteen wives of Kashyapa. They are borne by Diti as Asuras in order
to destroy Indra, chief of the devas. However, Indra succeeds in entering Diti's womb and
cuts the foetus into seven parts, which multiply seven-fold to form the forty-nine Maruts,
who are later converted into devas by Indra and led by him. In *RV* V,58,7 Earth is said to be
impregnated by Indra's host, the Maruts. The birth of the Maruts resembles that of Skanda
(see below p.240).

against the dragon Vrtra and Mitra are described as companions with contrary characteristics: "One with his might and thunderbolt slays Vrtra; the other (Mitra) as a Sage stands near in troubles" Mitra is typically the "brāhmanical" god, since he is originally the same as Brahman. Indra, on the other hand, is the "kshatriya".

In the Avesta, Xvarenah is the force of the Lord of Earth. This is made clear by the fact that the Zamyad Yasht which is dedicated to the Lord of Earth is actually addressed to Xvarenah. Xvarenah is, in Zamyad Yast (XIX),18, said to belong to all the Amesha (immortal) Spentas (blessed spirits) "who are the makers and governors, the shapers and overseers, the keepers and preservers of these creations of Ahura Mazda". Yima (called the ruler of the universe, the "sevenfold earth" in the same Yasht,31),[1238] for instance, succeeds for a while in retaining this xvarenah, but loses it once falsehood enters his mind, at which point the xwarenah flies out of him in the form of a falcon (wareghna), which happens also to be the seventh incarnation of Verethraghna (Bahram Yasht (XIV),19ff).[1239] Yima, the ancestor of the present human race, is, we may remember, the counterpart of the seventh Manu of the Padmakalpa, Manu Vaivasvata. So the falcon form of Verethraghna is related to the seventh Manu of our cosmic age. However, Yima's rulership over Earth suggests that he is ultimately the same as the First Man and identifiable with Ptah-Tatenen.[1240]

In its falcon form Xvarenah first flies to Mithra (35), then to Thraetaona, and finally to Keresaspa,[1241] son of Thraetaona. Mithra seems to be the same as Horus the Younger. Thraetaona[1242] is said to battle the monster Asi Dahaka[1243] (Zamyad Yasht XIX,37; Fargard XX) for the possession of this precious substance. In Zamyad Yasht VIII,45,52, Atar combats the same serpent for the Xvarenah, so Thraetona must be closely related to Atar. In Zamyad Yasht XIX,51ff, Atar succeeds in restoring the

---

[1238] The xvarenah is said to belong particularly to "the Aryan countries" (Yasht XIX,56).

[1239] Of the ten incarnations of Verethraghna, the first is as Vāyu (the Wind), then as a bull, a horse, a camel, a boar, a youth, a falcon, a ram, a goat and, finally, a man. Since the falcon is a typical symbol of the sun of ours system, it is possible that each incarnation corresponds to an Indian "manvantara". However, the ten incarnations cannot be easily made to correspond to the fourteen manvantaras. Also, these incarnations do not correspond exactly to the ten of Vishnu in the Purānas. Further, in *BP* II,7, Vishnu is given more than ten incarnations.

[1240] See above p.168. Tatenen is the later, universal form of the cosmic Ptah. So the seventh Manu too is a form of the first. That is why the name Ymir is used for the first Manu, the macroanthropos, in the Germanic Edda (see above p.182).

[1241] Keresaspa may be the Iranian original of the Sanskrit Kashyapa (see below p.307).

[1242] It is not certain if Thraetona is related to the Traitona of *RV* I,158,5.

[1243] Asi Dahaka is the same as the Sumerian Asakku (see below p.297).

Xvarenah to the Vouru-Kasha sea (the Abyss). Atar is the same as Seth/
Teshup/Ganesha, and, as we have seen, also identifiable with Heka/
Brahmanaspati.[1244] In the Avesta, Atar is called a son of the primal god
Ahura Mazda (Yasna 62,7).[1245] Atar may also be identified with the deity
called "Apām Napāt" (child of the waters) who is also equivalent to Agni,
particularly as the incipient sun. Atar is thus the stormy-force (Ganesha/
Seth) in the underworld that helps in the formation of the sun of our
system.[1246] Thraetona is also called Āthwya[1247] and may thus be the same as
Trita Āptya, who is a form of Agni[1248] that helps Indra in his fight against
the monstrous Vishvarupa for the release of the solar force (*SB* I,ii,3,1-2).[1249]
For Thrita too is referred to in Yasna IX,10 as smiting the serpent Dahaka,
which equates Dahaka with Vishvarūpā.

When Thraetona's son Keresaspa takes possession of the xvarenah,
he similarly does battle with the serpent as well as with "the golden-heeled
Gandareva that was rushing with open jaws, eager to destroy the living
world of the good principle" (Yasht XIX,41).[1250] When it finally reaches the
Vouru-kasha sea,[1251]where is no doubt situated the cosmic tree representing
the new universe, it is guarded by Apām Napāt (Agni as the child of the
waters), who bestows it then to the material world, along with "the waters"
and the "mighty Wind" and the "frawashis [souls][1252] of the faithfull" (Tir
Yasht (VIII), 34).[1253]

[1244]   See above p.208.

[1245]   See above p.156.

[1246]   Since Brahmanaspati is also identical with Seth/Ganesha, it is not surprising that he is
called "Atharvan" in *AV* IV,1,6.

[1247]   See A.K. Lahiri, *op.cit.*, p.188.

[1248]   The three Āptya forms are Ekata ("the first"), Dvita ("the second"), and Trita ("the
third") (*SB* I,ii,3,1).

[1249]   In *RV* X,8,8 Trita Āptya is said to have killed the three-headed son of Tvashtr, while
in *RV* X,8,9, Indra too is credited with this deed. However, Trita Āptya is, in *SB* I,ii,3,2,
characterised as a brāhmanical force (just as Mitra is; see above p.222) in contrast to Indra,
the kshatriya. In *SB* IV,i,4,4, kshatram (sovereignty) is attributed to Varuna, who is equivalent
to Indra. In *SB* IX,iii,4,18, Brahmanaspati similarly symbolises the priesthood, while Indra
represents the nobility. (The Zoroastrians seem ignorant of the original partnership between
the Vedic Indra and Atar/Brahmanaspati).

[1250]   Gandharvas are heavenly singers in the Vedas and it is interesting to note they too are
included as enemies of the fire-god in the Avesta.

[1251]   In the Sumerian and Indic literature Enki and Varuna are especially connected to the
Tree of Life in the Abyss (see below p.274).

[1252]   The Iranian term "frawashi" is related to the Sanskrit "urwashi" meaning a female spirit.

[1253]   We see here that Agni/Atar takes the place of Indra as purveyor of fire to our universe.

The Lordship of the Abyss in the Iranian religion is thus represented by the fire-god in the extreme fiery form of Xvarenah. In Mihr Yasht (X),127 Xvarenah is represented as going before Verethraghna (Vishnu),[1254] who himself precedes Mithra – who heralds the sun, Hvare. Verethraghna himself is preceded by Atar, who, we have just seen, is identifiable with Seth/Brahmanaspati. In Mihr Yasht (X),70, we find Verethraghna/Vishnu, as Mithra's herald in the form of a boar (the original form of the wind Vāyu through which Vishnu first extracts Earth from the Abyss). That Vāyu is a form of Verethraghna/Vishnu futher confirms the solar quality of Vāyu/Enlil as the second incarnation (birth) of Agni. In Mihr Yasht X,13, too, the sun Hvare follows Mithra. Thus we see that the order of the solar formation, Xvarenah (Agni), Verethraghna (Vāyu), Mithra (Āditya) is the same in the Avesta as in the Vedas. This order is, besides, a repetition in the underworld of the cosmic sequence which produced the Heavenly Light of Brahman.

That the Sumerians also possessed a notion of three sun-gods is suggested by the fact that the rising sun is descried as a form of Enlil (Vāyu), and the setting as a form of Enki (Agni).[1255] This latter must be the same as the sun called Utu.Di.Mush, the sun of Earth.[1256] Enki is the Lord of the setting sun and of Earth, and his seat is generally regarded to be in the "netherworld". In one of the predecessors of the An-Anum god-list, A.O. 5373,[1257] Ninabzu (the Lady of the Abyss) is called Ereshkigal, the queen of the underworld, and since Nun-abzu is an epithet of Enki, we may assume that Ereshkigal is his consort, though she is normally the consort of Nergal (the counterpart of Horus the Younger, and a form of Ninurta)[1258] as well. In the Hittite treaties too, Ereshkigal is a substitute for Damkina, the consort of Enki.[1259] This establishes that Enki and Nergal (the solar force in the underworld) are the same god. This is why the title Lord of Earth, Urash/Ninurash is used to name both Enki and Ninurta.

We have seen that Indra is indistinguishable from Shiva, who is the first form of Agni according to the Purānas (see above p.213).

[1254] That Verethraghna corresponds to Vishnu/Varuna is made clear by the fact that in the Verethraghna Yasht (14), 2, Vāyu is the first incarnation of Verethraghna (see above p.222n), Vāyu being the form that the deity assumes to operate on the waters (see above Ch.VI).

[1255] The third sun must be the sun of the heavens.

[1256] See M. Rutten, "Les Religions Asianiques", in *Histoire des Religions*, 4, Paris: Bloud et Gay, p.40.

[1257] See H. de Genouillac, "Grande Liste de Noms Divins Sumeriens", *RA* 20, p.105.

[1258] See below p.248.

[1259] See CTH 42, CTH 106 (see D. Yoshida, *op.cit.*, p.40).

Enki, like Varuna, is called "the King of the Apsu, the lord of the source"[1260] and also Nun-abzu.[1261] We have noted also that Enki is the source of the Greek name 'Okeanos' for the ocean which surrounds Earth. And we have seen that Osiris encircles the underworld of Earth in the form of a serpent.

According to the *Enuma Elish*, Enki battles Apsu to gain possession of the primal waters and establish his seat in the centre of the waters, Eridu. He thereby absorbs the role of Apsu. At the same time, Enki also supersedes Mummu,[1262] the formative force of the Abyss, and is often called Ninildu,[1263] the "carpenter" god who forges the storm-weapon of his son Ninurta/Marduk. This carpenter god is a reappearance in the underworld of Tvashtr, the formative aspect of the Cosmic Man.[1264] Ninildu is said to be the "carpenter" or fabricative aspect of An (Horus the Elder-Osiris). As the efficient force of An/Atum, Ninildu may indeed be considered the creative aspect of Enki (Osiris), "Nudimmud", who is Ea/Enki as "the moulder", "ša nabnite".[1265]

Further, it is Ninildu who builds the bow which Ninurta uses in his battle with the rebels. It is interesting to note that in the Vedas, the weapon, vajra, which Indra uses against the dragon Vrtra is indeed forged by Tvashtr, who, along with the Avestan Tvoreshtar, is a counterpart of Ninildu. The fact that the Greek equivalent of Tvashtr is Tartarus (a region deep in Earth, according to Hesiod)[1266] suggests that the weapon that is used to combat the forces which inhibit the rise of the light is developed in the darkness of Earth. We have seen that the "weapon" is indeed a flood which bears the solar force aloft after it has destroyed the serpent.[1267] Now the serpent Typhoeus which is the Greek counterpart of Vrtra is itself a son of Tartarus and Earth (*Theogony* ll.820-80).[1268] Thus the serpent and the weapon used

---

[1260] K 170+Rm520 obv. (see A. Livingstone, *op.cit.*, p.31).

[1261] CT 24,14,26 (see A. Deimel, *Pantheon,* p.194).

[1262] *EE* I,98.

[1263] Ninildu is given as one of the names of Enki in the 'An=Anum' list.

[1264] See above Ch.V.

[1265] See above p.218n; cf. also CT 24,14,19; 24,14,38; 24,27,8, and J. Hehn, *op.cit.*, p.27. T. Jacobsen (*Treasures of Darkness,* p.111) cites a passage from the myth "Enki and the World Order", ll.52-7, which points especially to Enki's virtue as "the power in amniotic fluid". In Egypt, Osiris is called the "lord of the sexual seed" (Pyr. 510c-d). In several passages (see K. Tallquist, *op.cit,* p.408) Ninildu seems to be mentioned as a separate figure from Enki, even though he is but an aspect of the latter.

[1266] See *Theogony* ll.119,721.

[1267] See above p.199.

[1268] Cf. Apollodorus, *Bibliotheca,* I,39ff.

to destroy it are both created by Tartarus/Tvashtr. And, as Güterbock has pointed out, Zeus again descends to Tartarus before he can fight the Titans, just as Teshup, the Hurrian Zeus, also descends to the Abyss to obtain the help of Ea in the Hurrian tale of Ullikummi.[1269]

En-me-šar-ra and Nin-me-šar-ra, 'Lord-' and 'Lady of the totality of the 'me's', are titles of Enki and his consort in the god-list from the Isin Dynasty.[1270] Enmesharra is identified also with Kingu, the second consort of Tiamat in *Enuma Elish*, in an Assyrian ritual text.[1271] Kingu however is defeated and killed by Enki's son Marduk.[1272] Since Enmesharra is also identified with the underworld god, Nergal, a form of Ninurta/Marduk,[1273] we may assume that the latter absorbs the role of Kingu. Besides, Marduk is, in the *EE* VII,120, finally identifiable with his father Ea, since he is the counterpart of Horus the Younger, who is equally identical to his father Osiris.

A temple hymn W.B.161 declares that Enki's temple, the "e-engur-ra" was first built in Enlil's city Nippur,[1274] which suggests that Eridu was perhaps founded after an earlier settlement at Nippur. Besides this possible literal historical significance, it is likely that the cosmological priority of Enlil is also being highlighted here since, as we have seen, Enlil is the primordial wind which retrieves Earth (the later domain of Enki) from the base of the cosmic ocean. Indeed, it is at Nippur that the fate of the Enki temple at Eridu is decreed. And Enlil declares:

> "My son has built a temple, the King Enki!
> Eridu, like a mountain, has he from the earth produced".[1275]

Enki's temple possesses the primordial 'me's' and is also called the sanctuary of the me's, Es-abzu. These primordial me's are the most powerful and sometimes represented as given to Enki (Osiris) by his "father", An (Horus the Elder), who is, more properly, his brother.[1276] Enki is sometimes also

---

[1269] See H.G. Güterbock, *Kumarbi*, p.103.

[1270] See H. de Genouillac, "Grande Liste", *RA* 20, p.97.

[1271] A.O. 17626 (RA 41 31) (see A. Livingstone, *op.cit.*, p.199).

[1272] Kingu himself is replaced, in the *Atrahasis* epic, I,223, by a god called Wê-ilu, "who has personality", and is ultimately sacrificed to produce mankind (see W.G. Lambert and A.R. Millard, *Atrahasis*, p.59; cf. p.186 above).

[1273] See A. Deimel, *op.cit.*, p.118.

[1274] See H. Wohlstein, *op.cit.*, p.54.

[1275] *Ibid.*, p.55.

[1276] An as Brahman is prior to Varuna/Enki. Though An is also a form of Girra/Agni

called the "leading 'son' of An [Dyaus] … who directs justice alongside An; the king, on the dais of An … decrees the fates alongside Enlil".[1277] Enki is to be imagined in this formula in his underworld form rather than as the primal lord of the cosmos. In Sumer, as in the Vedas, the cosmic waters which are created by the lord of the Abyss and constitute the basis of the physical life of the universe (Earth) are infused with the source of all morality and order, the me's (rta), which direct the course of the entire universe. The me's, which are the substance of the Abyss, are first manifested in the underworld (Earth), just as the solar light too is first formed there. Enki is the lord of the me's, just as in the Vedas, Varuna, along with Mitra (who is but another aspect of himself), is the lord of Rta.[1278]

In the poem, 'Enki and Ninhursag', we get a glimpse of the creation of universal life by Enki as the revivified Lord of the Underworld. He is described as creating, through Ninhursag, eight deities who manifest various parts of his own hidden body. It is interesting to note that Enki is, like the Egyptian Atum-Re/Amun, represented as creating through masturbation.[1279] However, his female partners are said to be Ninsikilla (Damkina) as well as Ninhursag, the Lady of the Base of the Mountain (wife of Enlil, Kurgal, the 'great Mountain').[1280] This close identity of Enki and Enlil is apparent in the fact that Marduk is sometimes considered the son of Enlil, rather than of Enki.[1281]

The eight divine creations of Enki may correspond to the universal manifestations of the Purānic, and phallic, Agni.[1282] The first of the eight deities brought to birth in Ninhursag's womb is Abu, the lord of plantal life, the second Nintulla, lord of Magan, and the last is called Ensag, lord of Dilmun, who is represented as a date-palm representing the cosmic tree.[1283] We will note, below, the association of the Tree of Life with Ninurta, one

according to the Assyrian exegetical texts (A. Livingstone, *op.cit.*, p.74).

[1277] See "Enki and Inanna", ll.85ff, in S.N. Kramer and J. Mair, *The Myths of Enki, the Crafty God*, Oxford: OUP 1989, p.41.

[1278] In Egypt, Osiris is not surprisingly also called the Lord of Ma'at (PT 1520a-1523a).

[1279] See B. Alster, "Dilmun, Bahrain, and the alleged Paradise in Sumerian Myth and Literature", in *Dilmun: New Studies in the Archaeology and Early History of Bahrain*, ed. D.T. Potts, Berlin: Dietrich Reimer Verlag, 1983, p.59.

[1280] See A. Deimel, *Pantheon*, p.75.

[1281] See K 3476 obv. L.5 (in A. Livingstone, *op.cit.*, p.121) where Ninlil is revealed to be the mother of Marduk; cf. Kinnier Wilson, *op.cit.*, p.63.

[1282] See above p.213.

[1283] See. K. Al Nashef, "The Deities of Dilmun" in *Bahrain Through the Ages*, pp.344ff; cf. B. Alster, *op.cit.* p.59. In the poem "Enki and the World-Order", however, the deity placed in charge of Dilmun by Enki is Ninsikilla (ll.238-9), who is but Damkina.

of whose forms is Nabû.[1284] Ensag is a name of Nabû, the force within the moon, which we have seen is the deity which rules the Mind of the universe, which is a manifestation of the highest level of divine energy, the sattvic. [1285]

In the poem 'Enki and Inanna', Enki is depicted embarking on a "magur" boat, also called "the Ibex of the Abzu", which is a symbol of Enki's shrine itself. It may also be the Sumerian counterpart of the sun-barque in Egypt. Enki's voyage, in the myth, does not take him on a patently solar course but moves from region to region in "Mesopotamia" and the surrounding lands.[1286] We shall see later, in our consideration of Ninurta, that the boat of the latter too is called the "magur".[1287] Once again the close identity of Ninurta (Marduk) to Enki as the underworld forms of the solar force is apparent.

Among the Hurrians, we have seen that the first ruler of heaven is, in the epic of 'The Kingship in Heaven',[1288] called Alalu, who rules for "nine counted years" before his dominion is replaced by that of Anu.[1289] Alalu is dragged by Anu into the realm of Earth. The Lord of Earth (Enki) is thus the same as Alala, the cosmic Man, deposed to Earth.[1290] This would explain the resemblance of the dead Osiris to the Ideal Man (Vishnu) asleep on the serpent Sesha in the Purānas.[1291]

Among the Hittites, we notice a Sun-god of Earth, as well as a Sun-goddess of the Waters and a Sun-god of the Heavens. In the Hittite treaties, the sun-god of Heaven is followed by the sun-goddess of Arinna (called Wurunsema in Hatti),[1292] who represents the Goddess of Earth,[1293] and her name is most likely related to "aruna" meaning the ocean. The sun-goddess

---

[1284]   See below p.248.

[1285]   See above p.110.

[1286]   See S.N. Kramer and J. Maier, *op.cit.*, pp.42ff. But the fact that the name of Sumer is itself probably derived from that of the primordial mountain at the centre of Earth (see above p.164n) makes it likely that these geographical regions reflect cosmological ones.

[1287]   See below p.298.

[1288]   See H.G. Güterbock, "Hittite Mythology", in S. Kramer (ed.), *Mythologies*, pp.155ff.; cf. H.G. Güterbock, *Kumarbi*, p.99.

[1289]   See H.G. Güterbock, "Hittite Mythology", pp.155ff.

[1290]   Enlil's town Nippur is, interestingly, mentioned in close relation to Kumarbi/Chronos/Enki in the fragments of the Kumarbi epic (see H.G. Güterbock, "Hittite Mythology", p.157).

[1291]   See above p.77.

[1292]   'Wurun' is most likely related to Varuna and 'sema' to 'Shamash'. The Hattic/Canaanite/Hamitic origin of these gods (see above p.27) is made clear here. 'Arinna' is equally a form of Varuna (see p.62 above, p.310 below).

[1293]   See V. Haas, *Geschichte*, p.423.

of Arinna is identified with Teshup's consort, Hebat.[1294] This means that the sun-god of Heaven is the same as Teshup/Seth. The son of the sun-goddess of Arinna is Telipinu, who corresponds to Horus the Younger in the Heliopolitan cosmogony.[1295] Since, in Egypt, Horus the Younger is the son of Osiris, Wurunsema/Aruna is clearly the same as Varuna.

The Hittite Sun-god of Earth is a god of the underworld. In KBo V 3 i 53, the Sun-god of the earth (taknaš ^{d}UTU-us)[1296] is mentioned in association with dAl-la-tum, who is the same as Ereshkigal, or Queen of the Underworld.[1297] Ereshkigal is the name of the consort of both Enki and Nergal/Marduk. This is of course due to the fact that Enki and Nergal/Ninurta/Marduk are ultimately the same solar force. The Hittite sun-god of the earth is thus related to Enki as well as to Nergal,[1298] the Sumerian sun-god of the underworld. Also, Ereshkigal is identified with Damkina, consort of Enki, in the treaty of Mursilis II (CTH 67 and CTH/51/52).[1299] The sun-goddess of Earth is also called Allani[1300] and sometimes, even Hepat (CTH 106).[1301]

The Canaanite myth of Baal repeats the story of Osiris/Nergal in a form that is very similar to the myth of Osiris. After his conquest of Yamm, the sea-god (a son of El/Chronos), Baal ventures into the underworld in order to dominate Mot, a death-dispensing ruler of the Abyss,[1302] who is (like Baal himself) also a son of El.[1303] Baal, Yamm and Mot are thus brothers. Yamm may be the same as Okeanos (itself a serpentine form of Enki/Osiris), while Mot may represent the deadly aspect of the passionate Seth. Before entering the underworld, Baal first produces a calf by mating with a cow in order that he may have a successor in the case of his death.

[1294]   *Ibid.* p.425.

[1295]   *Ibid.*, p.443. Telipinu is a deity of Hattic origins (see E. Laroche, *op.cit.*, p.34; cf. O.R. Gurney, *op.cit.*).

[1296]   In KUB XVII 14 iv 21, the Sun-god of Earth is mentioned in the company of the "lower" gods (Anunnaki) as opposed to the "upper" (Igigi) (see E. Tenner, "Tages- und Nachtsonne bei den Hethitern", *ZA* 38 (1929), p.187).

[1297]   See D. Yoshida, op.cit., p.317.

[1298]   See E. Laroche, *op.cit.*, p.34 (see also p.224 above).

[1299]   See D. Yoshida, *op.cit.*, p.20.

[1300]   Cf. V. Haas, *op.cit.*, p.132. Allani is the Hurrian version of the Babylonian Allatum.

[1301]   In the time of Hattusilis III, the sun-goddess of Arinna was equated with Teshup's consort, Hepat (KUB 21.27 = Vs.I 1-6) (see V. Haas, *op.cit.*, p.425).

[1302]   Mot is either a serpent himself or accompanied by a seven-headed hydra called Leviathan (see C. Gordon, "Canaanite Mythology", in S. Kramer (ed.) *Mythologies*, p.200).

[1303]   We have seen that Seth is a brother and *alter ego* of Osiris, and both Seth and Apopis are related to Re (see below p.290).

This calf may be the counterpart of Nannar in the Sumerian Enlil myth, in which case we remark the identity of Baal and Enlil.[1304] When he encounters Mot in the underworld, Baal is killed by the latter, exactly as Osiris is by Seth. Baal's corpse is found by Anat, his consort, along with the sun-goddess Shapsh [from Akk. Shamash], exactly as Isis bears the body of Osiris with the help of Horus the Younger. Anat succeeds in killing Mot and in resurrecting the body of her beloved Baal.[1305] It is important to note, however, that Baal himself is later associated with Teshup/Zeus/Seth,[1306] showing that Horus the Younger and Seth are indeed different aspects of the same solar energy that finally emerges as the sun of our system.

Since Dionysus is also represented as descending into the underworld, he is also a counterpart of Osiris, who is revived as the sun by both Seth and Horus the Younger.[1307] At the same time, Dionysus' association with wine is similar to Seth's with beer.[1308] The orgiastic cult of this Thraco-Phrygian deity and his association with wine-festivals (late substitutes for the soma-celebrations of the Āryan priesthood) are well known. The symbolism of wine in Dionysiac ritual is clearly the same as that of soma in the Vedic or of beer in the Sethian context. This is made especially clear in his appellation as "Dionysus in the tree",[1309] signifying the vital sap of the tree of life which he represents. The Dionysiac religion, however, is, like the Indian, a deeply philosophical one since it aims at saving men from the cycle of reincarnation. This is evident in the Orphic account of Dionysus' effort, after his resurrection, to save men from rebirth with the aid of his mother Kore/Persephone.[1310]

The Sumerian god Enki may have been the original of the Nordic god of the ocean, Aegir. However, there is little in the actual role Aegir plays – of host to the gods – that would allow us to recognize in him the primal deity of Mesopotamia, except for the fact that he "brews ale" for the Aesir[1311] which may be a distant reference to the "sweet waters" of Enki.

[1304]   Enlil and Enki are once again identifiable with each other.

[1305]   See M. Hütter, *Altorientalische Vorstellungen von der Unterwelt: Literar- und religionsgeschichtliche Überlegungen zu 'Nergal und Ereškigal'*, Freiburg: Universitätsverlag, 1985, 130-46.

[1306]   See H. te Velde, *op.cit.*, pp.120ff. For Baal, see A.R.W. Green, *op.cit.*, Ch.III.

[1307]   The ultimate co-operation between the solar and storm god is indeed reflected in the coupling of Shamash with Adad in the An-Anum god-list as well as in the royal name Shamshi-Adad (see above p.201).

[1308]   See above p.194.

[1309]   Plutarch, *Quaestiones Convivales*, V,3.

[1310]   Kore is the mistress of Zeus (see M.L. West, *Orphic Poems*, p.74; cf. p.95).

[1311]   See, for instance, 'Loki's Quarrel' in the *Poetic Edda*.

XVIII: ADITI

THE MATERIAL MATRIX OF THE UNIVERSE:
HUH–HUHET, HATHOR, NAMMU, TIAMAT

Varuna in the underworld is the lord of the waters, just as Osiris and Enki too are. In the Vedic literature there are indications that the waters are not just fluid expanses, but, give rise to sound-waves which enunciate the sacred Law of the universe.[1312] At *KYV* V,6,8, Earth is associated with "speech", just as the Mid-region is with "breath", and Heaven with "the eye". These correspond to the domains of Agni, Vāyu and Āditya. At *KYV* V,5,4, the waters, which are the "wives"of Varuna, are considered the birth-place of Agni as Vāk, the Word, the deity who creates and sustains the universe.[1313] We have seen that Agni also ruled speech in the ideal Macroanthropos.

The watery consort of Varuna is Aditi. The gods of the universe are all produced in the basic element of Aditi: "In her Prajāpati [Dyaus as god of generation] made effort. He produced the gods, Vāsus, Rudras, and Ādityas [sons of Aditi]" (*KYV* VII,1,4).[1314] The consort of Aditi, Varuna, is

---

[1312] These sound-waves must be related to the radio energy which has been observed emerging from the dark nucleus of a galaxy, the so-called "black hole" (*EB*, Macropedia, 16:635).

[1313] *RV* X,125 (Vāk Sūkta); cf. U. Choudhuri, *op.cit.*, p.43. Agni as the Word is the prototype of the philosophical hypostasis of the Logos in Greek and hellenised Christian philosophy.

[1314] In *BAU*, IX,2,ff. the eight Vasus are called "fire, earth, air, the sky, the sun, the heavens, the moon, the stars", the eleven Rudras are called "the ten breaths along with the mind" and the twelve Ādityas are called the "twelve months of the year", keeping in mind that the "year" is the same as the "universe", for the Ādityas are indeed the suns of different universes (see below).

According to *RV* X,72,8 there are eight Adityas, of which one, Mārtanda, died soon after birth. They are, according to the commentator Sāyana: Mitra, Varuna, Dhatar, Aryaman, Amsha, Bhaga, Vivasvān, Āditya. The names of the first and last two Ādityas confirm that they are indeed all solar phenomena, and *RV* IX,114,2: "Seven regions have their several suns ... seven are the Āditya deities", suggests that they are the suns of the seven "islands" or "continents" (galaxies) which constitute Earth (see above p.163).

sometimes called Vishnu since Vishnu represents the solar force that has been forced into the underworld and that will eventually rise as the sun of our system.[1315] One of the typical forms of Aditi as goddess of Earth is as a Cow (Prishnī).[1316]

In Egypt, the Earth-flood Mehet Ouret which bears the sun aloft is also represented as a cow.[1317] Mehet Ouret is identical to Huh-Huhet, the Earth-flood which we have already noted as one of the constituents of the egg.[1318] Both Mht wr.t and Huh-Huhet are accompanied by the pitch darkness (Kuk) that characterises the Abyss of the underworld (as well as

---

Sometimes the number of the Ādityas is given as six, with six female consorts so that the total number is enlarged to twelve. In *BP* VI,6,39 the Ādityas are twelve in number and all male, called Vivasvān, Aryama (Vedic Aryaman), Pusha (Pushan), Tvashta (Tvashtr), Savita (Savitr), Bhaga, Dhata, Vidhata, Varuna, Mitra, Sakra, Urukrama (Vāmana). In *BrdP* I,ii,24,33, the twelve suns are named Indra, Dhātr, Bhaga, Pūsan, Mitra, Varuna, Aryaman, Amshu, Vivasvān, Tvashtr, Savitr and Vishnu.

In Greece, the Ādityas, who are called Titans, include, in Hesiod, six male deities, Okeanus, Coeus, Crius, Hyperion, Iapetus, Cronos, and six goddesses Theia, Themis, Rheia, Tethys, Mnemosyne, and Phoebe. Of these we may recognize Cronos, Okeanus, and Hyperion as being identical to Shiva/Indra, Varuna (*AV* I,33,2) and Mitra. Hyperion's children include Eos, Helios and Selene, that is, dawn, and the "twins", the sun and the moon. In the *RV* too (VI,49,2), the sun and the moon are called Indra/Rudra's two "daughters", showing the solar (Mitra/Hyperion) quality of Indra in Vedic literature (cf. also p.294 below). The Titans are combatted and vanquished by Zeus (GaneshaTeshup/Seth). This defeat may correspond to that of the Asuras by the gods (also led by Indra) as well as to the killing of Osiris by Seth.

In the Avesta and the *Bundahishn*, the Ādityas, except Mithra and Airyaman, are absent, but vaguely reflected in the six Amesha Spentas, the "well-doing ones", Vohu-mano (good thought), Asha Vahista (excellent holiness, or the holy order of the universe corresponding to the Vedic rta), Kshathra Vairya (perfect sovereignty), Spenta Armaiti (divine piety, who reappears in the *RV* V,43,6 as "the great Aramati … who knoweth Holy Law"), Harvatat (health) and Ameretat (immortality), all ruled by Ahura Mazda. The Amesha Spentas are opposed by six evil counterparts [daevas] created by Angra Mainyu: Indra (or Andar), Akomano (evil thought), who opposes Vohu-mano; Sauru (Vedic Sarva; see above), who opposes Kshatra Vairya; Naunhaithya (Skt. Nāsatyas), who oppose Spenta Armaiti, Tarich and Zerich (*Bundahishn* XXVIII,7).

[1315]   See *KYV* VII,5,14.

[1316]   Prshni, the consort of Rudra, who is called the Cow in *RV* VI,66,1, is identifiable with Aditi (see Sāyana's commentary to *RV* II,34). In the Avesta, the Kine represent the "pure" [=pristine] animal creation (Yasna 35,3).; cf. pp.135,139 above. The creator of the Cow must be Tvoreshtar, who is the same as Spenta Mainyu, the creative aspect of Ahura Mazda (see above p.125).

[1317]   See above p.53. Cf. *Esna* III,31 (206,7) and III,33 (206,13) (see *LÄ* IV:4); cf. also S. Bickel, *op.cit.*, p.65.

[1318]   In the 'Morning Hymn' of Text 37 of tomb 33 (Petamenophis) (see J. Assmann, *op.cit.*, p.19), Huh and Huhet are represented as holding the emergent sun-god Re in their arms.

the cosmos before the appearance of the heavenly light, Horus the Elder), for there is a reference to "the darkness in the night which is Mht wr.t".[1319]

Another deity that appears as a ruler of the underworld is Hathor, who is naturally associated with Osiris, the ruler of the underworld. Indeed, dead women were believed to be transformed into Hathor just as dead men were into Osiris.[1320] Hathor is thus identified with Isis, consort of Osiris.[1321]

Hathor/Aditi is indeed the material basis in which the sun is born, and her name seems to have been understood to mean "house of Horus". The cosmic flood, Hathor/Aditi and the goddess of Dawn, Isis/Usha, are both forms of each other, and both of them are represented as a cow with horns.[1322] Hathor especially is transformed into an abundantly nourishing milch-cow, Earth, and bears the sun between her horns. The sun between her horns points to the significance of the solar light as the goal of the creation.

The greatest significance of Mht wr.t is, thus, her giving birth to the sun, Horus the Younger, in his early form as Harsomtus, "Horus who unites the two lands".[1323] The "two lands" in this title are originally clearly heaven and earth, since the domain of the sun is typically the region in between, and has connections to both heaven and earth. The transposition of this cosmological title of the sun to Upper and Lower Egypt is a later religio-political one.[1324]

Hathor is further associated with Seshat, the consort of Thoth, who, as we have seen, is the god of wisdom and hieroglyphs, and associated with Nun. As Sethe has noted, Nun, Nunet and Thoth form a triad, just as Amun, Amunet and Ptah form another.[1325] We have seen that Thoth is an aspect also of the primal Enki/Varuna/Osiris, since he represents the "tongue"

[1319] See E.A.W. Budge, *The Book of the Dead*, 1951, 124:17.

1320 See C.J. Bleeker, *Hathor and Thoth*, p.45.

[1321] See E. Hornung, *Conceptions of God*, pp.93-6 for the various references to this event in ancient Egyptian literature; cf. the Morning hymn mentioned above (J. Assmann, *op.cit.*, p.19), where the king identified with the sun-god is called the son of Osiris. This Re must be the same as Horus the Younger/Harakhte. The first form of Re as the rising sun is Khepera (see J. Assmann, *op.cit.*, p.48f).

[1322] Aditi (Hathor) is the source of that watery radiance consequent on the separation of heaven and earth which is personified by the Dawn, Usha/Isis. Usha as the goddess who goes before Sūrya must represent the incipient sunlight (just as Hathor is sometimes called the "sun-eye" (see M.E. Lefebure, *Tombeau de Seti I*, IV, 15-18; cf. C.J. Bleeker, *Hathor and Toth*, p.50) and is but a form of Aditi, consort of the Lord of the Waters, Varuna (Osiris).

[1323] See C.J. Bleeker, *op.cit.*, p.63.

[1324] See below p.260f.

[1325] See K. Sethe, *op.cit.*, p.77.

of the manifesting deity. The moon, the "greater" light that precedes the emergence of the sun, is also an effect of Thoth, and Hathor's association with him as a predecessor of the solar light shows that both the moon and the sun arise from the waters represented by Hathor/Aditi.[1326]

The moon, we shall see, is in Iranian mythology said to be the repository of the seed of the Bull of Heaven after it is slaughtered by Angra Mainyu. Hence it is called Soma[1327] itself in the Vedas. It is significant that, just as Agni is said to have consumed the (sexually) invigorating Soma while cradled in Aditi, so also Hathor's characterisation as a goddess of inebriety suggests the potent nourishment provided by her to the infant solar force called Horus.[1328]

Hathor is, further, called "the mistress of the sycamore"[1329] (representing the universal tree – filled with the sap of life – which holds the sun aloft above its uppermost branches). This is akin to Aditi's development of Indra [the Soma-filled solar force] as the cosmic Tree of Life in the Vedas.[1330]

In Sumer, according to the Tammuz passage in CT XVI,46,183ff,[1331] the goddess of the waters is represented by Nammu, who is located in Earth (the floods of Mehet Ouret). We have seen that Nammu also represents the primal waters in which the cosmic man lies and in which the Cosmic Egg constituted of heaven and earth is formed.[1332] Nammu is also called Belet-ili, the "mistress of the gods" and identified with Ishtar (Isis), the goddess of the Dawn, who is the sister-wife of the sun. Nammu is thus a counterpart of Aditi and Hathor,[1333] both of whom represent both the waters of the

---

[1326]   Thoth being associated with Tvoresthtar/Tvaštr/Tartarus (see above Ch.V) must be a god who rises from the total darkness of Kuk-Kuket.

[1327]   'Soma' is related to the Germanic "Samen" (seed).

[1328]   See S. Schott, *Das schöne Fest vom Wüstentale, Festbräuche einer Totenstadt*, Wiesbaden: F. Steiner, 1953.

[1329]   *WAS*, II:282.

[1330]   See below pp.275ff.

[1331]   See below p.281.

[1332]   See above p.104f.

[1333]   The original waters are represented as a mother goddess who bears heaven and earth [i.e. of our universe] in an undifferentiated complex surrounded by an ocean (see E.O. James, *op.cit.*, p.11). This "ocean" is the same as Okeanos (the Greek corruption of the name of the Sumerian lord of Earth, Enki), who is, like his consort Tethys, represented as a Titan 'child' of Ouranos (Dyaus) and Ge (Prithvī). The identity of Enki/Okeanos and Osiris is confirmed by Plutarch (*De Iside et Osiride*, 364d), which declares that the Egyptian priests "explain Oceanus as Osiris and Tethys as Isis" (tr. J.G. Griffiths). Oceanos/Osiris is thus the same as Varuna and Tethys/Isis identical to Aditi. The name Aditi, however, is more closely related to Hathor than to Isis, who is a later manifestation of the former, and equal to the Vedic Usha.

underworld and the Dawn (consort of the solar deity). That Ishtar is the same as Aditi/Hathor/Isis is made clearer by the fact that she was, like the latter, represented as a "wild cow".[1334]

At the same time, Inanna/Ishtar, like Nammu, though normally called the "daughter" of An, is originally the same as his consort, Antum (CT 24, 20, 19). In AO 6458 we get a description of the ceremony whereby Ishtar is elevated to her original form as Antum, consort of An:

> To the goddess Inanna, whom Thou loved hast,
> Transmit the direction of Thy "dispositions"
> May she be Antum, Thy equal consort.[1335]

Ishtar is represented as both the virgin mother and consort of Tammuz, who, as we have seen, is identical to An.[1336] Both An and Inanna were worshipped at the ancient Sumerian centre of Uruk.[1337] She is also an *alter ego* of the goddess of Dawn, Aia (who appears after Tammuz is resurrected as the sun). Indeed, she was also called Esha, "goddess of the sea",[1338] and this may be the source of the names Usha, Isis, Eos, all representing the goddess of Dawn. As such, she is considered the sister of Shamash and daughter of the moon, Nannar. Ishtar/Venus is also called "merciful sister of Marduk",[1339] which confirms Marduk's solar character. In the Ur dynasty, her name was read phonetically as Iš-ha-ra, with the variant Išhura, the latter using the sign "asar" which is associated with Enki and Marduk.[1340]

In the *Enuma Elish*, Apsu is "overthrown" by Ea/Enki, but the final triumph over Tiamat is, as we shall see, reserved for Enki's son, Marduk (Horus the Younger/Ninurta), a role assigned in the Sumerian original of the Babylonian epic probably to Ninurta, who undertakes similar exploits against Asakku in the epic *Lugal-e*.[1341] Marduk splits Tiamat into two halves forming heaven and earth, since the waters of the Abyss are originally constituted of unseparated earthly and heavenly elements.

[1334]   See S. Langdon, *op.cit.*, p.55.

[1335]   A.O. 6458 in H. Wohlstein, *op.cit.*, p.111.

[1336]   See above p.179.

[1337]   See S. Langdon, *op.cit.*, p.95.

[1338]   *Ibid.*, p.47; cf. CT 26, 42a, 10: [ilat] iš-ha-ra ti-amat.

[1339]   *Ibid.*, p.176.

[1340]   *Ibid,,* p.125.

[1341]   See W. Lambert, "Ninurta Mythology in the Babylonian Epic of Creation" in *Keilschriftliche Literaturen, Ausgewählte Vorträge der XXXII RAI*, Berlin: D. Reimer, 1985, pp.55-60; cf. p.297 below.

Significantly, Tiamat is equated with Ereshkigal, the goddess of the underworld, Earth, in an Assyrian ritual text (O 175),[1342] Ereshkigal being synonymous with Damkina, consort of Enki. However, since Nergal, the sun of the underworld, is also commonly described as the husband of Ereshkigal, we see again that Nergal (a form of Ninurta) is the same as Enki, just as Horus the Younger is indeed Osiris-Horus the Elder. And Nergal is equated with Enki's son, Marduk, as well, in Babylon (KAR 142 rec.iii 28).[1343] So that Tiamat/Ereshkigal must be a consort of Marduk/Nergal as well as of his father Enki/Osiris. But we have seen that Ishtar/Isis is the consort of An/ Horus the Elder as well, which suggests once again the identity of Horus the Elder with Osiris. The identification of Tiamat with Ereshkigal is repeated in the Sumerian identification of Asakku with Antum.[1344]

The waters of the primeval ocean surround not only earth, which is formed first from it but also the brilliant heaven above it. In fact, heaven is considered to be constituted "of water" (ša me).[1345] In Jewish and Moslem traditions which retain fragments of the cosmological conceptions of the Babylonians too, Tehom [from Tiamat] is considered as both the waters lying beneath and the waters of heaven.[1346] The waters of the Abyss are considered sweet and life-giving, and exorcisms in Babylon were practised by means of water from Eridu.[1347] However, rabbinical literature preserves a concept of the difference between the waters of the netherworld and those of heaven, the former being considered feminine and the latter masculine.[1348] The Ocean (Enki/Osiris) which surrounds Earth however is represented as dark and deadly and bears the form of a gigantic serpent.[1349]

In Iran, the counterpart of the waters of the Abyss is the Vouru-kasha Sea, the name of which may be the source of the Sanskritic term 'vrksha' for 'tree', since the roots of the cosmic tree that arises from Aditi/Hathor and is sustained by Varuna/Enki are based in the Abyss.[1350] The image of the Cow also appears in the Iranian Yasna 31,9 where Ahura Mazda is said to have created the Cow [Earth] for the "husbandman" and the "herdsman"

[1342]   See A. Livingstone, *op. cit.*, p.191.

[1343]   *Ibid.*, p.235.

[1344]   See below p.297.

[1345]   *Ibid.*, pp.32f.

[1346]   See A.J. Wensinck, "The Ocean", pp.15ff.

[1347]   *Ibid.*, p.60.

[1348]   *Ibid.*, p.61f.

[1349]   *Ibid.*, p.25.

[1350]   See Ch.XXIII below.

[Heaven].[1351] The primal Cow is, as we have seen above, the impregnated form of the extended Earth.

[1351] See above p.157.

XIX: SKANDA

THE SOLAR FORCE: NINURTA, MARDUK

Since Osiris represents the solar light felled by Ganesha/Seth and forced into the underworld of Earth, he is consequently represented as a "dying god" and the god of Earth (Enki). However, the reviving solar nature of Osiris is confirmed in the passage in CT 335 IV 192/3a-c: "Yesterday is Osiris: tomorrow is Atum", since it is Osiris who is resurrected as Horus the Younger and the other full-fledged forms of the sun.[1352]

This revivifying force is contained in the seed of the divine phallus which is personified by the Sumerian Ninurta, Babylonian Marduk and the Indian Skanda. In the AB, Prajāpati's seed falls when Rudra (Shiva)'s arrow pierces him and from this seed arises a lake surrounded by fire[1353] which is then agitated by the winds and the force of Agni. The kindled seed that ultimately turns into the sun is the same as Skanda. Although the seed is said to be that of Prajāpati, we have noted that Prajāpati and Shiva are the same as the First Man, just as Ouranos and Chronos are equally aspects of the Ideal Man.[1354] Indeed, just as Ninurta is considered the semen of the "great mountain" Enlil, Skanda, the son of Shiva (Enlil) in Indic mythology, has a name signifying "jet of semen".

The seminal solar force is virtually the same as the original Light of Brahman itself since, like the latter, Skanda too is born of an Egg. In the MBh, Āranyakaparva (IX,43,14ff), the story of the birth of Shiva's son Skanda reports that the daughter of Daksha (Aditi/Narmada/Parvathi)[1355]

[1352]   We have seen above (p.104) that the possible meaning of Osiris is indeed "life".

[1353]   Cf. the Isle of Flames in the Egyptian solar mythology, above p.153.

[1354]   See above p.141.

[1355]   Aditi is the daughter of Daksha and Akshini (see below p.307) and the resemblance of Aditi to Nammu, who is the counterpart of Narmada/Parvathi has already been noted (above p.234).

made love to Agni/Shiva six times (in spite of Shiva's famed asceticism), taking the guise of the wives of six of the seven sages (who, as we have seen, represent the wisdom of the previous cosmic ages), and then, taking his seed in her hand, flew in the form of a Gārudī bird[1356] to a golden lake[1357] on the peak of the "white mountain"[1358] guarded by Shiva-Rudra's armies. The seed of Shiva turns into an embryo [or egg] and the mountain itself turns into gold, while Earth is infused with metals of diverse colours.[1359] From this embryo is born Skanda (Muruga/Marukka), who, representing the jet of divine semen, emerges from atop a mountain, Shiva/Enlil being typically called Parvatha/Kur/Mountain.[1360] That Skanda is the same also as Ninurta/Marduk is clear from the similarity of the description of the metallic composition of Earth in both the *MBh* and the *Lugal e*,[1361] as well as from the fact that Skanda is a martial god like Ninurta and, in fact, the "commander" of the gods.[1362]

In the *MBh*, the birth of Skanda is described as being accompanied by terrific storms and blizzards.[1363] The gods are at first disturbed by the violence of his birth and suspect the infant of being a potential usurper of their role.[1364] The reason of the unusual violence accompanying the birth of Skanda is that his father Shiva is a powerful ascetic whose child is imbued with an extraordinary amount of "tejasic" or solar virtue.[1365] So Indra as the leader of the gods attempts to kill Skanda with the aid of the 'Mothers', the

---

[1356]   The Gārudī bird is the female of the Garuda, which, iconographically represented in fierce form, is an early manifestation of the sun (see below p.301). For the bird-imagery of the sun in Western Asia, including that of the cock, vulture, phoenix, and eagle, see A.J. Wensinck, "Tree and Bird as Cosmological Symbols in Western Asia", *Verhandelingen der Koninklijke Akademie van Wetenschappen*, Vol.22 (1921), pp.36ff.

[1357]   In the *Haracharitachintāmani* of Jayaratha, the lake itself is formed when Agni vomits after swallowing the powerful seed of Shiva (see W. O'Flaherty, *op.cit.*, p.274). The swallowing of Shiva's seed by Agni is represented in the Brāhmanical rituals by the insertion of oblations into the sacred fire (see W. O'Flaherty, *op.cit.*, p.278).

[1358]   In Kālidāsa's *Kumārasambhava*, V, the mountain itself and the lake of the forest of reeds, Saravana, were formed of Agni's entrance into the semen of Shiva (who is himself a form of Agni, as we have noted above p.213) when it was dropped onto Earth. It is interesting to note the reference to "reeds" here as well as in *Atrahasis*.

[1359]   cf. Kālidāsa, *Kumārasambhava* V.

[1360]   Vāyu, the god of Wind, is also, much like Enlil (lord Wind), called "Parvatha", Mountain, in *RV* I,132, 6.

[1361]   See below p.298.

[1362]   See *Kumārasambhava* V; *MBh* III,228.

[1363]   *MBh* IX, 44.

[1364]   *Ibid.*

[1365]   *MBh* XIII,83,45;47–8 (cf. W. O'Flaherty, *op.cit.*, p.268).

seven cosmic streams, who act as Skanda's nurses. However, the latter refuse to follow Indra's instructions and instead protect the infant against Indra's attacks. Finally, Indra concedes his impotence against the invincibility of Skanda and appoints him as his general.

In the account of the birth of Skanda in the *MBh*, we note that Skanda is distinguished from Indra, who, as leader of the gods, serves as his adversary. We may detect a resemblance of Skanda's birth to that of Zeus, who is more precisely the counterpart of Skanda's violent brother, Ganesha.[1366] However, Skanda and Ganesha are but two aspects of the same deity, just as Shamash (Suwalliyat) and Adad (Hanish), and Osiris and Seth too are.[1367] As Skanda represents the solar virtue of the seed of Brahman, so Ganesha bears the violent and envious nature of Shiva/Chronos. We know that it is indeed Ganesha/Zeus who attacks Brahman/Phanes, the cosmic light, and swallows his phallus.[1368] However, the solar force that Zeus bears within himself is revived as the sun of our universe.

As for Indra's murderous intentions against Skanda, we shall see that, in spite of his malevolence against Skanda, Indra himself, like Zeus/Seth, helps in the formation of the sun in the underworld, since it is Indra who possesses the solar power, "kshatram".[1369] At the stage when the divine Light itself is moribund as Osiris, it is Indra/Zeus/Seth who bear the vital solar source. Hence we find that, in the underworld, Indra/Zeus/Seth/Ganesha are fused with Ninurta/Suwalliyat/ Marduk/Muruga – who are indeed counterparts of Skanda. We have also noticed that Indra is a name used to describe the soul of the primal Purusha as well as the androgynous first Man.[1370] Since Indra is equally identifiable with Angra Manyu, who attacks the First Man, we see that Indra/Ganesha and Skanda/Muruga are indeed ultimately the same force, just as Osiris and Seth also are.

Among the Dravidians, Skanda is called Muruga, a name that is possibly related to the nominal variant "Marukka" for Marduk in the An=Anum god-list, Tablet II.[1371] Just as Marduk is four-headed,[1372] and Ninurta is called Sagash (six-headed),[1373] Muruka too is six-headed and

---

[1366] See above Ch.XIV.

[1367] See above p.193f.

[1368] See above p.196.

[1369] Cf. p.22 above.

[1370] See above pp.114, 181.

[1371] The name is spelled "Ma-ru-uk-ka" (see R. Litke, *op.cit.*, p.91).

[1372] See EE I:95; Varuna, the counterpart of Enki, is similarly four-faced (see above p.43).

[1373] See K. Tallquist, *op.cit.*, p.422.

therefore called Shanmukha ("the Six-faced"),[1374] since he is born of Pārvatī in the six-fold form of the wives of six of the seven sages.

The counterpart of Osiris in Sumer, Enki, is the same as his "son" Ninurta, just as Marduk is ultimately identical to Ea.[1375] In fact, the name Enki, Lord of Earth, has the same meaning as Ninurta, "Lord of Earth". But Ninurta is also related to and sometimes identified with Suwalliyat,[1376] the cosmic light of An/Horus the Elder.

Ninurta is, at the same time, the first-born son of Enlil, and is literally considered to be his seed. In the myth "Lugal-e", Ningirsu (Ninurta as Lord of the Flood) is represented as the reddish floodwaters of the mountains and equated to the mountain's "semen".[1377] It is interesting that the flood of which Ningirsu is lord is both the semen of his father, Enlil, and the cosmic flood from which the sun will arise. This shows that, while Ninurta is derived from the cosmic light, he is particulary that force within it which will emerge as the sun.

The final universal form of Ninurta is evident in his resemblance to Atum, for Ninurta's eyes are praised as "the twins, Sin and Šamaš",[1378] just as Ptah too is.[1379] On another occasion, he, again like Ptah, is hymned in fuller terms as a macroanthropos: "His face is the heavens, his form the god ..., his eyes Enlil and Ninlil, the pupils of his eyes Gula and Belit-ile, the iris of his eyes Sin, etc."[1380] We note here the same appellation of the heavens as the "face" of the supreme deity, Atum, that we have noticed in Egypt, so we may

---

[1374] SP V.1.34; I.1.27, etc. (see above p.240).

[1375] See below p.266.

[1376] See H.G. Güterbock, "The God Suwalliyat", p.4. Suwalliyat (Skt. Sūrya/Hurrian Tashmisu) is considered to be the "pure brother" of Teshup in Kbo V2 (*ibid.*).

[1377] See T. Jacobsen, *op.cit* p.131. We see that the attribute "mountain" regularly applied to Enlil is a phallic one and that Ninurta represents Enlil/Vāyu's seed. Cf. also the hymn to Enlil where Enlil's divine residence in Nippur, the Ekur (Mountain Temple), is called "the Lofty Seat of the Overflow" (A. Falkenstein, *Sumerische Götterlieder*, Heidelberg: Carl Winter Universitätsverlag, 1959, I, 21).

[1378] KAR 102, 10-19. Both Nergal and Sin are called "bull of heaven". In *RV* VI,49,2, however, the sun and the moon are called Shiva/Rudra[Enlil/Shu]'s two "daughters". Among the Hittites the sun is mostly female, and among the Lulubi too, the sun was considered a female deity and paired with the male moon, as in the list of gods invoked in the inscription of Anubanini, the Lulubi king: "Anu and Antum, Bel and Belit, Immer and Innina, Sin and Šamaš" (P.A. Schollmeyer, *Sumerisch-babylonische Hymnen und Gebete an Šamaš*, Paderborn: Ferdinand Schoeningh, 1912, p.5).

[1379] See above p.177f

[1380] KAR 102, 10ff., (see B. Meissner, *Babylonien und Assyrien*, Heidelberg: Winter, 1920-25, II:49; cf. A. Jeremias, *Handbuch der altorientalischen Geisteskultur*, Leipzig, 1929, 2 330, ATAT2 250).

assume that the rest of the symbols are related to the Egyptian conventions highlighted in the Ramesside theology.[1381]

We have noted that in Babylon Marduk – like Teshup, a deity that is born of An's seed in the body of Kumarbi[1382] – is the counterpart of Ninurta/Skanda. Thus, Marduk too is the object of macroanthropomorphic adoration in KAR 304,337.[1383] Both Ninurta and Marduk, like Zeus and Indra, represent the vital force of the solar force which helps in the formation of the universe as well as its sun.[1384]

[1381] See above p.98.

[1382] See H.G. Güterbock, *op.cit.*, p.158. Mention is made of several deities conceived in Kumarbi's body, but only three are named, Teshup, Marduk and a deity called KA.ZAL (lust). The sun–god mentioned along with Tashmisu and Teshup in the "Ullikummi" epic may be another reference to Marduk.

[1383] See A. Livingstone, *op.cit.*, p.101.

[1384] See below Ch.XXII.

XX: AGNI

THE UNDERWORLD SUN: NERGAL, GILGAMESH

Although the solar force is contained in the seed of the divine phallus in the the underworld and gradually begins to be transformed there into our sun, the first form of the sun, the sun of earth, is formed in the underworld only after the moon is first formed therein and elevated into the Mid-region of our universe. In Sumer, Nergal is the twin surrogate for the moon in the underworld while the latter is raised into the upper world by Enlil.[1385] Thus we have frequent references to the sun and moon as the 'mashtabbagalgal', the great twins.[1386] The moon is indeed termed the "great light", Gishnugal,[1387] since it appears before the sun of the heavens, which is called Gishnu.

The underworld sun is a child of Enlil (Shu), Nergal, created as an underworld substitute for Enlil's first son, the moon Nannar, when the latter is placed in the heavens by Enlil.[1388] In BMS 27,8, Nergal (Tammuz) is associated with Sin (Ningiszida)[1389] as one of the two guardians of the universe. Utu (Shamash), the heavenly sun, is formed after the moon. In an ancient manual on astronomy and astrology, as Hehn has pointed out, it is

---

[1385]   See H. Behrens, op.cit., pp.220ff.

[1386]   "ilSin u ilNergal" (A. Deimel, Pantheon, p.178); cf. H. Behrens, op.cit.; also the "Enlil and Ninlil" myth in E. Chiera, Sumerian Epics and Myths, 76,77; S.N. Kramer, Sumerian Literary Texts from Nippur, 19; T. Jacobsen, Treasures of Darkness, p.104. The "lesser twins" are formed by the son of Nannar, Ningublaga and Nannar's vizier Alammuš (see "Mondgott" in RLA VIII:365).

[1387]   See above p.20.

[1388]   The other two children begotten by Enlil in the underworld are Ninazu, the surveyor of fields, and Enbilulu, the inspector of canals.

[1389]   Cf. the reference to Tammuz and Ningishzida as the guardians of the gates of heaven in the Adapa myth (p.270 below).

stated that "Shamash (the risen sun) and Nergal are one".[1390] This reminds us once again that the different names of the sun denote the various stages of the developing sun.

In the Sumerian poem of *Nergal and Ereshkigal,* Nergal himself is represented as a god of the heavens who is forced to descend into the underworld at the behest of Ereshkigal. This identifies Nergal once again with Enlil/Enki. Although any immigrant into the underworld is doomed to stay there forever, Nergal succeeds in leaving. But due to Ereshkigal's repeated insistence before the great god Anu, the latter is forced to send Nergal once again into the underworld. This time Nergal succeeds in dominating Ereshkigal once and for all and in assuming the authority of the underworld as the consort of Ereshkigal.[1391] Nergal as the male counterpart of Ereshkigal, the goddess of the underworld (who is identified in the Hittite pantheon with the "sun-goddess of Arinna") makes him virtually the same as Enki, whose consort too is said to be Ereshkigal.[1392] Since Enlil also descends into the underworld, and is, further, said to be the form of Utu when the latter rises,[1393] we see again the virtual identity of Enki and Enlil and their son Ninurta/Nergal. We have seen already that Marduk is both son of Enlil and of Enki. Thus Nergal too is considered a son of Enlil as well as that of Enki.[1394]

According to a Babylonian exegetical text, Kiurash (the god of earth) is the form of the sun when it sets. This is the same as Enki. Nergal is equally called the "King of the setting sun" in BL 196,[1395] which suggests that he takes the part of Osiris in Egypt. Nergal is also called Enlilbanda, "Enlil the Younger" (SRT 12,19), just as Enki too is (CT 25, 33,18).[1396] We have noticed the ultimate identity of Marduk and Enki above and it is not surprising that Nergal (Ninurta) is also identical to Enki, for Ninurta and Marduk are the same solar force. Enki is hymned as being both glorious in both the heavens and in the underworld,[1397] just as Osiris/Ninurta/Marduk also are. Nergal is

---

[1390]   Sp.I 131 Rs.54 (see J. Hehn, *op.cit.,* p.79).

[1391]   M. Hütter, *op.cit.,* p.101-114.

[1392]   See above p.224.

[1393]   Weidner, *AfO,* 19, 110; cf. A. Livingstone, *op.cit.,* p.47.

[1394]   See M. Hütter, *op.cit.,* p.71. It is likely that the virginal mother of Nergal/Ninurta, Kutusur, is also the same as Ereshkigal (Earth), consort of Enki, who however, is identifiable with Nergal himself. We have seen (above p.231f) that Vishnu is both the son and consort of Aditi.

[1395]   See S.H. Langdon, *Babylonian Liturgies: Sumerian Texts from the Early Period and from the Library of Asshurbanipal,* Paris, 1913, 196, vs.27 (cf. M.K. Schretter, *op.cit.,* p.108).

[1396]   See A. Livingstone, *op.cit.,* p.46.

[1397]   See L.W. King, *Babylonian Magic and Sorcery,* London, 1986, no.27.

also called Lugalgalabzu, the great king of the Abyss, or Lugalaabba, king of the (underworld) ocean, thereby showing his ultimate identity with Enki/Osiris. However, we shall note Nergal's identity with Horus the Younger as well.[1398] In the myth of Nergal and Ereshkigal (EA 357:44, ANSt.10, 120 iv 31', 124 v 40) Enki is termed his "father", just as Horus the Younger is considered the "son" of Osiris.

Nergal's close association with his father, Enlil/Vāyu, is apparent from the fact that fever is generally said to emerge from Ekur, the house of Enlil.[1399] The malevolent character of the chthonic solar deities does not preclude their beneficent virtues, for Nergal as god of fever, plagues and death can also cure and revive dying men.[1400] Not surprisingly, Nergal and Nusku are both identified with Girra,[1401] the god of fire. Nergal shares many qualities with the god of fire, Agni, especially since the latter is the first form of the solar force in the underworld.[1402] In this context, the two names of Nergal, Meslamtea[1403] and Lugalirra, may refer to the beneficial and baneful aspects of this deity, since they are represented in a Sumerian hymn as the "white raven" and the "black raven".[1404] We may remember also that the Germanic Wotan is also accompanied by two such ravens.[1405]

[1398]   See below p.248.

[1399]   CT 17:12,3; 25:1,2; 26:52.

[1400]   See J. Hehn, *op.cit.*, p.81.

[1401]   For Nergal see IV R 24, no.1, 12f. (J. Hehn, *op.cit.*, p.80); for Nusku see the Maqlû series (Deimel, *op.cit.*, p.195). Nusku is particularly the light of the night. Hence he is considered to be the son of the moon, Nannar (see S.A. Cook, *op.cit.*, p.120; cf. *RLA* VIII:631).

[1402]   See below p.250 (cf. F Hrozny, *op.cit.*). The Urartian counterpart of Agni is Haldi (see below p.307f). It is possible that Haldi is related to the Greek Hades, who represents the (sun-)god of the underworld, just as his brothers Poseidon and Zeus represent the sun-gods of the waters and the heavens.

[1403]   T. Jacobsen (*Treasures of Darkness*, p.17) interprets the name to mean "He who issues from the thriving mesu tree". This tree may be equated with the tree of life planted in the Apsu by Enki/Varuna (see below p.274).

[1404]   In fact, Nergal has, according to some accounts (KAR 142 iii 27ff.), seven forms, which may even identifiable with the seven warriors that act as his armed force (Epic of Erra, 32-93). These may be the same as the seven Asakku demons engendered by Anu through earth (see below p.297n). It is interesting that Nergal's *alter ego*, Ninurta, too has seven forms. It may also be noted that the "seven gods" in Mesopotamia are called the "seven gods of Elam" (An=Anum VI 183), showing their eastern affiliations. These "seven gods" may be the same as the deities hymned in the Vedas as "sāmānya", meaning "all gods", since "seven", being a number of perfection, has the significance of "all" in Sumerian.

[1405]   See 'Grimnismal', 20 (cf. p.214 above). We may assume that the Germans got this mythology of Enlil and his children from the "Trojans", or Hittites.

Nergal as the force of the sun in all regions is the same as Enlil's "son", Ninurta/Marduk/Muruga.[1406] According to KAR 142, I, 22ff, Ninurta appears in seven forms as dIB (Urash), Nin-urta, Za-ba-ba [Marduk], Na-bi-um [the force within the moon], Ne-iri-gal [the underworld sun], Sa-kud and Pa-bil-sag.[1407] Nergal's identity with Ninurta is made clear in the hymn to Ninurta where the god is addressed as one who "goes about in the night as Irra [i.e.Nergal]".[1408]

Ninurta in Ekur,[1409] who may be identified with Nergal, is, like Horus the Younger, called the one who "avenged his father" (VAT 9817 rev.20-5,1).[1410] Nergal, who is also called "the avenger of his father", is himself the leader of the "rebellious" gods of the underworld, the Anunnaki.[1411] Also, Nergal, is worshipped sometimes as a god of war who destroys all hostile forces including the great serpent.[1412] Nergal is usually represented by a martial "sword-god", U-gur,[1413] who may also have been deified independently as his vizier.[1414]

Gilgamesh in the 'Epic of Gilgamesh'[1415] also represents the god Nergal, as the Assyrian ritual text O 175, obv., makes clear: "Meslamtea is Gilgamesh. Gilgamesh is Nergal, who dwells in the underworld".[1416]

[1406]   One of the names of dUTU is dMi-it-ra (CT 25.25.10) which, being an Emesal form, would have been the counterpart of Sumerian dGidra, which may be related to the name Gi-dar which Dumézil (see above p.196n) identified with Indra.

[1407]   K. Tallquist, op.cit., p. 421. In the Gula hymn of Bullutsa-rabi, the goddess' husband is called successively Ninurta, Ningirsu, Ninazu, Zababa, Utulu and Lugalbanda (Kinnier Wilson, op.cit., p.85).

[1408]   See A. Falkenstein, Sumerische und Akkadische Hymnen und Gebete, Zürich: Artemis Verlag, 1953, p.60.

[1409]   Ekur, which means 'mountain-house', must refer to the earth of our universe which arises from the underworld.

[1410]   See A. Livingstone, op.cit., p.125. For Nergal/Erra, see K.D. Macmillan, "Some Cuneiform Tablets bearing on the Religion of Babylonia and Assyria" BA 5 (1906), 642f., vs.5f (cf. M.K. Schretter, op.cit., p.53).

[1411]   AGH 112, 2-4 (see J.V. Kinnier Wilson, op.cit., p.38).

[1412]   As we have seen, Ninurta represents the entire range of Enlil's progeny, Nergal (Agni), Sin (Soma) and Utu (Sūrya), that is, all the forms of solar energy.

[1413]   See K. Tallquist, op.cit., p.389. The warlike Scythians, according to Herodotus (Histories, IV,62), too worshipped Ares, god of war, in the form of a sword. Ares is indeed the counterpart of Vishnu/Verethragna (see below p.308).

[1414]   Cf. W. Lambert, Bi Or, 30 (1973) 356; An=Anum V, 52.

[1415]   The original Sumerian name, Bilgamesh, is possibly a contraction of Gishbilgamesh (see A. Deimel, Pantheon, p.95).

[1416]   See A. Livingstone, op.cit., p.191. Enkidu, Gilgamesh's companion in the poem, may be the same as the deity, Enkimdu, who is listed as a "god of canals" in the god-list edited by

Gilgamesh, like Nergal, is designated at the end of the epic to be the judge of the underworld. However, Gilgamesh is also the one who kills the Bull of Heaven which is sent by the scorned Inanna to plague the earth with its fiery devastatations. Gilgamesh is thus identifiable with the Adad/Seth/Angra Manyu aspect of Ninurta/Osiris/Indra as well as with the solar (Shamash/Horus).

Among the Hittites, Telipinu, the son of the Hatti bull-god Taru/Teshup and the sun-goddess of Arinna,[1417] is the same as Nergal. It is possible that the Hittite Telipinu was also considered the sun-god of Earth.[1418] There is also a reference in the Hittite Telipinu myth (KUB XVII 10 iv ll8ff)[1419] to the "way of the sun-god of the earth" (taknaš ^{d}UTU-us), which is contrasted to the "kingly path" (kas lugal) followed by the sun-god of heaven (l.12). The paths of the three suns in Hittite religion may be related to the three steps taken by Vishnu through heaven, the mid-region and earth, called paramapada (the supreme step), pitrayāna (the step of the manes), and devayāna (the step of the gods).[1420] If they are, then the kingly path of the Hittite sun-god of heaven must correspond to the paramapada, the way of the sun-god of earth to the devayāna, and the path of the sun-god of the waters to the pitrayāna. This may be confirmed by the description of the 'mešu tree' as the "flesh of the gods" in the 'Poem of Erra', l.150,[1421] for the trunk of the cosmic tree represents earth.[1422] This is also the pathway of Enki – who holds the Tree of Life – to mankind.[1423]

It should be noted that, in Hittite, while the fire-god is commonly referred to as ^{d}Pahhur (from Sumerian pah-har),[1424] there are some ritual

---

Genouillac (see H. de Genouillac, "Grande Liste de Noms Divins Sumeriens", *RA* 20 (1923), p.96). Enkimdu may be the same as Enbililu, one of the underworld sons of Enlil (see above p.245n).

[1417] See V. Haas, *op.cit.*, p.322, p.443.

[1418] The original form of Telipinu was "ta-a-li-i-pi-in-nu" (see E. Laroche, "Recherches", p.34). Since -pinu means 'son' in Hatti, we may assume that 'tali' is a corruption of "taru" and his name means Calf, just as that of Marduk (sun-calf) also does. The daughter of the sun-goddess of Arinna and Teshup is also called Tappinu (or Mezzulla) – who is coupled with Hulla (see V. Haas, *Geschichte*, pp.426ff.). It is possible that the daughter and the son of the sun-goddess of Earth and the weather-god represent the same early form of the sun.

[1419] See E. Tenner, *op.cit.*, p.189.

[1420] See below p.265.

[1421] See L Cagni, *The Poem of Erra*, Malibu, CA: Undena Publications, 1977, p.32.

[1422] See below p.273.

[1423] See below p.265.

[1424] The Sumerian meaning of "gatherer" identifies this fire-god with Horus the Younger, who is also called "one who gathereth together all seed" (E.A.W. Budge, *op.cit.*, I:341), which

texts which refer to ᵈAkni as well.[1425] Agni, in these Hittite texts, seems to be an appellation of Fire in its destructive aspects and related to Nergal, who is also characterized by intense brightness.[1426] What is especially interesting is that the ritual texts in KBo XI and KBo XIII seem to equate Agni with the sun-god,[1427] which must here be the sun-god of the earth.[1428]

In the Vedas (*KYV* I,3,14), the solar fire Agni (Re/Girra) which is the Desire (Kāma) of the One (Soul/Amun) the supreme deity, is said to be manifest in a trifold form as Agni-Vāyu-Āditya, Agni being the solar force born of the Light of Heaven in the underworld, Vāyu the fire that informs our universe, and Āditya the sun of our system. The first birth of Agni is as Agni, the nascent solar form that develops from Varuna. In *KYV* IV,2,2, the first birth of Agni is referred to thus:

> From the sky [Dyaus]was Agni first born
> ....
> We know thy highest name is secret;
> We know the spring whence thou hast come.

At *KYV* IV,2,2, we get a glimpse of the rule of Agni in the realm of Earth:

> Agni hath cried, like Dyaus thundering,
> Licking the earth, devouring the plants;
> Straightway on earth he shone aflame.

---

suggests the generative power of the fire and sun. "Pah-hur/pahhur is clearly the source of the Greek 'pur'=fire. The Sanskrit epithet of Surya (the sun), "pāvaka", meaning 'the purifier', may be related to it, since the sun purifies the seed of the slaughtered first Man in the Iranian cosmogony (see below p.259).

[1425] This was first discovered by F. Hrozny, "Un dieu hittite Ak/Nis", *RA* 18 (1921), 34-36; cf. J. Friedrich, "Agniš," *RLA* I:42; F. Sommer, Review of H. Eheloff, *Keilschrifturkunden aus Boghazköi*, Heft XXX, *OLZ* 1939, p.688; H.Otten and M. Mayrhofer, "Der Gott Akni in den hethitischen Texten und seine indoarische Herkunft", *OLZ*, 1965, 11/12, p.545-52. The Sumerian word for fire, Girra, is probably also related to the Sanskrit 'agni', since the original form of 'agni', according to SB VI,i,1,xi is 'agri' (see U.C. Pandey, *The Cosmogonic Legends of the Brahmanas*, Gorakahpur: Shivaniketan, 1991/2, p.32).

[1426] See J.V. Kinnier Wilson, *op.cit.*, p.38. H. Otten and M. Mayrhofer (*op.cit.*, p.549) suggest that Agni was imported into Hattusa from the south-eastern part of Anatolia.

[1427] See H. Otten and M. Mayrhofer, *op.cit.*, p.548.

[1428] This close similarity of the Hittite religion to the Indic (represented in the ancient Near East by the Mitanni kingdom) suggests that the Hittites may be considered as part of the Indo-Iranian Āryan culture in spite of their centum language. The Kassites also seem to have been an Indo-Āryan people (see pp.92n,145n,1491n).

Nergal is, in the Graeco-Roman period, also equated with Herakles,[1429] who is the counterpart of Vishnu and Verethreghna,[1430] for all of them are characterised by a series of incarnations which represent the "toils" of the incipient sun. This points once again to the contradictions of the Zoroastrian reform, which retains the worship of Verethragna at the same time as it ostracizes Indra, of whom Vishnu-Verethreghna is the first solar form.

[1429]   See C. Bonnet, *Studia Phoenicia*, 7 (1988), pp.148-55; cf. E. Lipinski, *ibid.*, 14 (1995), p.242.

[1430]   Verethreghna is designated on the tomb of King Antiochos I as "Artagnes [=Verethreghna], Herakles, Ares" (see P. Kretschmer, *op.cit.*, p.313).

XXI: SOMA

THE "MOON" AND THE LIFE OF THE UNIVERSE:

SOMA, KHONSU, THOTH, NANNAR

Before the sun is free to rise into the Mid-region of our universe, the moon is established therein bearing within it the life of the universe. Hence, as we have seen, the moon is considered the elder or the great light in Sumer (Gishnugal), as well as in Egypt.[1431] In all the cosmologies that we are studying, the moon bears the seeds of life. While the "moon" bears the seeds of universal life, the sun which is borne by it bears the seed only of man (Manu, the son of the sun).

In *BP* V,22,8, the "moon" is said to be located above the sun ("in the north"), just as the twenty eight constellations are situated above the moon (V,22,11) suggesting that our galaxy is arranged in an oblique position between heaven and earth.[1432] At *RV* IX,113, Yama's dwelling is described as being in "the third sphere of inmost heaven where lucid worlds are full of light ... the region of the radiant Moon, where food and full delight are found". We know that Yama rules the lower of the three heavens, while the moon, or Soma, is located in the highest heaven. The moon is thus at the northernmost point of the sun's revolution, while Yama is at the southernmost.

In Mesopotamia, the force within the moon is represented by a form of Ninurta, Nabû, who was originally considered Marduk's "vizier", or "forerunner", though later he came to be considered to be his "son". If we compare the Heliopolitan myth of Thoth emerging from the brow of Seth, we may posit this event before the rise of Horus from the "horizon"

[1431] See above p.20.

[1432] At *BP* V,23,4ff. the heavenly bodies are said to be arranged in the shape of a downward hanging alligator "in a curved position". The tip of the tail of the alligator is at the highest heavenly body, the Pole Star. The sun is located at the chest (heart) and the moon at the head (mind) of the alligator (V,23,7). Since the moon is considered as being situated "north"of the sun, we may envision the head of the alligator as being turned backwards from its neck.

as Re-Harakhty. We know that Nabû is one of the seven forms of Ninurta/ Marduk,[1433] taking over indeed many of the characteristics of Ninurta.[1434] The real significance of Nabû, however, is revealed in VAT 8917 rev.5, where Nabû is called "the one inside Sin", just as Marduk is the "one inside Šamaš".[1435] As Marduk is the force that becomes Shamash, so too Nabû is the force that emerges as the moon, Nannar. The pairing of Sin and Nergal (or Lugalgìrra and Meslamtaéa)[1436] is thus matched by the pairing of Nabû and Marduk,[1437] whose solar force is first manifest in the underworld.

We shall see that Nabû is the deity who "searches" for Marduk when the latter is imprisoned in the underworld.[1438] Like the Egyptian moon-god Thoth, Nabû is also the scribal god and associated with wisdom and learning.[1439] This role he shares with Hermes, though he is identified – rather loosely – also with Apollo (Vishnu/Nergal/Marduk) by Strabo and other Greeks.[1440]

Nabû is also identifiable with another deity called Ningishzida, since the latter is represented by the double snake symbol typical of Thoth/Hermes.[1441] Ningishzida is, like Thoth/Hermes, also a scribal deity. Ningishzida is called the "son" of Nergal,[1442] just as Nabû came to be called the son of Marduk.

Ningishzida is also called the son of Ninazu, another of the three sons of Enlil born in the underworld.[1443] Ninazu is himself a form of Ninurta[1444]

[1433]   See below p.280. Nabû, like Thoth (Hermes Trismegistes), is identified astronomically with Mercury. Nergal is allied to Mars, and Marduk to Jupiter. Ninurta himself is allied to Saturn (see S. Langdon, *op.cit.*, p.79n; cf. H. Zimmern, *op.cit.*, p.400), showing his close affinity with his father Enlil/Shiva/Kumarbi/Chronos.

[1434]   See A. Livingstone, *op.cit.*, p.155. Just as Marduk is the "force within the sun", his vizier is the "one inside Sin", the moon-god. H. Zimmern (*op.cit.*, II:369) suggested that Marduk, Ninib [Ninurta], Nabû, Nergal may be phases of the sun as the spring-, summer-, autumn- and winter-sun, respectively. However, Nabû is clearly not a sun-god but, rather, the force within the moon, and all these gods are aspects of the son of Enlil, Ninurta, as we have seen.

[1435]   See A. Livingstone, *op. cit.*, p.83.

[1436]   See A. Deimel, *Pantheon*, p.178.

[1437]   *Ibid.*, p.186.

[1438]   See A. Livingstone, *op.cit.*, Ch.VI.

[1439]   See F. Pomponio, "Nabû" in *RLA* IX:21f.; cf. A. Deimel, *Pantheon*, p.185.

[1440]   See Pomponio, *op.cit.*, p.23.

[1441]   See S. Langdon, *op.cit.*p.122. Astrological texts identify both Nabû and Ningishzida with Mercury (see E. D. van Buren, "The god Ningizzida", *Iraq*, I (1934), p.62).

[1442]   In Egypt it is Horus the Younger's seed that impregnates Seth with Thoth.

[1443]   See above p.245n.

[1444]   See below p.248n.

and identified with Tishpak/Teshup,[1445] that is, with Seth, so that the lunar Thoth is a "son", as it were, of Seth, as well as of the sun of the underworld, Nergal/Horus the Younger. This confirms that the three "sons" of Enlil in the underworld are but three aspects of the chief son of Enlil/Shu-Ninurta/Osiris, and the moon is the product of two of these aspects Nergal/Horus the Younger and Teshup/Seth.

In the Adapa myth, Ningishzida and Tammuz, representing no doubt the forces within the moon and the sun, guard the gates to heaven, An (here the heaven of our universe).[1446] Ningishzida's wife is Geshtinanna, the sister of Inanna[1447] who sojourns in the underworld along with Tammuz.[1448] We have seen that Sin and Nergal as the moon and sun are considered "twins" in Sumer. So too are the forces within them. Ningishzida[1449] and Ningirsu [Ninurta as the lord of the Flood] are, as early solar forces, also sometimes considered (loosely) as the spring "sun" (i.e. from the winter to the summer solstice), while Nergal is the winter sun. [1450] On the other hand, Ningishzida is sometimes called the father of Tammuz.[1451] Indeed, Tammuz's original name may have been 'tu–mu umun [=nin] mu [=gis]–zi–da', or the son of Ningishzida.[1452] However, this must only be an indication of the earlier emergence of Ningishzida as the moon in the Mid-region than that of Tammuz as the sun.

The moon-god itself has the same character as the force within it. The moon is the first son of Enlil's and called Nannar (the counterpart of the Indo-Iranian Soma/Haoma). Nannar, as the great light, has priority over the rising sun, Utu (Shamash). The Moon is the first son of Enlil to be raised to the upper world while Nergal remains in the underworld as a substitute for it. It is also referred to as Magur$_8$, referring to the "makurru" ship of Ninurta as he rises as the sun.[1453] Since we have learnt that the barque is the barque of earth,[1454] we may assume that the vitality of the earth, or the material universe, is that which is concentrated in the moon.

[1445] See E. D. van Buren, *op.cit.*, p.64.

[1446] See E.O. James, *op.cit.*, p.10.

[1447] See E.D. van Buren, *ibid.*

[1448] See below p.269.

[1449] Like Ninurta, Ningishzida is also called "lord of the drum" (*ibid.*, p.70).

[1450] See S. Langdon, *ibid.* p.30.

[1451] See A. Deimel, *op.cit.*, pp.204, 203.

[1452] See S. Langdon, *op.cit.*, p.7n.

[1453] See K. Tallquist, *op.cit.*, p.443; cf. Maqlu III,123ff.; see above p.220.

[1454] See above p.161.

The form of Nannar's Akkadian counterpart, Sin, like that of Indra, is that of a bull. In Hurrian and Middle Assyrian ritual literature, Sin is typically associated with the impregnation of a cow,[1455] which may represent the material substance of the earth. Like Soma, Sin is particularly associated with the sources of life, which he guards as a "herdsman" of "cows".[1456] The myth of "Nannar's journey to Nippur", for instance, relates how Nannar milked his cows, poured their "milk" into churns and gave his father Enlil the best of his pure products.[1457] One of the attributes of Enannatum, the high-priestess of Nannar is indeed "the bearer of the life-giving egg",[1458] since the high-priestess is considered to be the spouse of her god, who represents the generative potency inherent in the moon. Again, in a Sumerian 'ersemma' hymn to Nannar, we find the following verse emphasising the intoxicating quality of the life-force stored in the moon:

> When you, father Nanna, rise to the shining sanctuary,
> Father Nanna, when you travel on the high flood as on a ship,
> When you travel there, when you travel there, when you travel there,
> When you travel there, when you pour out the intoxicating drink, when you travel there,
>
> When you feast yourself lavishly on the intoxicant that has been poured out, ...

We may compare this to the Vedic hymn to Soma (also called Indhu) who represents the life–force or seed stored in the moon as well as the vital substance of the light:[1459]

[1455]   See N. Veldhuis, *A Cow of Sin*, Groningen: Styx Publications, 1991; cf. V. Haas, *Geschichte*, p.316. The complaint of the cow in the Iranian Yasna 29 is also for a protector, whom she obtains in the form of Zarathustra/Ziusudra, the first man.

[1456]   The moon bears the seed of the murdered Bull of Heaven (representing all animal life), or Hoama, in the Avesta (Fargard XXI, 9). The seed of the waters, of the earth and of the plants, on the other hand, is stored in the stars (Fargard XXI, 13).

[1457]   See T. Jacobsen, *op.cit.*, p.127.

[1458]   en-sal-nunuz-zi ᵈNannar (SAK 206 b2,1; see A. Deimel, *Pantheon*, p.236f).

[1459]   The association of Soma with the moon which is typical of Indo-Āryan mythology is thus also observable in the mythology of Nannar among the Sumerians. In *SB* I,vi,3,22; III,iv,2,3, Soma is represented, much like Indra, as all the gods since they represent the vitality of Agni.

These rapid Soma-streams have stirred themselves to motion like strong steeds,

....

Immortal, cleansed, these drops, since first they flowed, have never wearied,
fain
To reach the regions and their paths.
Advancing they have travelled o'er the ridges of the earth and heaven,

And this the highest realm of all (*RV* IX, 22)

and

Swift Soma drops have been effused in streams of meath, the gladdening drink,
For sacred lore of every kin.
Hither to newer resting–place the ancient Living Ones [Soma drops] are come.
They made the Sun that he might shine. (23)[1460]

Just as Nannar is said to have milked his cows, Soma too is described as rich in cows that have been milked: "Down to the waters Soma, rich in kine, hath flowed with cows, with cows that have been milked" (*RV* IX,107,9). Soma is the life-force of the universe and the Purānas equate it with the tears which are shed by the creating god. In the Purānas (*PP* V,12, 1-13; *MP* XXIII,1-10)) these tears are received by the sky to form Soma.

The animal life of the universe, as we have noted from the Iranian evidence, is stored in the moon. In *RV* IX,93,1, it is interesting to note that Soma is called the "child of Sūrya", since this may be related to the Egyptian doctrine of the moon's being formed of the seed of Horus the Younger through the stimulation of Seth. However, the Vedic passage does not clearly distinguish the sun of the underworld (Vishnu) from that of the heavens (Sūrya), nor the latter from its original form as the cosmic light, Brahman. According to *RV* IX,42,1, Soma is considered as the progenitor of the sun, just as Ningishzida is also called the father of Tammuz. This is no doubt due to its chronological priority to the sun. The moon itself is said to be formed by the infusion of Soma into the waters (*SB* IV,vi,7,12). Soma

---

[1460] The conception of the moon-god as a cow-herd is carried over into the mythology of Krishna (who is considered one of the later incarnations of Vishnu), since Krishna is descended of the *lunar* Aila dynasty (see *BP* XIV,XXIV).

then engenders the sun in floods along with the other stars. Soma here is clearly identical to Indra/Ninurta filled with Soma. Indeed, in *RV* IX,5, Soma is hymned as the bull and the "self" of Indra himself.

Exactly as in the Iranian sacred literature,[1461] the pressing of Soma is considered as a sacrifice of the god. Soma is indeed identified with the primal Prajāpati himself in *SB* III,9,4,17, since we have seen that his sacrifice is essentially a castration of his seed-filled phallus. Soma is commonly understood to be an intoxicant pressed from the soma plant and consumed by the Āryan priests during the ritual.[1462] The Scythians, as we have noted, are indeed called "haomavarga Sakas", or soma-drinking Scythians,[1463] and archaeological finds at the BMAC in Afghanistan include vessels stained with plant-juice. But the real significance of Soma in the Āryan literature is as the life-force of the macroanthropos. Indra's establishment of the solar force in the heavens is due to the potency derived from the Soma within him.

We may note in passing a popular legend which recounts the insemination of Pārvatī by Agni. When Shiva, her husband, sees her writhing in pain with the fiery seed of Agni (here the underworld god), he sheds tears, and from his tears is produced a "little man who used a torch and incense to smoke Agni out of the body of Pārvati".[1464] In *MP* 23,1-10, Atri, one of the seven sages created by Brahman, sheds tears from which Soma is formed as a young boy.[1465] The homunculus in the first account may thus represent the infant moon.[1466] Shiva is also frequently represented with the moon arising from his head just as Thoth does from Seth's.[1467] The moon contains the Soma with which Shiva/Indra/Seth himself is infused.

In the *Bundahishn*, the seed of the Bull (representing all animal life)[1468] slaughtered by Angra Mainyu is purified and stored in the moon,[1469]

[1461]   See below p.259.

[1462]   The Vedic sacrifice involving the extraction of soma is called "kratu", while that without it is a "yajna".

[1463]   So in the inscriptions of Darius I (see P.O. Skjaervo in G. Erdosy, *op.cit.*, p.157).

[1464]   See A. Miles, *Land of the Lingam*, London, 1933, p.219f. (cf. W. O'Flaherty, *op.cit.*, p.107).

[1465]   Cf. *PP* V,12,1-13.

[1466]   Interestingly, in Egypt, mankind itself is formed from the tears of Re (CT 1130 VII 465a, CT 714 VI 344f-g; see S. Bickel, *op.cit.*, p.199). Re sheds tears when his eye (the sun) goes out from him. This must refer to its manifestation in our universe. In an Orphic hymn to Helios too, it is stated that "Thy tears are the race of suffering mortals" (see M.L. West, *Orphic Poems*, p.213).

[1467]   See W. O'Flaherty, *op.cit.*, p.50.

[1468]   The seed of the dead Bull stored in the moon is the same as the life of the universe preserved after the "deluge" by the first man, Yima/Ziusudra/Manu.

[1469]   See *Bundahishn* X, 1-2; cf. *Fargard* XXI,9 and *Sirozah* I,12.

just as the seed of the slaughtered First Man (representing all human life) is stored in the sun.[1470] The Bull is thus, in the *Greater Bundahishn*,[1471] likened to the shining Moon just as, in Egypt, the seed of Horus reappears on Seth's forehead as the moon, Thoth. Similarly the First Man is likened to the shining sun (where his seed will be purified). In the Haoma-sacrifice, Hoama is represented anthropomorphically, for the pressing of the soma plant in this sacrifice is represented as a slaying of a primal god, Haoma or his anthropomorphic form Duroasha (or Frashmi), in order to extract his productive essence.[1472] Duraosha is said to have been in existence even before Vivanghvant, the solar father of Yima.[1473] Yima (Manu) is indeed the one who corrupts the Haoma rite by burning the sacred plant (Yasna XXXII,8). Haoma is said to have been prepared for the corporeal world first by Vivanghavant (the sun) (Hom Yast IX, 3), and fourthly by Pourushaspa, father of Zarathustra. Duraosha is sacrificed so that the vital force of Soma may be expressed in the world. In the haoma-sacrifice, the pressing of the soma plant thus symbolises the extraction of the life-force of Haoma/Soma.

Haoma is considered by the Zoroastrians to be not only a source of immortality but also a destroyer of the Daevas (I,6). In the Vedas, Indra is the chief of the Devas, who, as we have seen, kills Vrtra. However, the moon and also Soma are themselves often identified with Vrtra,[1474] the serpent killed by Indra, just as Seth and Apop are identified with each other in Egypt.[1475] Vrtra and Soma may represent the powerful sexual force which sustains the universe. Indeed, Soma, symbolising the moon is said to be the "food" of the sun (also a form of Indra) (*SB* I,vi,4,18), since the sun "consumes" its soma.

It is in Egypt that we get the clearest account of the birth of the moon. Horus the Younger is said to have been violated by his "uncle" Seth, the storm-god, with the result that Horus is sexually excited and emits his seed. Isis, however, contrives to collect the seed of Horus on lettuce which Seth, a lover of lettuce, subsequently eats. "Pregnant" with the seed of Horus, Seth then "gives birth", significantly from his forehead, to the golden disk of the moon, called Thoth.[1476] Thoth is also identified with the moon-god

[1470]   *Bundahishn* XV.

[1471]   See RC. Zaehner, *op.cit.*, p.40.

[1472]   See E.O. James, *op.cit.*, p.26.

[1473]   Yasna IX,17,27; X, 21; XLIII,5.

[1474]   See A.K. Lahiri, *op.cit.*, pp.172-87.

[1475]   See below p.290.

[1476]   See H. te Velde, *op.cit.*, p.43f.

Aah-Tehuti,[1477] and he and Re, as the moon and the sun, are considered the two eyes of Horus (the Elder). Thoth, as the primal god of Thebes, is also sometimes addressed as Temu (Atem), for Thoth, as we have seen, is also the formative aspect of Ptah.

In some versions of the story of Horus and Seth,[1478] Seth too in seducing Horus emits or "loses" his seed, an action which may have been interpreted as loss of sexual power or castration. The eye of Horus and the testicles of Seth are related to each other in a causal connection of light and life. In the town of Saka, Seth as a bull undergoes self-castration and, in the Pap. d'Orbiney, Seth (called Bata in Saka), castrates himself in order to avoid the sexual advances of his sister-in-law, and then goes into exile in foreign lands.[1479] This reinforces the significance of Soma as Purusha that is stressed in the Hoama sacrifice mentioned above. Thus it may also be related to the legends of Shiva/Indra in the Indian Purānas[1480] and of Attis in Syria.[1481]

The phallic importance of Seth, however, is not diminished in this story of seduction and punishment since, even though the moon (Thoth) that is created from the union of Horus and Seth is called the "eye of Horus" (being formed of his seed), it is the phallus (called sometimes politely "finger")[1482] of Seth which is finally required to instil light in it.[1483] The force of light is thus intimately connected to that of life,[1484] which Seth, like Indra, eminently embodies. Thus finally, after the separation by Re[1485] of Horus and Seth locked in sexual union, the two gods are reconciled, as Horus the sun, representing the light of earth in the Mid-region,[1486] and Seth, the stormy life-force embodied in the thunder of the higher region of heaven. In historical terms, Horus and Seth were united as the rulers of Lower and

---

[1477]   E.A.W. Budge, I, 412.

[1478]   For instance, Pap. Jumilhac (see H. te Velde, *op.cit.*, p.41).

[1479]   See H. te Velde, *ibid.*

[1480]   See A. Daniélou, *Shiva and Dionysus,* p.62.

[1481]   See the reference to Lucian, *De Dea Syria* above p.194n.

[1482]   The typical depiction of the young Horus (Harpocrates) with a finger in his mouth, generally considered an indication of his infant nature, may also be a suggestion of the phallic infusion of Horus by Seth.

[1483]   PT 48 (see H. te Velde, *op.cit.*, p. 49).

[1484]   See H. te Velde, *op.cit.*, p.51

[1485]   Pap. Boulaq 17; in the "Contendings of Horus and Seth", it is Thoth who separates his "parents" Horus and Seth (see H. te Velde, *op.cit.*, p.61).

[1486]   Though the sun is primarily situated in the Mid-region, it begins as a light of earth, that is, in the underworld.

Upper Egypt. However, Horus came to acquire a greater standing in Egypt, and Seth began to be considered a rather alien god related as he was to the Hurrian Teshup and to the Canaanite Baal.[1487]

Moreover, in Pap. Hearst XIV, 2-4, Isis brings the moon "to her son [Horus, the incipient sun] to purge his body [after his sexual initiation by Seth]" in order to purify "the evil which was in his body".[1488] We have noted that, in the Avesta, the seed of the bull of heaven (Osiris) which is killed by Angra Mainyu (Seth) is concentrated and purified in the moon. We see that the moon is considered in Egypt too as a purificatory body and note once again a similarity between the Egyptian and Iranian theologies.

In the Theban cosmology, Khonsu is the moon-god, counterpart of Nannar. Khonsu is called the "great light,[1489] just as, in Sumer too, the moon is called Gishnugal, the great light, since it is elder than the sun. Indeed, Khonsu is not merely the moon but also a twin of the solar force in the underworld, Horus the Younger.[1490] In Hermopolis, Khonsu is the son of Amun whose pneumatic virtue is similar to that of the Heliopolitan Shu/Enlil. Khonsu is borne by Hathor as the wife/mother[1491] of Amun-Ra, indicating that he is born in the waters of the underworld.[1492]

In Hermopolis, Amun engenders the moon-god Khonsu through his union with Mut/Hathor.[1493] Shu is also closely associated with Khonsu, the moon-god or the "great light".[1494] We know that Atum himself (Horus

---

[1487] The demonisation of Seth did not begin until the early 18th dynasty, as a reaction to the hateful domination of Egypt by the Hyksos, who worshipped a god identified with Seth (see H. te Velde, op.cit., pp.61, 68, 121, 141). According to Plutarch, De Iside et Osiride, 30, Seth is also said to have escaped on his ass, during one of his battles, to a place of safety and to have begotten two sons, Hierosolymus and Judaeus. The legend clearly associates Seth with the Hebrew god Yahwe and mocks the Jewish account of "the flight of Moses out of Egypt, and of the settlement of the Jews about Hierusalem and Judaea" (See E.A.W. Budge, op.cit., II:254). The identity of Yahwe to the storm-gods under consideration is highlighted by the "wrathful" nature frequently attributed to him in the OT (cf. A.R.W. Green, op.cit., Ch.IV).

[1488] See H. te Velde, op.cit., p.48

[1489] See K. Sethe, op.cit., p.114.

[1490] We may remember that Sin and Nergal are called the "great twins" mashtabba-galgal in Sumer (see above p.245).

[1491] Hathor is also called Mut, mother. As mother of Khonsu, Hathor must be identical to Ninlil, the wife of Enlil.

[1492] See E.O. James, op.cit., p. 177.

[1493] Mut is particularly a form of Hathor in the underworld, where the moon is born (see E.A.W. Budge, op.cit., II:29).

[1494] K. Sethe, op.cit., pp.31,114. In Sumer, too, the moon is called Vishnugal, the great light (since the moon is senior to the sun, Utu).

the Elder) as the son of Amun-Re and Hathor, is identifiable with Shu.[1495] since the process of the formation of the moon and sun in the underworld repeats that which produced the cosmic light (Atum/Horus the Elder), and Horus the Elder and Horus the Younger are the same force at different stages of solar evolution. Khonsu, as the son begotten of Hathor (in her form as Mut), and Amun-Re in the underworld also shares in the virtue of Shu, since Shu indeed represents the force which provides the luminosity of the moon. We have seen that Nabû, the lunar form of Enlil's son, Ninurta/Enki, is also identifiable with Thoth.[1496]

Khonsu, son of Amen-Ra and Hathor/Mut, like Enlil's "son" Nannar and the Vedic "moon"-god Soma, is a repository of the vital power of generation. Thus Khonsu is a god of fertility who causes women to conceive, cattle to become fecund, and the germ to grow in the egg.[1497]

Among the Hurrians and Hittites, the Egyptian moon-god Khonsu was worshipped as Kusuh, and his identity with Nannar (Sin) is made clear by the fact that his consort is called Ningal.[1498] In the Hittite religion, the moon-god of the waters (dEn.Zu u-i-te-e-ni),[1499] is mentioned along with dUTU u-i-te-e-ni (the sun-god of the waters) (Kbo V 2 ii 13),[1500] since both the sun and the moon are born of the waters of the "underworld".

[1495]   See E.A.W. Budge, *op.cit.*, I:466-8; cf. K. Sethe, *op.cit.*, p.31.

[1496]   See above p.254.

[1497]   See E.A.W. Budge, *op.cit.*, II:35.

[1498]   See V. Haas, *Geschichte*, p.374.

[1499]   Kbo V 2 ii l.11. In another text (KUB VII 5 I i 24ff.), the author beseeches the moon-god and stars to bring the sun-god of Earth along with them.

[1500]   See E. Tenner, *op.cit.*, p.186. dUTU me.e (KUB V 6 i l.6. ii l.14) is also a term for the sun-god of the water (*ibid.*).

XXII: INDRA-VISHNU

THE INCIPIENT SUN: HORUS THE YOUNGER, VISHNU, MARDUK

In the underworld, Osiris' potency is revived by Re as the universe and his "son" Horus the Younger[1501] also begins to rise as the sun. However, Horus the Younger, who bears the name of his father the heavenly light, Horus the Elder (who is the solar counterpart of the vital force of Osiris), continues to be opposed by Seth in several cosmic contests, though these contests end in reconciliation.[1502] Seth is said to have violated Horus and it is the latter's seed swallowed by Seth that produces the moon from Seth's forehead, as Thoth. We know that, in Sumer, it is Enlil/Enki who descends into the underworld and creates the moon. The equation of Horus the Younger with Shu (the counterpart of Enlil-Enki) emphasizes the instrumental force of the wind-god in the creation of the life of our universe. Horus the Younger, like Horus the Elder, is a form not only of Re but also of Amun.[1503] Indeed the Sumerian identification of the rising sun with Enlil[1504] is repeated in the identification of Re-Harakhty with Shu in the early Egyptian formulas (UC 69).[1505] So we may infer that Horus the Younger also represents a later form of Shu. Indeed, Osiris himself is a form of Shu, according to CT 80.[1506] Thus we have another confirmation that Horus the Elder-Osiris and Horus the Younger are but the same deity.

[1501]   Cf. Sidney Smith's notion (p.118n above) that Osiris may be related to Marduk. Marduk is the counterpart of Osiris' "son" Horus the Younger, who is nevertheless the same as his father.

[1502]   See H. te Velde, *op.cit.*, pp.32ff.

[1503]   See A. Barucq and F. Daumas, *op.cit.*, p.156.

[1504]   See below p.309.

[1505]   See S. Quirke, *op.cit.*, p.161f.

[1506]   See J.P. Allen, *op.cit.*, p.23.

During his battles with Seth, Horus is deprived of his "eye" (which is another term for his solar force) and Seth of his testicles (his life-force). In one battle with Seth, Horus succeeds in capturing Seth, but Isis sets him free. Enraged, Horus cuts off the head of his mother and Thoth intervenes to save her life by substituting a cow's head in place of her own (we remember that Aditi and Usha are also called the Cow in Vedic literature). In some accounts, the younger Horus however is said to avenge the murder of his father, by subduing the forces of Seth.[1507] Horus the Younger indeed helps in the resuscitation of his father,[1508] but it is Osiris' own life-giving fluids that are administered by his son to Osiris, as is evident in the royal funerary ritual which resembles the Christian Mass.[1509]

If we examine the myths related to Seth, we will note that both the descent of Osiris into the underworld and the development of the infant Horus the Younger as the sun are caused by the tempestuous interventions of Seth (Indra/Zeus), who may thus represent the most vital aspect of the heavenly light. That is why Seth/Teshup/Indra/Zeus were the chief gods of the Egyptians, Hurrians, Indians, and

Greeks. Seth's force is also, as we have seen, necessary for battling the serpent on the sun-barque.

However, once liberated, the new sun, Horus the Younger, is represented as coursing through all three regions of the universe. Indeed, šnw n Hr (the circuit of Horus) means the universe in Egyptian.[1510] Horus the Younger, is (exactly as Vishnu also is) particularly characterised by his large strides: "in your name of 'The Runner'/ You traverse millions and hundreds of thousands of nomes (schenes)".[1511]

In India, the counterpart of Horus the Younger is indeed the solar form of the deity, Vishnu.[1512] Vishnu is not only a son of Aditi but also her consort, that is, both Horus the Younger and Osiris. In *KYV* VII,5,14, Aditi is described as Vishnu's consort. Aditi, we have seen, is a daughter

---

[1507] So in Pap. Jumilhac (see H. te Velde, *op.cit.*, p.66).

[1508] The Avestan Mithra, who resembles Harakhte (see below p.265) is also said in Mihir Yasht XXIII,90 to have been the first to have "lifted up Haomas, in a mortar inlaid with stars and made of heavenly substance", which may be a reference to the lifting up of the sacrificed Osiris.

[1509] See J.G. Griffiths, *op.cit.*, p.151–8.

[1510] See S. Mercer, *op.cit.*, p.194.

[1511] See A. Barucq and F. Daumas, *op.cit.* p.176; cf also p.50: "Horus arrives! The Runner with the Large Strides comes!" (Pyr. 852-56), and p.123. The term "schenes" (šnz) refers to a particular ancient Egyptian nome (see *LÄ* V:576).

[1512] We shall encounter this name in the Sumerian god-list CT 25,25,8 (see below p.308).

of Daksha, one of the seven sages created intellectually by Brahma.[1513] Vishnu's major contribution to Indra's cosmic accomplishment is the three tremendous steps with which he traverses the three worlds [i.e. Heaven, Earth and the Mid-region][1514] that have been covered by the serpent Vrtra. Vishnu thereby "establishes the spaces" (*AV* VII,25,1). Vishnu's encompassing the three worlds represents the pervasiveness of the solar energy in the expanded universe.[1515] The three steps of Vishnu are called 'devayāna'[1516] (the path of the gods), 'pitrayāna'[1517] (the path of the fathers or manes), and 'paramapada' (the supreme step). One of these, most probably the first, corresponds to the pathway of Enki (Lord of Earth) to mankind described in the Sumerian hymn discussed below.[1518] *RV* I,154 describes the highest point in the manifest universe as the region of Vishnu (representing his 'paramapada'). Again, in *KYV* V,5,1, Vishnu is said to be the highest form of Agni (=Varuna).

According to the Avestan Mihir Yasht, the sun is preceded by Mithra (Horus the Younger/Harakhte). Mithra does not appear as one of the Amesha Spentas, but rather as the son of Ahura, who therefore corresponds particularly to Horus the Elder-Osiris and Brahman. Like the Vedic Mitra, Mithra is a priestly (Brāhmanical) god (89). At 127 Mithra is described as being accompanied by Atar "all in a blaze" and the "awful king Glory" [Xvarenah-Varuna/Agni]. Mithra, who heralds Hvare, is himself preceded by Verethraghna (Vāyu/Indra), and Xvarenah (Varuna/Agni).

Mithra is often adored in the form of a bull (86) and is said to be "the lord of wide pastures", which is clearly a reference to the wide-ranging extent of his course as a "bull". We recall that Horus the Younger and Vishnu are also often admired for their wide strides. Mithra is said to move through all the seven continents (karshvares) of Earth (16). He is created by Ahura Mazda "possessing the most xwarenah of the supernatural gods" (Zamyad Yasht, 35), and is represented as bestowing the xvarenah upon all the seven continents (Mihir Yasht, 16).

Mithra moves in a chariot driven by "four stallions" (124-5) and is represented as a god of war (35-43). The solar force is originally invested with this martial virtue since, as we have seen, it has to battle the demons

---

[1513] See below p.307; cf. p.147, where Daksha is identifiable with Agni.

[1514] See *RV* I,154–6; *AV* VII,26,1.

[1515] In *RV* I,154,4 Vishnu is said to uphold Earth, Heaven and the Mid-region; cf. *RV* VI,49,13.

[1516] *RV* I,72,7; 183,6; 184,6.

[1517] *RV* X,2,7.

[1518] See below p.279.

of darkness in order to maintain its glory. Mithra is also supposed to have a "thousand eyes" (or "spies") (82) with which he observes and judges the actions of man. Mithra is accompanied (41) by Rashnu (Justice) and Sraosha (Faith).[1519]

In Babylon, Marduk, like the Sumerian Dumuzi, is always called the son of Enki (Osiris). That he is also the counterpart of Horus the Younger, the early sun, Harakhte, is suggested by the original form of Marduk's name Amarutuk, sun-calf.[1520] Marduk is also the son of Enlil/Shu, since he is said to have been created by Nunamnir, that is, Enlil, in a hymn to Marduk.[1521] We have already noticed the Sumerian account of Enlil's parentage of Nergal.[1522]

Further, just as Horus the Younger bears the name of his father Horus-Osiris, so also the last of the fifty names given to Marduk in the concluding section of *EE* is in fact Ea itself. This Ea is Osiris, the "brother" of Horus the Elder. That Ea is coeval with and a "brother" (rather than "son") of An is made clear by the fact that both An (Horus the Elder) and Ea (Osiris) have Anshar as their father (*EE* I,14; II,8).

It is interesting to note that one of the fifty names of Marduk in EE is "Asari", which may be a contraction of 'Asarluhi', a southern Sumerian deity associated, and later identified, with Marduk,[1523] since Asarluhu too seems to have been worshipped as the son of Enki.[1524] Though the meaning of Asarluhi is uncertain,[1525] it is mentioned, in a Sippar hymn to Marduk, as an epithet of Marduk "in the pure Abyss".[1526] Marduk's consort Zarpanit is also called Me-absu, that is, the holy truths or me's (Sanskrit 'rta') of the Abyss,[1527] which inform all morality in the universe. Marduk thus is a god who emerges from the Abyss just as Tammuz (Dumuzi-absu) too is.

Marduk is also virtually the same as Osiris/Enki, since he is forced to descend into the underworld, according to the fragmentary myth,

---

[1519]   In Srosh Yasht, Sraosha is called "the incarnate Word". In Vedic literature, Sūrya's daughter is called Shraddhā (Faith), according to *SB* XII,vii,3,11.

[1520]   W. Lambert, "Studies in Marduk", *BSOAS*, 47, p.8.

[1521]   W.G. Lambert, "Three literary Prayers of the Babylonians", *AfO* 19 (1959-60), p.62; cf. Kinnier Wilson, *op.cit.*, p.63

[1522]   See above p.245f.

[1523]   See W. Sommerfeld, *Der Aufstieg Marduks*, Kevelaer: Butzon & Bercker, 1982, p.18.

[1524]   See W. Sommerfeld, "Marduk" in *RLA* VII: 362.

[1525]   See W. Sommerfeld, *Aufstieg*, p.13ff.

[1526]   *Ibid.*; cf. *RLA* VII:368.

[1527]   We remember the appellation of the waters as the "wives of Varuna" in *KYV* V,5,4, (see above p.138).

"Marduk's Ordeal", mentioned above.[1528] The banishment of Marduk to the underworld is ascribed, in these fragments, to Anshar.[1529] And the crime for which he is so punished must be his violence against his father Anu.[1530] Since the descent of the solar force is due to Seth/Teshup/Zeus, we see that Marduk embodies both the solar and stormy aspects of Seth and Horus the Younger respectively.[1531] The one who searches for Marduk is his "vizier", Nabû, who will emerge first from the underworld as the moon, and then allow Marduk to rise as the sun. Marduk's passion in the underworld as depicted in the fragments relating to "Marduk's Ordeal"[1532] reveals the similarity between Marduk, Nergal, Gilgamesh, and even Tammuz.

Marduk as the counterpart of Nergal is called the "one inside Šamaš", just as Nabû, his vizier, or forerunner, is "the one inside Sin".[1533] In an inscription from the second century B.C. Marduk is associated with the day as Nabû is with the night.[1534] Marduk, Nergal and Nabû, as we have seen, are but different aspects of Ninurta.

We have noted that Tammuz is a counterpart of Osiris. The story of the descent of Tammuz into the underworld is essentially the same story as that of Osiris and Isis. According to the famous legend of Tammuz and Ishtar, the former is destroyed by a "raging flood" and taken to the underworld,[1535] where Ishtar follows him to seek and restore him. The reference to a storm-flood reminds us of Ram/Adad/Seth as the possible cause of his destruction. At the same time, the "son" of An, Tammuz, is

---

[1528] See above p.160.

[1529] In the Egyptian Osirian mythology, we know that Seth, who causes Osiris' similar descent, is but the stormy aspect of Osiris, the solar energy itself. The stormy aspect of Ninurta/Marduk is Adad. Just as Adad and Shamash are regularly evoked together in prayers, so also are Marduk and Shamash (C.A.H., pl.i, 226b) (see S. A. Cook, *op.cit.*, p.42).

[1530] We have noted above (p.185n) the reference to Marduk's cutting off Anu's neck.

[1531] We have seen above (p.230) that Baal too is at once a storm-god and a solar one.

[1532] See A. Livingstone, *ibid.* That this sojourn of Marduk in the underworld is the source of the account of Christ's death and resurrection has already been pointed out by H. Zimmern, 'Religion und Sprache', pp.384ff. We see thus that Christ is in the final analysis a Babylonian mythological figure representing the solar force. That Christ is synonymous with Marduk, Bel, Baal, may be one of the reasons for the original orthodox Jewish antipathy to Christianity. The pre-Islamic Allah too is derived from Baal since like the latter, he is said to have three daughters (see *Moslem World*, 23, 1 (1943); cf. C.H. Gordon, "Canaanite Mythology", in S. Kramer (ed.), *Mythologies*, p.196).

[1533] VAT 8917 rev.5 (see A. Livingstone, *op.cit.*, p.83).

[1534] See J. Epping and J.N. Strassmeier, "Neue babylonische Planeten-Tafeln", ZA, 6 (1891), 241.2-9; cf. X. Kugler, *Im Bannkreis Babels*, p.63.

[1535] See S. Langdon, *op.cit.*, p.12; in SRT 31, obv.13ff. it is stated that Tammuz "perished in the Rebellion" (see J.V. Kinnier Wilson, *op.cit.*, p.65).

virtually the same as An himself, since the consort of Tammuz is Inanna, who is at once his mother and sister.[1536] In the Assyrian text A.O. 17626 obv.,[1537] An is indeed identified with Dumuzi(d)-Abzu (abbreviated as Tammuz),[1538] meaning the child of the Abyss.

However, Tammuz is, more particularly than An, the solar force which transforms itself into the sun of our system. In a hymn to Tammuz (IV R 30, no.2), the latter's solar identity is made clear in the verse: "In his childhood he lies in a sunken ship".[1539] Tammuz' facial features are said to be of pure lapis lazuli (the azure light of the universe), which extends beyond the Ocean[1540] that surrounds Earth. That Tammuz is not yet the fully risen sun Shamash, is suggested by the fact that Tammuz is represented as guarding the roots of the "kishkanu" tree along with Shamash.[1541] Rather, Tammuz is here identifiable with Ninurta/Nergal, as the sun of the underworld,[1542] in which case he is a counterpart also of Marduk/Horus the Younger.

Our knowledge of the flood myths, as well as the myths of Osiris' death and of Marduk's ordeal, suggests that the sun of the new universe is first formed in the depths of the underworld to which the light of Heaven descends. It is also likely that Ishtar is responsible for the various metamorphoses of Tammuz (Horus/Hercules/Verethraghna/Vishnu).[1543] This is indeed the reproach that Gilgamesh makes to Ishtar in the sixth book of the Gilgamesh epic.[1544]

Tammuz was most likely represented as bound with an "evil" companion in the underworld, just as Marduk (and later Jesus) are found in the company of a "criminal", this evil companion perhaps representing

---

[1536] See S. Langdon, op.cit., p.29.

[1537] See A. Livingstone, op.cit, p.199.

[1538] The original form of Dumuzi would have been Dumu-zi(d)-abzu, good son of the Abzu (SAK 18,6,2; see A. Deimel, Pantheon, p.104).

[1539] See H. Zimmern, op.cit., p.398n.; the text continues: "grown up he lies in the immersed fruit of the field", wherein Tammuz's character as a vegetation god is revealed.

[1540] E. Ebeling, 'Heiliger Baum', in RLA, IV:435.

[1541] See S. Langdon, Tammuz and Ishtar, p.31.

[1542] Langdon pointed out that Ningirsu and Ningiszida came to represent the spring sun, while Nergal the sun of the period between the summer solstice and the winter solstice (ibid., p.30). This does not obviate the original lunar significance of Ningiszida, since the flood represented by Ningirsu and the moon are forms of Ninurta which precede the sun, Babbar/Shamash.

[1543] See, for instance, the incarnations of Verethreghna above p.222n.

[1544] See S. Langdon, op.cit., p.83ff.

the Sumerian counterpart of Seth/Teshup.[1545] Ishtar succeeds in raising Tammuz from the dead and returns to the heavens with the young god in her bosom, at which triumphant moment the liturgies especially celebrate the return of the light: "In heaven there is light, on earth there is light."[1546] Tammuz is said to have risen "from the flood" and to "create the rising waters".[1547] The third birth of Agni, as we shall see below, is similarly said to be "from the waters".[1548]

According to the myth of Inanna's descent into the underworld, Inanna's ascent from the underworld with the life-giving powers of Enki is followed by the need to find a substitute for herself in the underworld. As such a substitute, Inanna sends Dumuzi (An – who is, however, the same as Enki), whereupon he loses his life in the underworld. This myth therefore duplicates the story of the descent of the divine light into the underworld considering Enki and Dumuzi as two different figures). To rescue him, Dumuzi's sister Geshtinanna (lady of the vine, of the "tree of life") follows him into the underworld, and wins his release but only on the condition that she stay behind, so that finally the two siblings take turns sojourning in the underworld.[1549]

This reflects the episode in the Sumerian story of "Enlil and Ninlil" where Nergal, the underworld sun, is formed as a substitute for the moon when the latter has to be ejected into our universe. Tammuz is said to have grown up in Eridu (i.e. the Abyss), and his dwelling is Earth, where Nammu, representing the cosmic streams, lies. Tammuz, who is a form of Ninurta, and originally the guardian of the tree (as Nergal) in the underworld, is gradually identified, like Ninurta, with the tree itself.[1550]

Tammuz is also identified with the universal forms of Ninurta, especially Ningirsu (Lord of the Flood which bears the sun).[1551] That Tammuz/An is ultimately the same as Ninurta, who is indeed the source of both the moon (as Nabû) and the sun (as Nergal/Ningirsu), is clear from

---

[1545] See the ritual text in S. Langdon, *op.cit.*, p.35, where a morbid suppliant appeals to Tammuz to be freed of the "evil spy, the adversary" who is bound with him, so that he may live.

[1546] *Ibid,*. p.22.

[1547] *Ibid.*, p.32. Langdon noted that Innini (Ishtar) of Assur, Nineveh, and Arbela may have been originally worshipped by the Mitanni of that area (*op.cit.*, p.67n). We shall note below the possible Central Asian origin of the cedar associated with Tammuz as well (below p.281n).

[1548] See below p.305.

[1549] *Ibid.*, pp.116–30.

[1550] See below p.281.

[1551] S. Langdon, *ibid.*, p.6n (cf. p.242 above).

the passage where Tammuz is called both Nannar, the moon, (Nergal's "great twin") and Shamash.[1552] Tammuz is also represented as a guardian of the gates of heaven.[1553]along with Ningishzida (Lord of the true wood/tree), who, as we have seen, is associated with Thoth, 'the tongue' of Ptah,[1554] and the moon. Ninurta/Marduk are equally considered the son of Enki/Osiris and are virtually identical with their father, the cosmic light. The force of the cosmic light, however, is the vivifying life-force of the universe, Enlil.[1555]

It may be noted in this connection that the Cretan Zeus, son of Chronos, in the original Cretan tradition, is believed to have died and been buried in Crete.[1556] This Zeus is the same as Dionysus/Tammuz/An. Dionysus is considered a son of Kore/Persephone.[1557] Kore herself is the child of Zeus Aitherios (Chronos)'s mating with Rhea-Demeter (whom Plutarch identified with Nut as he did Geb with Chronos). Kore/Persephone is therefore identical to Isis, daughter of Nut, and consort of Osiris. Kore is equally the counterpart of Inanna who, as we have seen, is also forced to descend into the underworld.[1558] This suggests that the Dionysus who is the son of Kore is Horus the Younger.

The salvation story related to Dionysus may have served as a source of the rituals of the cult of the Christ, for a 3rd c. B.C. papyrus which gives instructions for a religious rite contains the following version of the familiar communion formulae: "[Let him] collect the raw pieces [of the mutilated Dionysus]… on account of the sacrament. Accept ye my [offering] as the payment [for my lawless] fathers".[1559] The passion, resurrection and ascension of Christ, which may have originally been derived directly from the Babylonian Ordeal of Marduk, as we have already noticed, was also probably influenced by the Thraco-Phrygian version of it. The Christian

---

[1552]   *Ibid.*

[1553]   See above p.255.

[1554]   See above p.254.

[1555]   Ishtar, Tammuz's consort, is associated, perhaps in a familial relationship, with ᵈAmanna of Uruk, who is called the Enlil of Suruppak (see S. Langdon, *op.cit.*,p.100). This association suggests that An begins to be manifest as a result of the powerful wind-god Enlil. Both Tammuz and An (Brahman) may be related to the Egyptian Amun (Ātman) (whose first, and typical, manifest form is that of Shu/Enlil). For, like Amun, Tammuz is symbolized in Elamite art by a ram (see S. Langdon, *op.cit.*, p.162).

[1556]   See A.B. Cook, *Zeus*, I:157.

[1557]   According to some Orphic theogonies, "Zeus" is indeed considered to be Dionysus' father (see M.L. West, *op.cit.*, p.74), but this must be Zeus Aitherios/Chronos. Sometimes, Dionysus is represented as a son of Zeus and Semele (see above p.180).

[1558]   See above p.269.

[1559]   See M.L. West, *op.cit.*, p.170.

drama is also obviously related to the Egyptian account of the killing of Osiris and his resurrection as Horus the Younger. The essential identity of Horus the Younger to Osiris and of Marduk to Ea is no doubt the reason of the metaphysical identification of Christ with his "Father" in some Christian theologies.

XXIII: ASHVATTHA

THE TREE OF LIFE: INDRA, YGGDRASIL, NINURTA

We have seen that, in the sixth hour of the *Amduat*, when Re passes over Osiris he becomes ithyphallic. This betokens the rise of the universal life contained in the phallus of Heaven (Horus the Elder-Osiris) into the Mid-Region between the heaven and earth of our universe. We know also that the divine phallus was absorbed by Zeus/Teshup/Seth so that the entire universe moved into his "stomach". This suggests once again that Seth is indeed the life-force of Osiris. The rising phallus is also often represented as a "tree" of life. Tammuz and Dionysus and Ninurta are all admired as a Tree of Life, which is indeed symbolic of the entire universe.

The universal tree has its roots in the Abyss while its trunk represents earth and branches the Mid-region. Atop its branches, in the heavens, will emerge the sun. The 'ashvattha' fig-tree is considered to be inverted, so that its roots grow upwards and its branches spread downwards.[1560] That the tree is an analogue of the phallus is made clear by the reference in *LP* 17ff to the phallus too as an endless column of fire which fills the universe, and at the top of which is Brahma in the solar form of a swan (hamsa) and at the base of which is Vishnu in the form of a boar. We have seen that, in Mesopotamia, Shamash and Tammuz, representing the sun of heaven and the sun of earth, are similarly represented as the guardians of the Tree of Life.[1561] The sun-god (Sūrya) is a later manifestation within our universe of the original light of the universe which appeared above the "lotus" of Earth. The representation of Vishnu as a boar corresponds to Vāyu as the life of the universe, for we have seen that the boar form of Verethreghna indeed heralds Mithra in the Avesta.[1562]

[1560] *Katha Upanishad*, VI,1.

[1561] See below p.268.

[1562] See above p.224.

In India, as in Sumer, the tree of life spans the entire universe comprising the three regions of earth, the mid-region, and the heavens, which are dominated respectively by the three forms of solar energy, Agni, Vāyu, Āditya.[1563] Agni is, in *KYV* V,5,1, called "the lowest of deities", while Vishnu (Āditya) is the highest. In the case of the German Yggdrasil,[1564] the roots of this tree reach heaven, earth and the Abyss equally. In the *Maitri Upanishad* (VI,4) the tree (called metonymously "Brahman") is called "three-footed", and from the evidence of the Germanic Edda we may consider these feet or roots as not restricted to heaven but as equally embracing heaven, earth and the Mid-Region. Moslem literature too retains the image of a downward tending cosmic tree which reaches to the lowest heaven. A similar tree growing from the lowest depths of Hell, however, grows upwards.[1565]

In the *Maitreya Upanishad*, VI,6, the universe is called the "gross form" of Purusha, where Heaven is his head, the atmosphere [or Mid-region between Heaven and Earth] is his navel, and the sun his eye. According to the *Shvetāsvatara Upanishad*, III,9, the Purusha himself "stands like a tree established in heaven; by Him, the Purusha, is this whole universe filled". This Purusha is, as we have seen, the First Man, rather than the Ideal macroanthropos.

Just as the Sumerian Enki does, so too Varuna, in *RV* I,24,7, "sustaineth erect the Tree's stem in the baseless region [the Abyss, apsu]", for Varuna is the Lord of the Abyss. The roots of the tree arise from deep within the Abyss, while the trunk represents Earth. The branches of the Tree of Life represent the Mid-region of the manifest universe and the sun which arises from atop them rules this region as well.[1566] The passage from the *Maitri Upanishad* mentioned above further makes clear that the "branches", which represent the Mid-region of the manifest universe, contain "space, wind, fire, water, earth and the like". The summit of the tree, that is, the highest point of its branches, represents heaven, the domain of the gods. The highest of the three heavens serves as the seat of the gods (*AV* V,4,3,4). There the Ādityas enjoy their nectar of immortality,[1567] while Yama (*RV* X,135,1) is ruler of the lowest heaven. According to *AV* V,4,3, the original location of

---

[1563] See Chs.XX,XXV.

[1564] See below p.283.

[1565] See A.J. Wensinck, "Tree and Bird", pp.33,35.

[1566] See below p.317.

[1567] The first of the Ādityas, Mitra-Varuna, are the lords of rta, or the me's, of the universe, the waters in which they were born being the seat of these me's. Similarly, the other Ādityas represent various divine virtues (see above p.231n).

Soma, which infuses the entire Tree, is in the highest heavens. In the *MBh*, the infant Vishnu is found *under* an "asvattha" tree during the flood, which may be a depiction of the sun of the underworld since the roots of the tree are in the Abyss.[1568]

The use of Vishnu as the deity at the base of the phallus [tree] in the LP is particularly significant since Vishnu (Verethraghna) is represented as a boar in the Avesta. In fact the Tree is the locus of the second birth of Agni in our universe as Vāyu, the Wind-god. In the Vedic literature, Agni is said to have been born in the Earth (SB, VII,iv,1,9: "this earth is — the birthplace of Agni"), or in the navel of the Earth (SB VII,vi,3,9), as also in the waters (his third birth, as Mitra/Aditya) and from Heaven (his first birth as Agni/Varuna). In KYV IV,2,2, the second birth of Agni from Earth is described thus:

From us[1569] secondly [was born] he who knoweth all

The reference to the god "who knoweth all" is clarified by the Eddic reference to Wotan's acquisition of supreme knowledge on the Yggdrasil.[1570] And Wotan is the Germanic counterpart of Wāta/Vāyu.

In the RV X, 31, 6-10, the impregnation of Aditi by Agni is said to cause her to give birth to the ashvattha fig tree which holds heaven and earth together:[1571]

When suddenly called the cow that erst was barren, she, self-protected, ended all her troubles.

Earth, when the first son sprang from sire and mother, cast up the Sami [the asvatta fig], that which men were seeking.

The preciousness of the tree is, of course, due to its bearing the sap of immortality, Soma.

[1568] Within the human microcosm, Rele identifies Vishnu with the spinal cord itself (see V.G. Rele, *op.cit.*, pp.71-3).

[1569] The first person form assumed by the priests at this point indicates their exalted status as Mitra-Varuna priests, Mitra and Varuna being forms of Agni, the elemental form of the solar energy.

[1570] See below p.284.

[1571] A pictorial representation of this event is to be found among the Indus seals, showing that the civilization of the Indus Valley is at once Āryan and Dravidian, the contacts between the two cultures extending perhaps to the earliest history of the proto-Hurrians in Elam and Mesopotamia.

The tree of life holds heaven and earth together and is also identified with Indra,[1572] who, as we have seen, is the same as the Ideal Man as well as the First Man.[1573] Indra is called "the Bull" who has drunk the powerful Soma:

> 6. This Bull's most gracious far-extended favour existed first of all in full abundance.
> By his support they [the Ādityas] are maintained in common who in the Asura's mansions dwell together.
>
> 7. What was the tree, what wood,[1574] in sooth, produced it, from which they fashioned forth the Earth and Heaven?
> These Twain [earth and heaven] stand fast and wax not old for ever: ...
> ... He is the Bull, the Heaven's and Earth's supporter.

In *AV* IV,11,2 Indra is called the "draft ox" who sustains the earth and heaven.

In *RV* III,31, Indra develops into a universal tree as a result of his consumption of soma and this soma-inspired growth holds earth and heaven together:

> 11. For [Indra] the Cow [Aditi], noble and far-extending, poured pleasant juices, bringing oil and sweetness.
>
> 12. They [the kine] made a mansion for their Father [their protector, Indra], deftly provided him a great and glorious dwelling/ With firm support parted and stayed the Parents [Heaven and Earth], and sitting, fixed him there erected, mighty.
>
> 13. What time the ample chalice [of soma] had impelled him, swift waxing, vast, to pierce the earth and heaven.

And *RV* II,15:

[1572] Indra is the mystical name of Indha, which, according to *SB* VI,i,1,2, means "the blower", a name that relates Indra to Vāyu.

[1573] See above pp.114,181.

[1574] This particular curiosity with regard to the "wood" of the tree is clearly addressed to the erection of the phallus as well.

High heaven unsupported in space he stablished: he filled the two worlds [earth and heaven] and the air's Mid-region.

Earth he upheld, and gave it wide expansion. These things did Indra in the Soma's rapture.

Indra is indeed represented as the vital force of Agni in all its three forms, in the underworld, the mid-region, and the heavens (*RV* X,31):

8. ... With power divine he makes his skin a filter, when the Bay Coursers bear him on as Surya [=Āditya]

He passes o'er the broad Earth like a Stega:[1575] he penetrates the world as Wind [=Vāyu] the mist-cloud.

He balmed with oil, near Varuna and Mitra, like Agni in the wood, hath shot forth splendour.

Indra is always closely associated with the "Soma" or seminal fluid of the universe and he is called the "lord of the seed".[1576] Indra is said to have imbibed the sap of life, Soma (seed), in the dwelling of Tvashtr, who is an aspect of Dyaus. Soma is described in RV III,48,2-3 as that milk which Indra's mother, Aditi, "poured for thee [Indra] in thy mighty Father's dwelling./ Desiring food he came unto his Mother, and on her breast beheld the pungent Soma."[1577] At RV III,I,7, the infant "Agni" is said to be nourished by the "milch-kine" (solar rays) which are present in the seven cosmic rivers which issue out of the mountain when Indra destroys the serpent Vrtra. The "cows" (the water of Aditi) are said to be impregnated by the "bull". At RV I,84,15 the "milch-kine" are said to have recognized their lord as Tvashtr's Bull in the mansion of the moon, the moon being the heavenly body in which the Soma will be finally stored.[1578]

[1575] The meaning of this word is uncertain, though it may refer to the penetrating power of Agni.

[1576] *MBh* I, 57, 1-27.

[1577] In *RV* III,30,14, the Cow "bearing ripe milk [i.e. soma; see above p.221n]" is used as a synonym for Usha, the goddess of the Dawn. In Egypt, Isis revives Osiris with "life-giving milk" (see H. Junker, "Das Götterdekret über das Abaton", *DAWW* 56 (1913); cf. "Isis", *LÄ* III:194). That soma is ultimately the same as (Ger.) Samen/seed, which infuses Indra as the "Tree" of Life, is clear from this reference to Indra consuming soma at his mother's breast, since, according to the *Bundahishn* Ch.XVI,5, the woman's milk is produced by the male seed just as blood is produced by the female.

[1578] See above p.258.

In RV IX,99,5, Agni is said to impregnate the Cow [Prshni, i.e. Aditi][1579] specifically as Soma, which represents the seminal force of Indra. At RV III,22,1, the potency of the Soma which Indra consumed is said to be Agni itself. At AV III,21,2, Agni – Fire – is said to be inherent in Soma (identified with the moon god) as well as in all animals.[1580] At RV III,48,4, Indra is said to have conquered his father and borne off the Soma in beakers thereafter. This reference to the destruction of his father by Indra reminds us of the swallowing of Ouranos' phallus by Chronos' son, Zeus.

In SB I,vi,3,22; III,iv,2,3, Soma, much like Indra, is represented as all the gods since they are both the vital form of the all-pervasive Agni. In RV IX,109,5, Soma too, much like Indra, is called the "sustainer of the sky". In KYV I, 8,22, Soma, along with Pushan,[1581] is called the creator of heaven and earth, that is, the force that impelled their separation, as well as the "navel of immortality", Soma being considered a source of life immortal. Soma is also said to make the thunder (IX,61,16).

Indra's intoxication with Soma is indeed the prototype of the Dionysiac and Bacchic wine-rituals.[1582] Soma thus represents the creative potency of fire which is responsible for the formation of our universe but must nevertheless be dompted in order to allow the sun to emerge as the ruler of the universe. In this context, it may be noted that, in the Brāhmanas, the moon (SB I,vi,4,18) as well as Soma (SB III,iv,3,13) is called Vrtra,[1583] the serpent, which we shall see is also infused with Soma and Agni. The moon, which is always associated with Soma, is indeed considered to be a form of Agni as Kāma (Desire).

It has been suggested, also, that, in the human microcosmos, the Tree may be manifest as the central nervous system.[1584] The squirrel Ratatosk

---

[1579]   Agni here is the same as Varuna.

[1580]   Agni is called the "begetter of offspring" in *KYV* II,2,10.

[1581]   Pushan is a solar Āditya, so that Soma and Pushan, who are referred to in *RV* II,40,1, as the "twins" may refer to the moon and the sun (cf. the reference to Sin and Shamash as twins above p.242). However, it must be noted that, in *RV* II,40,4, Pushan is said to rule Heaven, while Soma rules the Mid-region (as the moon) and Earth (as the lord of plantal life). But we shall see (below p.306) that Aton/Re who represents the highest form of the sun is the same as Indra – who is also a storm-god. Thus Pushan must represent the highest solar form of Indra himself, which is to be distinguished from those of Mitra (Nergal/Horus the Younger) and Savitr (Khepera). We have noted also that Sin and Nergal too are considered to be "the great twins" (see above p.245).

[1582]   See above p.230. The fact that the cosmological significance of this intoxication is lost in Asia Minor and Greece shows that the western Āryan religions are indeed later forms of the Indo-Āryan and Sumero-Egyptian.

[1583]   See A.K. Lahiri, *op.cit.*, pp.181,183.

[1584]   For an understanding of the tree within the human microcosm as the structure of the

which runs up and down the Germanic Yggdrasil conveying the message of the eagle symbolising the sun to the serpent Nidhogg below[1585] may indeed be representative, in the microcosm, of the nerve-impulses which move from the brain, through the descending tract of neurons in the nervous system, in order to stimulate motor neurons or to initiate glandular secretions. Since the base of the spinal cord is the seat of unconscious, as well as of sexual, activity, it is indeed the task of spiritual man to rise to supraconsciousness by mastering the "serpent". The tree which sustains the microcosmos as well as the macrocosmos is, indeed, filled with the seed of desire which, when it succeeds in producing the clear light of consciousness (Brahman) in enlightened man, at once prompts the destruction of the tree itself as an illusion.[1586]

In the Sumerian poem, "Enki and the World-Order", the roots of the cosmic tree are generated by Enki in the Abyss. Enki is called (l.3) the son of Enlil (Shu) and of An (Horus the Elder), though he is the same as both. Enki is said to have planted the "me tree" or the tree of life in the Abzu. This tree, called a "kishkanu" (Sumerian "gishkin") tree in an Akkadian hymn to the "tree of Eridu", extends from the depths of the apsu, where Enki dwells, to the heights of heaven, and represents at the same time the pathway of Enki to mankind.[1587] In the 'Epic of Gilgamesh' (IX,164ff) too, the hero finds a tree of "cornelian"and "lapis lazuli" at the eastern end of Earth, from whence the sun, Shamash, ascends to the heavens.[1588] The protective shade of the tree is said to spread over the entire universe. At l.69 of "Enki and the World-Order" Enki is called the "great light who rises over the great below", as well as the "great lord of Sumer".[1589]

---

entire nervous system itself see V.G. Rele, *op.cit.*, pp.26f. The two hemispheres of the brain are considered by Rele as symbolic of the two heavens, while the base of the spinal cord represents Earth. The recognition of the forces represented by the several Vedic deities within the microcosm is justified by the Purānic description of the constitution of the Macroanthropos (see above p.110); cf. A. Daniélou, *Hindu Polytheism*, London: Routledge and Kegan Paul, 1964, pp.98f.

[1585] See below p.283.

[1586] This characteristic Indo-European spirituality is recovered in the West in the philosophy of Arthur Schopenhauer (especially in his masterwork, *Die Welt als Wille und Vorstellung*).

[1587] See 'The Poem of Erra', I,150; cf. M. Rutten, "Les Religions Asianiques", p. 98f.

[1588] See A.J. Wensinck, "Tree and Bird", p.3. In *Daniel* 4:10-17, Nebuchadnezzar describes a dream of a similar cosmic tree, and so too does Ezekiel in *Ezekiel* 31:3 (cf. A.J. Wensinck, *ibid.*, pp.25f.).

[1589] Sumer itself is most probably the name of the "primordial hill" of the central island of Earth, through which the solar force of the universe emerges since Sumer is called "the great mountain, the land of the universe" in l.192. Sumeru ('Holy Meru') is also a name of Mt. Meru in *BrdP* I,ii,15,42. The names of the other lands around Sumer – Ur, Meluhha, Dilmun,

That Ninurta is only a continuation of Enki is made clear by the reference to Enki's 'makurru' boat (1.107), the sun-barque which is featured prominently as Ninurta's own in Lugal e. In fact, Enki is said to have received the "lofty sun-disk" in Eridu (1.121) showing that as ruler of the underworld he is identical to the "dead" Osiris who is transformed into Horus the Younger. Since Ninurta is a counterpart of Marduk, it is not surprising that Marduk is also called "Ea" in EE, VII,120. However, as we shall see, Marduk is particularly the force of the incipient sun in the underworld.

Ninurta is also admired as the axis of the universe or tree of life. That the tree of life is a symbol of Enlil's warrior son, or "strong arm",[1590] Ninurta, is made clear in the epic Lugal e (1.189), where Ninurta is called "the cedar which grows in the Abzu" (1.189)[1591] as well as "the great Meš tree" (1.310).[1592] Ninurta is also called the "date-palm" in the An=Anum god-list, Tablet I, dLugal.giš.gišimmar (ŠA6).[1593] The mešu tree is like the kishkanu tree since, in the Irra myth,[1594] its roots are said to be in the Ocean and its top touches the heavens. The mešu tree is called the "flesh of the gods" (Poem of Erra, I,150), since, as we have seen, its trunk represents 'earth', the material substance of the universe.[1595]

We have seen that Indra is infused with the powerful seminal force of Soma, It is not surprising that Ninurta, like Shiva's son, Skanda, represents the seed of Enlil.[1596] Ninurta is, like his father Enlil, also said to be a great "mountain" [i.e. phallus] which extends from earth to heaven.[1597] According to KAR 142,I,22ff, Ninurta's seminal force appears in seven forms as dIB (Urash),[1598] Nin-urta, Za-ba-ba,[1599] Na-bi-um, Ne-iri-gal, Sa-kud and Pa-bil-

---

Elam-Marhasi, and Martu – which Enki blesses in the poem of "Enki and the World-Order" may have similar cosmological significances.

[1590]   See J. Van Dijk, *Lugal ud me-lam-bi Nir-gal*, Leiden: E.J. Brill, 1983, p.29. The strong arm of Ninurta is itself personified as Adad/Sarur (see above p.199).

[1591]   *Ibid.*, p.75.

[1592]   *Ibid.*, p.90.

[1593]   See R. Litke, *op.cit.*, p.46.

[1594]   See E. Ebeling, KARI, 168, Rs.I, l.28ff.

[1595]   See above p.274.

[1596]   See above p.239.

[1597]   Ninurta is precisely, the force, 'semen,' of his father Enili, 'the great mountain' (see above p.239.

[1598]   Urash is the name of Enki as well (see above p.139), showing the same assimilation of son and father that we find in the case of Shiva and Skanda.

[1599]   This is also an appellation of Marduk (See K. Tallquist, *Akkadische Götterepitheta*, p.364).

sag.[1600] (Similarly, in the Gula hymn of Bullutsa-rabi, the goddess' husband is called successively Ninurta, Ningirsu, Ninazu, Zababa, Utulu and Lugalbanda).[1601] The Dilmunite[1602] name of Nabû, d.En-sa6-ag, in the myth of "Enki and Ninhursag" also contains a reference to the date-palm, just as the date-palm branch engraved on the left side of a Rimum inscription also hints at this metaphorical name of Nabû.[1603] Nabû, like Ningishzida,[1604] is, particularly the force within the moon (Soma).

The cedar tree is sacred to Tammuz, since we have seen that, like Ninurta/Marduk, he is identifiable with both the original light of the cosmos (An) and the sun of the underworld. Tammuz' mother and consort is Antum/Ishtar consort of An as well as of the mistress of the underworld (just as Isis is Osiris' wife). Ishtar is also the mistress who bears the cedar tree.[1605] In CT XVI,46,183ff., Tammuz is, like Ninurta, identified with the Tree itself.

In Egypt, both Hathor and Nut (heaven) are associated with the cosmic sycamore, showing that they are the same deity at different stages of cosmic evolution.[1606] We have seen that Hathor is indeed called the "mistress of the sycamore".[1607] Nut the goddess of the sky, and mother of Osiris, is also in charge of the sycamore tree located in Heliopolis, which is surrounded at its base by the serpent Apop. The solar god, her son, Osiris, moves out from between this tree and another like it when the sun begins its journey across the skies. However, it is strictly Horus the Younger who is the sun of our universe and Hathor/Isis who is his mother. Like the Soma-bearing tree of the Indians, the sycamore contains the water and air of immortality which the dead thirst for in the underworld.[1608] That this sap of the sycamore is the same as the Vedic Soma, which also bears immortal life, is patent. Osiris is frequently referred to as bearing the divine life-giving fluid.[1609]

[1600] See K. Tallquist, op.cit., p. 421

[1601] See Kinnier Wilson, op.cit., p.85.

[1602] We have seen already that Dilmun itself signifies the spot at which the sun rises, and is the paradise (the lower heavens) to which Ziusudra, the survivor of the cosmic flood (Yima/Manu), is sent at the end of his life.

[1603] See K. Al-Nashef, "The Deities of Dilmun", in Bahrain Through the Ages, p.346.

[1604] See above p.253f.

[1605] Ibid., p.10; pp.50ff. It is interesting to note that the cedar is not indigenous to Sumer, unlike the date-palm. This may be an indication that the founders of the Tammuz cult originated in Central Asia.

[1606] See above p.176.

[1607] See above p.234.

[1608] See E.A.W. Budge, op.cit., II:106f.

[1609] See E.O. James, op.cit., p.6.

The material matrix of the universe called Earth is also symbolised by the Djed column. In the Edfu temple records (E VI,184,18),[1610] the Djed pillar, which is made of reeds, seems similar to the lotus Earth (Geb), on which the divine Light rests. In the Ramesseum dramatic text in honour of Sesostris I, the Djed column is particularly identified with Geb's son Seth (Teshup), who represents the passionate element of Osiris, while the branches of the 'jm3' tree wound around it are called "Osiris",[1611] the solar force, thus symbolising perhaps the two most powerful gods associated with the rise of our universe. In the Edfu documents, the presiding deities of the so-called Island of Trampling also rest on Djed pillars.[1612]

On the Indic Mitanni seals of the second millennium B.C., the winged disk representing the emergence of the sun[1613] is sometimes supported on a sacred pillar, while on other seals the wings of the disk are transformed into the branches of a tree. We have seen that the branches of the Tree of Life represent the Mid-Region between heaven and earth, and the bird itself must represent the eagle of the Avesta.[1614] In Assyria, too, Ashur is frequently represented by a winged disk hovering over a tree.[1615] We have seen above that Assur (Anshar) is the Assyrian Enlil (Vāyu).[1616] In the biblical book of *Ezechiel* 31:3, Assur, the Assyrian king, is also described in the image of a cosmic "cedar of Lebanon".

In the Avesta (Rashn Yasht, XII,17), it is stated that, in the centre of the Vouru-kasha Sea, stands "the tree of the eagle … that is called the tree of good remedies … on which rest the seeds of all plants".[1617] At the base of the tree is a "lizard" created by Ahriman to destroy the tree. However ten fish save the tree by continually swimming around it.[1618]

[1610] See E.A.E. Reymond, *op.cit.*, p.88.

[1611] See "Djed Pfeiler"in *LÄ*, I, 1101.

[1612] See E.A.E. Reymond, *op.cit.*, pp.124f.

[1613] The wings are those of a falcon, which, in Egyptian as well as Avestan religion, represents a solar form of the divine energy.

[1614] See below.

[1615] See E.O. James, *op.cit.*, pp.43,97. If Ashur as the divine power of the sun seems to resemble here the Babylonian Marduk ("the one within the sun"), that is due to the ultimate identity of Marduk and Ea (*EE* II,8), who, as we have seen, is but a form of Enlil (see above p.144).

[1616] We have seen that Vāyu is the second incarnation of Agni at the stage of the manifestation of the universe (see above p.275).

[1617] Yasna 42,4 also mentions a sacred [unicorn] beast which stands in the Vouru-kasha sea; cf. *Bundahishn*, XIX, which refers to a three-legged ass with one horn; and the Indus seals with their many representations of a beast resembling a unicorn bull.

[1618] See *Bundahishn*, XVIII,2.

In the poetic Edda, the name of the Yggdrasil ash-tree may be phonetically related to the Vedic Indra.[1619] We may note the similarity of the description of this tree in "Voluspa" and "Grimnismal" to those in the Vedas, and in Mesopotamian and Egyptian cosmological literature:

> I know an ash-tree stands called Yggdrasill,
> a high tree, soaked with shining loam.[1620]

and:

> Three roots there grow in three directions
> under the ash of Yggdrasil;
> Hel lives under one, under the second the frost-giants,
> the third humankind.

> Ratatosk is the squirrel's name who has to run
> upon the ash of Yggdrasil;
> the eagle's word he must bring from above
> and tell to Nidhogg below.[1621]

Like the Indian tree, the Yggdrasil also grows downwards, since one of its roots is said to be based in the heavens, where the gods (Aesir) hold court. Under this root is the well of Urd.[1622] In one region of heaven called Valaskjalf (the hall of the slain) is to be found the seat of Odin, called Hlidskjalf, whence he surveys the nine worlds covered by the tree [there being three heavens, as well as three mid-regions and earths].

The second root reaches the Ginnungagap (the Abyss), where the "frost ogres" dwell. Here is to be found an oracular spring guarded by the

---

[1619] The popular interpretation of Yggdrasil, however (see, for instance, R. Cook, *op.cit.*, p.23), is as "steed of Odin", from Ygg, one of the names of this god meaning "the terrible" (see 'Grimnismal', st.54). The tree is associated with the horse in the Odin myth as well as in shamanistic rituals which depict the "ride" or "ascent" of the shaman to heaven (see M. Eliade, *Shamanism*, p.270). Indeed, the Vedic term "ashvattha" for the fig-tree itself contains the word for horse "ashva" (see J. Miller, *op.cit.*, pp.249f.). The conflation of arboreal and equestrian symbolism is perhaps related to the original conception of the universe as a phallus. In the royal horse-sacrifice of the Indo-Āryans, the horse is said to be produced from the "left eye" of Prajāpati (*SB* XIII,iii,1,1) so that the sacrifice of the horse is meant to restore this eye to its proper place. The eye is here clearly a symbol of the sun.

[1620] Voluspa, 19, in *The Poetic Edda*, tr. C. Larrington, Oxford: OUP, 1996, p.6. The "shining loam" is the same as "soma", the life-giving sap of the cosmic tree.

[1621] Grimnismal, 31-32, in C. Larrington, *op.cit.*, p.56.

[1622] "Gylfaginning" ("The Deluding of Gylfi") in *The Prose Edda*, tr. J.I. Young, p.42f.

sage Mimir.[1623] This region represents the waters from which the sun is born (just as it is born also from Heaven and from Earth). The third root ends in Hel, or Niflheim, which is Earth as well as the land of the dead, the underworld. At the base of this region dwells the serpent Nidhogg[1624] in the well called Hvergelmir.

We may assume that between Niflheim and heaven is the realm of Ymir, which is the Mid-region of the material universe. In Indic literature, the lower heavens is ruled by Yama, who is also the king of the dead.[1625] The "squirrel" which bears the "word" of the eagle in the branches of the cosmic ash to the serpent below must, as we have noted above,[1626] represent the disciplined energy of the yogi in the Kundalini-Yoga system. That the Nordic tree also represents the axis from which the sun is born is made clear in the verses that refer to "Arvak and Alsvid", two horses which "must pull wearily the sun from here".[1627]

The tree also serves as the locus of the great self-sacrifice of the god Odin/Wotan/Wata to himself, which may be a repetition of the original killing of Ymir, the First Man:[1628]

> I know that I hung on a windy tree[1629]
> nine long nights,
> wounded with a spear, dedicated to Odin,
> myself to myself.[1630]

It is as a result of this sacrifice – so akin to yogic penance – that Odin achieves mastery of the magical runes, no doubt related to the esoteric sources of light, Heka, and the "brahman" prayer. This episode is also similar

---

[1623] A spring is found also at the base of the sacred oak of the Pelasgian Zeus at Dodona (cf. E.O. James, *op.cit.*, p.29). Mimir may be the Germanic version of Mummu in the Babylonian *Enuma Elish*.

[1624] The name "Nidhogg" means "striker that destroys" (cf. *The Prose Edda*, p.43). It is interesting to note that the serpent is said to be situated at the bottom of Niflheim rather than of the Abyss, as in the other mythologies.

[1625] See above p.88.

[1626] See above p.278f.

[1627] 'Grimnismal', 37. The name of the shield of the sun, "Svalin", in 'Grimnismol', 38, may be derived from the same root ("svar") which gave Suwalliyat/Sūrya.

[1628] See above p.182. We have seen also that the second birth of the sun, from Earth, is that of the wind-form (Vāyu) of the supreme god.

[1629] We see the reference to the tree as being "windy" once again and remember the lilith demon as well as Sura and Asakku in the mountain (see below p.299ff).

[1630] 'Havamal', 138.

to Shiva's burning of his erotic aspect Kāma in the form of a tree.[1631] The reference to the "windy" tree reminds us of Wotan's own nature as wind-god as well as of the Purānic accounts of the deluge which accompanies the birth of the sun, where Manu/Mārkandeya/Shiva are, like Wotan, depicted as the only ones that achieve knowledge of the true nature of the universe.[1632]

As in India, and possibly also in Babylon, the destruction of the Yggdrasil, which represents the universe, heralds the end of a cosmic age, *Ragnarok*, which however will be followed by a renewed creation of the universe from the life-bearing trunk (earth) of the tree.[1633]

In Homeric mythology, we find the cosmic tree represented as a lofty pine-tree which has its roots in Tartarus[1634] while its branches bear Zeus[-Apollo] in the form of a [sun-] bird, which corresponds to the eagle in the related mythologies.[1635] In the nuptial rites of the 'Anacalyteria' (unveiling of the bride), too, the symbolic robe was hung on a "winged oak", a tree that represents the substructure over which the universe is wrapped.[1636] The oak is thus another form of the Tree of Life representing the universe. Further, as Wensinck has pointed out,[1637] Nonnus' *Dionysiaca* and Philostratus' *Life of Apollonius* too refer to a fiery "olive" tree in Tyre and Gades, respectively, the latter of the two having close associations with Herakles, the counterpart of Vishnu, the solar force whose Iranian counterpart, Verethraghna, is represented in his first incarnation by Vāyu and in his fifth by the boar-form of the same god.[1638]

[1631]   See below p.302.

[1632]   See above p.86.

[1633]   'Voluspa', 45ff.; cf. *The Prose Edda*, 'Gylfaginning'.

[1634]   Tartarus is, as mentioned above, the Greek form of Tvashtr, who is a form of Varuna/Enki, who holds the roots of the Tree in the Abyss.

[1635]   *Iliad*, 1.288.

[1636]   See E.O. James, *op.cit.*, p.158f.

[1637]   See A.J. Wensinck, *op.cit.*, pp.17-20.

[1638]   See above p.222n.

XXIV: VRTRA-GARUDA

THE LIBERATION OF THE UNIVERSE

The rise of the solar force in the underworld into the Mid-region of our universe as the sun is not possible until the serpent at the foot of the Tree, in the depths of the Abyss, is destroyed. This serpent, which represents the force of earthly constraint, is destroyed not by the solar god himself, since he is at first moribund in the underworld (as Osiris) and then puerile, as the incipient sun (Horus the Younger), but rather by the storm-god (Seth, Teshup, Zeus) who was initially the adversary of his solar counterpart, Osiris. The vital force which fells the fiery sky or solar force and causes the latter to descend into the "underworld" is, thus, not an entirely inimical one since it is the same that will destroy the serpent, separate the earth from heaven in our universe and allow, first, the moon and, then, the sun to rise to the Mid-region of the stars.

The serpent at the base of the cosmic tree may represent the tāmasic force which is a persistence of the dull material aspect of the deity which brought about the first cosmic manifestations through its Māya, or power of illusion, which was also represented as the serpent Sesha on which the Ideal Man (Vishnu) reposes.[1639] In the Eddas, the Midgard serpent is represented as encircling the earth.[1640] In Sumer, a fish with the head of a 'dara', or mountain goat, is symbolic of the shrine of Enki.[1641] In Islamic literature, we find that a "stormy wind with two heads ... wound itself like a serpent on the spot of the sacred house" (sanctuary).[1642]

The serpentine form of Ocean which surrounds the Earth is not exactly the same as the serpent at the base of the tree though it is related

---

[1639] See above p.77.

[1640] *The Prose Edda*, Ch.47; cf. "The Deluding of Gylfi".

[1641] F. X. Steinmetzer, *Sachau Festschrift*, pp.62ff., quoted in A.J. Wensinck, "The Ocean", p.65.

[1642] See A. Wensinck, *ibid.*

to it. We shall see that the Greek proto-Stoic tradition distinguishes the dangerous serpent Ophioneus from Okeanos.[1643] Also, Tehom-Leviathan, which, in *Isaiah* 27:1, is referred to as a "serpent",[1644] is elsewhere in Jewish tradition distinguished from Ocean. According to one Jewish text, "the Ocean surrounds the world as a vault surrounds a large pillar. The world itself is placed in its circular form on the fins of the Leviathan".[1645] Leviathan is thus specifically the serpent of the underworld.

In the Hurrian cosmology, the serpent that Teshup combats is the monster Illuyanka, who first succeeds in defeating the storm-god. The latter, however, then enlists the seductive powers of his daughter, Inara, and her human assistant, Hupasiyas. Inara and Hupasiyas succeed in drugging the serpent with intoxicants and binding it until Teshup arrives and kills it in the "sea" (aruni/Varuna/Enki/Okeanos). There are suggestions that the killing of Illuyanka causes the waters to flow, since, after this act, Inara puts the control of the subterranean waters in the hands of the reigning King of Nerik.[1646] This may be a counterpart of the Vrtra episode in the Vedas as well as those of Typhon and Apop. For, just as Iluyanka is paralysed by Inara, *RV* X,113,8 also relates that Agni/Shiva "ate Vrtra, the dragon, maimed by Indra's deadly dart".

We have noted abote Przyluski's suggestion that the Hittite deity Inara may be a female version of Indra The fact that Inara appears in the Hittite dragon story as the "daughter" of Teshup – who is the counterpart of Seth and *alter ego* of Tashmisu/Ninurta/Skanda/Muruga/Marduk – suggests that Inara is, like, Ninurta's weapon, Adad, a storm-force. This stormy element is no doubt derived from Kumarbi/Chronos/Shiva, who is the father of Teshup. We have seen that Shiva himself is identifiable with the First Man divided into male and female (corresponding to the first Manu and his wife Shatarūpā),[1647] since he is often represented in androgynous form (Ardhanārīshwara). The transference of Shiva/Kumarbi's characteristics to Teshup's "daughter" may be a local Hurrian variant of the original androgyny of the First Man.

In the Egyptian text entitled "The Book of Knowing the Evolutions of Ra, and of Overthrowing Apepi" (Papyrus BM, no.10,188) dated around 312

[1643] See below p.296f.

[1644] That Yahweh is a counterpart of Seth is made clear from the fact that the former too undertakes a battle against the monsters of the deep, Rahab and Leviathan, in *Isaiah* 51:9 and 27:1.

[1645] A. Jellinek, *Bet ha-Midrasch*, Jerusalem: Sifre Waherman, 1967, I:63, quoted in A.J. Wensinck, *op.cit.*, p.62.

[1646] See A.K. Lahiri, *op.cit.*, p.108f.

[1647] See above p.181.

B.C., the birth of the sun is described rather elaborately. Shu and Tefnut were enclosed for several aeons in the watery mass of Nun hiding within themselves the sun. After Shu and Tefnut were raised up from their original matrix by Kephera,[1648] the sun was able to emerge as the eye of Nun. The sun, however, is not liberated without a battle waged against the monster of darkness, Apop, which obscures the waters of Nun. Apop may be subtly distinguished from another serpent which serves as a symbol of the primordial waters and of the supreme spirit which dwelt in them, that is, Amun himself.[1649] This primeval serpent is sometimes simply called Amun.[1650]

It is interesting to note that Osiris in the "underworld" is also enfolded, as if in mummy bindings, by the serpent Nehaher ("the Fearful Face").[1651] In the *Amduat* the eleventh hour marks the encirclement of the corpse of the dead Osiris (representing the solar light) in the coils of the serpent called "the World-Encircler".[1652] Even though the latter is normally considered inimical to the solar light, the serpent preserves Osiris' corpse and is gradually cast off as Osiris revives and emerges as the light of the universe in the twelfth hour from the mound of Earth. Osiris (as Enki/Okeanos) too is identified with a serpent, as the following PT 1146 makes clear:

> I am the outflow of the Primeval Flood,
> He who emerged from the waters,
> I am the "Provider of Attributes" serpent with its many coils ...[1653]

The serpentine Ocean (Okeanos) coiled around Earth is thus a primordial form of the deity of the primordial waters (Osiris/Enki). Osiris is indeed sometimes represented as encircling the underworld.[1654] Sito the serpent that surrounds the primeval Hill is also called "son of Earth", as Osiris also is.[1655] And, as *BD*, 175, reminds us, at the end of time, the universe will revert to its primal state of chaos and the divinity will reassume the form of the serpent.

[1648] This account is important for stressing the importance of Shu (Enlil) and Tefnut in the formation of the sun.

[1649] See R.T. Rundle Clark, *op.cit.*, p.53.

[1650] PT 434 (see R.T. Rundle Clark, *op.cit.*, p.241).

[1651] *Ibid.*, pp.167ff.

[1652] See E. Hornung, *op.cit.*, p.41; cf. p.220 above.

[1653] *Ibid.*, p.50.

[1654] See R.T. Rundle Clark, *op.cit.*, p.249.

[1655] *Ibid.*, p.240.

In the tenth and eleventh hours of the *Book of Gates* the solar odyssey is marked by a battle against the serpent Apop.[1656] Apop itself is said to have originated from the spittle of Re's mother Neith in the primordial waters and taken the form of an enormous snake that revolted against Re. That Apop is, in his origin, related to Re is not surprising since we shall see that Vrtra too, like Agni, is born of Tvashtr. Vrtra is also infused with Agni.[1657]

In fact, Apop is on occasion identified also with Seth, just as Ninurta[1658] and Marduk are symbolised as dragons themselves. Ninurta in Sumer and Marduk in Babylon too assume the stormy aspect of the son of Chronos, even though they are the same as Enki/Osiris. Marduk and Shamash are invoked together in prayers (C.A.H., pl.i, 226b), exactly as Adad (Seth) and Shamash are. We have seen that Seth represents the passionate element just as the serpent does the lingering earthly aspect of the solar force. The serpent's obstruction of the emergence of the latter in the universe however can be combatted only by the storm-god himself. Once again the contest is an internal one, just as the sacrifice of the Cosmic Man, as well as that of the First Man, was also a self-sacrifice.

Although Seth is the one who is represented as battling the serpent Apop, Thoth is sometimes considered the agent who dispelled the darkness spread over the sun by "Seth" and "brought the Eye of Ra alive and whole, and sound, and without defect[1659] to its lord" (*BD* Ch.17,69ff.). Since this is the achievement of Indra in the Vedas, we see that Thoth, the formative aspect of the Cosmic Man, is also that of the moribund Osiris, and that Apop is an aspect of Seth himself, though he is the slayer of Apop.

In the Heliopolitan myth of the sun too, Seth, though the murderer of Osiris, the divine Light, helps Horus the Younger fight Apop on the barque of Re in order to ensure Re's emergence as the solar light.[1660] The barque itself represents the material universe, which bears the light of the universe, Re, and is called the "barque of the earth" in the *Book of the Gates*.[1661] Seth overcomes Apop using his characteristic rage (nšn),[1662] corresponding to the

---

[1656] See E. Hornung, op.cit., p.64.

[1657] See below p.292.

[1658] BE XXIX 1, rev.iii, 9; see J.V.Kinnier Wilson, *op.cit.*, p.17.

[1659] The "defect" referred to is possibly the corruption it may have suffered from its contact with Seth (*BD* 17,71).

[1660] See H. te Velde, *op.cit.*, Ch.4.

[1661] See E.T. Hornung, *Ancient Egyptian Books*, p.60.

[1662] See H. te Velde, *op.cit.*, p.101.

Indic 'manyu' and Iranian 'mainyu' which, as we have seen, are associated with Shiva/Indra.[1663]

Seth and Osiris are two aspects of the same solar light. Seth and Horus the Younger (the solar product of Osiris) are equally regarded as the rulers of Heaven and Earth, or of Upper and Lower Egypt respectively, in which rule we note that it is Seth who rules Heaven while Horus the Younger as the sun rules only the underworld Earth where he is born and, later, the Mid-region between Heaven and Earth.

In the Indian system of Kundalini Yoga, the Kundalini serpent (which is analogous to Vrtra)[1664] is represented in the microcosm as the force of vitality as well as of sexuality coiled at the base of the spinal cord.[1665] The aim of the yogic discipline is, as Cook puts it,

> to awaken this sleeping force and get it to climb the spinal tree, piercing the various spiritual centres (chakras) along its way, until finally it is released [like Brahman from atop the petals of the lotus in the Puranas or the sun from atop the sycamore in Egypt] from the Sahasra Chakra, the Thousand-petalled Lotus, at the top of the head. At this point the heavy material forces of the earth and the waters, ... take flight... The mythical eagle Garuda carries off Kundalini in its beak; heaven and earth, light and darkness, spirit and flesh are finally, ecstatically united.[1666]

The sublimation of the serpentine force marks the rise of the soul, Ātman, to its original brilliance as the divine Consciousness, Brahman. Further, in *BP* V,25,1, the serpent Sesha is described as being the tāmasic or Māya-associated aspect of the supreme lord which sustains this universe by the magical effect of sympathy.

In the Vedas, Vrtra is a serpentine cosmic phenomenon represented as being located within a turbulent wind. Vrtra is a demon of resistance which prevents the "mountain" from ejecting its life-giving seed. In

---

[1663]   See above Ch.XIII.

[1664]   See above p.219.

[1665]   See R. Cook. *op.cit.*, p.25. The fact that the serpent provides Adam and Eve with sexual awareness in Genesis reveals the ultimate reliance of the Hebrew Bible on proto–Indic sources, even though the spiritual significance of the story of the cosmic man is entirely ignored by the priestly redactors of the Bible.

[1666]   See R. Cook, *ibid.* That this process is akin to a sexual orgasm is not surprising considering the significance of the phallus even in the macrocosmic creation. The "flood" which accompanies the emergence of the sun in our universe (see below p.295) is thus naturally related to the waves of pleasure that suffuse our mind in sexual ecstasy.

KYV II,5,2, Vrtra is said to be called Vrtra because "he enveloped these worlds".[1667] In *TS* II,iv,12,2, Vrtra is said to have grown and enveloped the three worlds.[1668] Indra is the hero chosen by the gods to defeat the dragon, Vrtra, when all of the Adityas, Vasus, Rudras and gods were paralysed by the monster (*RV* 10,48,11). Indeed, Indra's freeing of the waters from the restriction imposed on them by the dragon Vrtra is associated with the creation of our heaven and earth, which are formed out of Vrtra's body (*RV* I,36,8).

Vrtra is considered as one of the Dānavas (the Asuras born of the female deity Dana, rather than of Aditi, whose sons are Ādityas), so that the Devas, or gods, opposed to Vrtra, represent the emanative solar impulse of the universe, while the Dānavas must represent the contrary restricting force. That Vrtra however hides Agni (Shiva) within itself is confirmed by *AV* III, 21,1 where there is particular reference to the form of Agni within Vrtra along with those within the waters, man, stones, herbs, and forest trees. We have seen that Agni is, like Vrtra, a creation of Tvashtr,[1669] and that Apop is also related to Re.[1670]

In *BP* VI,9,18, Vrtra is said to cover the universe in darkness, which is not surprising considering that his father Tvashtr is the same as Tartarus, who, according to the Greek tradition, is the parent of Typhon.[1671] In *RV* V,40,5, there is a reference to Indra's dispelling of the magical spell of the Asura "Svarbhānu" which surrounded the sun with darkness.[1672] These passages thus seem to refer to the liberation of the solar energy from its original concealment in gaseous matter. Indra is thus associated with the discovery of the "lights" for the benefit of living creatures and men in particular (*RV* VIII,15,5). *RV* III,39,6 further states that Indra "took the light, discerning it from darkness". Indra is said to have discovered Agni (meaning here primarily Agni's Rudra form which rules the sun)[1673] among the waters. In *AV* XIII,1,33, the sun is called "the calf of Virāj". Virāj, who is

---

[1667]   The etymology of the word, however, is more accurately preserved in the Avestan "Vrθra" meaning "resistance" (see A.K. Lahiri, *op.cit.*, p.73).

[1668]   It is in order to combat this control of the three worlds by Vrtra that Vishnu expands through these worlds with his three gigantic steps (see above p.265) and thus allows Indra to hurl his thunderbolt against the monster (see A.K. Lahiri, *op.cit.*, p.195).

[1669]   See above p.125.

[1670]   See above p.290.

[1671]   See below p.296.

[1672]   Indra is aided in his fight against Svarbhānu by Atri (*RV* V,40,8; cf. *RV* I,51,3), who is one of the seven sages, and who himself is helped by the Ashwins (*RV* VIII,62; *RV* X,143). Atri may also be associated with the Angirasas, who typically help Brahmanaspati.

[1673]   See above p.213.

represented as a cow in *AV* VIII,10,24 (cf. XI,8,30), signifies the waters of Earth/the underworld represented by Aditi, for we know that the third birth of Agni as Āditya is from the waters.[1674]

Vrtra is indeed an Asuric creation of Tvashtr (just as Typhon is a child of Tartarus) who developed this monster of resistance when Indra felled his first offspring, Vishvarūpa (*RV* II,11,19), who is represented as a "three-headed" monster.[1675] Vishvarūpa is perhaps the counterpart of the Iranian Asi Dahaka and the Sumerian Asakku, though the latter resembles Vrtra as well. However, Indra is also considered the "protector" in the Vedas (*KYV* IV,6,2).[1676] So his slaughter of the monstrous Vishvarūpa must have been conducted mainly to control the material substratum of animal life represented by it.[1677] The Manyu of Indra thus represents both the destructive and creative aspect of the emergent solar force.

Indra also succeeds in freeing the "cows" from the "vala", a rocky enclosure in which they are hidden by the evil Panis.[1678] The "cows" in the vala myth (10.67,1-12) symbolise the radiant solar energy, since *RV* I,164,3 suggests that this is the secret name of the rays of the dawn.[1679] In *RV* X, 108, 5, the "cows" are described as "flying around to the ends of the sky". The Panis themselves are described in *BP* V,24,30 as serpentine, Asuric creations of Diti and Danu and inhabit Rasātala, the sixth of the seven subterranean regions of the material universe bordering on the last, called Pātāla, below which lies the serpent Sesha.[1680] The Panis are thus related to Sesha/Vrtra. "Vala", significantly, is the same term that is used in the Avesta ("vara") for the ark which bears Yima during the flood which accompanies the birth of the sun.[1681] And we have seen that the barque of Re is the "barque of earth".

[1674]   See below p.305.

[1675]   See *RV* I,161,6; cf. *KV* II,5,1; *BP* VI,9,11.

[1676]   See above p.126.

[1677]   Cf. p.297f below.

[1678]   In the Vrtra myth (*RV* I, 32,11) the waters confined by Vrtra are compared to the cows confined in the vala by the Panis. However, the Panis are here called 'Dasyus' and not 'Dānavas', as in *BP*.

[1679]   H.-P. Schmidt, *op.cit.*, p.222.

[1680]   In the Egyptian *Book of the Heavenly Cow* the underworld is described as being populated by serpents supervised by Geb [earth] (see E. Hornung, *op.cit.*, p.149).

[1681]   The Vedic vala myth is thus a cosmological archetype of the Flood story. The animals saved from the deluge in the later Sumerian and Indo-Iranian Flood stories, as well as in the account of Noah in the Hebrew Bible derived from them, are, unlike the elements of solar energy symbolically referred to in *RV* as "cows", real animals, and therefore associated with the seeds of all animal life borne by the Vedic Cow [Earth], as well as by the Iranian Bull.

It is apparent thus that the separation of primal Heaven from Earth by Kāla/Chronos is repeated in the underworld ("earth") by Indra in order to allow the rise of the solar energy from there into the Mid-region of the stars. In *RV* VII, 23,3, it is stated that "Indra when he had slain resistless foemen, forced with his might the two world-halves asunder". In *RV* VI,8, this act of separation of heaven from earth, normally attributed to Indra, is ascribed to Mitra (Horus), since Mitra is but the early form of Indra as the sun:[1682] "Wonderful Mitra propped the heaven and earth apart, … He made the two bowls [i.e. earth and heaven] part asunder like two skins".[1683]

Vishnu is also credited with the accomplishment of this feat (*RV* VII,99,3), for we have seen that Indra and Vishnu bear the common epithet Vrtrahan/ Weretraghna, in the Vedas and the Avesta. Vishnu represents the expansive and sustaining form of Agni much like Vāyu (Shu). In *RV* VII,99, Vishnu (like Marduk in *EE*, and Shu in the Heliopolitan cosmogony, who is sustains the separated heaven and earth)[1684] is said to firmly support the two halves of the universe, heaven and earth, while he holds fast Earth among the waters (Okeanos) which surround it by fixing it with "pegs". According to *SB* XI,viii,1, the "pegs" are "mountains" and "rivers": "He sets this [Earth] firmly with the help of mountains and rivers". These mountains and rivers are clearly not terrestrial any more than Earth itself is, since, as we have noted above, the mountain is the source from which the material universe as well as its light arises, while the rivers are the seven streams whence the galaxies are formed.[1685] The universe is said to have been spread out through Vishnu's sacrificial fervour, since it is spiritual intensity which causes spatial expansion. Vishnu is called the lord of the sacrifice since he represents the expansive force of Prajāpati.

In *RV* V, 85, the separation of the heavens from the earth normally attributed to Indra is associated with Varuna, who is (like Indra and Shiva) said to have spread forth the earthly element "as a skin to spread in front of Surya" and "standing in the firmament hath meted the earth out with the sun as with a measure". In *KYV* I, 2, 14, Varuna is called the bull that "hath stablished the sky, the atmosphere/ Hath meted the breadth of the earth" (I, 2,8), for "All these are Varuna's ordinances".

In *AV* IV,I, Brahmanaspati (Heka) who, as we have seen, is particularly associated with Ganesha/Seth, is identified as the force of Indra

---

[1682] See below p.306.

[1683] This recalls particularly the brutal image of Marduk's splitting of Apsu's consort, Tiamat (Aditi), into heaven and earth in (*EE* IV,137).

[1684] See above p.132.

[1685] See above p.277.

in the separation of heaven from earth. Brahmanaspati is described as the essential "divinity" of the deity separating heaven from earth:

> For he of the heaven, he of the earth the right-stander, fixed [as his] abode the (two) great firmaments; the great one, when born, fixed apart the (two) great ones, the heaven [as] seat[1686] and the earthly space.[1687]

> He from the fundamental birth hath attained unto the summit; Brahmanaspati, the universal ruler, [is] the divinity of him...

We see, therefore, that Ganesha possesses the potency of Indra/Shiva, just as Seth possesses that of Horus the Elder/Osiris and Adad represents that of Ninurta.

The slaying of Vrtra not only forms heaven and earth out of the latter's body but also allows the elevation of the sun to the mid-region between them: "As you, Indra, killed Vrtra with power, you raised the sun in heaven to be seen" (*RV* I,51,4).[1688] In the *AV* IV,10,5, the sun is said to be "born from the ocean, born from Vrtra".[1689] According to *RV* X,121,7, it is Indra's deliverance of the waters from the grasp of Vrtra and their subsequent outflow which allow the waters to give birth to Agni (i.e. his third form as the sun). The waters flow out as seven cosmic streams which are called "mothers" (*RV* II,12,3; X,17,10; VIII,96,1), since, as we have seen, they guarded the birth of Shiva's son, Skanda (Marduk).[1690] The vital solar energy too rises from the depths of the Abyss in this flood, since Indra/Soma is said in *RV* IX,42,1[1691] to engender the sun in "floods" along with the other stars.[1692] Thus the flood is the result of the splitting of the universe as well as the condition of the creation of its light. The final identification of

---

[1686] The reference to heaven as the "seat" of the gods is familiar to us from Hesiod's *Theogony* as well (see above p.140n).

[1687] The reference to earthly "space" should make it clear that "earth" does not in ancient mythology mean our planet but, rather, the fundament of the universe.

[1688] See A.K. Lahiri, *op.cit.*, p.103.

[1689] cf. *SB* V,v,5,1-5.

[1690] See above p.240f.

[1691] Soma is the potency imbibed by Indra (see above p.276).

[1692] See *RV* II,19,3:
"Indra, this mighty one, the dragon's slayer, sent forth the flood of waters to the ocean,
He gave the sun his life, he found the cattle".

Indra with the sun of the heavens is seen in several passages of the *RV*.[1693] Indra is therefore the hero who facilitates the birth of our universe as well as releases the solar energy from the icy forces of resistance represented by the Panis and Vrtra.

In the Avesta, as in the Vedas, there are two monsters, Asi Dahaka and Apaosa. Thraetaona (Skt. Traitona) is said to battle the monster Asi Dahaka for possession of the Xvarenah (Zamyad Yasht XIX,37; Fargard XX). Asi Dahaka is referred to in the Vedas (*RV* VI,29,2;X,113,3) as Ahi and is perhaps the same (even etymologically) as the Sumerian Asakku. In Zamyad Yasht VIII,45,52, Atar combats the same monstrous form. So Thraetona (who is related to Trita Āptya)[1694] must be closely related to Atar. Indeed, in Zamyad Yasht XIX,51ff, Atar succeeds in restoring the Xvarenah to the Vouru-Kasha sea (the Abyss).

Indra's destruction of Vrtra, the second "monster" created by Tvashtr, is celebrated with equal fervour by the Zoroastrians as an achievement not of Indra himself but, rather, of Verethraghna (Destroyer of Vrtra), who, as we have seen, corresponds to Indra's solar form, Vishnu. We may assume that Verethra is the "lizard" at the base of the Vouru-kasha sea, the Iranian equivalent of the Abyss.[1695] In the Tir Yasht devoted to the god Tisthrya, the release of the waters is due to the destruction of Apaosha (Yasht VIII,29) (a name which may be related to the Egyptian Apop)[1696] as well as of the Pairikas (Yasht VIII, 40) (evil spirits that may correspond to the Panis of the Vedas). It is interesting to note that the waters when released are described as flowing into the Vouru-kasha sea (Yasht VIII,47). This suggests that the Vouru-kasha sea is a particular region of the waters of the underworld which represents the energetic fluid of the universe that bears the sun.

In Hesiod, Typhoeus is the monster created by Gaia (Prithvī) and Tartarus (Tvashtr) and whose ambitions to rule the cosmos are thwarted by Zeus (Seth/Brahmanaspati-Ganesha), the "son" of Chronos/Shiva. In the *Theogony*, 820-68, after Zeus battles with Typhoeus, he forces him down into Tartarus, whence he emerged.[1697] In Pherecydes, it is Chronos (Shiva/Kumarbi) himself who battles a serpent called Ophioneus who is pushed

---

[1693]   See, for instance, *RV* VIII,6,24,30; I,83,5; III,39,7; VIII,69,2; X,55,3; X,111,7. The solar imagery associated with Indra is noticeable also in *RV* I,84,1, where his particular virtue (indriyam) is said to fill the deity as the sun's rays fill the darkness.

[1694]   See *RV* I,158,5.

[1695]   See above p.236.

[1696]   The resemblance of Apaosha to the Egyptian Apop offers a further confirmation of the Iranian origins of the Heliopolitan religion (see above p.48).

[1697]   It is possible that this serpent is located at the base of the Greek tree of life as well (see above p.285).

into the ocean by the former and thereafter associated with Okeanos. The name Ophioneus too is probably related etymologically to Apop and Apaosa.

In the Sumerian epic *Lugal e*, the outflow of waters resulting from Indra's defeat of Vrtra is reflected in Ninurta's causing a flood that accompanies the emergence of the sun.[1698] Like Indra and Adad, Ninurta is considered the "strong arm" of Enlil – who himself has a stormy character and both threatens the heavens and devastates the "lands that offer resistance".[1699] However, Ninurta is also the solar force, and one of his seven forms is indeed Nergal, the sun of the underworld.[1700] In the *Lugal e* epic, Ninurta is represented, much like Indra in the Vedas, as battling a monstrous creation (hidden in a mountain) of unseparated earth and heaven[1701] called Asakku (who may be a form of Antum, Earth itself),[1702] which constrains, through its frigid force, the solar energy (the life-giving "waters") contained in the mountain.[1703] The defeat of Asakku as well as of the Mountain which Asakku has dominated results in the separation of Heaven and Earth and a flood of cosmic waters which threatens to destroy all life in the cosmos.[1704] Ninurta therefore constructs a dam out of the stony and metallic materials of the corpse of Asakku. This dam is called "hursag",

---

[1698]   Cf. above p.199. The flood that accompanies Ninurta's resurrection of the sun may be distinguished from that which causes the initial descent of the solar force (An/Tammuz) (see above p.179).

[1699]   See the hymn to Enlil, in A. Falkenstein, *Sumerische Götterlieder*, p.98 (cf. p.199n above for the term "resistance"). As Assmann has pointed out (*op.cit.*, pp.42,53), the resistance that is offered by Apop is both a physical withholding of light and life and a symbol of evil itself which has to be destroyed so that Maat (Rta), the divine order of the cosmos may be established; cf. the 19th Dynasty hymn to Amun where it is stated that each of "those who transgress [this] written order is a rebel against Re" (A. Barucq and F. Daumas, *op.cit.*, p.229).

[1700]   See above p.248.

[1701]   Asakku is a dragon like the Babylonian Tiamat, Avestan Aši Dahaka and Vedic Vishvarūpa. Ninurta may thus be considered as a "dragon-slayer" just as Marduk his Babylonian counterpart too is (see below p.299).

[1702]   Cf. the liturgical commentary O175 where Asakku is equated with Antum (F. Thureau-Dangin, "An acte de donation de Marduk-Zâkir-Šumi", *RA* 16 (1919), 144ff). Ninurta's destruction of Asakku then would be comparable to Marduk's destruction of Tiamat (see below p.299). This is confirmed also by the other correspondences between the Ninurta mythology and the Marduk (see W.G. Lambert, "Ninurta Mythology", 55-60; cf. also J. Day, *God's Conflict with the Dragon and the Sea*, Cambridge: Cambridge University Press, 1985).

[1703]   In KAR 142 seven Asakku demons, sons of Anu – corresponding no doubt to the seven malevolent demons engendered by Anu from Earth (see above p.247n) – are said to be prisoners of Ninurta (see H. Wohlstein, *op.cit.*, p.158).

[1704]   This cataclysm which precedes the emergence of our sun is similar but not identical to the destruction of the cosmos at the end of a cosmic age.

or the foothills, and Ninmah, Enlil's wife and Ninurta's mother, is thus, at the end of the *Lugal e* myth, called Ninhursag, or Lady of the Foothills, which represent the earth of the material universe to which Ninurta has now directed the waters of the cosmic streams.

The mountain rising from the foothills is the Mid-region of the universe, and the seed of the "primordial hill", Ninurta himself,[1705] will finally emerge atop it as the sun of our system. Indeed, in the epic, Ninurta, having accomplished his great deed, finally assumes his natural role as the sun by boarding a barque, a vehicle that will be familiar to us from the Egyptian solar theology:

> The Hero had crushed the Mountain; when he moved in the steppes, he appeared as the [S]un (?),
>
> ....
>
> Ninurta went joyously towards the "magur", his beloved boat,
> The Lord set his foot on the Makarnunta'e (boat).[1706]

The poem continues with Ninurta's disposition of the various elementary metals constituting the "hursag" according to their beneficent or baneful properties (*Lugal e*, ll.416ff.). From the similar reference to the metallic constitution of earth at the birth of Skanda (as the sun) in the *Mahābhārata* discussed above,[1707] we may surmise that the destruction of Asakku is related to the formation of the universe as well as of the sun.

Ninurta's defeat of Asakku releases the life-giving seminal waters for the vivification and illumination of the universe.[1708] We have seen that Ninurta's mighty battle against the mountainous "regions of resistance"[1709] is conducted with the aid of the mace fashioned for him by Ninildu that is identified with the stormy wind, Rihamun.[1710] But since Ramman and

---

[1705] Ninmah is said to have borne Ninurta in the Mountain itself (*Lugal e*, ll.390ff).

[1706] J. Van Dijk, *Lugal e*, p.137 (my English translation of van Dijk's French). The term 'utuaula'/ 'ut-tu gis-gal-a' used for Ninurta in *Lugal e* as well as in the Genouillac god-list (H. de Genouillac, *op.cit.*, p.100) may refer either to the tempestuous storm which Ninurta sails over in his sun–barque or to his own stormy nature.

[1707] See above p.240.

[1708] See S. Kramer, "Review of A. Hendel, *The Babylonian Genesis: The Story of Creation*", *JAOS*, 63 (1943), pp.70ff.

[1709] See J.V.Kinnier Wilson, *op.cit.*, p.51.

[1710] Similarly, Indra's thunderbolt, or Vajra (which, in *RV* III,30,17, is characterised as a "burning weapon"), is said to have been fashioned by Tvashtr, the creative aspect of Varuna (Enki)

Adad are identifiable with Seth, we see again that Ninurta, who is identical to Suwalliyat (Horus the Younger) and his stormy aspect are but the same deity. Hence also the frequent identification of Adad,[1711] and Seth[1712] with the sun, Shamash/Re. The storm-wind is necessary for the destruction of the serpentine force of resistance which itself is contained in a windy "mountain".

In the *EE* IV, the son of Enki,[1713] Marduk, is the valiant warrior who defeats the watery dragon Tiamat, and her second consort, Kingu, in battle. Marduk, like Indra and Seth, is represented as a dragon-slayer,[1714] since Tiamat has the monstrous dragon-form of the serpent at the bottom of the underworld of Earth.[1715] Tiamat therefore is a counterpart of Vrtra, rather than of Vishvarūpā.

Both Asakku and Tiamat offer the same obstruction to the rise of the solar force. Indeed, Marduk himself is said, in Šurpu IV, 1-3, to have vanquished Asakku. Just as Ninurta in *Lugal-e* does, so also Marduk "fixes a bolt" and stations a watchman around the corpse of Tiamat so as "not to let her waters come forth".[1716] Tiamat and Asakku are primal chaotic forms of Antum, or earth, which needs to be separated from heaven.

It is interesting to note that Marduk combats Tiamat with a collection of winds which "disturb the inwards parts of Tiamat", as well as with the "thunderbolt, his mighty weapon" and his chariot "the storm". This is exactly like the use of Rihamun by Ninurta in his battle against Asakku.[1717]

In the *EE*, it is by dividing the corpse of Tiamat into two parts that the division of heaven and earth in our universe is effected. The Assyrian ritual text K 3476 rev. l.9 reveals the phallic role of Marduk in this aggression: "Marduk, who with his penis ... Tiamat".[1718] The separation of

---

[1711]   Cf. the Assyrian royal name, Shamsi-Adad, meaning "Adad is my sun" (above p.201).

[1712]   See above p.219.

[1713]   See, for instance, Codex Hammurabi. I, 1-26.

[1714]   The account of Marduk's battle with the dragon is preserved in CT XIII, pl.33f. Rm.282 (cf. *Enuma Elish: the Seven Tablets of Creation*, ed. L.W. King, London: Luzac and Co., 1902, pp.118ff.).

[1715]   For the imagery of the fight between the eagle, representing the solar force, and the dragon, representing the primeval watery element, see A.J. Wensinck, "Tree and Bird", pp.46f.

[1716]   Cf. *Proverbs* 8:29: "[God] gave the sea his decree that the waters should not pass his commandment"; and *Job* 26:10.

[1717]   We may remember that Shiva in the *PP* too initially destroys the cosmos with storm-winds and that these thunderbolts are in fact those of his alter ego, or "assistant", Indra (see above p.83).

[1718]   See A. Livingstone, *op.cit.*, p.123.

heaven and earth resultant on the destruction of the serpent facilitates the rise of the sun to its position between them. After his control of the waters of Tiamat, Marduk is indeed able to construct the three heavens distributed among An, Enki and Enlil (*EE*, IV). Marduk's splitting open of Tiamat's body into two in the *EE* is also remarkably like the description, in the Tamil *Akam*, 59, ll.10-11, of Murugan's "vel" cutting "in two the side of Sura's body".[1719]

In the Germanic *Prose Edda* ("The Deluding of Gylfi"), the slaying of the serpent is represented in the battle of Thor against the Midgard serpent, which is, in the end, consigned to the ocean around earth, which it then encircles. The root of the Yggdrasil tree that reaches to Niflheim also harbours the serpent Nidhögg, which must be related to the Midgard serpent.

The Peacock and the Sun–Bird

The serpent at the bottom of the Tree of Life is not the only obstacle to the rise of the sun of our universe. The "bird" in the branches of the Tree of Life also has to be destroyed since it represents an early unruly form of the sun. In the Sumerian literature, the Anzu bird atop the "huluppu" tree is, like Asakku, one of the foes that Ninurta battles. The extraordinary power of the bird is revealed in the 'Lugalbanda Epic', where the cry of the bird is said to cause heaven and earth to tremble.[1720] Yet, Ninurta is also closely related to the Anzu bird as an earlier form of himself,[1721] even though he is seen later to battle this bird. We have seen that in the epic *Lugal-e,* Asakku is a form of Antum, the earth. The Anzu bird too is a product of it ("The [broad] earth conceived him"),[1722] though, as an earlier form of Ninurta, it possesses a solar aspect as well. Ninurta's battles with Anzu as well with Asakku may thus highlight the tremendous spiritual domination of original matter required for the release of the perfect light of the sun.

In the Dravidian and Sumerian literature, this avian form of the sun is indeed considered an early obstacle to the rise of the perfected sun. In the Dravidian *Kantapurānam*, after Muruga destroys the Asura Surapadman's first monstrous form, Surapadman transforms himself into a mango-tree.

[1719] See K. Zvelebil, *op.cit.*, p.80.

[1720] See C. Wilcke, *Das Lugalbandaepos*, Wiesbaden: O. Harrassowitz, 1969, p.95.

[1721] See T. Jacobsen, *Treasures of Darkness,* p.128.

[1722] See the *Epic of Anzu*, I,52-3 (A. Annus, *op.cit.*, p.x). It is interesting to note that, according to one Muslim tradition, earth is considered to have been created in the form of a bird (see A.J. Wensinck, "Tree and Bird", p.37).

Muruga casts his "vel", the Maya-destroying lance, against it. This changes the tree into a cock and peacock. The cock and the peacock which are associated with the mango-tree in the Dravidian myths are symbols of death and the netherworld.[1723] In the SP V,2,14, 2-30, the peacock is the form assumed by Shiva when he absorbs the deadly poison which first emerges from the cosmic ocean as it is being churned for the nectar of immorality/ Soma. It is significant that the peacock is also the vehicle of the erotic aspect of Shiva, Kāma.[1724] The battles undertaken by the leader of the gods, Ninurta/Marduk/Muruga, may thus be directed to the purification of the initial passionate, or Asuric, quality of the cosmos. Muruga too succeeds in dompting these birds and in harnessing the peacock as his vehicle. These birds may be an analogue of the Anzu bird in the Ninurta myths of Sumer.

They are also closely related to the Garuda bird, which, however, has a more benevolent aspect. In the MBh, the female of this bird, Gārudī, is, as we have seen, associated with the pregnant consort of Shiva, whose seed she carries to the primordial mountain in this avian form.[1725] The seed of Shiva which she bears as a bird produces the solar force called Skanda. Garuda is itself clearly related to the sun since his father, like that of the Ādityas,[1726] is Kashyapa (PP I,47,44). Indra himself is called an eagle who bears Soma[1727] and once assumes the form of a falcon during a rivalry over the Soma.[1728] However, Garuda, like the Anzu bird, is also described in PP I,47,148ff. as being attacked by Indra for having robbed the divine nectar. It is stated that Garuda required this nectar only because his mother was held hostage by a demoness and her serpentine sons who had turned the sun's horse black and whom this demoness wished to make immortal. Once Garuda obtained the nectar and his mother yielded it up to the demoness, who then gave it to her sons, Indra however intervened and transformed the nectar into poison which thus rendered the serpents baneful and mortal.

We have noted that, in the Heliopolitan cosmology, Osiris remerges through the separated elements of heaven and earth as the phoenix-falcon

---

[1723] For the resemblance of the cock-image to that of the cosmic Tree in Muslim tradition, see A.J. Wensinck, "Tree and Bird", p.36.

[1724] See W. O'Flaherty, op.cit., p.167.

[1725] See above p.240. In the Bundahishn XIX, the bird Kamros is said to be located at the top of Mt. Alburz which represents the Iranian counterpart of Mt. Meru (see above p.164). This bird, like the Garuda, is considered to be a beneficent one.

[1726] See below p.307.

[1727] O'Flaherty (op.cit., p.277) suggests that this may be related to the Greek tradition of representing the phallus as winged.

[1728] SB III,ix,4,10; RV X,99,8.

Bennu. The sun-bird, bnw,[1729] which is a form of Atum himself,[1730] is considered the pneumatic form, or "ba", of the sun and its flight is that of Horus the Younger through the three regions, earth, the Mid-region, and the heavens. Like the Garuda, it is not considered as a baneful or unruly bird. Indeed, even the Anzu bird is a form of Ninurta itself, so it is possible that all these birds symbolise an early form of the emerging sun.

The Felling of the Tree

In all these combats what we witness is in fact a process whereby the solar force, which has been forced into the underworld by the storm-force, is gradually cleansed of its material elements. This purification which allows the sun to acquire its tremendous power in our universe is inextricably allied to the more general *contemptus mundi* and asceticism which underlie the theology of the solar religions, especially the Indic and the Dionysian-Orphic, as well as the Pythagorean-Platonic.[1731] We have seen that the Tree of Life may represent both the infrastructure of the material universe and the internal nervous structure and erotic force of microcosmic man. The material universe being considered a result of the illusion of the divine Māya and incomparably inferior to the original Cosmic Light and Intellect, it is the duty of the pious Hindu to detach himself from it by "cutting down" the Tree of Life. The Tree is itself thus represented as being cut down or displaced in some of the legends of the mythologies under consideration. Since the "tree" is an analogue for the divine phallus itself, the exhortation to asceticism in these mythic accounts is clearly comprehensible. In the *SP* I,1,21,82-99, Kāma, who is Shiva's own erotic aspect and burnt down by Shiva in the form of a tree, is called the "evil at the root of all misery".[1732]

[1729]   CT 335 IV 198a-201a (see S. Bickel, *op.cit.*, p.240). We may note that Thoth is also commonly represented as a bird understood to be an "ibis".

[1730]   See CT 76 II 3h-4c, where Shu says that Atum first "came into *existence*" when he, Shu, was spat out by Atum "when I was surrounded by the breath of life in the throat of the phoenix" (S. Bickel, *op.cit.*, p.240).

[1731]   For the Orphic religion see W.K.C. Guthrie, *Orpheus and Greek Religion: A Study of the Orphic Movement*, London: Methuen, 1952, p.156f. It is interesting to note that according to Hecateus of Abdera Orpheus introduced the mysteries of Dionysus and Demeter into Greece which were modelled on those of Osiris and Isis in Egypt (see M.L. West, *Orphic Poems*, p.26). For the Pythagorean doctrines see J.A. Philip, *Pythagoras and Early Pythagoreanism*, Toronto: University of Toronto Press, 1966, p.137f.. We have also noticed the ritual castration in the cult of the Phrygian Attis (see above p.194).

[1732]   See W.D. O'Flaherty, *op.cit.*, p.159.

Here the contest is plainly between the ascetic Shiva and the erotic passion which engenders and sustains the illusion of the universe.

In the *MBh (Bhagavad Gita)*, too, Krishna counsels Arjuna to cut down the ashvattha tree since the tree represents the world of sense-experience, *samsara*.[1733] The baneful aspect of the material manifestation of the cosmos is to be found in the Dravidian version of the *SP, Kantapurānam*. Here, the mango tree situated in the midst of the ocean is the second form taken by the demon Surapadman who himself is concealed in a mountain (exactly as Asakku is in *Lugal-e*,[1734] or Vrtra in the Vedas). The first form assumed by Surapadman is a monstrous multiform mockery of the Purusha characterised by a thousand arms and legs,[1735] corresponding no doubt to the Vedic Vishvarūpā.[1736] The son of Shiva born especially for the martial purpose of defeating the Asura Surapadman is Muruga, or Skanda, the counterpart of Marduk/Ninurta. Muruga destroys Surapadman's first form by revealing his own true, and eternal, form as the Purusha. Surapadman's second form, that of the "mango" tree, is also cloven into two by Muruga.

Just as Muruga in the Dravidian version of the myth is said to have cloven the "mango" tree,[1737] Marduk too is said to have altered the position of the tree, in the *Poem of Erra*, I,148.[1738] We note that Muruga/Marduk/Ninurta oppose the Tree though they themselves represent the Ideal form of it as the divine phallus.

The Sumerian kishkanu tree bears three inimical creatures in itself which have to be overcome before the light of the universe may be released. The Anzu bird nests in its upper branches (representing an obstacle to the emergence of the sun of heaven or its first inchoate form),[1739] a serpent at its base (representing the dragon of resistance that the underworld sun has to combat), and a wind-demon, Lilith, in its trunk.[1740] In the myth of the

---

[1733] See E.O. James, *op.cit.*, p.257.

[1734] The lilith demon in the Sumerian tree of life may also be a counterpart of the same phenomenon.

[1735] See D. Handelman, "Myths of Murugan: Asymmetry and Hierarchy in a South Indian Puranic Cosmology", *History of Religions*, 27, no.2, p.143.

[1736] See above p.293.

[1737] See D. Shulman, "Murukan, the Mango and Ekambaresvara-Siva Fragments of a Tamil Creation Myth", *Indo-Iranian Journal* 21 (1979), p.32.

[1738] See L. Cagni, *The Poem of Erra*, p.32.

[1739] In the *Epic of Anzu*, the bird is said to be a source of the waters which may bear the sun. However, the bird becomes traitorous to Enlil, and causes the waters to flood uncontrollably and steals the tablets of destinies from Enlil (*Epic of Anzu*, I). Thus it is killed by Ninurta, who then retrieves the tablets of destines from it.

[1740] We have seen that the trunk of the tree represents earth (see above p.273).

"huluppu" tree, Gilgamesh (Nergal) destroys all these creatures, the bird, the wind-demon and the serpent.[1741]

We have seen that the serpent at the bottom of the Abyss from whence the tree emerges is identifiable with the Māyā of the supreme deity as well as – microcosmically – with the Kundalini serpent at the base of the spinal cord. The injunction to cut down the tree therefore signifies the severing of the illusion of Egoity which lies at the base of the axis of the universe through the abjuration of the sexual force (Kāma, Desire) represented by the Kundalini serpent.

[1741]   See D. Wolkstein and S. Kramer, *Inanna, Queen of Heaven and Earth: Her Stories and Hymns from Sumer*, N.Y.: Harper and Row, 1983, p.9.

XXV: SŪRYA

THE SUN: SŪRYA, UTU, HARAKHTE-KHEPERA-ATON-ATUM

With the purification of the solar force from the underworld elements which long encumbered it, the sun is finally free to rise to its present life-giving position in our system. The source of the third birth of Agni is the waters of the Abyss or the underworld into which the solar force had descended. In the Vedas (*KYV* IV, 2,2), it is stated that

> In the waters thirdly [was Agni born] the manly
> ....
> The Manly souled [Indra-Soma] kindleth thee in the ocean, in the waters,
> In the breast of the sky, O Agni, he who gazeth on men.
> Thee [Agni] standing in the third region,
> In the birthplace of holy order [Rta], the steers [Mitra-Varuna] inspirited.

The third region is the mid-Region, which is ruled by the sun. The form of Agni as the one "who gazeth on men" is that of the sun-god of the heavens called Āditya (son of Aditi) or Sūrya. At *AV* IV,39,6, Sūrya is called the "calf of the cow Heaven", just as Horus the Younger is the son of Nut/Hathor. At *RV* X,72,7, the sun is said to be born of the waters and located in the highest heaven, surrounded by the waters.[1742] The "waters" which give birth to the light of the heavens are the waters of the "underworld".

Indra is the god "who gave being to the Sun, and Morning [Dawn], who leads the waters" (*RV* II,12,7). In *RV* IX,86,22, it is stated that the consumption of Soma, the "seed", or life-force, of Agni, by Indra results in the rise of the sun to its place in the universe: "Sinking into the throat of

---

Indra with a roar, led by the men, thou madest Surya mount to heaven". Indra's establishment of the solar force in the heavens is thus due to the potency derived from his consumption of Soma. In *RV* IX,42,1, Soma, identified with Indra, engenders the sun in floods along with the other stars. We have already in the second chapter studied the "floods" which accompany the birth of the sun.

The sun is fixed in our heavens by Indra (*RV* II,21,4). In *RV* IX,63,8 Indra is said to make the sun move by yoking ten coursers to it. In *RV* I,24,8, the path of the sun in the system is said to be ordained by Varuna, who is but a form of Agni/Shiva/Indra and the counterpart of Osiris. The sun is also set in motion (*RV* VII,86,1) and established in its course (*RV* VII, 87,1) by Varuna. At *RV* I, 1145,5 the sun of the Heavens, Sūrya, is said to be the manifest form of Varuna. When the sun sets, it is said to become one with Varuna (*KB* XVIII,9). This is the same as the identification of the setting sun with Osiris, "chief of the western [gods]" in Egypt. In *RV* VII,99,4 Sūrya (the sun of heaven), Dawn and Agni (here the sun of earth) are said to be the children of Vishnu.

In *AV* XIII,3,13 the different forms of the sun of our system are described in a way that recalls the Egyptian solar gods:

> This Agni becomes Varuna in the evening; in the morning, rising he becomes Mitra; he, having become Savitar, goes through the atmosphere; he, having become Indra, burns through the midst of the sky.

Here Varuna is the counterpart of Osiris, Mitra of Harakhte, Savitr of Khepera and Indra of Aton-Re.[1743] However, as we shall see below, the terms "morning" and "evening" do not refer to terrestrial time but rather to solar.[1744] And the "sun" which is adored in several forms, as the rising sun, the risen, the mid-day sun and the setting sun, is not really the star itself, but rather the changing solar energies that characterise it in these several phases.

Like the Avestan Mithra,[1745] the Vedic god Mitra is the same as Horus the Younger. In *RV* V,3,1, Mitra and Varuna are said to be the quiescent and enflamed states of Agni: "Thou at thy birth art Varuna, O Agni; when thou art kindled thou becomest Mitra".[1746] Mitra is, on one occasion (*RV*

[1743] See below p.311.

[1744] See below p.318.

[1745] See above p.265.

[1746] Cf. *RV* VII,88,2: "And now as I am come before his presence, I take the face of Varuna

VIII,25,4,), called a Deva (god), whereas his counterpart, Varuna, is in the same passage called an Asura, since the latter rules the underworld. Varuna is the quiet setting sun whereas Mitra is the rising. In *MBh* IX,44,5, Mitra is accompanied by two companions, Suvrata (true to his vows) and Satyasamdha (true to his contracts).[1747]

The Ādityas themselves are reported in the *BP* VI,6,25-39 as resulting from the union of Aditi – who is a daughter of Daksha (one of the sages created intellectually by Brahma) and Akshini – and Kashyapa, in the seventh manvantara, which is our own. We may infer from this that the first seven manvantaras of the second Kalpa (Padmakalpa) begin with the emergence of Brahman, the divine light and end with the Flood and the establishment of our solar system (at the commencement of the present manvantara).

According to the Avesta, the sun arises from the Hara mountain (Mihr Yasht, X,13) preceded by Mithra (Horus the Younger/Harakhte).[1748] The sun of the heavens is called Hvare, which is the Avestan form of Svar (the shining one), another name of Sūrya.[1749] We may note incidentally that the xvarenah when flying out of Yima, once he has become sinful, takes the form of a falcon, the typical form of the Egyptian Horus. Yima is himself representative of the seventh manvantara, according to the evidence of *BP* VIII,13.[1750] The symbolic importance of the falcon is most evident in the Horus cult of Egypt and, since the name of Horus is itself, as we have seen, probably derived from the Iranian Hvare, this is another indication that the people who developed the Horus cult in Egypt from Elam and Mesopotamia were probably closely allied to the Iranian Āryans. The cult of Seth in the south, on the other hand, seems to bear a resemblance to the worship of Teshup among the Hurrians, of Ganesha among the Indians and of Zeus among the Greeks.[1751]

The Armenians distinguish between a "Great Mher [Mihir/Mithra/Horus the Younger]" and "Mher the Younger" (the sun-god, Hvare). These two 'Mher's are Zoroastrian names for Urartian gods called originally

---

for Agni's".

[1747] These two companions correspond to those of the Akkadian Shamash, Kittum (fidelity) and Nigsisa (justice) (see below p.309).

[1748] See above p.265.

[1749] cf. the Hittite/Hurrian form, Suwalliyat, above pp.131,179, as well as the Kassite Šuriaš, above p.201n.

[1750] See above p.78.

[1751] See above Ch.XIV.

Haldi[1752] and Siwini (Shamash) respectively. Haldi is called Vahagn by
the later Armenians, and Vahagn may be the Armenian counterpart of
the Iranian Verethragna[1753] (Vishnu), which is the name of the solar force
which rises from the underworld. The Great Mher is called "great" because
he is the force within the sun, which is represented by Siwini. The birth of
Vahagn is represented dramatically in the Armenian religious texts:

> Heaven and Earth were in labour,
> And in labour was the purple sea,
> And in labour was the red reed[1754] in the sea.
> Out of the reed smoke came forth,
> Out of the reed flames came forth,
> And out of the flames a blonde boy came forth.
> He had hair of fire,
> And a beard of flame,
> And his eyes were two suns.[1755]

In Sumer, the common name of the sun-god is Utu. The sun is also
sometimes called dGišnu (TCL 15, 10, 173; CT 25,25,8). We have seen
that Gishnugal meaning "the greater light" is an appellation of the moon,
Nannar (which also has a higher numerical value, 30, compared to the
sun, 20). Another name of Utu attested in Mesopotamia is Mitra-šúdú (CT
XXV,25,10), which may mean the perfect sceptre-bearer.[1756] We have seen
that Mitra is, in the Avesta as in the Vedas, especially used for the rising sun,
Harakhte. In the Sumerian myth of "Enki and Inanna: The Organisation of
the Universe", Mitra is called the "great herald of An",[1757] where An is the
same as Shamash the sun in its perfect form (Hvar/Svar/Sūrya), while Mitra
is the earlier, rising sun of the horizon. Thus also Harakhte heralds Khepera
and, more significantly, the full-fledged Re/Aton.

[1752] See above p.247n.

[1753] Verethraghna is called Bahram in the Pahlavi texts. The Bahram, or Varhran, fire is the
highest of all the fires worshipped by the Iranians (see J. Duchesne-Guillemin, *Religion of
Ancient Iran*, Bombay: Tata Press, 1973, pp.59ff.). It is not certain if the name Bahram may
be related to the Indic "Brahman".

[1754] We note again the mention of the "reed" as bearing the seed of universal life (see above
p.92).

[1755] See M. Kavoukjian, *Armenia, Subartu and Sumer: The Indo-European Homeland and
Ancient Mesopotamia*, tr. N. Ouzonian, Montreal: M. Kavoukjian, 1987, p.177f.

[1756] See P.A. Schollmeyer, *op.cit.*, p.12.

[1757] See S. Kramer and J. Maier, *Myths of Enki*, p.53.

Mitra is the one who acts as judge among the gods, since he oversees the universe. This may explain the reference to "sceptre-bearer" in the Sumerian "Mitra".[1758] However, we note that An himself is described as a sceptre-bearer in A.O.6461,[1759] showing once again the identity of the different forms of the sun. The association of Phanes, the Orphic counterpart of the cosmic light Brahman, with the sceptre is also clear in the Rhapsodic theogony: "for it was Phanes who first fashioned the sceptre".[1760] This suggests that the role of universal judge is equally that of the first cosmic light (Phanes/Horus the Elder) and of the light of our universe (Horus the Younger). The rising sun is also called Babbar, which name is explained as such in CT XII,6b,6.[1761] The sun is said to rise from a mountain in the east between two peaks.[1762]

Among the Akkadians the sun-god is called Shamash and Shamash' role as a judge is parallel to that of his "twin" Sin as "illuminator of the night".[1763] In the An=Anum list, one of the sons of Shamash is called Kittum [Fidelity] (CT 24, 31, 82), who is related to his vizier Niggina (CT 24, 31, 81). These two figures are in turn identifiable with Nigzida, who is one of Shamash's emissaries along with Nigsisa (Righteousness/Justice) (CT 24, 31, 74-75).[1764]

It is interesting that Enlil himself is considered the form of the rising sun, since we have observed that Enlil is the vital force of the entire manifest universe in the Mid-region between earth and heaven. According to a Babylonian exegetical text, Enlil is the form of Utu (the sun) when the latter rises, just as Kiurash (Enki, the lord of Earth) is his form when he

---

[1758] See A. Ungnad, "Ahura-Mazdah und Mithra in assyrischen Texten?", OL 1943 No.5/6, p.200. The Sanskritic derivation of Mitra from "mit" to unite (thus, "friend") is doubtful. It must be noted that the Iranian Mithra is also called Mihir (cf. Mihir Yasht), in which the "h" may be a characteristic Iranian substitution of an original "s" or "sh". If this be so, the name may be related to the Hittite adjective "mišriwant", which may mean either brilliant or perfect (see The Hittite Dictionary, III:27). On the other hand, the Hittite form of Mitra may have been Mezzulla (see below p.310).

[1759] See H. Wohlstein, op.cit., p.103.

[1760] See M.L. West, Orphic Poems, p.231f.

[1761] See P.A. Schollmeyer, op.cit., p.3.

[1762] Cylinder seal (British Museum no. 89,110) (see P.A. Schollmeyer, op.cit., p.5).

[1763] See the hymn to Marduk, CT 24, 50, 47406, obv.3-10: "Sīn is Marduk, the illuminator of the night,/ Shamash is Marduk of justice" (T. Jacobsen, op.cit., p.235).

[1764] Cf. H. Zimmern, op.cit., p.368; cf. P.A. Schollmeyer, op.cit., p.17. Nigsisa is also called Bunene (see 'Nigzida' in RLA IX:313). Among the Hittites, Mešaru (akk. Mišaru) and Bunene are the viziers of the sun-god (see V. Haas, op.cit., p.380). So Mešaru/Mišaru must be the same as Nigzida/Niggina/Kittum.

sets.[1765] Since the setting sun is the same as Osiris/Atum, the former may be equated with Harakhte/Utu. Indeed, Enlil is also the solar light of An due to the fact already noticed above that the supreme deity is in fact a trinity of An-Enlil-Enki (corresponding to Brahman-Shiva-Vishnu).[1766]

We have seen that, in an Assyrian exegetic work on Sumerian theology, the heavens (Akk. 'šame') are explained as being "of water", "ša me".[1767] However, among the Hittites, the sun is distinguished in two forms, as the sun of the waters and as the sun of the heavens. The first form of the sun is the Sun-god of the waters. ᵈUTU ME.E or ᵈUTU ú-it-e-e-ni,[1768] which corresponds to the rising sun (Harakhte). This is the Hittite counterpart of Shimige (the Hurrian version of the Akkadian Shamash),[1769] who, like the Hittite sun-god, is represented as riding on a bull. This may be a local adaptation of the familiar Iranian Mithraic iconography. The daughter of the sun-goddess of Arinna, who is perhaps the same as the sun-god of the waters (since Arinna is clearly related to the Ocean, "Arunas"), is also called Mezzulla, who may be a female form of Mitra.

The god-lists in the Hittite treaties[1770] begin with another form of the sun, dUTU SAME/ nepisas, the Sun-god of Heaven. This is the solar light which reigns in heaven after rising from the waters as the sun-god of the waters. Muwattalli's prayer in KUB VI 45 III, 13ff. addressed to the sun-god of the heavens runs: "you rise, sun-god of heaven, from the waters, and enter heaven".[1771] The Hittite sun-god of heaven must be the counterpart of Re/Aton/Sūrya/Hvare.

In Crete and the Aegean too, Zeus, the supreme solar god, was considered as a triple divinity, a Sky-god, a Water-god, and an Earth-god.[1772] This corresponds exactly to the three suns of the Hittites, the sun-god of

---

[1765] See Weidner, *AfO*, 19, 110 (see A. Livingstone, *op.cit.*, p.47).

[1766] See above p. 161. For identifications of An with Enlil, see H. Wohlstein, *op.cit.*, p.35. According to the Babylonian cosmology recounted by Damascius (*De Principiis*), Anos, Illinos and Aos are all sons of "Kissare and Assoron" (Kishar-Anshar) (see *ATAT*, p.138; cf. H. Wohlstein, *op.cit.*, p.10).

[1767] See A. Livingstone, *op.cit.*, p.33 (cf. above p.138n).

[1768] The waters from which the sun is born are represented by the sun-goddess of Arinna and ME.E/arunaz (see E. Tenner, *op.cit.*, p.186).

[1769] The original form of the name was Shimesgi, which is, like Tasmisu, derived from the Akkadian Shamash (Sumerian 'Utu').

[1770] See D. Yoshida, *op.cit.*, pp.12-29.

[1771] See E. Tenner, *op.cit.*, p.186.

[1772] See A.B. Cook, "Zeus, Jupiter and the Oak", *Classical Review*, 17 (1903), 403ff. These three forms of the supreme deity may correspond to the gods Zeus, Poseidon, Hades (see above p.247n).

Heaven, the sun-god of Earth and the sun-god of the Waters,[1773] as well as to Āditya, Vāyu, Agni of the Vedas. We see again that Vāyu/Enlil is identifiable with the sun that rises from the waters.

In Egypt, we have seen that the incipient sun in the underworld is called Horus the Younger, who represents the reviving Osiris. As the sun at the horizon (Re-Harakhte), he is called a falcon "who traverses the two heavens" and the "lower celestial vault".[1774] The first form of Horus the Younger is the sun of the horizon called Harakhte. The risen sun is called "the developer" Kephera (represented by the scarab beetle), while the mid-day sun is the full splendour of Re himself as the solar disk Aton or Aten. In Pap. Chester Beatty 9, BM 19689, Atum is said to have mastered the heavens as Re, the sun. However, Atum or Atem is properly the name of the setting sun. Atum's name is often used to denote the primal light of the universe, for Horus the Elder and Osiris (who "sets" or goes into the underworld) are virtually identical.

It is interesting that, in PT 587, Pyr.1587a-d, Khepera (the scarab which bears a sun between its legs) is also addressed as the primordial hill,[1775] which is the appellation of of Geb,[1776] though the scarab as representative of the sun actually emerges from the hill. In the Fifth Hour of the *Amduat*, the hill is represented as a tumulus over the grave of Osiris (in the desert of Rosetau) from which the sun will emerge – in the Twelfth hour – in the form of a scarab.[1777] In the Twelfth Hour of the *Amduat*, the scarab is indeed elevated into the daytime sky by Shu. In the Middle and New Kingdoms, especially under Akhenaton, Shu is identified also with the solar deity Re (equivalent to the noon-day sun Aton) itself, though he is more typically, as we have seen from the Mesopotamian evidence, the morning sun.[1778]

The role of divine judge in Egypt, however, is normally played by the sun-god's most brilliant form, Re/Aton.[1779] The scepter of the sun-god itself,

[1773] The close resemblance between the Indic, Hittite and early Greek cosmologies makes clear the close kinship between these early branches of the Āryan family. The association of the Indo-Āryans with the Iranians and Scythians has also been studied above p.64f.

[1774] See A. Barucq and F. Daumas, *op.cit.*, p.140.

[1775] See S. Bickel, *op.cit.*, p.44.

[1776] The Sumerian Enlil is also called "the great mountain" ("kurgal"; see above p.227). Indeed, one of the Egyptian terms for the hill, q3, is similar to the Sumerian 'kur'.

[1777] See E. Hornung, *Ancient Egyptian Books*, p.37.

[1778] See K. Sethe, *op. cit.*, p.112f.; cf. above p.230.

[1779] See J. Assmann, *op.cit.*, p.50.

which we have encountered in Sumer, is described also in the Egyptian text STG (pp.203-209) in relation to Amun-Re:

> The ames-sceptre is in your fist, its limits are unattainable;
> Its nature is secret,
> It is invisible, nobody knows what it is
>
> …
>
> It roams about, seeking to cause havoc,
> It deals blows to those who will attack it.[1780]

In the *Book of Caverns*, the sceptre of Atum, the setting sun, is similarly considered to have "created the netherworld [the place of judgement] and brought forth the realm of the dead".[1781] The inscriptions on the tombs of Seti I and Rameses IV in Thebes also mention the aging of Re (the mature sun), which causes him to ask Shu to take his place [as the sun of the Mid-region of our universe] while Nut [Shu's daughter] bears him on her back to heaven, where he reigns as sun-god of the heavens.[1782]

The Son of the Sun: Man

We have seen that the sun is the heavenly body in which the seed of the First Man Gayomaretan is purified after he is killed by Angra Mainyu (*Bundahishn* Ch.XIV). After Gayomaretan's seed is purified in the light of the sun, one part of it is received by Earth (Spandarmat), where it turns into androgynous twins called Mashye and Mashyane, whose erring conduct serves as the model for the story of Adam and Eve in the biblical *Genesis*.

The sun is also associated with Yima, who seems to be a duplicate of Mashye, who is born of the seed of the First Man. This explains the identification of the Germanic Ymir with Gayomaretan, the First Man.[1783] We have seen that Haoma too may have been considered in a macroanthropomorphic form called Duraosha, who was in existence before Vivanghvant.[1784] However, Hoama and Duraosha are more closely related to the Tree of Life than to either the First Man or the son of the sun.

[1780] *Ibid.*, p.203.

[1781] See E. Hornung, *op.cit.*, p.88.

[1782] See E.A.W. Budge, *op.cit.*, I:367.

[1783] See above p.182.

[1784] See above p.259.

Nevertheless it is interesting that even in the Avesta, Yima too is once (in the Zamyad Yasht, 46) described as having been cut into two by the agents of Angra Mainyu, exactly as if he, the counterpart of the seventh Manu, Vaivasvata, were the same as Gayomaretan, the counterpart of the first Swāyambhuva Manu/Purusha. However, just as Yama is distinguished from Purusha in the Vedas, in the Avesta too, Yima is generally distinguishable from Gayomaretan, the macroanthropos. In the Eddas, however, Ymir is used as the name of the early form of Brahman/Prajāpati as the first Manu, and his cosmic body itself[1785] is divided into Heaven, Earth and a Mid-Region, the three regions typical also of our universe.

Yima (Hom Yasht; Yasna 9,4) is considered as the son of Vivanghvant (the sun). Vivasvān is considered in the Vedas to be the Āditya most closely associated with human life.[1786] Yima survives the flood, preserving the life of the universe in the "ark" commissioned by Ahura Mazda. Yima is said to rule over the entire material universe called the "seven-fold Earth", which includes, as we have seen, the seven galactic "continents" of the universe. Yima is also said to be capable of expanding the earth when it becomes overcrowded (Vendidad 2, 9-19),[1787] which suggests that he is closely associated with the solar force Mithra, just as Ziusudra is with Ninurta.[1788]

At the same time, it must be noted that Yima himself, rather like Mashye in the *Bundahishn*, is said to have begun to "find delight in words of falsehood and untruth" in Zamyad Yasht (34). In the Indic *BP* (III,5,20), too, Yama is punished with human incarnation. This is possibly the reason why he is allotted, as we shall see, the southern point in the Mid-region and is, even in Vedic literature, generally considered the ruler of the realm of the dead along with Varuna (Osiris).[1789] The realm of Manu/Yama indeed borders on the waters of the Ocean surrounding Earth, which is the realm of Enki/Osiris/Varuna. The Moon (Soma), which is the eldest heavenly body, is, on the other hand, situated at the northern point in the Mid-

---

[1785] In the Indic mythology, it is the lotus formation of Earth which is divided by Brahman into the three regions (see above p.163).

[1786] In Indian mythology (*RV* X,10ff.), Yama is the son of Vivasvān (the Āditya) and Tvashtr's daughter, Saranyū. The children born of this union are the twins representing life and death, Yami and Yama (the Ymir of Nordic mythology must thus be the grandson of Tuisto/Tvaštr). Another son of Vivasvān, by another consort than Saranyū, is Manu, who was, however, worshipped as Mannus, 'the son [rather than grandson] of Tuisto [Tvashtr]', by the ancient Germans (Tacitus, *Germania*, Sec.2). In *MP* III,30-44, IV,11-21, Brahma impregnates his daughter Sāvitrī (the female form of Savitr, the sun of the heavens), who gives birth to Manu.

[1787] This expansion of our universe is reminiscent of Vāyu's initial extension of the material basis of the cosmos.

[1788] See above p.82.

[1789] See *HW* II:614.

region.[1790] In spite of the fall of Yima/Yama, Manu is represented as a great king in *BP*, and a sage whose purpose was the enlightenment of mankind. We have seen that, in the Vedas, Yama is blessed with immortal life, in the lower heavens.[1791] In Mesopotamia, too, Ziusudra and Atrahasis are holy men, just as Utnapishtim is promised eternal life in Dilmun (which may correspond to the beatitude of Yama's lower heaven).

In the *Atrahasis*, episode mentioned above[1792] the birth of mankind results from the sacrifice of the god Wê-ilu demanded by Enlil. Enki helps in the creation of semi-divine life from the slaughtered god. The divine substance (heaven) of the victim is, after his slaughter, mixed with clay (earth) to form mankind (I,213).

With the appearance of the first man, we have reached the final stage of the deluge story discussed in the first chapter. In spite of the minor variations that we have noted in the various accounts of the creation of human life on the planet after the formation of the sun, it is clear that this life is directly derived from the sun. The sun of our system is the purifier of the seed whereof we are born, just as the animal life of the universe is purified by the moon. Furthermore, the sun is, in the Vedas, considered to be the very soul (ātman) of "everything either moving or stationary" (*RV* I,115,1) as well as the supreme judge of the universe. This is because it is the manifest symbol of the Divine Consciousness, Brahman, within our universe. Purified by the severe passion undergone by the Divine Light in the underworld, the risen sun of the heavens represents the perfection of the manifest universe.

[1790] See below p.318.

[1791] See above p.284.

[1792] See above p.186.

XXVI: MAHĀVISHNU

THE LORD OF THE UNIVERSE

With the emergence of the sun in our system, the universe has achieved its final organisation. In the Vedas, the order of the establishment of the universe is suggested in *RV* V,85,5. Earth is formed first, and from it heaven and the Mid-region are said to have been "measured out" by the sun. *SB* VIII,iii,3,5 declares that "The mass is this world [earth], for this world was measured out as soon as it came into being; the front portion is the atmospheric [mid-region], for the atmospheric region was measured forwards from this world as soon as it came into being ... the corresponding portion is that world (heaven), for that world was measured out against the atmospheric region as soon as it came into being." That earth is above the waters of the underworld is made clear by *SB* XII,ix,2,8, which declares that "This earthly world is higher than the water".

In the *BrdP* III,iv,2,14ff. the total number of worlds is said to be seven, beginning with Bhū, Bhuvah, Svar (the three worlds of the universe), followed by Mahar, Jana, Tapah, and Satya. Mahar is the abode of the gods (Devas), Jana is the source of human life beginning with the Manus, Tapas is the realm of those who have practised sexual penance, and Satyaloka is the original realm of light of Brahman himself. In *BP* II,6,38ff, Bhurloka is said to occupy the region of the waist of the Ideal Man, Bhuvarloka his navel, Svarloka his heart, Maharloka his chest, Janaloka his neck, Tapoloka his two lips and Satyaloka his head.[1793] Brahmaloka (or Vaikuntha) itself is transcendent and not associated with any part of the anthropomorphic form of the deity. Earth or Bhurloka is said to rotate, just as our planet does (*BrdP* III,iv,2,37bff.). The Bhuvarloka or the Mid-region of the stars is said to have the sun itself at its upper limit and Svar [heaven] is the realm

---

[1793] Similarly, the underworlds represent the lower part of the macroanthropos, Atala his hip, Vitala his thighs, Sutala his knees, Talātala his forelegs, Mahātala his ankles, Rasātala the top of his feet, and Pātala the lower part of his feet.

between the sun and the Pole Star (*ibid.*). The sun is more than a 100,000 yojanas[1794] above earth, and the moon, which is above the sun, is 200,000 yojanas above the latter. The Maharloka is above the Pole Star, Janaloka is 2 crore[1795] yojanas above Maharloka, Tapakoka above the Maharloka and Satyaloka 600,000 yojanas above Tapaloka (*BrdP* III,iv,138ff.). The world of Shiva is called the "eighth" world, though it is the realm of Māya (cosmic illusion) itself. Here the supreme Lord is said to be present as in the minutest of atoms (Paramānu) (*BrdP* III,iv,2,227).

The seed of the Lord that developed into the Cosmic Egg is the individuated soul of Brahman himself and called 'kshetrajna'. This is the seed that develops into Prajāpati. Prakriti (Nature) is the same as the cosmic womb (yoni) and reappears in the lowest realm of the manifest universe, Bhurloka, or earth (*BrdP* III,iv,2,235). It is also called Nārāyana (*BrdP* III,iv,2,231), since the egg is originally formed within his "navel". The Cosmic Egg itself is said to extend 15,000,000 yojanas beyond, that is, outside, the Brahmaloka (*BrdP* III,iv,2,224).

In the *BP* V,20,43, the entire universe including the underworld, earth, intermediate region and the heavens emerges from the golden egg formed in the Hiranyagarbha ("golden womb"). In *BP* V,21,2, heaven (again, as in Hesiod) is a covering of earth that is exactly as extensive as the latter. The region between the two is called Antariksha (the Mid-region) and is ruled by the sun, which is "the brightest of all the luminaries,[1796] heating and illumining the three regions – the earth, the middle region and heaven" (3).

The lotus-formation that grows through the navel of the Lord[1797] appears in the manifest universe primarily as earth, and is constituted, as we have seen, of seven "islands".[1798] At the centre of the material universe is our "island" called Jambudweepa, which is surrounded by Plakshadweepa, Salmaladweepa, Kushadweepa, Kraunchadweepa, Sakadweepa and Pushkaradweepa. In *BP* V,20,29, the last dweepa, or island, of earth is

---

[1794]   A yojana is computed to be around 8 miles (see *HW*, "Weights and Measures", II:594ff.).

[1795]   A crore is 10,000,000.

[1796]   That the sun is the most powerful star is made clear in the *SB*, which maintains that the sun has deprived the other stars of their power (kshatra) and therefore are they called "nakshatras" (stars) (see B.R. Yadava, *Vedic Cosmogony*, Aligarh: Vijnana Prakasana Press, 1987, p.154).

[1797]   The Moslems use the image of the lotus interchangeably with that of the cosmic tree in their sacred literature (see A.J. Wensinck, *op.cit.*, p.31). However, the lotus is actually only a symbol of earth, whereas the tree symbolises the entire universe.

[1798]   See above Ch.XI. This seven-fold formation of Earth is certainly the basis of the form of the Hebrew menorah, which H. Gunkel (*Schöpfung und Chaos*, Göttingen, 1895, p.124ff.) identified with the Tree of Life.

surrounded by an ocean of pure water (corresponding to Okeanos in the Greek mythology). Since Bhāratvarsha is the outermost of the nine regions of Jambudweepa and is described as being "alone ... the field of Karma, or the place where a Jiva (life) can acquire merit and demerit by work" (V,17,11), it is probable that it represents the matrix of our own planet,[1799] which latter, however, is to be located in the Mid-region ruled by the sun. The entire "island" of Jambu must then be related to our solar system especially since the axle-tree of the chariot of the sun is attached to the top of Mt. Meru, which is at the centre of Jambudweepa (V,21,13). The other dweepas encircling Jambudweepa must bear similar solar systems or galaxies within their enormous ranges.

The organisation of the Mid-region of the stars is given in detail in *BP* V,21-23. The moon which "satisfies the hunger, the life-principle in all beings – devas, pitrs, men, animals, birds, serpents, trees, creepers, etc." gives food and energy to all" (*BP* V,22,10) is said to be "more than a lakh[1800] of yojanas above the sun" (*BP* V,22,8), while the 28 constellations are located "three lakhs of yojanas above the moon" (*BP* V,22,11), and still further above them are Venus, Mercury, Mars, Jupiter, Saturn, and the Seven Sages (Great Bear). Thirteen lakhs of yojanas above the Great Bear is the Pole Star, Dhruva, to which all the constellations and planets are fixed (V,23,3). The Pole Star is envisaged, as we have seen,[1801] as occupying the tip of the tail of a downward hanging alligator, at whose chest is located the sun, and in whose head is the moon (V,23,7).

Though located in the Mid-region between earth and heaven, the sun illuminates all the regions of the universe, the waters, the Mid-region, and the heavens. In the *AV* XIII,2,30, the sun is called a "bird which shines in the heavens, the atmosphere, on the earth and in the waters". In another passage (*AV* II,143,9), the sun is called "the Bull of Heaven, the Atmosphere, and the Earth". Indeed, the sun is not stationary but has an extremely vast circuit. Furthermore, at *BP* V,22,2 the solar system is described as revolving in the opposite direction to that of the other galaxies.

In *BP* V,21,7, the sun is said to move from the city of Indra [representing the "arms" of the macroanthropos whose torso and head encompass the universe] in the east, to Yama's [the "navel"] in the south, to Varuna's [the "tongue"] in the west,[1802] and finally to Soma's [mind] in the north (7). We see that Indra/Shiva represents the rising sun just as Enlil

---

[1799] The name Bhārat thus is originally not restricted to India, as it is today.

[1800] A lakh is 100,000.

[1801] See above p.253n.

[1802] The Ideal Man is to be imagined as supine and facing westwards.

and Shu too do, even though the exact counterpart of the latter is Vāyu. Indra must thus be closely related to Vāyu, which is perhaps why he is called Indha, "the blower".[1803] Yama, who is identified with the "navel" of the supreme lord, is, as we have seen, situated in the "lower heavens". Yama is thus the southernmost point in the revolution of the sun, the western being Varuna, the northern Soma and the eastern Indra. The Yama which is considered the "southern" terminus of the sun's revolution is perhaps to be located in the regions of earth, since he also rules as lord of the dead. Soma, the "northern" limit of the sun's revolution, is at the border of the lower heavens.

We have seen that in the *AV* the rising sun, that is, of the east, is called Mitra, and this must be equated with the Indra of the *BP*. The terms "rising", "risen" and "noon-day" are not quite accurate since the phases under consideration are not related to the sun's apparent daily motion but rather to its galactic. Since the sun is represented as revolving, we may consider the entire universe constituted of Earth, the Mid-region and Heaven as revolving about the focal point of the Abyss, which extends far beneath Earth, constituted of seven subterranean regions and the profoundest base wherein the serpent Sesha lies.

The Vedas envisage three earths, three heavens, and three intermediate regions.[1804] According to *AV* XIX,27,4f., there are, along with "three heavenly vaults", also "three oceans … three atmospheric regions". *RV* I,35,6 states that, of the three heavens, two, the higher, are "Savitr's[1805] adjacent", while the third is in "Yama's world, the home of heroes". We may infer that the realm of Yama, who is identifiable with the seventh Manu, ranges from the lower heavens through the Mid-region to earth, or, more precisely, to upper and middle earth.[1806] At *RV* IX,113, we find Yama's dwelling described as "the third sphere of inmost heaven where lucid worlds are full of light … the region of the radiant Moon, where food and full delight are found". The region of Yama must therefore extends from that of the moon, which is, as we have seen, "north" of the sun, while Soma, representing the substance of the moon, is the northernmost point of the sun's revolution.[1807]

The organisation of the universe in the Babylonian *EE* IV,135-46 is modelled after the Abyss. We have seen that our heaven and earth are

---

[1803]   See above p.276n.

[1804]   See W. Kirfel, *op.cit.*, p.14f.

[1805]   See E.A.W. Budge, *op.cit.*, I:293ff.

[1806]   Cf. the Babylonian scheme of the universe in VAT 8917.

[1807]   In the cosmological 'Romance of Alexander', on the other hand, the South is represented by the "Mountain of the Moon" (see A.J. Wensinck, "The Ocean", p.35).

formed out of Tiamat's body. Marduk is described as fashioning the abodes of Enki (Eshgalla, earth) – modelled on the Apsu, abode of the Lord of the Abyss – of An (the heavens) – also modelled on the Apsu – and of Enlil (Esharra, the mid–region) – modelled on the Eshgalla.[1808] We note that the Apsu is the prototype of the three universal regions.

In a fragment related to *EE*, VAT 8917 obv.30-rev.30, heaven is divided into an upper heaven (ruled by the solar An),[1809] a middle heaven (inhabited by the Igigi and ruled by Enlil/Marduk) and a lower (governed by the "stars"). We have seen that the region of the stars is considered to be the Mid-region in the Indic literature. We have seen also that the lower heavens are, in the Vedas, particularly the domain of the first man, Yama, who rules universal life. Earth is divided into upper earth (peopled by mankind), middle earth (ruled by Ea) and lower earth (the domain of the Anunnaki).[1810] Since there are only two major regions, heaven and earth, we may assume that the Mid-region of the Vedas is also governed by the stars which rule the lower heaven.

According to the Sumero-Akkadian poem of 'Gilgamesh and the "huluppu" tree', when heaven separated itself from the earth, Anu took over the rule of heaven, Enlil that of earth and Ereshkigal (wife of Nergal, as well as of Enki, lord of the underworld) that of the underworld.[1811] In the Sumerian fragments relating to the epic of Gilgamesh,[1812] too, An is said to rule heaven, Enlil earth and Enki the underworld. We see that Enlil, who rules the middle heaven in VAT 8917, is said to rule earth here. So the domain of Enlil must extend from the middle heaven to the upper earth, which is roughly that of Yama.

In the Babylonian fragments (BF 39099) relating to the *Atrahasis* epic, Anu and Adad (Seth/Zeus/Teshup) rule the upper regions,[1813] Sin and Nergal (the children of Enlil) "earth", and Ea the lower regions.[1814] The

---

[1808] *EE*, IV, 135ff.

[1809] Savitr (Khepera, the risen sun) is the counterpart of Anu here, as also in BF 39099 (see below).

[1810] See W. Lambert, "The Cosmology of Sumer and Babylon", p.58; cf. A. Livingstone, *op.cit.*, p.83. The waters of the "underworld" and the "primeval" world of the Anunnaki are, of course, related to the Abyss.

[1811] See D. Wolkstein and S. Kramer, *op.cit.*, p.4; cf. J.J.A. van Dijk, *Sumerische Religion: Handbuch der Religionsgeschichte*, Goettingen, 1971, p.453.

[1812] See A. George, *The Epic of Gilgamesh*, London: Allen Lane, 1999, 'Bilgamesh and the Netherworld', p.179.

[1813] The common coupling of Adad and Shamash in Babylonian oaths and prayers, as well as in the name Shamshi-Adad (see above p.201) reveals the equivalence of Shamash to Anu.

[1814] See W. Lambert and A.R. Millard (ed.), *Atrahasis*, p.10.

association of Adad with the realm of Enlil in VAT 8917 reminds us that the storm-gods are an aspect of the wind-god. The "earth" of this fragment obviously includes the Mid-region of the Indic astronomy, ranging from the lower heaven to the upper earth, which is peopled by mankind in VAT 8917. From the allotment of heaven to Seth and earth to Horus the Younger in Egypt, we may again deduce the correspondence of Adad to Seth, who is lord of Heaven. Since the lord of Earth is Horus the Younger, we may suppose that Nergal in this Babylonian fragment represents the same deity.

We see that the Vedic division of the cosmos into three heavens, earths and intermediate regions bears a general, though not exact, resemblance to the Babylonian cosmos of *EE*, as well as to that of the VAT 8917 fragment. The realm of Anu in the fragment is the same as the highest heaven of the Vedas assigned to Savitr. The middle heaven ruled, according to the *RV*, also by Savitr, corresponds to the realm of Enlil. The lower heaven is ruled by Yama in the Vedas and the region of the stars in VAT 8917 corresponds to the highest level of the Mid-region of the Vedas. The domain of Enlil called "earth" in the Sumero-Akkadian Gilgamesh literature – which, unlike the Babylonian, has a tripartite division of the universe resembling the Indian – seems to coincide with that of Yama and range over the Mid–region of our universe.

Among the Hittites, the heavens are divided into an upper heaven, ruled by Anu, a middle by Marduk, and a lower inhabited by the stars.[1815] The chief god of the universe is Teshup. Earth is also divided into three regions, an "upper earth" inhabited by mankind, animals and plants, a "middle earth" ruled by Ea, and a "lower earth" inhabited by the Anunnaki and ruled by Ea's consort Ereshkigal. This division of the universe seems to be derived from the Babylonian cosmology. We have seen that the middle earth and lower earth in the Babylonian cosmology too are ruled by Ea and the Anunnaki.

In Egypt, we have noted the crucial importance of the underworld in the regeneration of the solar energy. The netherworld itself is said to be created by the sceptre of Atum (who represents Horus the Elder/Brahman as well as Osiris/Varuna, Lord of the Underworld).[1816]

~

It is clear that the solar force which informs the entire universe is the focus of the worship of all the religions based on the cosmology we have

---

[1815] See V. Haas, *op.cit.*, p.126f.

[1816] The lower earth is said to be a creation of the aquatic god Hapi (identified with the Nile), who declares: "It is I who bore the Netherworld" (CT 318, IV, 136d; 140b).

studied. The adoration of Marduk as the organiser of the cosmos in *EE* signals the ascendancy of this energy after its sojourn in the underworld. Marduk/ Muruga/ Ninurta, who are but forms of Shiva/Enki-Enlil/Osiris, and their stormy aspects, Ganesha/Adad/ Seth/ Zeus/ Thor, indeed play the role of "chief gods" in these cultures. These are the gods who make our universe manifest, inform it with divine vitality and establish the rule of the sun. The sun, however, is just the final manifestation in our universe of the divine light of Brahman which once suffused the cosmos. This perfect light is the supreme Consciousness of the supreme deity himself as the Ideal macroanthropos. The destiny of enlightened mankind, as sons of the sun, is clearly to aspire to this divine consciousness. This may be achieved only through the recognition of the illusory nature of the divine Māyā which produces the entire creation, cosmic as well as universal. The enlightened man is not distracted by the phenomenal diversity of the divine manifestation and seeks, instead, to abjure it, concentrating on the unique reality of the primal Soul (Ātman), which is the One beyond its own Desire.[1817] For, indeed, as *RV* VIII (Vālakhilya hymns),58,2 points out,[1818]

> Kindled in many a spot, still One is Agni;
> Sūrya is One though high o'er all he shineth.
> Illumining this All, still One is Ušas.[1819]
> That which is only One hath into All developed.

[1817] Cf. the ascetic and purificatory aspects of the solar drama (p.302ff above), where the solar force is purified of its chthonic elements before it attains the universal empire of the sun.

[1818] The Upanishadic character of this Vedic passage reveals that the Upanishads are not really much later works than the Vedas, but, rather, contemporaneous with them, as their esoteric exegeses.

[1819] Agni, Ushas, and Sūrya correspond to Agni, Vāyu, Āditya, Vāyu (Enlil/Shu) being the impetus to the rising sun (see above p.246), and, like Usha (Dawn), the herald of the sun of the heavens.

BIBLIOGRAPHY

PRIMARY SOURCES

Indic

Atharva-Veda Samhita, tr. W.D. Whitney, 2 vols., Cambridge, MA: Harvard University Press, 1905.
The Hymns of the Atharva-Veda, tr. R.T.H. Grifffith, 2 vols., Benares: E.J. Lazarus,1895-6.
The Hymns of the Rgveda, tr. R.T.H. Griffith, Benares: E.J. Lazarus, 1889.
The Veda of the Black Yajus School entitled Taittiriya Samhita, tr. A.B. Keith, Cambridge. MA: Harvard University Press, 1914.
Rigveda Brahmanas: The Aitareya and Kauśitaki Brahmanas of the Rigveda, tr. A.B. Keith, Cambridge, MA: Harvard University Press, 1920.
The Śatapatha-Brahmana according to the text of the Mādhyandina School, tr. J. Eggeling, 5 vols., Oxford: Clarendon Press, 1882-1900.
Bhagavata Purana, 5 vols., tr. G.V. Tagare, Delhi: Motilal Banarsidass, 2002.
Srimad Bhagavata: The Holy Book of God, tr. Swami Tapasyananda, 4 vols., Madras: Sri Ramakrishna Math, 1980-82.
Brahma Purana, 4 vols., Delhi: Motilal Banarsidass, 2002.
Brahmanda Purana, 5 vols, Delhi: Motilal Banarsidass, 1984.
Brahmavaivarta Purana, 2 vols., Delhi: Motilal Banarsidass, 2001.
Linga Purana, 2 vols., Delhi: Motilal Banarsidass, 1973.
Padma Purana, tr. N.A. Deshpande, Delhi: Motilal Banarsidass, 1988-90.
Shiva Purana, 4 vols., Delhi: Motilal Banarsidass, 1970.
S. Shastri, *The Flood Legend in Sanskrit Literature*, Delhi: S. Chand and Co., 1950.
The Mahabharata, 11 vols., tr. P.C. Roy, Calcutta: Datta Bose and Co., 1924-31.
The Laws of Manu, translated with extracts from seven commentaries, by G. Bühler, Oxford: Clarendon Press, 1886.
The Complete Works of Kalidasa, ed. V.P. Joshi, Bombay: Lakhani Book Depot, 1976.
The Complete Works of Kalidasa, Vol.I, tr. C. Rajan, N.Delhi: Sahitya Akademi, 1997.
R.C. Majumdar, *The Classical Accounts of India*, Calcutta: Firma K.L. Mukhopadhyay, 1960.

Iranian

The Zend-Avesta, Part I, tr. J. Darmsteter, (Sacred Books of the East, Vol.4), Oxford: Clarendon Press, 1880.
The Zend-Avesta, Part II, tr. J. Darmsteter, (Sacred Books of the East, Vol.23) Oxford: Clarendon Press, 1883.
The Zend-Avesta, Part III, tr. L.H. Mills, (Sacred Books of the East, Vol.31), Oxford: Clarendon Press, 1887.
Pahlavi Texts, Part I, tr. E.W. West (Sacred Books of the East, Vol.5), Oxford: Clarendon Press, 1880.
W.W. Malandra, *An Introduction to ancient Iranian Religion: Readings from the Avesta and Achaemenid Inscriptions*, Minneapolis, MN: University of Minnesota Press, 1983.
R.C. Zaehner, *The Teachings of the Magi*, London: George Allen and Unwin Ltd., 1956.

Mesopotamian

A. Alberti, "A Reconstruction of the Abū Salābīkh God-List", *SEL* 2 (1985), 3-23.
A. Annus, *The Standard Babylonian Epic of Anzu*, Helsinki: The Neo-Assyrian Text Corpus Project, 2001.
H. Behrens, *Enlil und Ninlil: Ein Mythos aus Nippur*, Rome: Biblical Institute Press, 1978.
L. Cagni, *The Poem of Erra*, Malibu, CA: Undena Publications, 1977.
E. Chiera, *Sumerian Texts of varied Contents*, Chicago: University of Chicago Press, 1934.
J.S. Cooper, *Presargonic Inscriptions*, New Haven, CT: American Oriental Society, 1986
J.A. Craig *Assyrian and Babylonian Religious Texts*, 2 vols., Leipzig: J.C. Hinrichs, 1895-7.
J. Van Dijk, *Lugal ud me-lam-bi Nir-gal*, Leiden: E.J. Brill, 1983.
J. van Dijk, "Die Inschriftenfunde: II. Die Tontafeln aus dem res-Heiligtum" in *XVIII. vorläufiger Bericht über die von dem Deutschen Archaeologischen Institut und der Deutschen Orient-Gesellschaft aus Mitteln der Deutschen Forschungsgemeinschaft unternommenen Ausgrabungen in Uruk-Warka (1959/1960)*, Berlin: Heinrich J. Lenzen, 1962.
E. Dhorme *Choix de Textes Assyriens et Babyloniens*, Paris: Victor Lecoffre, 1907.
E. Ebeling *Die akkadische Gebetsserie "Handerhebung"*, Berlin: Akademie Verlag, 1953.
A. Falkenstein, *Sumerische und Akkadische Hymnen und Gebete*, Zuerich: Artemis Verlag, 1953.
A.Falkenstein, *Sumerische Götterlieder*, 2 vols., Heidelberg: Carl Winter Universitätsverlag, 1959.
Falkenstein, "Sumerische religiöse Texte", *ZA* 55 (1962), 11-67.
A. Falkenstein and W. von Soden, Sumerische Hymnen, Zürich, Artemis Verlag, 1953.
H. de Genouillac, *Textes religieux sumériens du Louvre*, 2 vols., Paris: Geuthner, 1930.

H. de Genouillac, "Grande Liste de Noms Divins Sumeriens", *RA* 20 (1923), 89-106.

A. George, *The Epic of Gilgamesh, the Babylonian epic poem and other texts in Akkadian and Sumerian*, London: Allen Lane, 1999.

H. Gressmann, *Altorientalische Texte und Bilder zum Alten Testamente*, 2 vols., Berlin: W. de Gruyter, 1926-7.

O.R. Gurney, J.J. Falkenstein, P. Hulin, *The Sultantepe Tablets*, 2 vols., London: British Institute of Archaeology at Ankara, 1957-64.

T. Jacobsen, *The Sumerian King-list*, Chicago: University of Chicago Press, 1939.

L.W. King, *Enuma Elish: the Seven Tablets of Creation*, London: Luzac and Co., 1902.

M.G. Kovacs (tr.), *The Epic of Gilgamesh*, Stanford: Stanford University Press, 1985.

S. N. Kramer, *Enmerkar and the Lord of Aratta*, Philadelphia: University Museum, 1952.

S.N. Kramer, *Sumerische literarische Texte aus Nippur*, 2 vols., Berlin: Akademie Verlag, 1961.

W.G. Lambert and A.R. Millard, *Atrahasis: The Babylonian Story of the Flood*, Oxford: Clarendon Press, 1969

W.G. Lambert, "Three literary Prayers of the Babylonians", *AfO* 19 (1959-60), 47-66.

S.H. Langdon, *Babylonian Liturgies: Sumerian Texts from the Early Period and from the Library of Asshurbanipal*, Paris, 1913.

R. Litke *A Reconstruction of the Assyro-Babylonian God-list An:^{d}A-nu-um and An: anu šá amēli*, New Haven, CT: Yale Babylonian Collection, 1998.

A. Livingstone, *Mystical and Mythological Explanatory Texts of Assyrian and Babylonian Scholars*, Oxford: Clarendon, 1986.

K.D. Macmillan, "Some Cuneiform Tablets bearing on the Religion of Babylonia and Assyria" *BA* 5 (1906),

A. Poebel, *Historical and Grammatical Texts*, Philadelphia: University Museum, 1914.

J.B. Pritchard, *Ancient Near Eastern Texts relating to the Old Testament*, Princeton: Princeton University Press, 1969.

H. Rawlinson, *The Cuneiform Inscriptions of Western Asia*, London: R.E. Bowler, 1861-84.

P.A. Schollmeyer, *Sumerisch-babylonische Hymnen und Gebete an Šamaš*, Paderborn: Ferdinand Schoeningh, 1912.

M.J. Seux, *Hymnes et Prières aux Dieux de Babylonie et d'Assyrie*, Paris : Editions du Cerf, 1976.

A.W. Sjoberg and E. Bergmann, *The Collection of the Sumerian Temple Hymns*, Locust Valley, N.Y.: J.J. Augustin, 1969.

H. Steible, *Die Altsumerischen Bau- und Weihinschriften*, Wiesbaden: F. Steiner, 1982 (FAOS 5).

F. Thureau-Dangin, *Die sumerischen und akkadischen Königsinschriften*, ed. Leipzig: J.C. Hinrichs, 1907.

C. Wilcke, *Das Lugalbandaepos*, Wiesbaden: O. Harrassowitz, 1969.

D. Wolkstein and S. Kramer, *Inanna, Queen of Heaven and Earth: Her Stories and Hymns from Sumer*, N.Y.: Harper and Row, 1983.

Egyptian

J. Assmann, Ägyptische Hymnen und Gebete, Zürich: Artemis Verlag, 1975.

A. Barucq and F. Daumas, Hymnes et Prières de l'Egypte ancienne, Paris: Cerf, 1980.

E.A.W. Budge, The Alexander Book in Ethiopia, London: OUP, 1933.

E. Drioton, Le texte dramatique d'Edfou, Cairo, 1948.

R.O. Faulkner, The Ancient Egptian Pyramid Texts, Oxford : Clarendon Press, 1969.

R.O. Faulkner, The Ancient Egyptian Coffin Texts, 3 vols., Warminster: Aris and Phillips, 1973-78.

E. Hornung, Das Amduat: Die Schrift des verborgenen Raumes, 3 vols., Wiesbaden: O. Harrassowitz, 1963-7.

E. Hornung, Das Totenbuch der Ägypter, Düsseldorf: Artemis und Winkler, 1990.

A. Mariette, Les papyrus égyptiennes du Musée de Boulaq, Paris, 1876.

C. Maystre, "Le Livre de la Vache du Ciel dans les Tombeaux de la Vallée des Rois", BIFAO, 40 (1941) 53-115.

K. Sethe, Dramatische Texte zu altägyptischen Mysterienspielen, Hildesheim: G. Olms, 1964.

G. P.Verbrugghe and J.M. Wickersham, Berossus and Manetho, Introduced and Translated: Native Traditions in Ancient Mesopotamia and Egypt, Ann Arbor, MI: University of Michigan Press, 1996.

Palestinian

Lucian, De Dea Syria, The Syrian Goddess, tr. H.W. Attridge and R.A. Oden, Missoula, MT: The Society of Biblical Literature, n.d.

Philo of Byblos, The Phoenician History, tr. H.W. Attridge and R.A. Oden Jr., Washington, D.C.: The Catholic Biblical Association of America, 1981.

The Holy Bible Containing the Old and New Testaments Translated Out of the Original Tongues, London, 1611.

Graeco–Latin

Apollodorus, The Library, 2 vols., tr. J.G. Frazer, London: William Heinemann, 1921.

Cicero, De Natura Deorum. Academica, tr. H. Rackham, London: William Heinemann, 1933.

H. Diels, Doxographi Graeci, Berlin: G. Reimer, 1879.

Herodotus, Histories, tr. A.D. Godley, 4 vols., London: William Heinemann, 1924-28.

Hesiod, The Homeric Hymns and Homerica, tr. H.G. Evelyn-White, London: William Heinemann, 1914.

Julian, Works, 3 vols. tr. W.C.Wright, London: W. Heinemann, 1913-23.

Nonnos, Dionysiaca, 3 vols., tr. W.H.D. Rouse, London: William Heinemann, 1940.

Plutarch, Moralia, V, tr. F.C. Babbit, London: William Heinemann, 1936.

Plutarch, De Iside et Osiride, tr. J.G. Griffiths, University of Wales Press, 1970.

Probus, M. Valerii Probi in Vergilii Bucolica et Georgica Commentarius, ed. H. Keil, Halle: Eduard Anton, 1848.

Porphyry, *De Abstinentia* in *Porphyrii Philosophi Platonici Opuscula Selecta*, ed. A. Nauck, Leipzig: B.G. Teubner, 1886.

Germanic

The Poetic Edda, tr. C. Larrington, Oxford: OUP, 1996.
The Prose Edda, of Snorri Sturlusson, tr. J.I. Young, Cambridge: Bowes and Bowes, 1954.
Tacitus, *Germania*, tr. M. Hutton, in *Dialogus, Agricola, Germania*, London: W. Heinemann, 1914.
Geoffrey of Monmouth *History of the Kings of Britain*, tr. L. Thorpe, Harmondsworth: Penguin, 1966.

SECONDARY SOURCES

H.-P. Adler *Das akkadische des Königs Tushratta von Mitanni*, Kevelaer: Butzon und Bercker, 1976.
G.W. Ahlström, *The History of Ancient Palestine*, Minneapolis, MN: Fortress Press, 1993.
W.F. Albright and P.E. Dumont, "A Parallel between Indic and Babylonian Sacrificial Ritual", *JAOS* 54 (1934), 107-28.
G. Algaze, *The Uruk World-System: The Dynamics of Expansion of early Mesopotamian Civilization*, Chicago: Chicago University Press, 1993.
B. and R. Allchin, *The Birth of Indian Civilization*, Harmondsworth: Penguin Books, 1968.
J.P. Allen, *Genesis in Egypt: The Philosophy of Ancient Egyptian Creation Accounts*, New Haven, CT: Yale University Press, 1988.
K. Al Nashef, "The Deities of Dilmun", in *Bahrain through the Ages: the Archaeology*, ed. S.H.A. Al Khalifa and M. Rice, London: KPI, 1986, 340-65.
A. Archi, "The Names of the Primeval Gods", *Orientalia* 59 (1990), 114-29.
J. Assmann, *Re und Amun: Die Krise der polytheistischen Weltbilds im Ägypten der 18.20. Dynastie*, Freiburg: Universitätsverlag, 1983.
J. Assmann, *Egyptian Solar Religion in the New Kingdom: Re, Amun and the Crisis of Polytheism*, tr. A. Alcock, London: Kegan Paul International, 1995.
C. Autran, *Sumérien et Indo-Européen*, Paris: Librairie Orientaliste Paul Geuthner, 1925.
T.P. van Baaren, "Pluriform Monotheism", *Ned.Theol. Tijdschr.* 20 (1965-66), 321-8.
A. Bergaigne, *La Religion Védique d'après les Hymnes du Rig-Veda*, Paris: Librairie Honoré Champion, 1963.
S. Bickel, *La Cosmogonie Egyptienne avant le Nouvel Empire*, Fribourg: Editions Universitaires, 1994.
K. Bittel, *Les Hittites*, Paris: Gallimard, 1976.
C.J. Bleeker, *Die Geburt eines Gottes: eine Studie über den aäyptischen Gott Min und sein Fest*, tr. M.J. Freie, Leiden: E.J. Brill, 1956.
C.J. Bleeker, *The Egyptian Goddess Neith*, Festschrift G. Scholem, 1968.

C.J. Bleeker, *Hathor and Thoth: Two key Figures of the Ancient Egyptian Religion*, Leiden: E.J. Brill, 1973.

C. Bonnet, *Studia Phoenicia*, 7 (1988), 148-55.

F. Bork, "Die Mitanni Sprache", *MVAG*, I and II, 1909.

J. Bottero, *Mesopotamia: Writing, Reasoning and the Gods*, tr. Z. Bahrani and M. van de Mieroop, Chicago: University of Chicago Press, 1992.

J. Bottero *Le problème des habiru*, Paris, 1954.

J.P. Brereton, *The Rgvedic Adityas*, New Haven, CT: American Oriental Society, 1981.

G.W. Brown, "The Possibility of a Connection between Mitanni and the Dravidian languages", *JAOS*, 50 (1930), 273-305.

H.K. Brugsch, *Religion und Mythologie der alten Ägypter,* Leipzig: J. Hinrich, 1891.

A. de Buck, "De godsdienstige opvatting van de slaap inszonderheid in het oude Egypte", *MVEOL* 4 (1939).

E.A.W. Budge, *The Gods of the Egyptians, or Studies in Egyptian Mythology*, 2 vols., London: Methuen and Co., 1904

E. D. van Buren, "The god Ningizzida", *Iraq*, I (1934), 60-89.

J. Cauvin, *Religions néolithiques de Syro-Palestine*, Paris: J. Maisonneuve, 1972.

J. Charpentier, "The Date of Zoroaster", *BSOS* 3 (1923-25), 747-55.

P. Charvat, *Mesopotamia Before History*, London: Routledge, 2002.

G. Childe, *The Dawn of European Civilization*, London: Routledge and Kegan Paul Ltd., 1961.

U. Chouduri, *Indra and Varuna in Indian Mythology*, Delhi : Nag Publishers, 1981.

A.B. Cook, *Zeus: A Study in Ancient Religion*, 2 vols. in 3, New York: Biblo and Tannen, 1964-5.

A.B. Cook, "Zeus, Jupiter and the Oak", *Classical Review* 17 (1903), 174-86; 268-78; 403-21; *Classical Review* 18 (1904), 75-89; 325-28; 360-75.

R. Cook, *The Tree of Life: Symbol of the Centre*, London: Thames and Hudson, 1974.

S.A. Cook, *The Religion of Ancient Palestine in the Light of Archaeology*, London: Oxford University Press, 1930.

J.S. Cooper, "Sumerian and Semitic Writing in most ancient Mesopotamia", in *Language and Cultures in Contact: At the Crossroads of Civilizations in the Syro-Mesopotamian Realm*, ed. K. van Lerberghe and G. Voet, Leuven: Uitgeverij Peeters, n.d., 61-77.

F. Cornelius, *Geistesgeschichte der Frühezeit*, 2 vols., Leiden: E.J. Brill, 1962.

F. Cornelius, "Erin-Manda", *Iraq* 25 (1963), 167-70.

A. Daniélou, *Hindu Polytheism*, London: Routledge and Kegan Paul, 1964.

A. Daniélou, *Shiva et Dionysos: La religion de la nature et le l'éros, de la préhistoire à l'avenir*, Paris: Fayard, 1979.

A. Daniélou, *Shiva and Dionysus*, tr. K.F. Hurry, London: East-West Publications, 1979.

J. Day, *God's Conflict with the Dragon and the Sea*, Cambridge: Cambridge University Press, 1985.

A. Deimel, *Pantheon Babylonicum: Nomina deorum e textibus cuneiformibus excerpta et ordine alphabetico distributa*, Rome: Pontifical Biblical Institute, 1914.

M.M. Deshpande and P.E. Hook (ed.) *Aryan and Non-Aryan in India*, Ann Arbor, MI: Center for South and Souteast Asian Studies, The University of Michigan, 1979.

G.V. Devasthali, *Religion and Mythology of the Brahmanas*, Poona: Poona University Press, 1965.

M. Dietrich and I. Kottsieper (ed.) *Und Mose schrieb dieses Lied auf: Studien zum alten Testament und zum alten Orient, Festschrift für Oswald Loretz*, Münster: Ugarit Verlag, 1998.

J.J.A. van Dijk, *Sumerische Religion: Handbuch der Religionsgeschichte*, Göttingen, 1971.

J. Duchesne-Guillemin, *Religion of Ancient Iran*, Bombay: Tata Press, 1973.

G. Dumézil, "Dieux cassites et védiques à propos d'un bronze du Louristan", *RHA* 52 (1950), 16-37.

A. Dundes (ed.), *The Flood Myth*, Berkeley: University of California Press, 1988.

M. Eliade, *Shamanism: Archaic Techniques of Ecstasy*, N.Y.: Pantheon Books, 1964.

J. Epping and J.N. Strassmeier, "Neue babylonische Planeten-Tafeln", *ZA* 6 (1891), 89-102.

G. Erdosy (ed.) *The Indo-Aryans of Ancient South Asia*, Berlin: Walter de Gruyter, 1995.

Ethnic Problems of the History of Central Asia in the Early Period (second millennium B.C.), Moscow, 1981.

J. Finegan, *Archaeological History of the Ancient Middle East*, Boulder, CO: Westview Press, 1979.

T. Folger, "The real Big Bang", *Discover*, Dec. 2002, 41-46.

E. Forrer, "Stratification des langues et des peuples dans le Proche-Orient préhistorique", *JA* 217 (1930), pp.227-52.

H. Frankfort, *Archaeology and the Sumerian Problem*, Chicago: Chicago University Press, 1932.

C.J. Gadd and L. Legrain, *Ur Excavations: Texts, Vol. I: Royal Inscriptions*, London, 1928.

H.D. Galter, *Der Gott Ea/Enki in der akkadischen Überlieferung* (Dissertationen der Karl-Franzens-Universität Graz), Graz, 1983.

G. Garbini *History and Ideology in Ancient Israel*, tr. J. Bowden, London: SCM Press, 1988.

I.J. Gelb, *Hurrians and Subarians*, Chicago: Chicago University Press, 1944.

K. Gerhardt, *Die Glockenbecherleute in Mittel- und Westdeutschland*, Stuttgart, 1953.

A. Ghose, *The Secret of the Veda*, in 'Sri Aurobindo Birth Centenary Library', vol.10, Pondicherry: Sri Aurobindo Ashram, 1971.

A. Ghose, "The Origins of Aryan Speech", in 'Sri Aurobindo Birth Centenary Library', vol.10.

G.S. Ghurye, *Indian Acculturation: Agasthya and Skandha*, Bombay: Popular Prakashan, 1977.

K-H. Golzio, *Der Tempel im alten Mesopotamien und seine Parallelen in Indien: eine religionshistorische Studie*, Leiden: E.J. Brill, 1983.

J. Gonda, *The Vedic God Mitra*, Leiden: E.J. Brill, 1972.

C.H. Gordon, "Canaanite Mythology", in S. Kramer, *Mythologies of the Ancient World*, 181-218.

H. Grapow, *Die bildlichen Ausdrücke des Aegyptischen: vom Denken und Dichten einer altorientalischen Sprache*, Leipzig, 1924.

A.C. Green, *The Storm-God in the Ancient Near East*, Winona Lake, IN: Eisenbrauns, 2003.

J.G. Griffiths, *The Conflict of Horus and Seth*, Liverpool: Liverpool University Press, 1960.

J.G.Griffiths, *The Origins of Osiris and his Cult*, Leiden: E.J. Brill, 1980.

H.G. Güterbock, *Kumarbi, Istanbuler Schriften* 16, 1946.

H.G. Güterbock, "The god Suwalliyat reconsidered", *RHA* 19 (1961), 1-18.

H.G. Güterbock, "Hittite Mythology", in S. Kramer, *Mythologies of the Ancient World*, 139-179.

J.F.H. Gunkel, *Schöpfung und Chaos: Eine religionsgeschichtliche Untersuchung über Gen.1 und Ap. Joh.12*, Göttingen, 1895.

O.R. Gurney, *Some Aspects of Hittite Religion*, Oxford: Oxford University Press, 1977.

W.K.C. Guthrie, *Orpheus and Greek Religion: A Study of the Ophic Movement*, London: Methuen, 1952.

V. Haas and G. Wilhelm, *Hurritische und luwische Riten aus Kizzuwattna*, Kevelaer: Butzon und Bercker, 1974.

V. Haas, *Geschichte der hethitischen Religion*, Leiden: E.J. Brill, 1994.

W.E. Hale, *Asura in Early Vedic Religion*, Delhi: Motilal Banarsidass, 1986.

D. Handelman, "Myths of Murugan: Asymmetry and Hierarchy in a South Indian Puranic Cosmology", *History of Religions*, 27, no.2, 133-70.

R.J. Harrison, *The Beaker Folk*, London: Thames and Hudson, 1980.

J. Haudry, *La religion cosmique des Indo-Europeans*, Milan, Paris: Arché, 1987.

J. Hehn, *Die biblische und babylonische Gottesidee*, Leipzig: J.C. Hinrichs, 1913.

W. Helck, *Urkunden der 18. Dynastie, Übersetzungen zu den Heften 17-22*, Berlin: Akademie Verlag, 1984.

H. Heras, *Studies in Proto-Indo-Mediterranean Culture*, Bombay: Indian Historical Research Institute, 1953.

W. Hinz, *The Lost World of Elam*, tr. J. Barnes, London: Sidgwick and Jackson, 1972.

S. Hood, *The Minoans: Crete in the Bronze Age*, London: Thames and Hudson, 1971.

J. Hornell, "The Origins and ethnological Significance of Indian Boat Designs", *Memoirs of the Asiatic Society of Bengal*, VII,3,139-256.

E. Hornung, *Conceptions of God*, tr. J. Baines, Ithaca: Cornell University Press, 1982.

E. Hornung, *The Ancient Egyptian Books of the Afterlife*, tr. D. Lorton, Ithaca: Cornell University Press, 1999.

W. Horowitz, "The Babylonian Map of the World", *Iraq*, 50 (1988), 147-66

F. Hrozny, "Un dieu Hittite Ak/niš", *RA* 18 (1921), 34-36.

F. Hrozny, "Hethiter und Inder", *ZA* 38 (1928), 184-85.

M. Hütter, *Altorientalische Vorstellungen von der Unterwelt: Literar- und religionsgeschichtliche Überlegungen zu 'Nergal und Ereškigal'*, Freiburg: Universitätsverlag, 1985.

The Interpreter's Bible, N.Y.: Abingdon Press, 1952.

A.V.W. Jackson, *Grundriss der iranischen Philologie*, 2 vols., Strassburg: K.J. Trübner, 1895-1904.

A. Jacob, "Cosmology and Ethics in the Religions of the Peoples of the Ancient Near East", *Mankind Quarterly*, Vol.140, No.1 (Fall 1999), 95-119.

T. Jacobsen, *Treasures of Darkness: A History of Mesopotamian Religion*, New Haven: Yale University Press, 1976.

E.O. James, *The Ancient Gods*, London: Weidenfeld and Nelson, 1960.

E.O. James, *The Tree of Life: An Archaeological Study*, Leiden: E.J. Brill, 1966.

M. Jansen, *Die Indus-Zivilisation: Wiederentdeckung einer frühen Hochkultur*, Köln: DuMont, 1986.

A. Jellinek, *Bet ha-Midrasch*, Jerusalem: Sifre Waherman, 1967.

P. Jensen "Assyrio-Hebraïca", *ZA* IV (1889), 268-80.

A. Jeremias, *Die babylonisch-assyrischen Vorstellungen vom Leben nach dem Tode, nach den Quellen mit Berücksichtigung der alttestamentlichen Parallen dargestellt*, Leipzig: Hinrichs, 1887.

A. Jeremias, *Handbuch der altorientalischen Geisteskultur*, Leipzig, 1929.

H. Junker, "Das Götterdekret über das Abaton", *DAWW* 56 (1913), No.4.

A. Kammenhuber, *Hippologia hethitica*, Wiesbaden: O. Harrassowitz, 1961.

A. Kammenhuber *Die Arier im vorderen Orient*, Heidelberg: Carl Winter Universitätsverlag, 1968.

M. Kavoukjian, *Armenia, Subartu and Sumer: The Indo-European Homeland and Ancient Mesopotamia*, tr. N. Ouzonian, Montreal: M. Kavoukjian, 1987.

H. Kees, "Kulttopographische und mythologische Beiträge", in *ZÄS* 65 (1930), 83-84.

W. Kirfel, *Die Kosmographie der Inder*, Hildesheim: G. Olms, 1967

L.W. King, *Babylonian Magic and Sorcery*, London, 1986.

J.V. Kinnier-Wilson *The Rebel Lands: An Investigation into the Origins of Early Mesopotamian Mythology*, Cambridge: Cambridge University Press, 1979.

J. Klinger, "Überlegungen zu den Anfang des Mitanni-Staates", in V. Haas (ed.) *Hurriter und Hurritisch*, Konstanz: Universitätsverlag Konstanz, 1988, 27-42.

A. Klasens, *A Magical Statue Base (Socle Behague) in the Museum of Antiquities at Leiden*, 1952.

J.A. Knudtzon, *Die El-Amarna-Tafeln*, 2 vols., Leipzig: Hinrichs, 1915.

S. Kramer, *Sumerian Mythology: A Study of spiritual and Literary Achievement in the Third Millennium B.C.*, N.Y.: Harper, 1961.

S. Kramer (ed.) *Mythologies of the Ancient World*, Garden City, NY: Doubleday, 1961.

S. Kramer, "Review of A. Hendel, *The Babylonian Genesis: The Story of Creation*", *JAOS*, 63 (1943), 69-73.

S.N. Kramer and J. Mair, *The Myths of Enki, the Crafty God*, Oxford: OUP 1989.

F.R. Kraus, "Nippur und Isin nach altbabylonischen Rechtskunden", *JCS* 3 (1949), 78-80.

P. Kretschmer, "Weiteres zur Urgeschichte der Inder", *Zeitschrift für vergleichende Sprachforschung* 55 (1928), 78-103.

P. Kretschmer, "Indra und der hethitische Gott Inaras", *Kleinasiatische Forschungen* I (1930), 297-317.

X. Kugler, *Im Bannkreis Babels: panbabylonistischen Konstruktionen und religionsgeschichtliche Tatsachen*, Münster: Aschendorff, 1910.

A.K. Lahiri, *Vedic Vrtra*, Delhi: Motilal Banarsidass, 1984.

W. Lambert, "The Cosmology of Sumer and Babylon", in *Ancient Cosmologies*, ed. C. Blacker and M. Loewe, London: George Allen and Unwin, 1975, 42-65.

W. Lambert, "Studies in Marduk", *BSOAS* 47(1984), 1-9.

W. Lambert, "Ninurta Mythology in the Babylonian Epic of Creation" in *Keilschriftliche Literaturen, Ausgewählte Vorträge der XXXII RAI*, Berlin: D. Reimer, 1985, 55-60.

B. Landsberger, *Three Essays on the Sumerians*, tr. M. DeJ. Ellis, Los Angeles: Undena Publications, n.d.

B. Landsberger and T. Bauer, "Zu neueröffentlichen Geschichtsquellen", *ZA* 37 (1927), 61-98.

D. Lang, *Armenia: Cradle of Civilization*, London: George Allen and Unwin, 1980.

S. Langdon and A.H. Gardiner, "The treaty of alliance between Hattusili, king of the Hittites, and the pharaoh Rameses II of Egypt", *JEA* 6 (1920).

S. Langdon, *Excavations at Kish*, I, Paris: Librairie Orientaliste Paul Geuthner, 1924.

S. Langdon, *Tammuz and Ishtar: A Monograph Upon Babylonian Religion and Theology Containing Extensive Extracts from the Tammuz Liturgies and all of the Arbela Oracles*, Oxford: Clarendon Press, 1914.

R. Largement, "La religion suméro-akkadienne" in M. Brilliant and R. Aigrain,119-76.

R. Largement, "La religion cananéene" in M. Brilliant and R. Aigrain, 177-99.

E. Laroche, *Recherches sur les noms divins hittites, RHA* VII, 45 (1946-7).

E. Laroche, "Les dénominations des dieux 'antiques' dans les texts hittites", in *Anatolian Studies presented to Hans Gustav Güterbock on the Occasion of his 65th Birthday*, Istanbul: Nederlands Historisch-Archaeologisch Instituut in Het Nabije Oosten, 1975, 175-85.

M. Lebeau (ed.), *About Subartu: Studies Devoted to Upper Mesopotamia* (Subartu IV,i-ii), Turnhout: Brepols, 1998.

M.E. Lefebure, *Le Tombeau de Seti* I, Paris, 1886.

G. Leick *Mesopotamia: The Invention of the City*, London: Penguin Books, 2000.

F.M.T. de Liagre Boehl, "Die Religion der Babylonier und Assyrier" in *Christus und die Religionen der Erde: Handbuch der Religionsgeschichte*, ed. F. König, 3 vols., Wien: Herder, 1961, II,

Bruce Lincoln, *Myth, Cosmos and Society: Indo-European Themes of Creation and Destruction*, Cambridge, MA: Harvard University Press, 1986.

E. Lipinski, *Dieux et Déesses de l'univers phénicien et punique (Studia Phoenicia* 14 (1995).

M. Liverani (ed.), *Akkad, the First World Empire*, Padova: Sargon, 1993.

La Lune: Mythes et Rites (Sources Orientales V) Paris: Éditions du Seuil, 1962.

H. Lüders (ed. L. Alsdorf), *Varuna*, 2 vols., Göttingen : Vandenhoeck und Ruprecht, 1951.

A.A. Macdonell, *A History of Sanskrit Literature*, Delhi: Munshiram Manoharlal, 1961.

V. Machek, "Name und Herkunft des Gottes Indra", *AO* 12 (1941), 143-54.

V.H. Mair (ed.) *The bronze age and early iron age Peoples of Eastern Central Asia*, 2 vols., Washington, D.C.: Institute for the Study of Man, 1998.

A. Mairette, *Dendérah: Description générale du grand temple de cette ville*, Paris : A. Franck, 1870-75.

J.P. Mallory, *In Search of the Indo-Europeans: Language, Archaeology and Myth*, London: Thames and Hudson, 1989.

J.P. Mallory and V.H. Mair, *The Tarim Mummies*, London: Thames and Hudson, 2000.

S. Marakhanova, "A Version of the Origins of the World in Egyptian, Orphic and Gnostic Cosmogonies", in *Ancient Egypt and Kush*, Moscow, 1993, 277-89.

S. Mark, *From Egypt to Mesopotamia: A Study of Predynastic Trade Routes*, College Station, TX: Texas A & M University Press, 1997.

G.C.C. Maspero, *Histoire ancienne des peuples de l'Orient classique*, 3 vols., Paris: Hachette, 1895-99.

F. Max-Mueller, *Selected Essays on Language, Mythology and Religion*, 2 vols., London: Longmans, Green and Co., 1881.

B. Meissner, *Beiträge zum altbabylonischen Privatrecht*, Leipzig: J.C. Hinrichs, 1893.

B. Meissner, *Babylonien und Assyrien,* Heidelberg: Winter, 1920-25.

J. Mellaart, *Çatal Huyuk: A Neolithic Town in Anatolia*, London: Thames and Hudson, 1967.

S. Mercer, *Horus Royal God of Egypt*, Grafton, MA: Society of Oriental Research, 1942.

A. Miles, *Land of the Lingam*, London, 1933.

J. Miller, *The Vision of Cosmic Order in the Vedas*, London: Routledge and Kegan Paul, 1985.

S. Morenz, *Aegyptische Religion*, Stuttgart: W. Kohlhammer, 1960.

S. Morenz and F. Schubert, *Der Gott auf der Blume*, Berlin, 1953.

J. de Morgan, *Kom Ombos*, Vienna, 1895-1909.

M.J. de Morgan, *Délégation en Perse*, Paris, 1900.

W.M. Mueller, "Der Bündnisvertrag Ramses' II und des Chetiterkönigs", *MVAG* 7 (1902),

K.L. Muttarayan, "Sumer:Tamil of the First Cankam", *Journal of Tamil Studies*, 8 (1975), 40-61.

K. Mysliwiec, *Studien zum Gott Atum*, 2 vols., Hildesheim: Gersternberg Verlag, 1979.

S.L. Nagar, *The Cult of Vinayaka*, N.Delhi: Intellectual Publishing House, 1992.

H. Nissen, *The Early History of the Ancient Near East 9000-2000 B.C.*, tr. E. Lutzeier and K.J. Northcott, Chicago: University of Chicago Press, 1988.

H. Nissen, P. Damerow, R.K. Englund, *Archaic Bookkeeping*, Chicago: University of Chicago Press, 1993.

H. Nissen, "Ortsnamen in den archaischen Texten aus Uruk", *Orientalia*, NS, 54, 228-30.

J. Oates, "Ur and Eridu, the Prehistory", *Iraq* 22 (1960), 32-50.

W.D. O'Flaherty, *Asceticism and Eroticism in the Mythology of Śiva,* London: Oxford University Press, 1973.

H. Oldenberg, *Die Religion des Vedas*, Stuttgart: J.G. Cotta, 1923.

H. Otten and M. Mayrhofer, "Der Gott Akni in den hethitischen Texten und seine indoarische Herkunft", *OLZ*, 1965, 11/12, p.545-52.

U.C. Pandey, *The Cosmogonic Legends of the Brahmanas*, Gorakahpur: Shivaniketan, 1991/2.

F.E. Pargiter, *Ancient Indian Historical Tradition*, London: Milford, 1922.

A. Parpola, "On the Proto-history of the Indian Languages in the Light of Archaeological, Linguistic and Religious Evidence: An Attempt at Integration", *South Asian Archaeology 1973*, Leiden: E.J. Brill,1974, 90-100.

A. Parpola, "Aryan Languages, Archaeological Cultures and Sinkiang: Where did Proto-Iranian come into being and how did it spread?", in V.H. Mair (ed.) *The Bronze Age and Early Iron Age Peoples of Eastern Central Asia*, Washington, D.C.: Institute for the Study of Man, 1998, I:114-47.

A. Parpola, "The Problem of the Aryans and the Soma", in G. Erdosy (ed.), *The Indo-Aryans of Ancient South Asia*, Berlin: Walter de Gruyter, 1995.

A. Parrot, *Sumer*, Paris: Gallimard, 1960.

W.M.F. Petrie and J.E. Quibell, *Naqada and Ballas*, London: Bernard Quaritch, 1896.

J.A. Philip, *Pythagoras and Early Pythagoreanism*, Toronto: University of Toronto Press, 1966.

A. Piankoff, *Le "Coeur" dans les Textes Egyptiens*, Paris: Librairie orientaliste Paul Geuthner, 1930.

S. Piggott, *Prehistoric India to 1000 B.C.*, London: Cassell, 1962.

A. Poebel, "Sumerische Untersuchungen", *ZA* 39 (1929), 129-64.

D.T. Potts, *Dilmun: New Studies in the Archaeology and early History of Bahrain*, Berlin: Dietrich Reimer Verlag, 1983.

D.T. Potts, *The Archaeology of Elam*, Cambridge: Cambridge University Press, 1999.

J. Przyluski, "Deva et asura", *Rocznik Orjentalistyczny* 8 (1931-2), 25-29.

J. Przyluski, "Inara et Indra", *RHA* V, Fasc. 36 (1939), 142-46.

S. Quirke, *The Cult of Ra: Sun-worship in Ancient Egypt*, London: Thames and Hudson, 2001.

C.K. Raja, *Survey of Sanskrit Literature*, Bombay: Bharatiya Vidya Bhavan, 1962.

A.E. Redgate, *The Armenians*, Oxford: Blackwell Publishers, 1998.

V.G. Rele, *The Vedic Gods as Figures of Biology*, Bombay: D.B. Taraporevala Sons, 1931.

E. Renan, *Histoire Générale et Système Comparé des Langues Sémitiques*, Paris: Levy, 1863.

E.A.E. Reymond, *The Mythical Origin of the Egyptian Temple*, Manchester: University of Manchester Press, 1969.

M. de Rochemonteix, *Le Temple d'Edfou*, Caire: Institut français d'archaeologie orientale du Caire, 1897.

L. Rocher, *The Puranas*, Wiesbaden: Otto Harrassowitz, 1986.

Y. Rosengarten, *Sumer et le sacré*, Paris: Editions E. de Broccard, 1977.

G. Roux, *Ancient Iraq*, London : George Allen and Unwin, 1964.

G. Rubio, "On the alleged 'Pre-Sumerian Substratum'", *JCS*, 51(1999), 1-16.

R.T. Rundle Clark, *Myth and Symbol in ancient Egypt*, London: Thames and Hudson, 1959.

M. Rutten, "Les Religions Asianiques", in *Histoire des Religions*, ed. M. Brilliant et R. Aigrain, Vol. 4, Paris: Bloud et Gay, 1953-6, 7-117.

Z. Saad, *Royal Excavations at Helwan*, Cairo, 1952.

M. Safar, M.A. Mustafa, S. Lloyd, *Eridu*, Baghdad: Ministry of Culture and Information, Republic of Iraq, 1981.

M. Salvini, "Un royaume hourrite en Mésopotamie du Nord à l'époque de Hattušili I", in M. Lebeau, IV,i,305-11.

M. Sandman-Holmberg, *The God Ptah*, Lund: C.W.K. Gleerup, 1946.

H.A. Schloegl, *Der Gott Tatenen*, Freiburg: Universitätsverlag Freiburg Schweiz, 1980.

H.-P. Schmidt, *Brhaspati und Indra*, Wiesbaden: Otto Harrassowitz, 1968.

S. Schott, *Das schöne Fest vom Wüstentale, Festbräuche einer Totenstadt*, Wiesbaden: F. Steiner, 1953.

E. Schrader, *Die Keilinschriften und das Alte Testament*, Berlin: Reuther und Reichard, 1903.

M.K. Schretter, *Alter Orient und Hellas*, Innsbruck: AMOE, 1974.

O. Schroeder, "Ein neues Götterlistentypus aus Assur", *ZA* 33 (1921), 123-47.

G. Sergi, *The Mediterranean Race: A Study of the Origin of European Peoples*, London: W. Scott, 1909.

K. Sethe, *Amun und die acht Urgötter von Hermopolis (Abhandlungen der preussischen Akademie der Wissenschaften*, 1929, Nr.4).

A.G. Shedid, *Die Felsgräber von Beni Hassan in Mittelägypten*, Mainz am Rhein: Verlag Philipp van Zabern, 1994.

M. Shendge, *The Aryas: Facts without Fancy and Fiction*, N. Delhi: Abhinav Publications, 1996.

D. Shulman, "Murukan, the Mango and Ekambaresvara-Siva Fragments of a Tamil Creation Myth", *Indo-Iranian Journal* 21 (1979), 27-40.

J. Siegelova, *Appu Märchen und Hedammu-Mythus (Studien zu den Bogazköy-Texten* 14), Wiesbaden: O. Harrassowitz, 1971.

H. Sköld, "Were the Asuras Assyrians?", *JRAS*, April 1924, 265-7.

H. Sköld, "Zu den altindischen Gottesnamen im Mitannivertrag", *OLZ* 6 (1926), 396-97.

G.E. Smith, *The Ancient Egyptians and the Origin of Civilization*, London: Harper, 1923.

S. Smith. *Early History of Assyria*, London: Chatto and Windus, 1928.

S. Smith, "The Relation of Marduk, Ashur, and Osiris", *JEA*, 8 (1922), 41-44.

S. Sörensen, *An Index to the Names in the Mahabharata*, London: Williams and Norgate, 1904.

F. Sommer, "Review of H. Eheloff, *Keilschrifturkunden aus Boghazköi*, Heft XXX", *OLZ* 1939, no.11, 678-88.

W. Sommerfeld, *Der Aufstieg Marduks*, Kevelaer: Butzon & Bercker, 1982.

E. Speiser, *Mesopotamian Origins*, Philadelphia: University of Pennsylvania Press, 1930.

E.A. Speiser, *Introduction to Hurrian*, AASOR XX (1941).

E.A. Speiser, "The Hurrian participation in the civilizations of Mesopotamia, Syria and Palestine", *Cahiers d'Histoire Mondiale*, I,2 (1953), 311-27.

P. Steinkeller, "Early Political Development in Mesopotamia and the Origins of the Sargonic Empire", in *Akkad, the First World Empire*, ed. M. Leverani, Padua: Sargon srl, 1993, 107-29.

F. X. Steinmetzer, "Die Sinnbilder auf dem Grenztstein des Nazi-Marutaš", in *Festschrift Eduard Sachau zum siebzigsten Geburtstage*, ed. G. Weil, Berlin: Georg Reimer, 1915, 62-71.

M. Streck, "Das Gebiet der heutigen Lanschaften Armenien, Kurdistan und Westpersien nach den babylonisch-assyrischen Keilinschriften", *ZA* XV (1900), 272-5.

G.G. Stroumsa, *Another Seed: Studies in Gnostic Mythology*, Leiden:E.J. Brill, 1984.

R.F.G. Sweet, "A New Look at the 'Sacred Marriage' in ancient Mesopotamia", in E. Robbins and S. Sandahl (ed.), *Corolla Torontonensis: Studies in honour of Ronald Morton Smith*, Toronto: Tsar, 1994, 85-104.

M. Taddei and G. de Marco (ed.), *South Asian Archaeology 1973*, Leiden: E.J. Brill, 1974.

K. Tallquist, *Neubabylonisches Namenbuch zu den Geschäftsurkunden aus der Zeit des Šamaššumukin bis Xerxes*, Helsinki, 1906.

K. Tallquist, *Akkadische Götterepitheta (Studia Orientalia 7)*, Helsinki, 1938.

E. Tenner, "Tages- und Nachtsonne bei den Hethitern", *ZA* 38 (1929), 186-90.

R.C. Thompson, *A Century of Exploration at Nineveh*, London: Luzac, 1929

F. Thureau-Dangin, *Rituels Accadiens*, Paris: Leroux, 1921.

F. Thureau-Dangin, "An acte de donation de Marduk-Zâkir-Šumi", *RA* 16 (1919), 117-56.

S. Tyler, "Dravidian and Uralian: the lexical Evidence", *Language* 44 (1968), pp.198-212.

A. Ungnad, *Subartu: Beiträge zur Kulturgeschichte und Völkerkunde Vorderasiens*, Berlin: Walter de Gruyter, 1936.

A. Ungnad, "Ahura-Mazdah und Mithra in assyrischen Texten?", *OLZ* 1943 No.5/6, 193-201.

H. Usener, *Die Sintfluthsagen*, Bonn: Friedrich Cohen, 1899.

H. te Velde, *Seth God of Confusion: A Study of his Role in Egyptian Mythology and Religion*, Leiden: E.J. Brill, 1967.

H. te Velde, "The God Heka in Egyptian Theology", *JEOL*, 21 (1970), 175-86.

N. Veldhuis, *A Cow of Sin*, Groningen: Styx Publications, 1991.

E. von Weiher, *Der babylonische Gott Nergal*, Kevelaer: Butzon und Bercker, 1979.

A.J. Wensinck, "The Ocean in the Literature of theWestern Semites", *Verhandelingen der Koninklijke Akademie van Wetenschappen*, XIX (1918), no.2.

A. Wensinck, "The Ideas of the Western Semites Concerning the Navel of the Earth", *Verhandelingen der Koninklijke Akademie van Wetenschappen*, XVII (1916), no.1.

A.J. Wensinck, "Tree and Bird as Cosmological Symbols in Western Asia", *Verhandelingen der Koninklijke Akademie van Wetenschappen*, XXII (1921), no.1.

M.L. West, *Early Greek Philosophy and the Orient*, Oxford: Clarendon Press, 1971.

M.L. West, *The Orphic Poems*, Oxford: Clarendon Press, 1983.

M.L. West, *The East Face of Helicon*, Oxford: Clarendon Press, 1997.

G. Wilhelm *Grundzüge der Geschichte und Kultur der Hurriter*, Darmstadt: Wissenschaftliche Buchgesellschaft, 1982.

G. Wilhelm, *The Hurrians*, tr. J. Barnes, Warminster: Aris and Phillips Ltd., 1989.

R.H. Wilkinson, *Symbol and Magic in Egyptian Art*, London: Thames and Hudson, 1994.

T. Wilkinson, *The Genesis of the Pharaohs*, London: Thames and Hudson, 2003.

H. Wohlstein, *The Sky-god An-Anu*, Jericho, NY: Paul A. Stroock, 1976.

B. R. Yadava, *Vedic Cosmogony*, Aligarh: Vijnana Prakasana, 1987.

D. Yoshida, *Untersuchungen zu den Sonnengottheiten bei den Hethitern*, Heidelberg: Universitätsverlag C. Winter, 1996.

J. Zandee, "Seth als Sturmgott", *ZÄS* 90 (1963), 144-56.

J. Zandee, "The Birth-Giving Gods in Ancient Egypt", in *Studies in Pharaonic Religion and Society in Honour of J. Gwyn Griffiths*, London: Egypt Exploration Society, 1992, 169-85.

H. Zimmern, "Religion und Sprache" in E. Schrader, 343-653.

H. Zimmern, "Biblische und babylonische Urgeschichte", *Der Alte Orient,* II (1901), no.3.

K. Zvelebil, *Tamil Traditions on Subrahmanya-Murugan*, Madras: Institute of Asian Studies, 1991.